VOLUME 2

SACRED NATURE

Reconnecting People to Our Planet

By Jonathan & Angela Scott

DESIGN BY
DAVID JOHN SCOTT

PUBLISHER
HPH PUBLISHING

If the sight of the blue skies fills you with joy, if a blade of grass springing up in the fields has power to move you, if the simple things of nature have a message that you understand, rejoice, for your soul is alive.

— Eleanora Duse

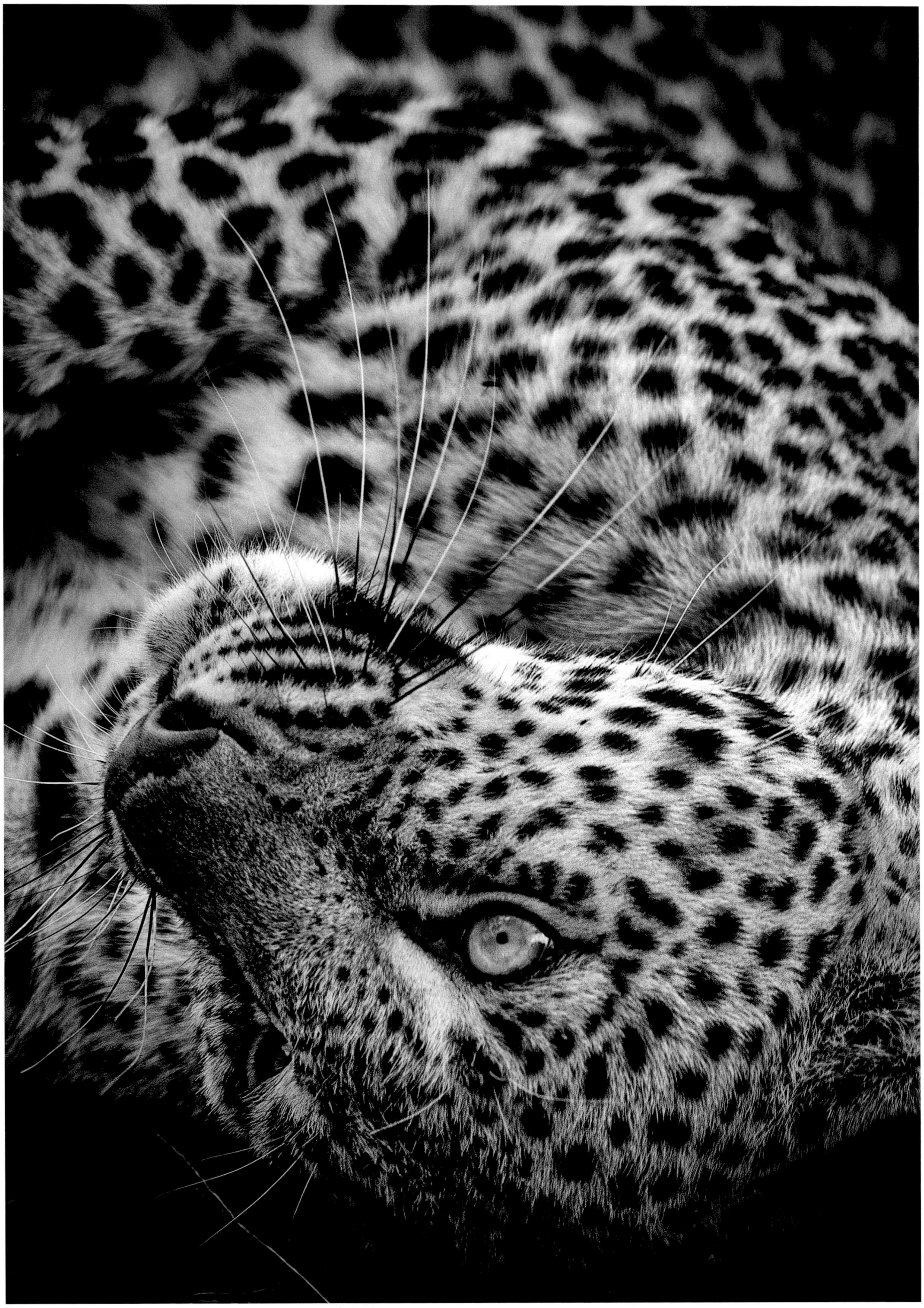

Contents

Attributed to Chief Seattle, Duwamish and Suquamish Nations

Humankind has not woven the web of life. We are but one thread within it. Whatever we do to the web, we do to ourselves. All things are bound together. All things connect.

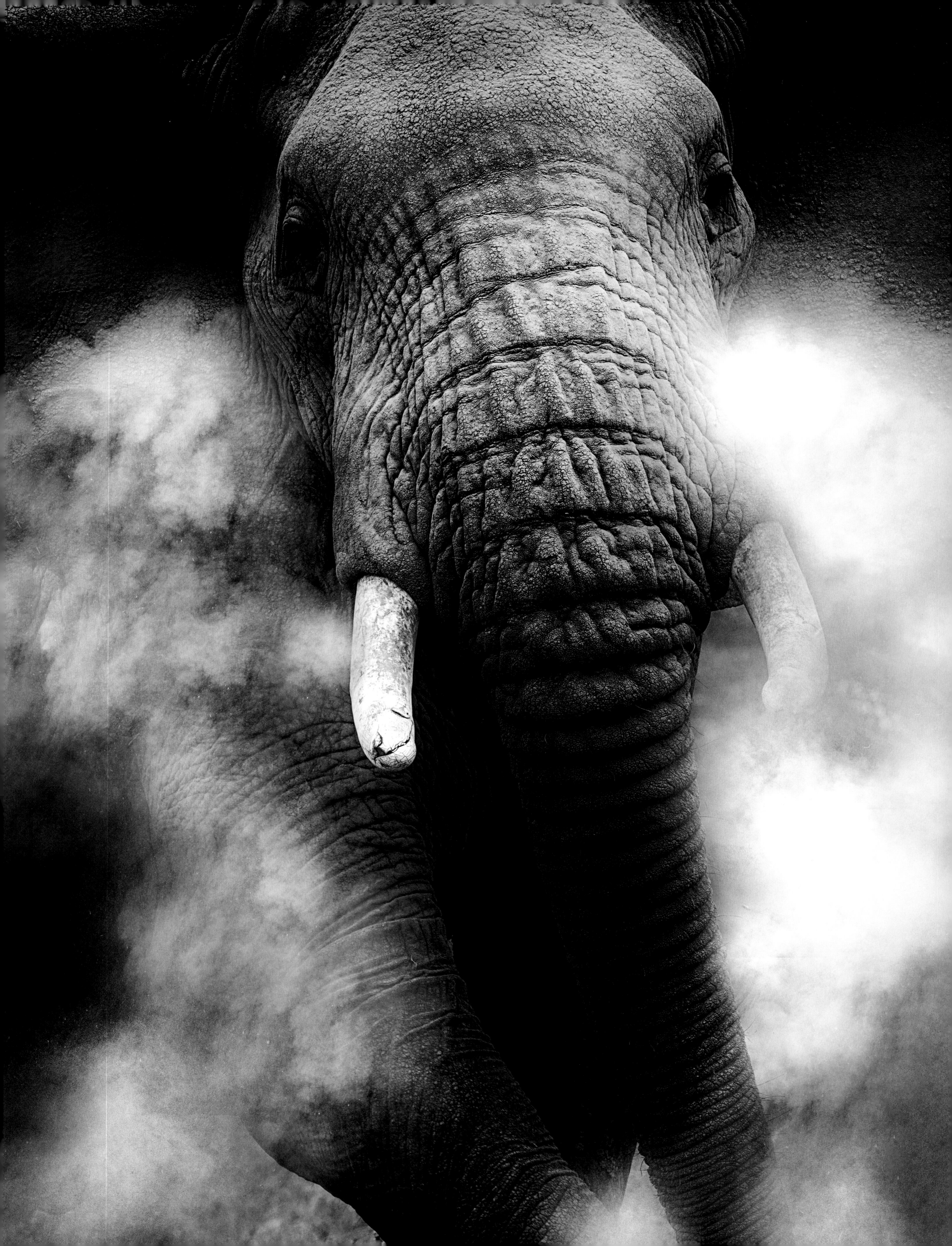

Introduction

PARADISE LOST

What I see in nature is a magnificent structure that we can comprehend only very imperfectly and that must fill a thinking person with a feeling of humility. This is a genuinely religious feeling that has nothing to do with mysticism.

— Albert Einstein

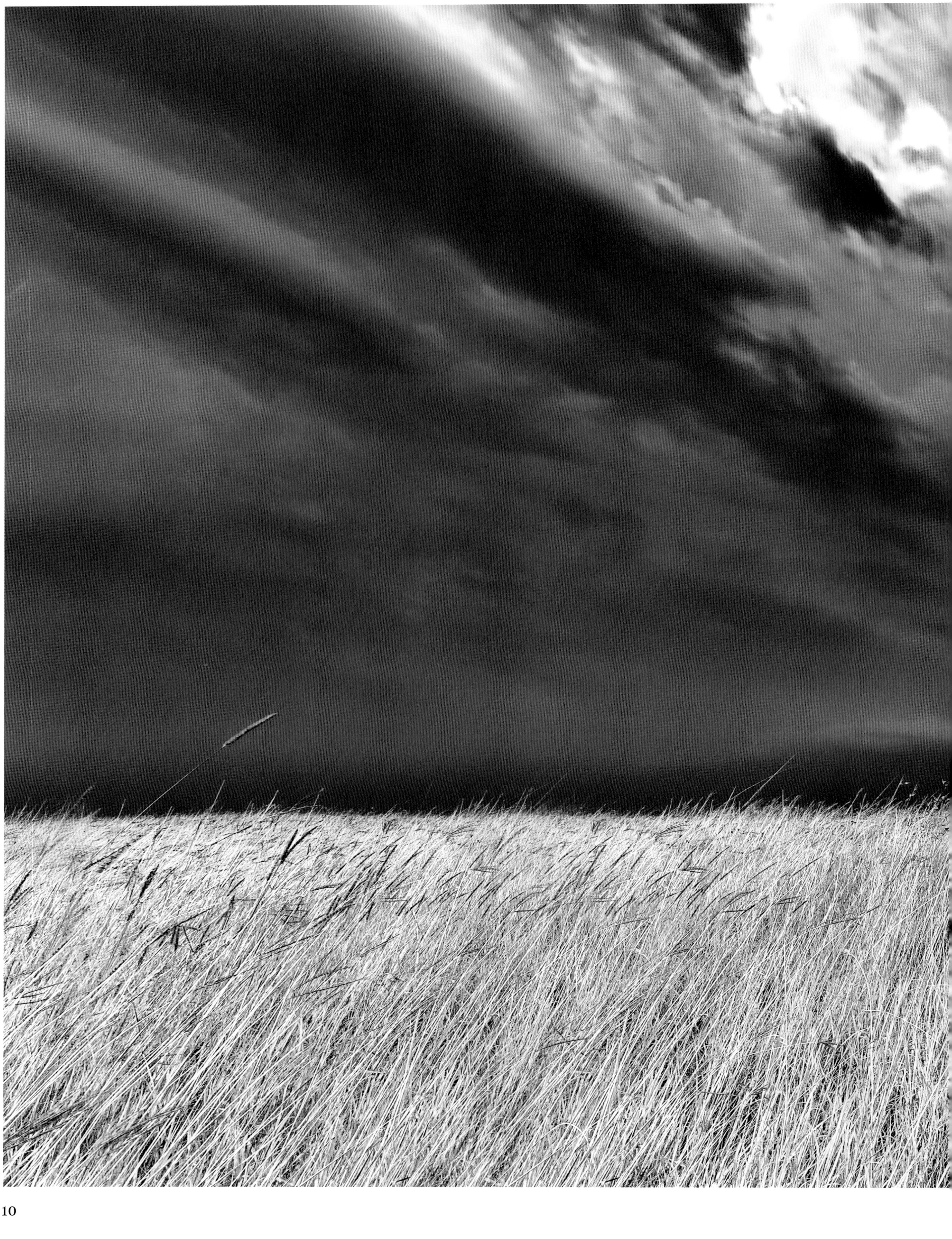

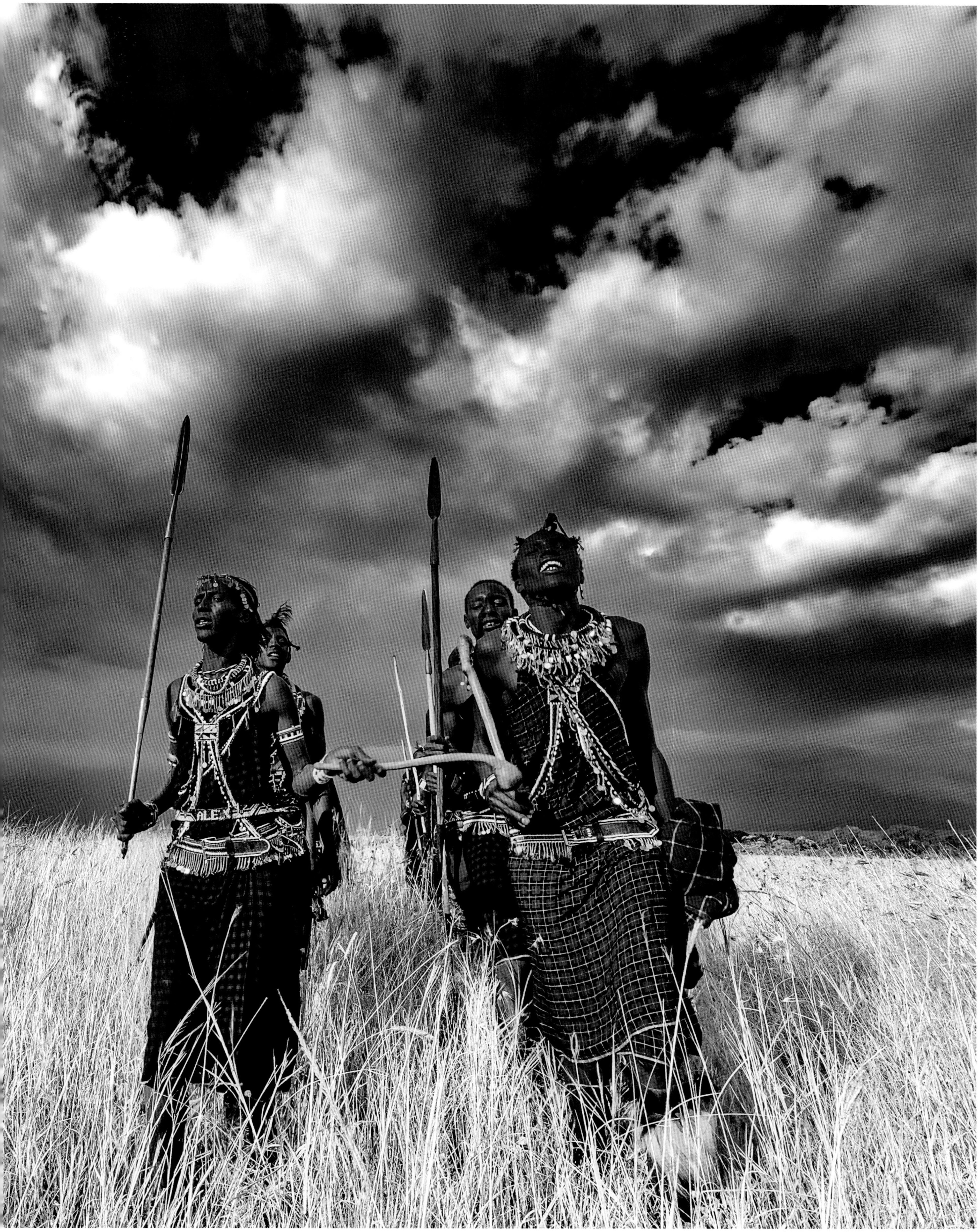
ALEX

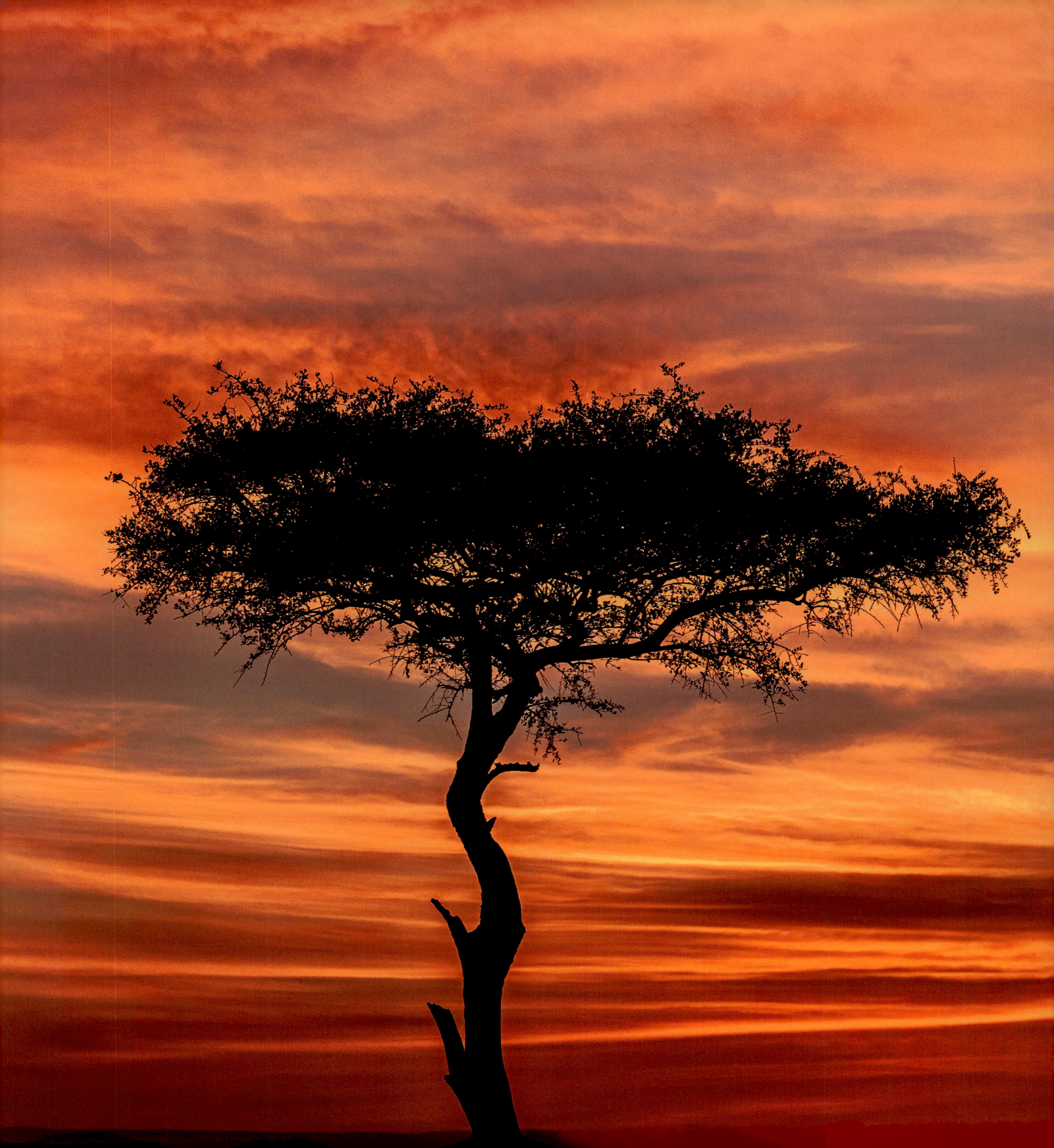

There was a time when 'out there' was every child's playground, somewhere they could cultivate an interest in the living world, where the rich smell of fresh earth and the intoxicating aroma of trees mingled with bird song and the haunting cry of a fox. It was a place to explore without grownups, a world infused with the promise of adventure and make-believe. It helped us to identify our strengths and weaknesses, building confidence and self-sufficiency. Bonding with nature offered the chance to challenge ourselves with the real or the imagined, a rite of passage that embedded a lifelong connection with the natural world, with the added benefit of ensuring healthier minds and bodies. Children who spend time in the great outdoors experience the echo of life as our early ancestors knew it: the need to find shelter, to hide from predators, learning how to track wild creatures, fashioning tools from sticks and stones, exploring the far horizon, embracing the darkness, marvelling at the star-filled sky. Being 'out there' allows us to learn courage and perseverance, to discover the key to our identity and our place in the natural order of things.

More than half the world's population now lives in cities. In an urbanised world, nature has come to mean something remote from everyday existence, a place that you drive through or visit occasionally (if at all), something taken for granted. This is witnessed by the lack of contact that many of our young people have with nature. If they do not experience it, they will not care. Meanwhile, with shutters tightly fastened to keep the wilderness at bay, our lives consumed by an insatiable desire for economic growth and wealth, the planet's wild and beautiful landscapes are under siege. Oceans are drowning in plastic, the wide open savannas fenced off into individual plots, mountains ripped open for their minerals, forests and jungles felled for timber, deserts desecrated for hidden treasures. Plants and animals of every description – birds, reptiles, mammals, marine creatures – are being driven to extinction. The bonds holding nature dear to us have been ruptured. No quiet and pristine corner of the Earth remains untouched by humankind; our ecological footprint is burnished deep into the ice and sand, mountain and ocean.

It is time for us to restore balance to our view of the natural world. Unless we limit the impact of the human population on the environment to sustainable levels, we will continue to jeopardise the health of the planet and the wellbeing of future generations. To quote artist and naturalist Jonathan Kingdon, 'Impoverishing an irreplaceable asset is a failure of mankind.'

The story of the origins of life on Earth is more spectacular than anything the human mind could have conceived. The universe is around 13,800 million years old (some believe it is younger, at 11,000 million years old). Time of this magnitude is beyond human comprehension, measured against a human life of three score years and 10. Our life-giving solar system is five billion years old, the Earth 4.6 billion. All life that ever existed evolved from a single-celled organism that came into being roughly 3.5 billion years ago, a fact first alluded to by Charles Darwin in his ground-breaking *On the Origin of Species* (1859). Origins stunned the world of science and delivered a body blow to formal religion by offering the world a new creation story: evolution through natural selection with only the fittest among species surviving. The ability to reproduce itself is the common thread in nature's miraculous living web, with deoxyribonucleic acid (DNA) carrying the genetic code for the development and reproduction of all known organisms and many viruses.

Simple proteins coded by DNA gave rise to the earliest plants and animals – first in the sea and then on land. In time, flying reptiles and birds also mastered the skies. Beneath our feet a handful of soil has more living organisms than the nearly eight billion people that today dominate Planet Earth. Nature capitalises on every opportunity, moulding life forms to every niche. The miracle of a termite colony composed of hundreds of millions of individuals co-operating as a single entity bridges life above and below ground, while the grand presence of a six-tonne bull elephant lumbering quietly across the African savanna provides yet another glimpse of the breadth of nature's creativity.

If the roll call of life on Earth is staggering, so too is its obituary. Between 10 and 14 million species of plants, animals, fungi and bacteria are thought to be alive today, though only a fraction of those – around 1.2 million – have been documented. This number is dwarfed by the fact that 99 per cent of all species that ever lived – over five billion – have gone extinct. Over the eons, there have been five mass extinctions. The first occurred 450 million years ago, most likely caused by a cold snap, while the worst dates to 250 million years ago: a cataclysmic volcanic event that released huge amounts of carbon dioxide into the atmosphere, wiping out 96 per cent of marine and 70 per cent of land species; a stark warning to humankind in these days of climate crisis. In recent times, the rate of extinction has increased a thousandfold, leading to a staggering loss of biodiversity. If that trend continues, 50 per cent of land and marine life will have become extinct by 2100. Scientists are already calling our era the Anthropocene or Sixth Mass Extinction, defined by a 'biological annihilation of wildlife' whose cause rests squarely on our shoulders, though seemingly not on our conscience.

Darwin was right in believing the chimpanzee is our closest living relative, though of just how much we are part of an ancient continuum dating back to the genesis of all forms of life still fails to resonate with significant parts of the population. Forty per cent of Americans believe God created humans in their present form 10,000 years ago. So at what point did humans begin to view themselves as apart from nature? The fossil record confirms that our primate ancestors evolved in Africa, forest-dwelling apes wrapped in a thick coat of fur to shield them from the chill night, powerful muscular arms and sturdy legs allowing them to navigate through the canopy during the hours of daylight. At times they stood up on their hind legs, reaching out for food items or to gain a better view through the dense foliage, plotting the way ahead. And then something happened to the weather.

Millions of years ago, sub-Saharan Africa was transformed by a prolonged dry spell. The great forested enclaves began to open up, the rainforests retreated to the equatorial belt and scattered strongholds in the north, giving way to savanna woodlands alternating with dry forests and grasslands. Looking out from the treetops, our primate relatives saw opportunity. Driven by the urge to explore new horizons and to exploit novel sources of food, the more adventurous among them emerged tentatively into the daylight, standing upright, albeit briefly at first, to peer cautiously over the long grass, scanning for danger. Initially they would have stayed close to the boundary between forest and grassland, running for the relative safety of the trees when alarmed and sleeping in the canopy as wild chimpanzees and gorillas do today.

These early hominids – small bands of relatives and friends – eked out a precarious existence as hunter-gatherers as they sought ever more sophisticated ways to shield themselves from the elements. They harnessed fire and crude weapons to tame the wilderness and keep predators at bay, sheltering in caves and rocky outcrops, huddled for warmth and security around the flickering embers of the camp fire. They depended entirely on the bounty of the wilderness, regarding the Earth as sacred and themselves as its beneficiaries. They saw the hand of the gods in the night sky, the expression of divine wrath

They depended entirely on the bounty of the wilderness, regarding the Earth as sacred and themselves as its beneficiaries.

in the sound of thunder and the crackle of lightning. Firelight illuminated the darkness as stories, dance and ritual shared around the hearth provided the fabric of society, a rich tapestry that gave meaning to their lives, binding generations together with a common purpose. Their large brains and increasingly complex language skills allowed them to decipher the intentions of group members and work out how best to live with neighbours. It enabled them to plan where it would be best to hunt tomorrow and how to outwit their prey.

While living in the present, we were learning to imagine the future, to participate in constructing and realising our dreams. We buried our dead and imagined an afterlife. We became more and more innovative, fashioning needles from sticks, stones and bone splinters to stitch together fur and hides, fastening them tight around our bodies to keep us warm during the deep freeze of ice ages. By 35,000 years ago, we were creating astonishing works of art such as the cave paintings at Chauvet in France and more recently at Lascaux. Equally evident is the devastating impact we had on other species as we spread across the globe, witnessed by mass extinctions of large mammals hunted by the first humans to reach Australia and America, perhaps 40,000 and 30,000 years ago respectively.

Our ancestors were unaware of the consequences of their actions. We no longer have that excuse. We can see clearly the effects of the choices we have made in the past and we can glimpse the future. At some point we began to believe we could survive with little regard to the fate of the natural world rather than as an integral part of it. A turning point was the advent of the Holocene period, characterised by warmer conditions and climate stability that encouraged a shift from hunter-gathering to agriculture around 12,000 years ago. The planting of crops and domestication of animals offered a more settled existence. Food could be stored to ensure survival during lean times for family and clan. We began to fashion a way of life predicated on taming nature, pushing back the wilderness and bending it to our will. We avoided the forests where real or imagined danger might lurk. We demonised predators and human rivals alike, as something other, something to be subjugated or destroyed.

With food production more assured, larger communities evolved: the towns, cities and nation states that define so much of our culture. By 2,000 years ago, the global population had increased from a few hundred thousand hunter-gatherers to 300 million farmers and urbanites. In the 18th century – fuelled by the exploitation of coal and oil – the Industrial Revolution transformed the workplace in Europe. A boom in technology gave birth to an economy built on machines, manpower and trade. But the real cost was the plunder of the world's resources. We came to view the natural environment as a commodity we could exploit to improve our health and comfort, with little regard for the future of the planet and its wild inhabitants. The price of civilisation has been the loss of our deeply spiritual connection to nature.

The elevation of humanity above all other life as sanctioned by the Christian church left the fate of the living world resting precariously in our hands. The biblical book of Genesis commands us to 'be fruitful and multiply and fill the Earth and subdue it and have dominion over ... every living thing that moves on the Earth'. Now the old gods have fallen silent. Science has brought us a new reality based on fact rather than fiction. But science alone cannot provide all the answers or sustain our spiritual needs. People yearn for a sacred narrative: we long to believe in something.

So today we need a new mythology. In the early 1970s, the British chemist and inventor James Lovelock and American biologist Lynn Margulis stirred the public imagination with what became known as the Gaia hypothesis, after the Greek goddess of the Earth. Gaia envisions Earth as a self-regulating entity balancing climate, atmosphere, soil and ocean in a way that is favourable to life. It resonates with the need for a global perspective acknowledging that life co-evolved with its environment. This vision is captured in the breathtaking image of Earth – all pristine blues, greens and whites – taken while orbiting the moon in 1968 by astronaut William Anders. 'Earthrise', as it became known, evokes a state of transcendent awe and identification with the planet. Viewed from so far away, humans and their egos become invisible, no more or less important than the rest of life on Earth, promoting a feeling of unity with nature which blurs the distinctions of race and politics that divide the world. The Russian cosmonaut Yuri Artyukhin summed it up perfectly: 'It isn't important in which sea or lake you observe a slick of pollution or in the forests of which country a fire breaks out, or on which continent a hurricane arises. You are standing guard over the whole of our Earth.'

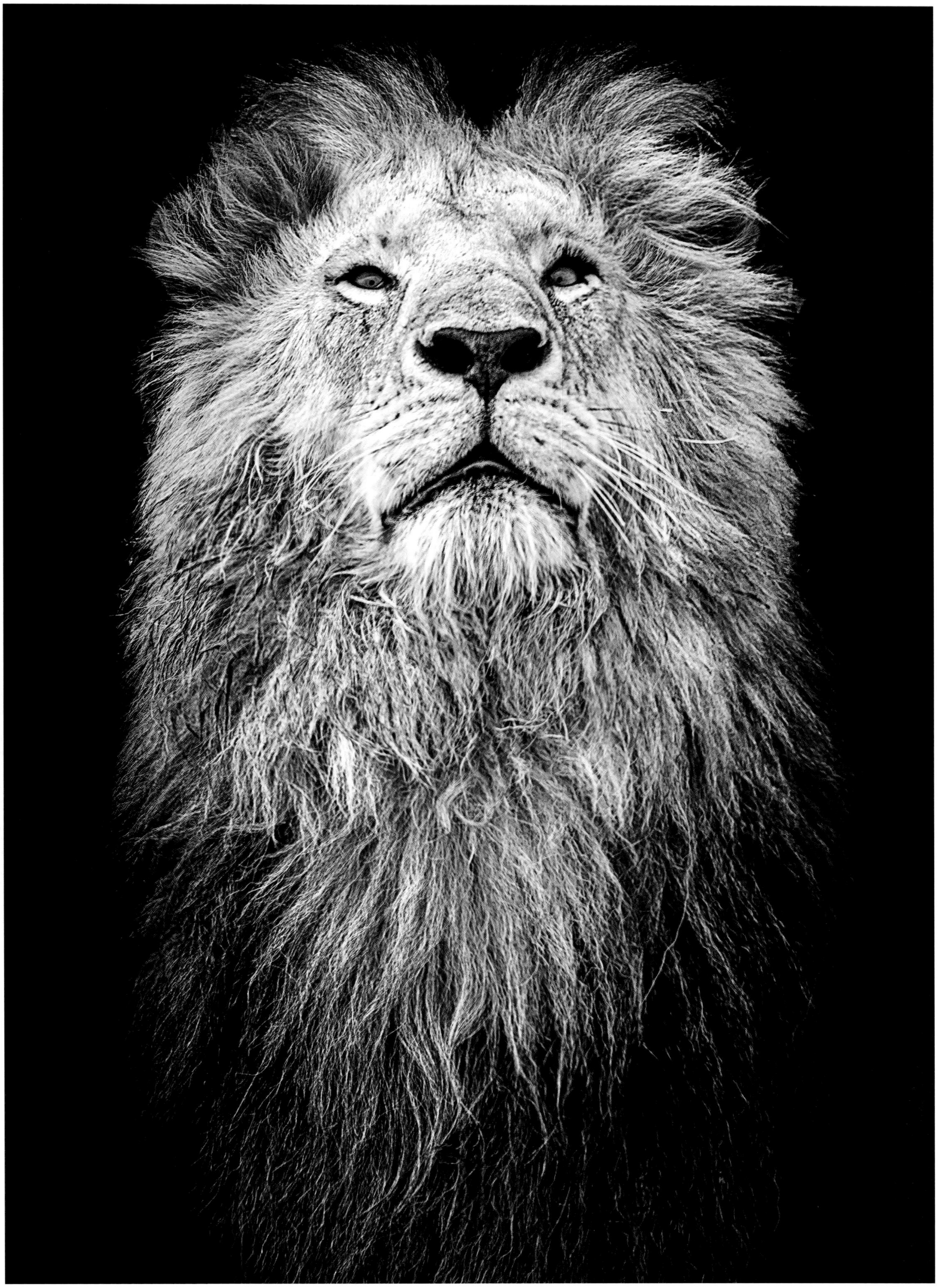

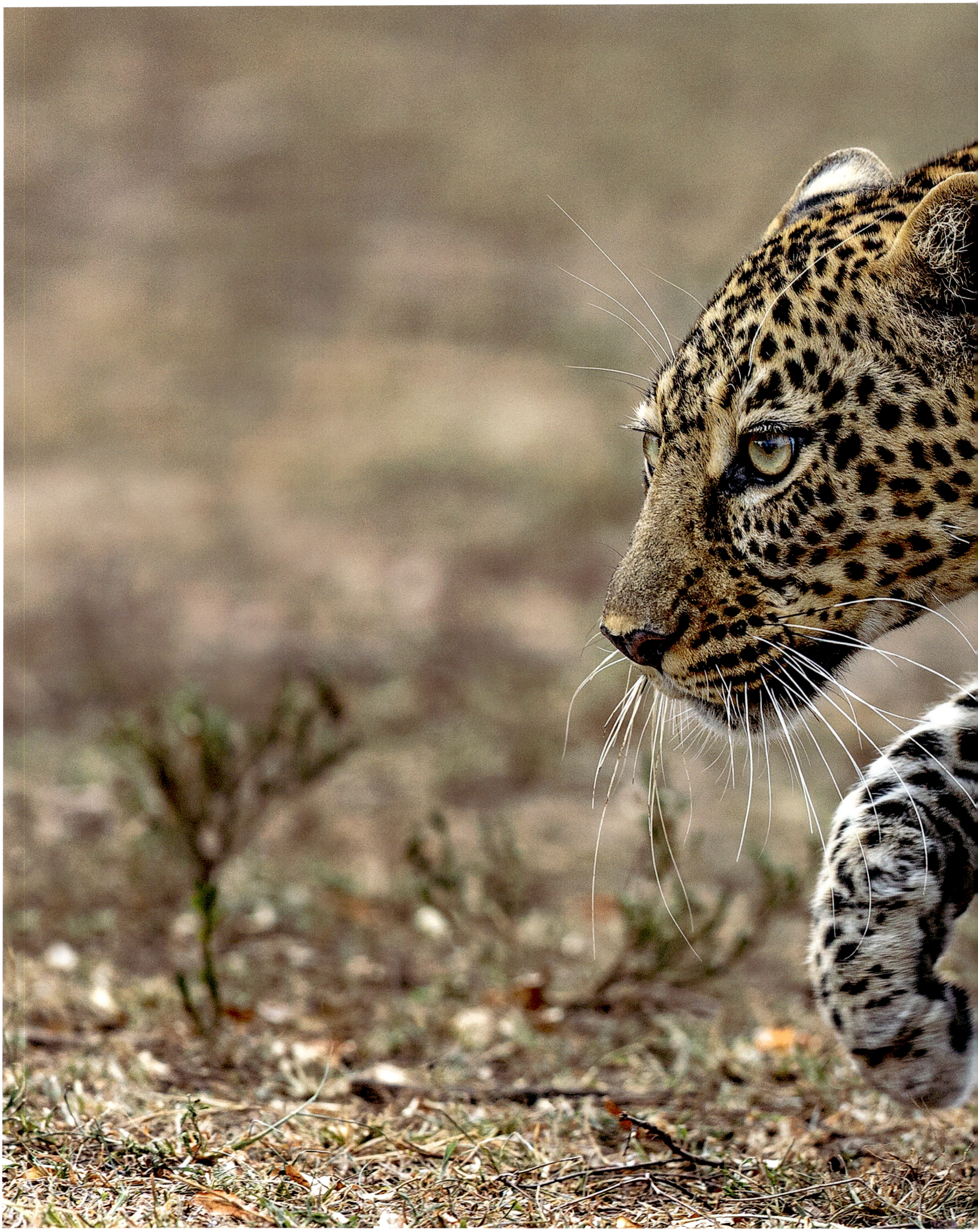

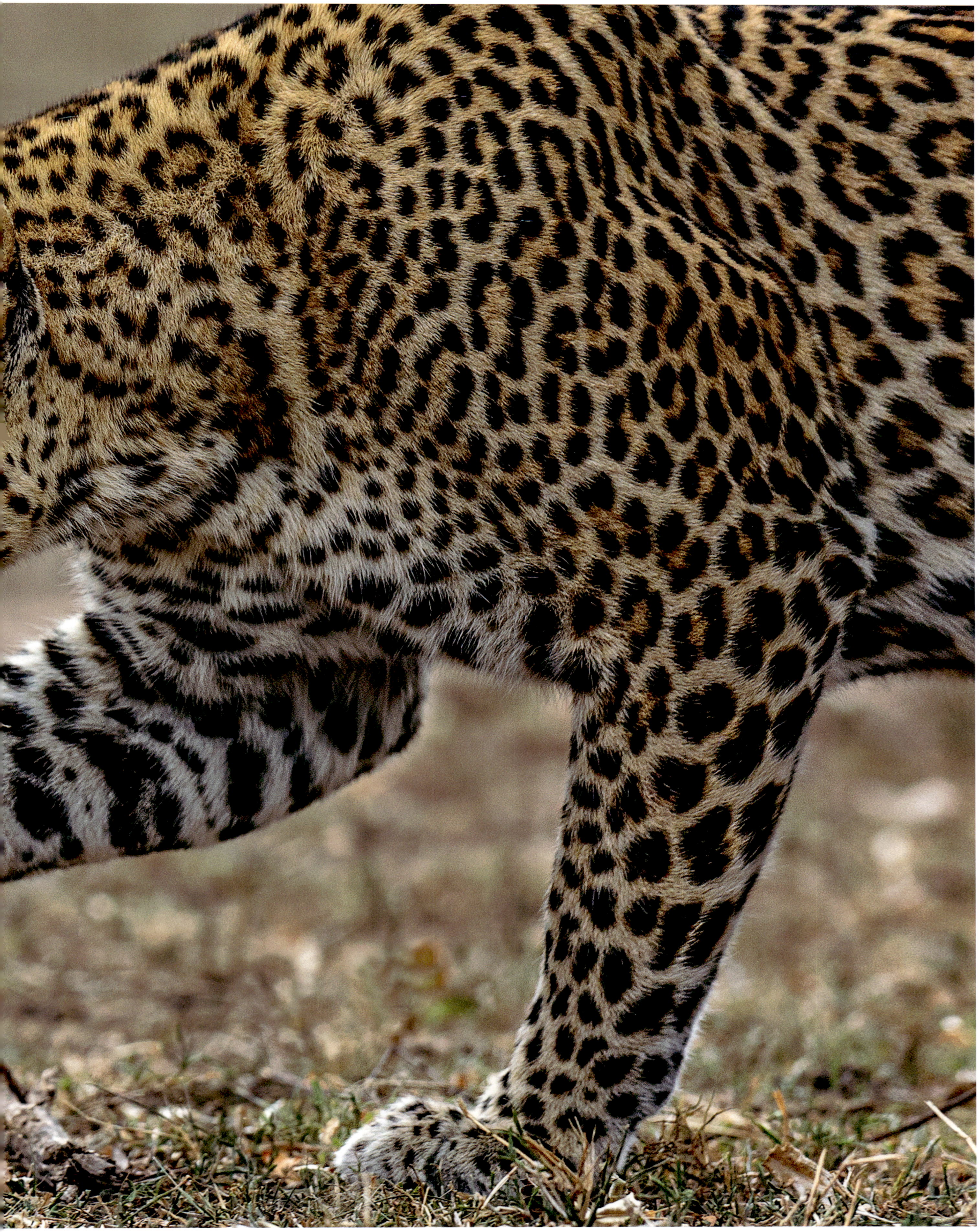

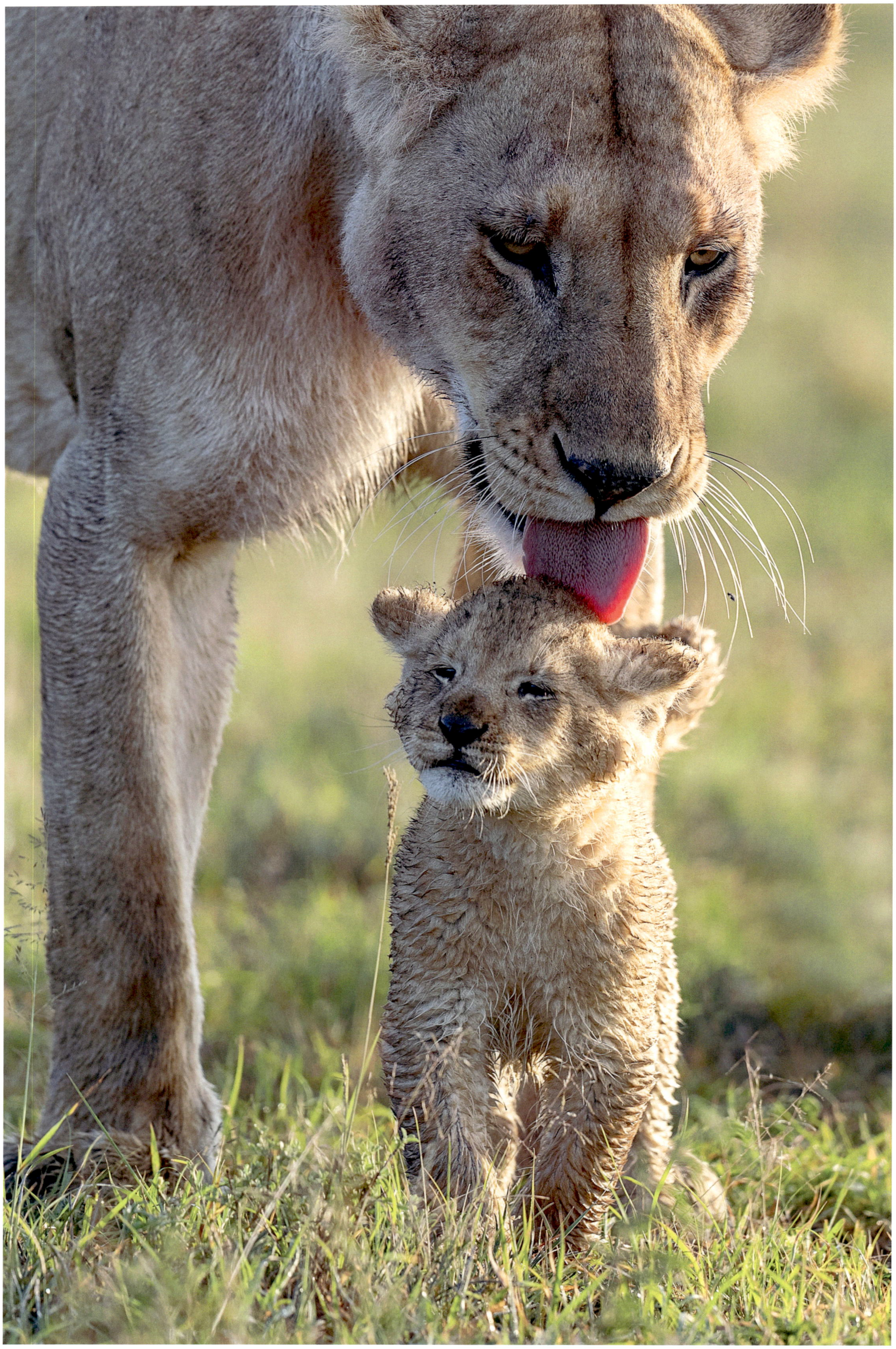

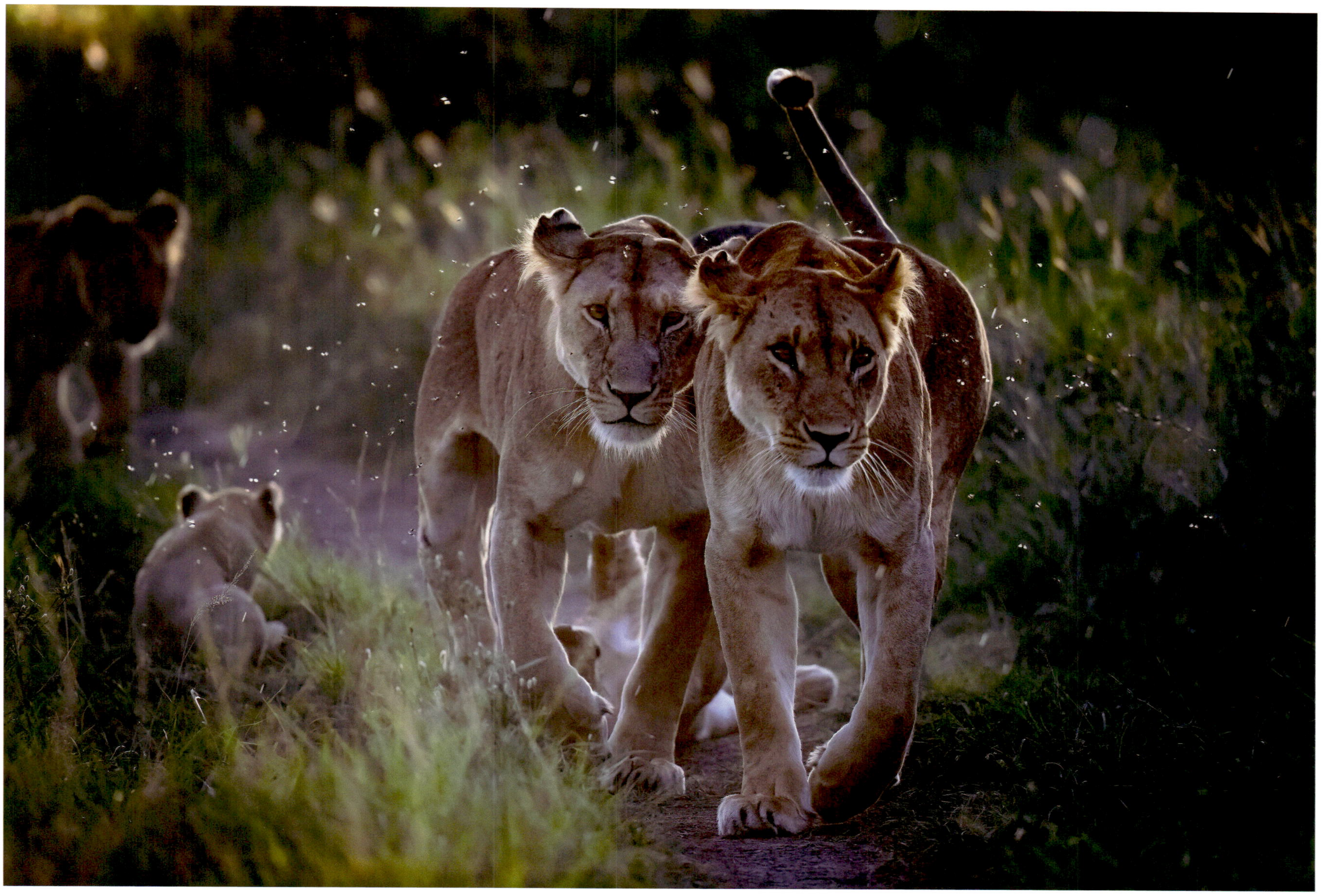

It is in the still silence of nature where one will find true bliss.

— *Unknown*

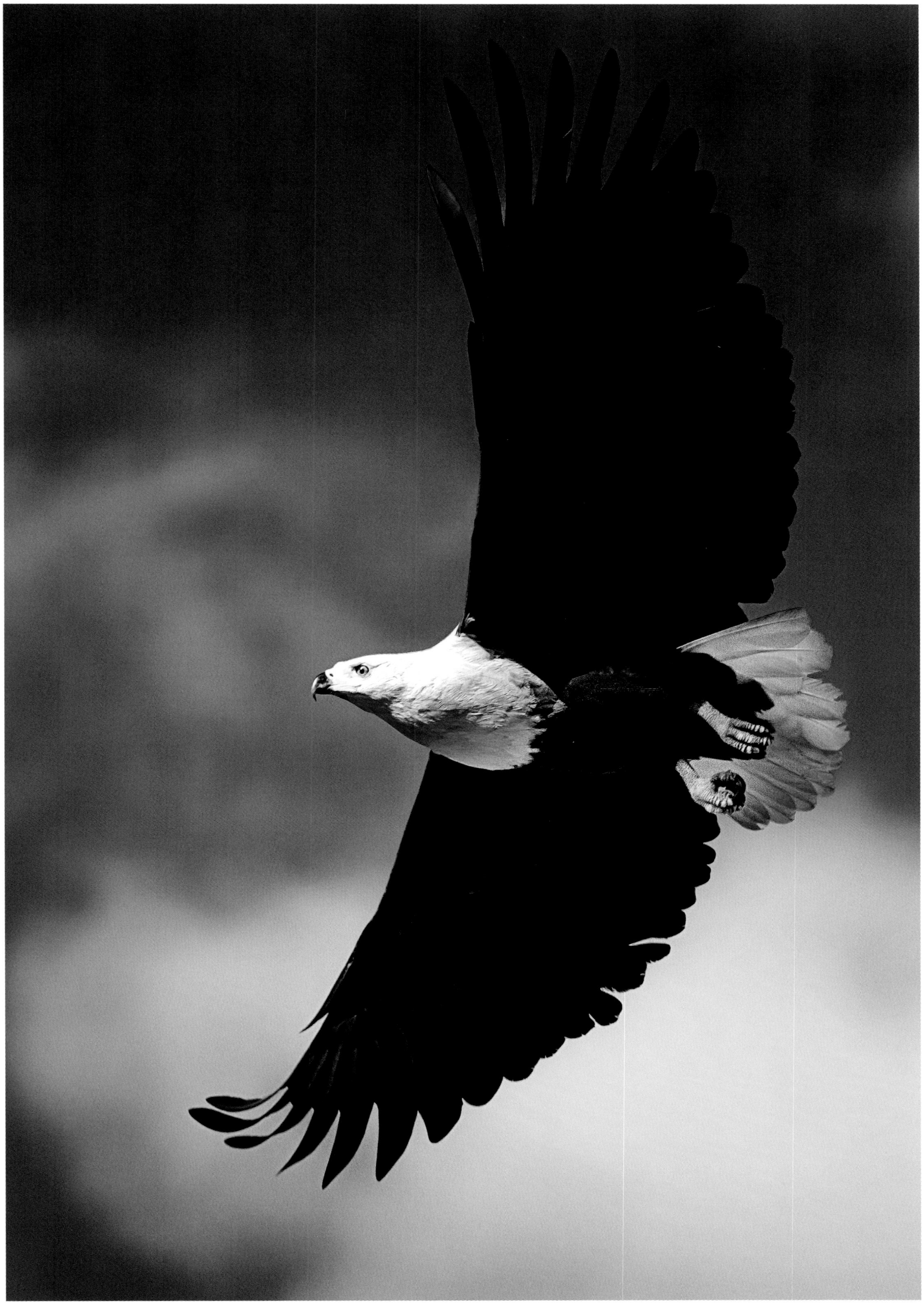

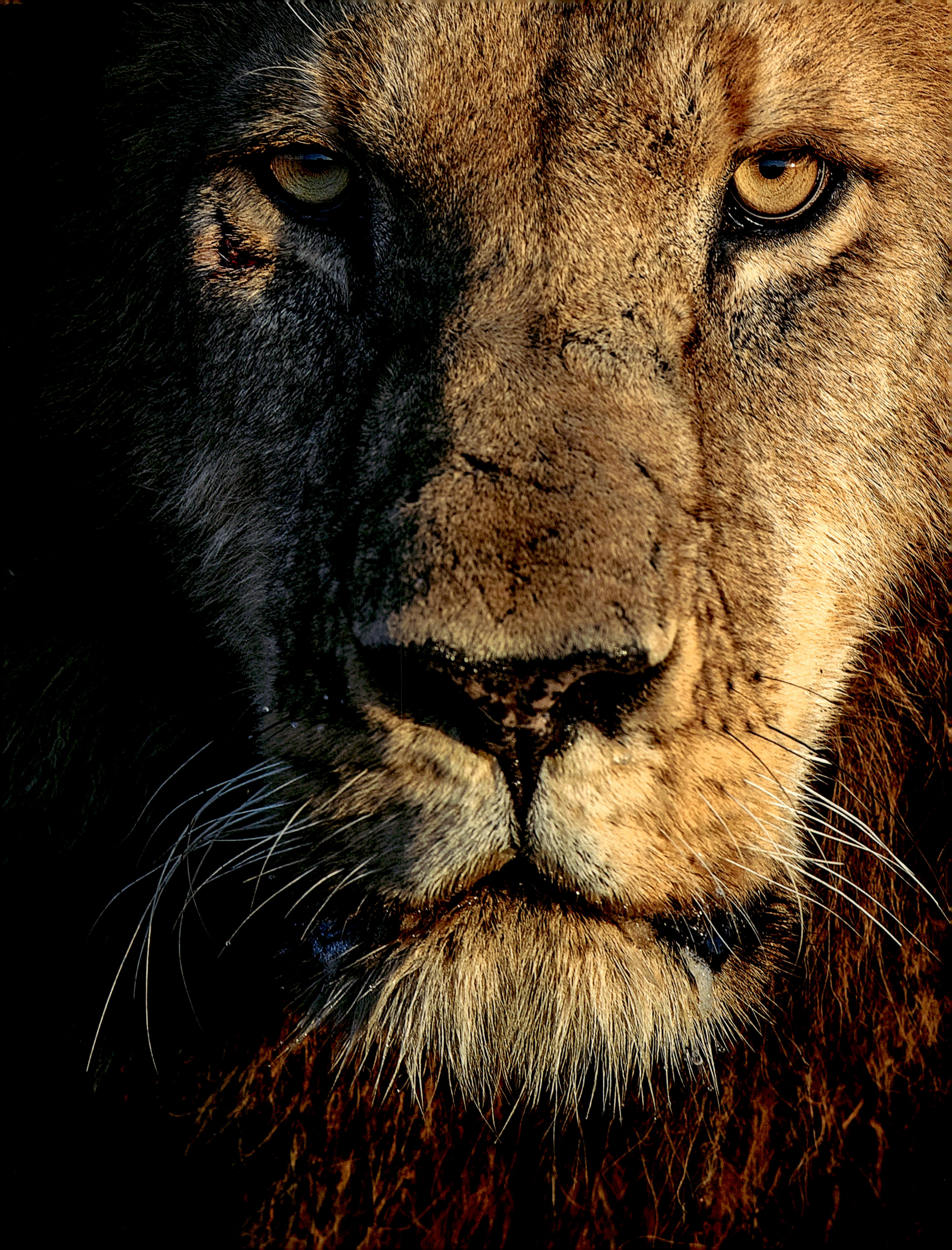

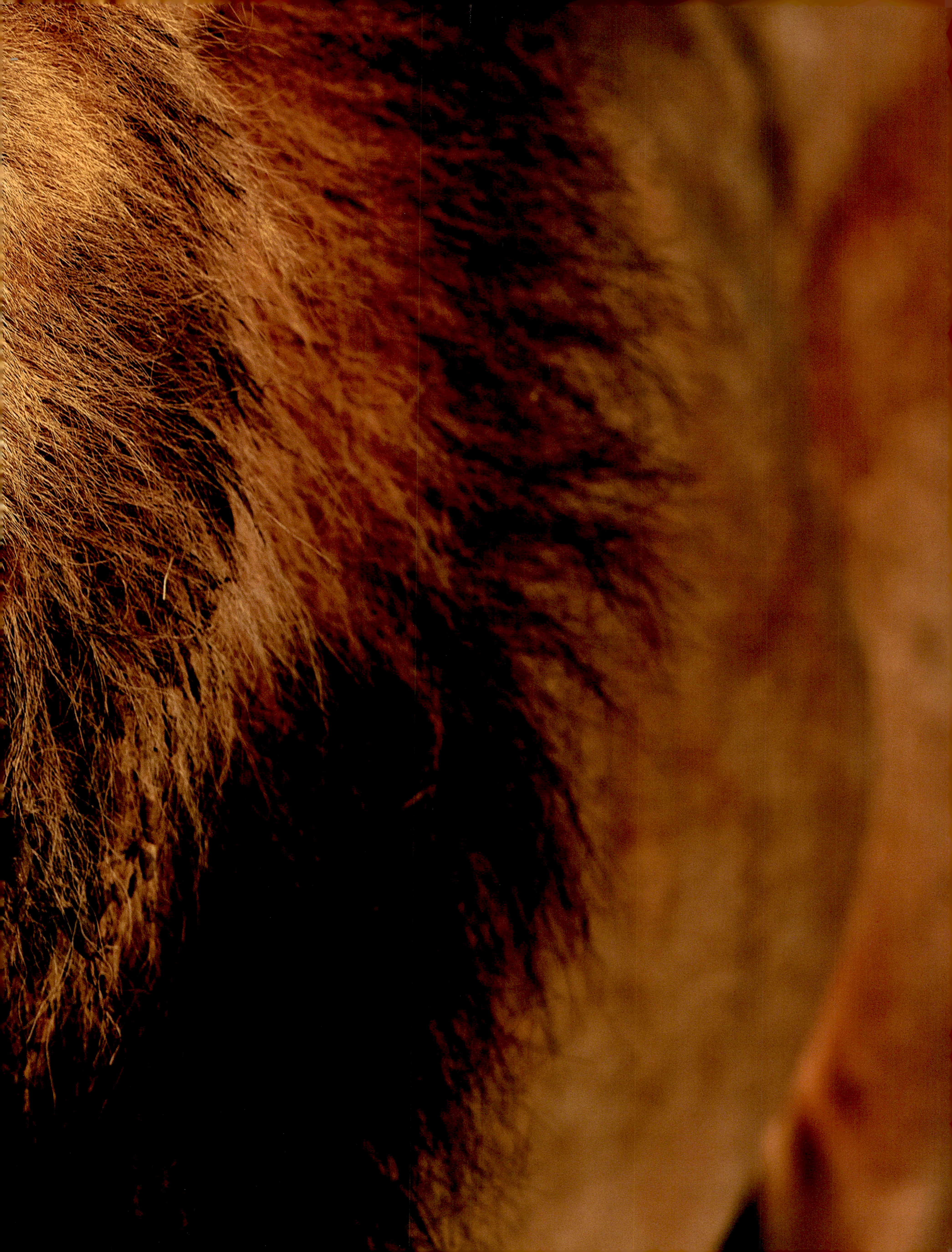

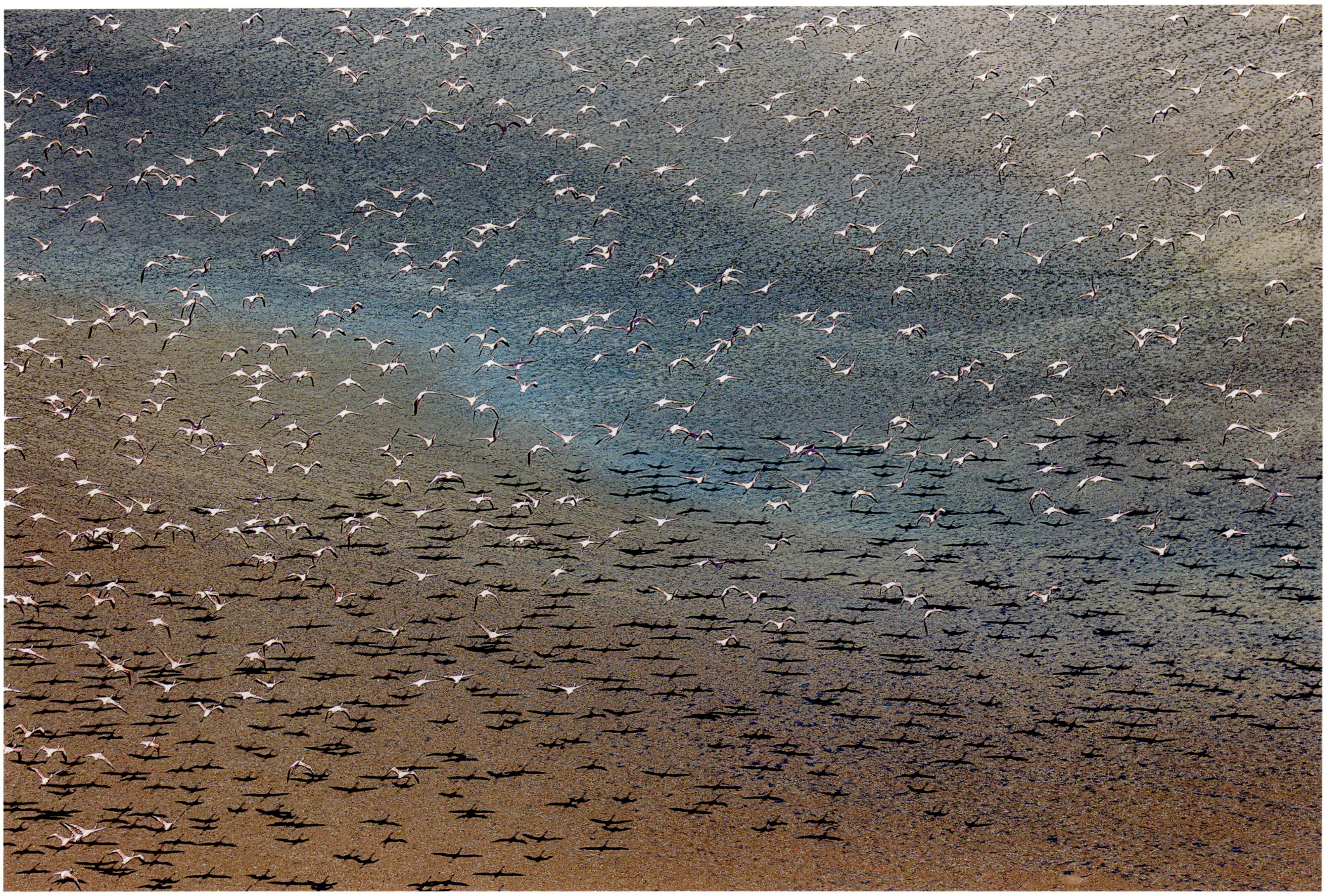

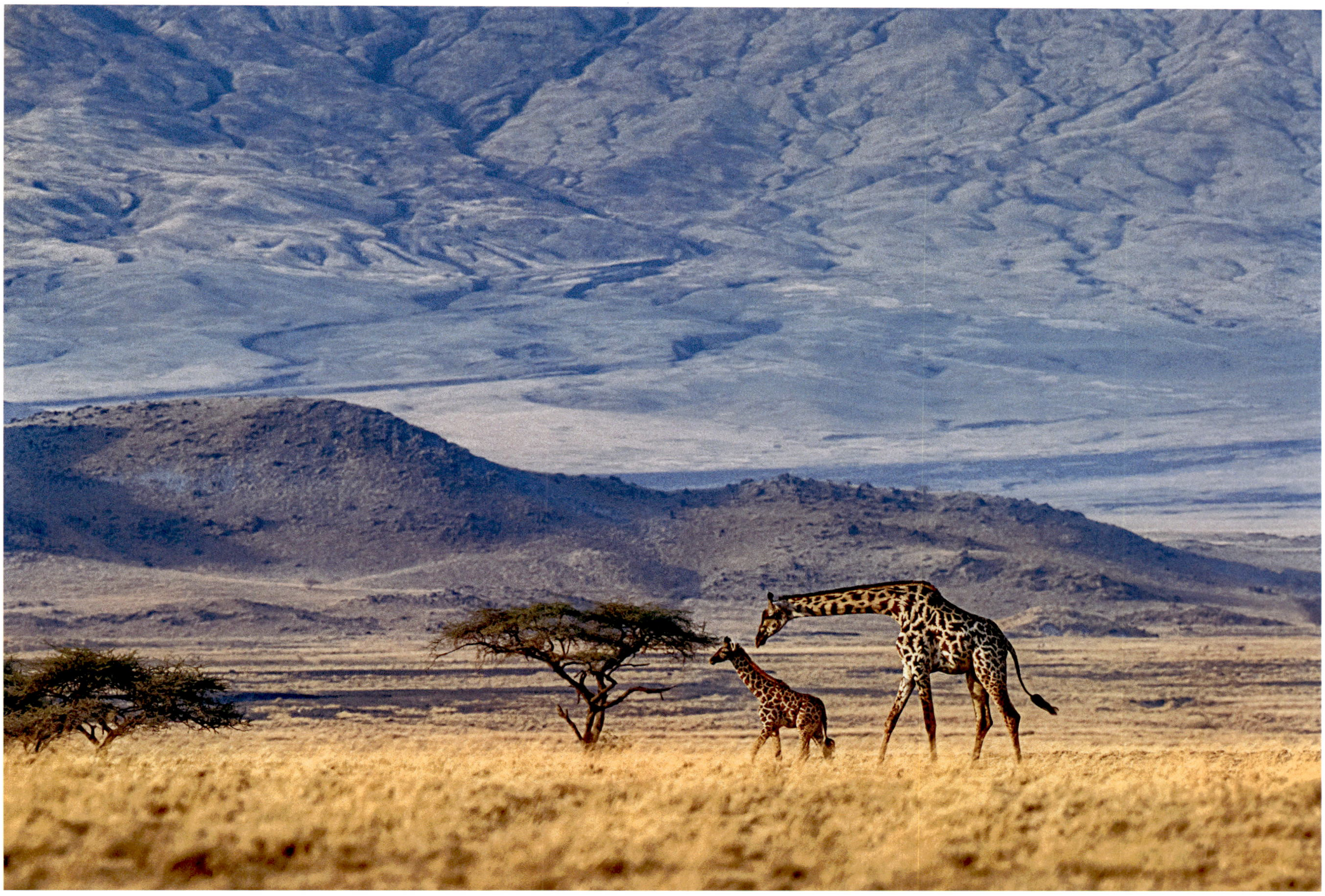

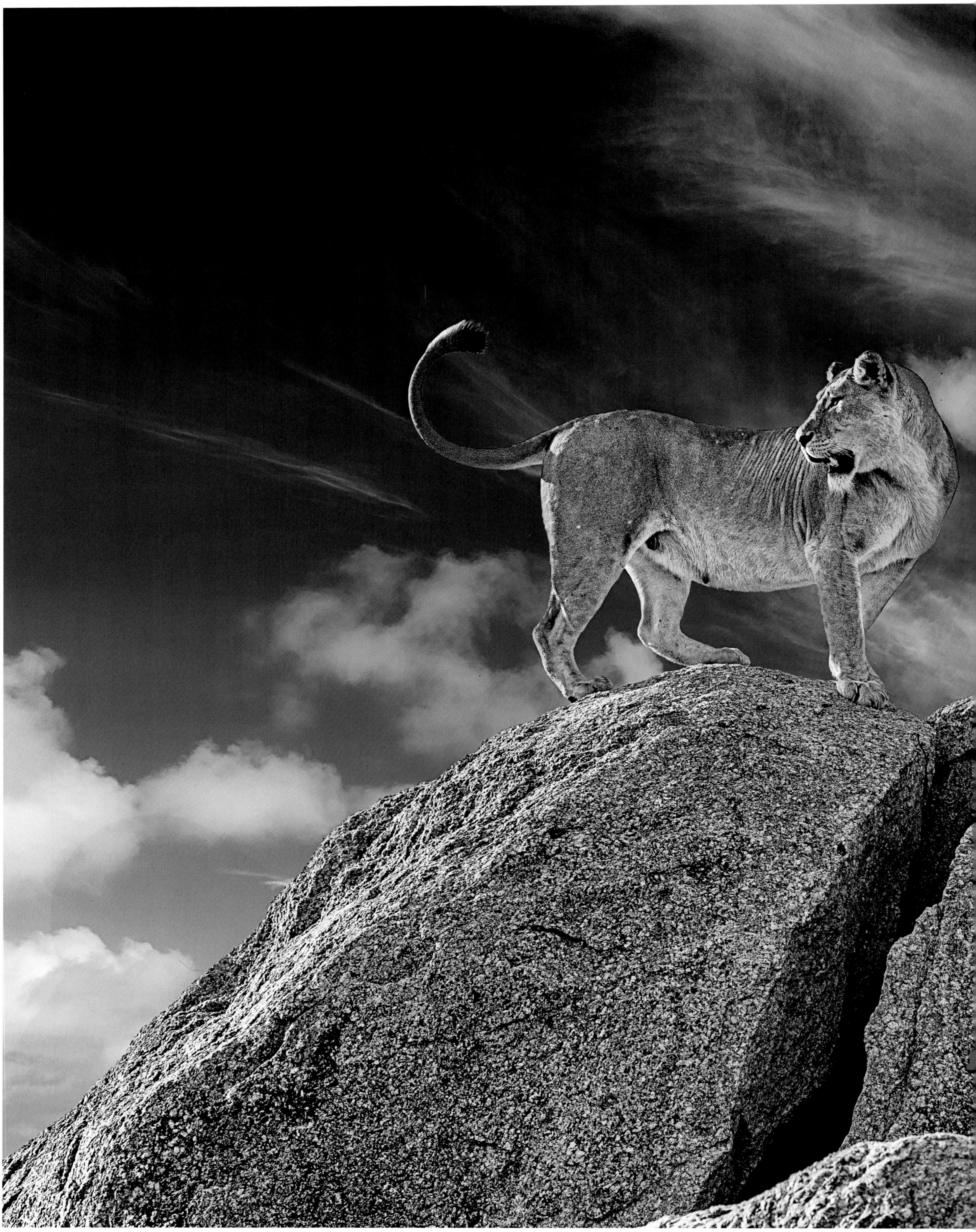

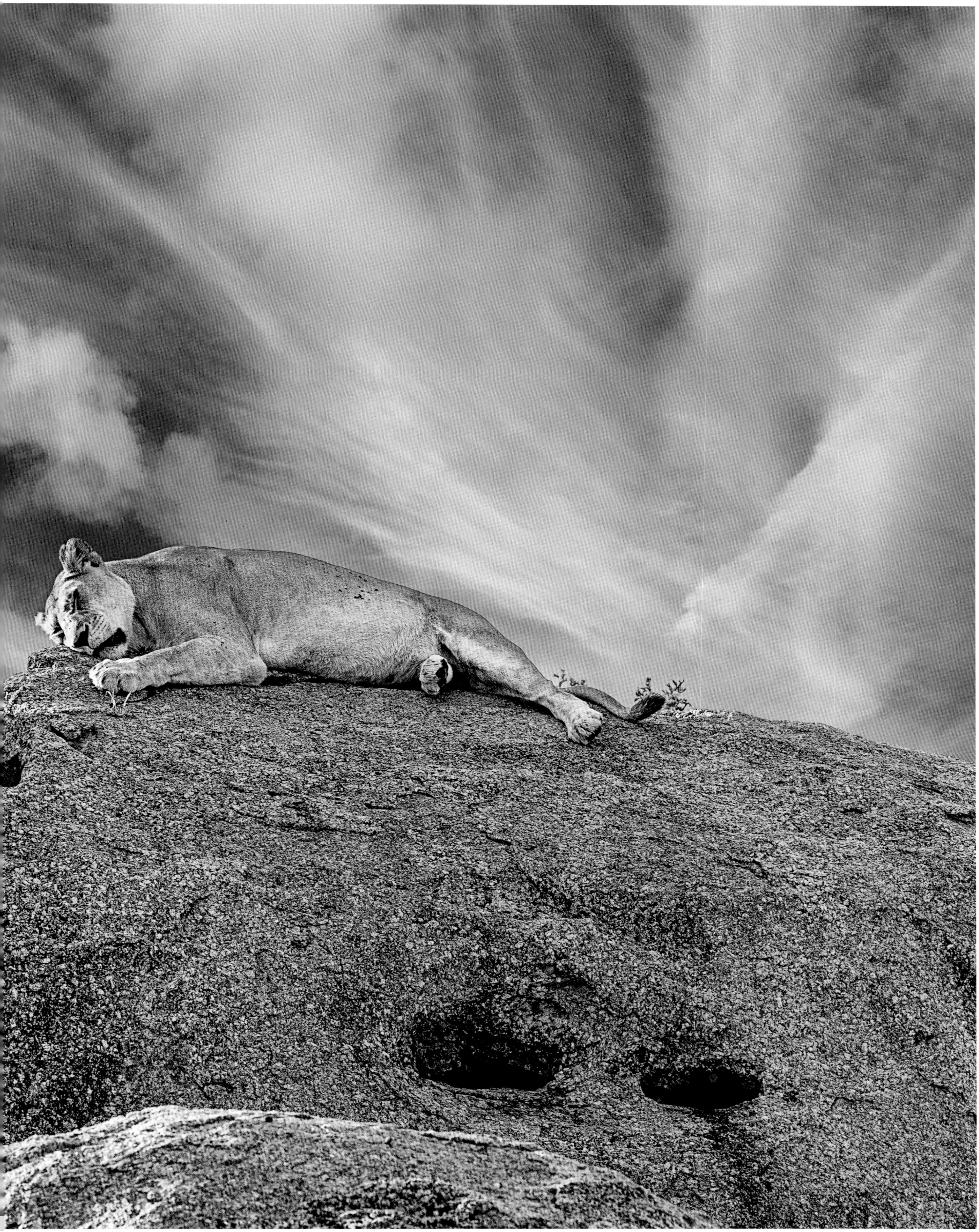

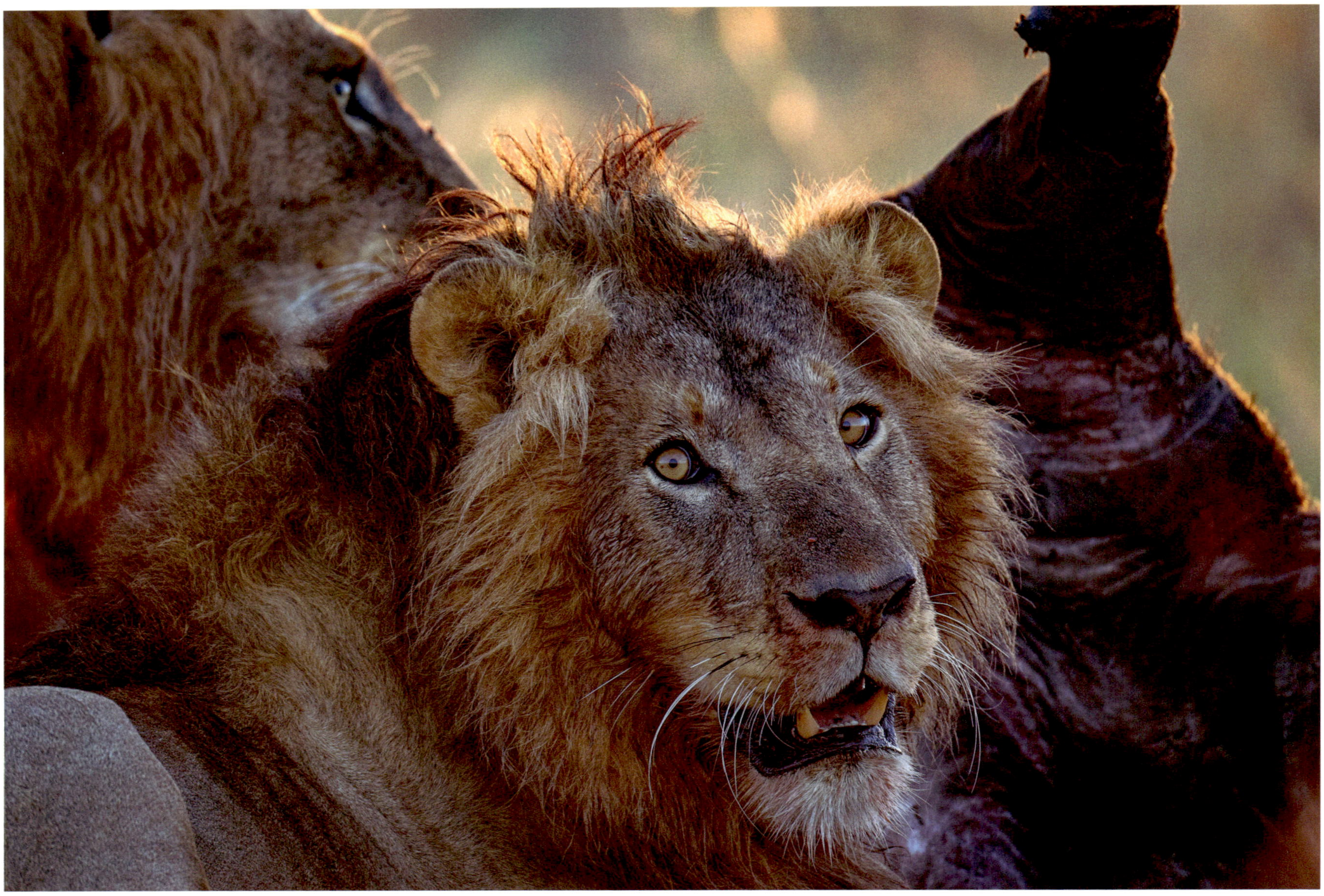

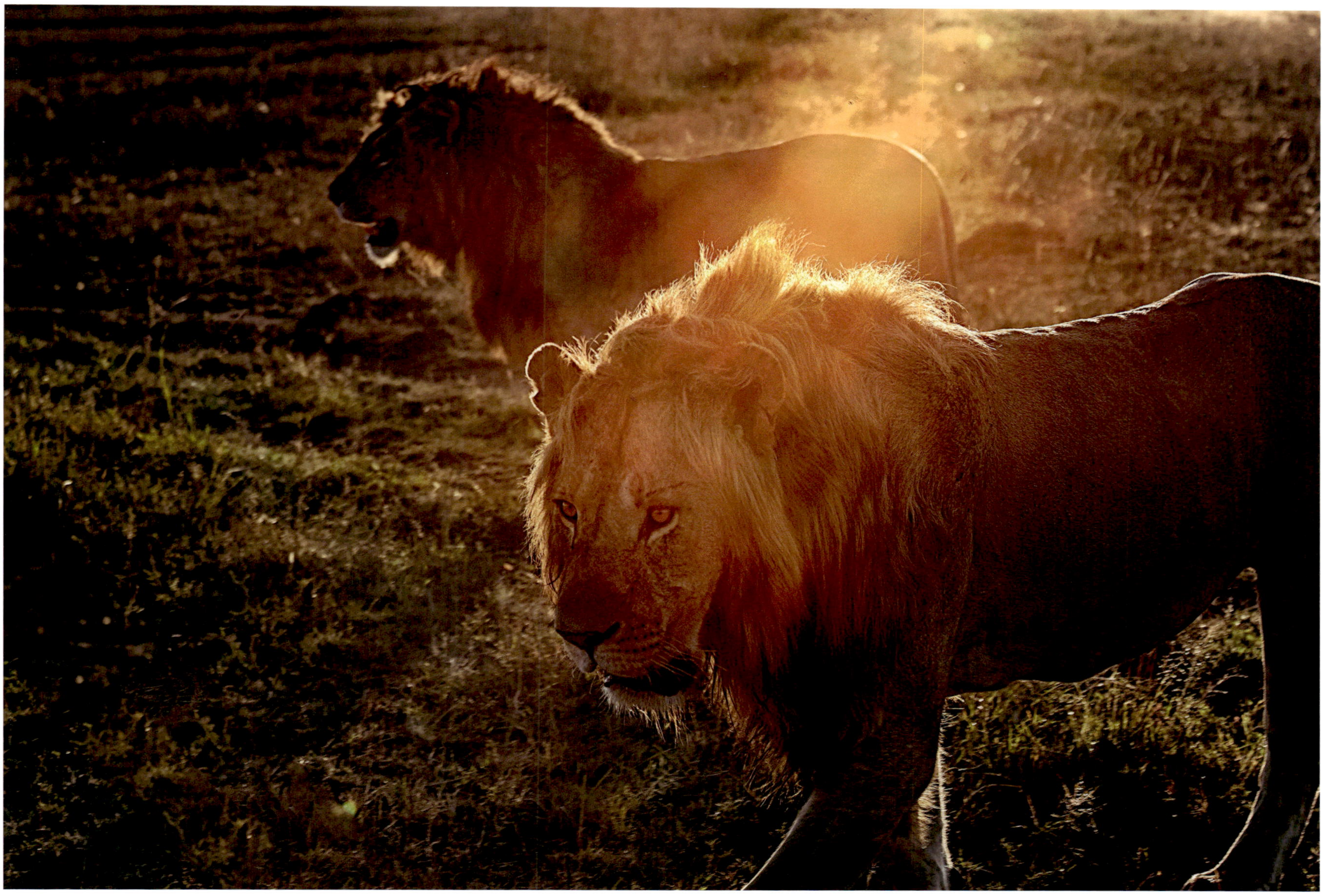

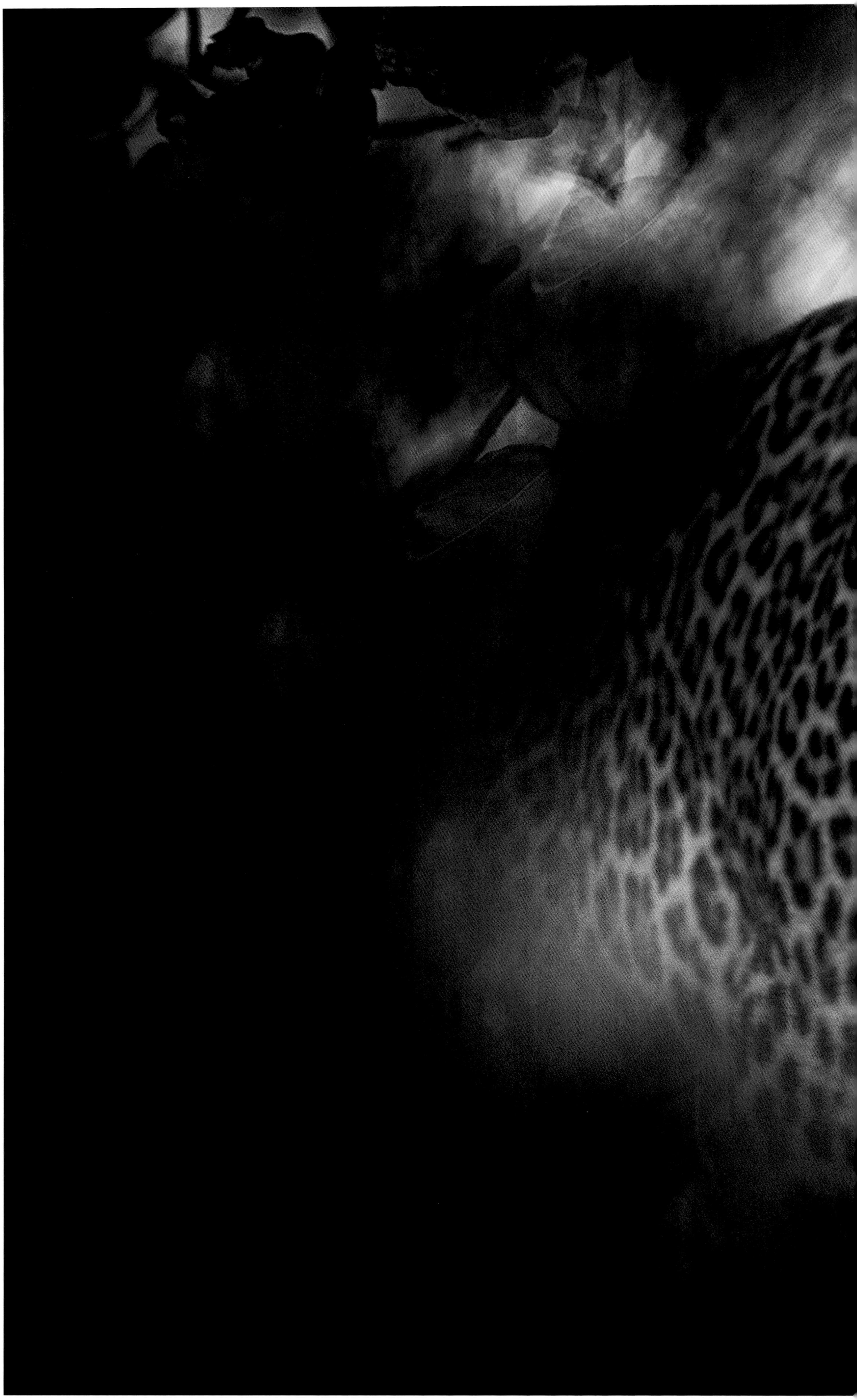

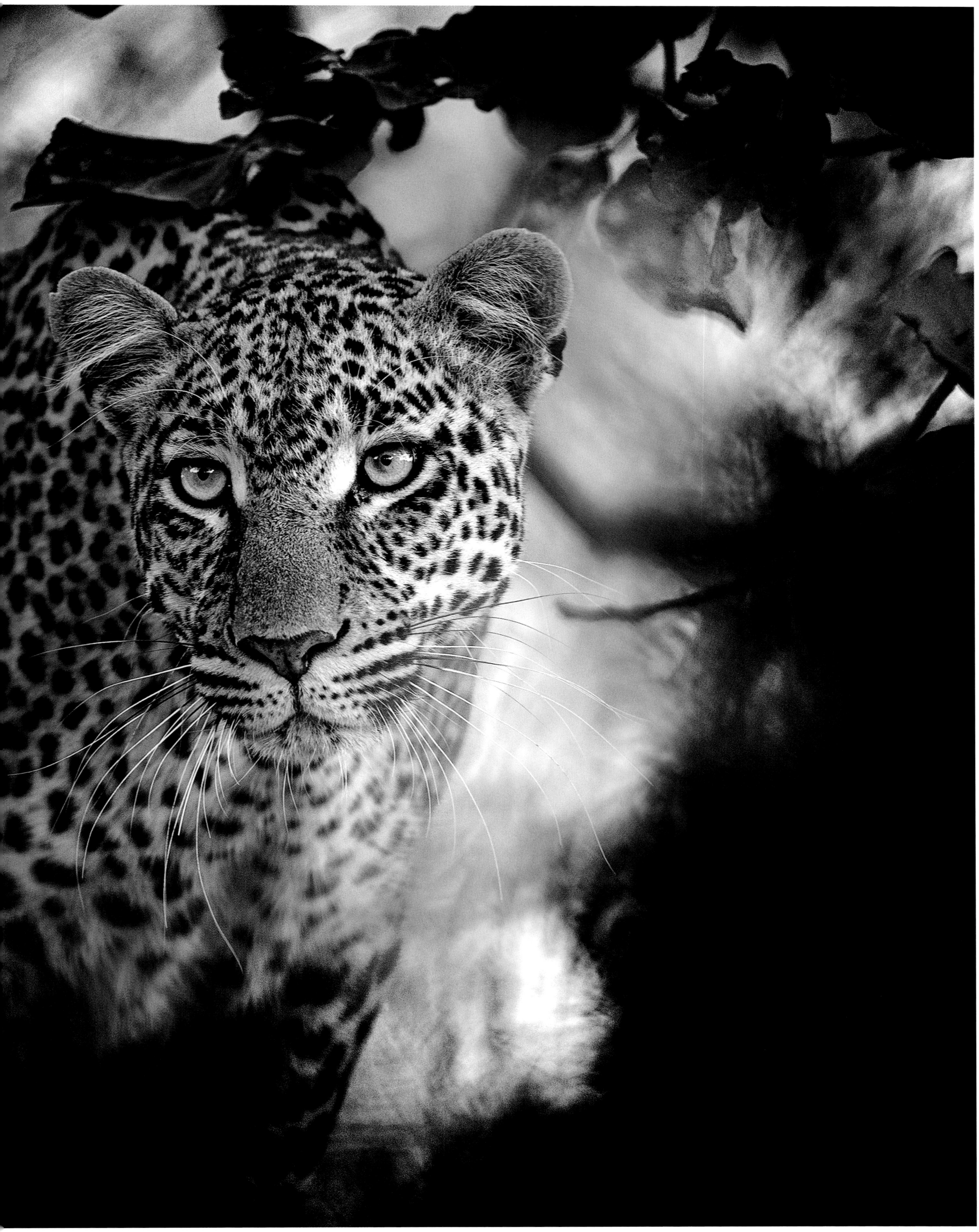

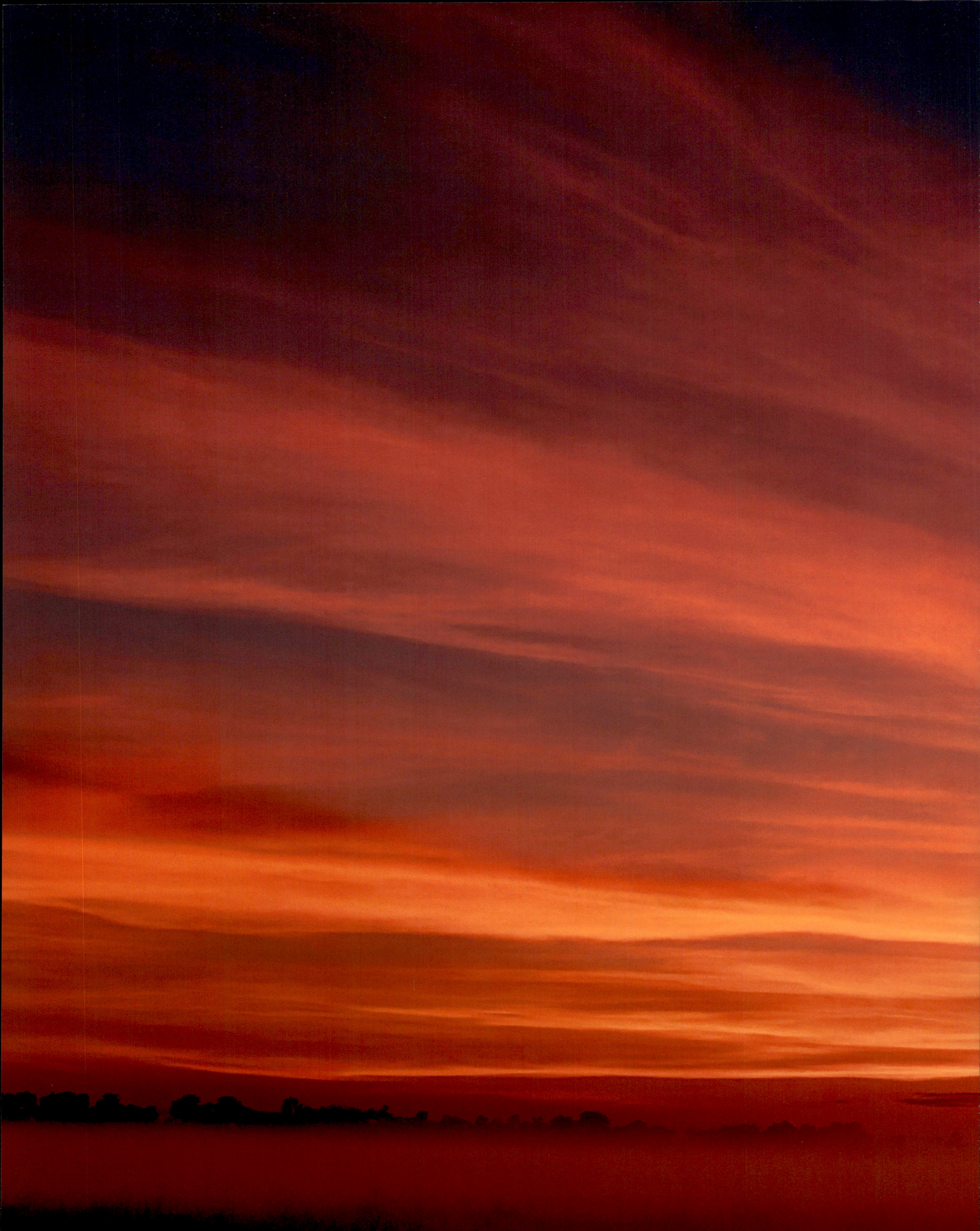

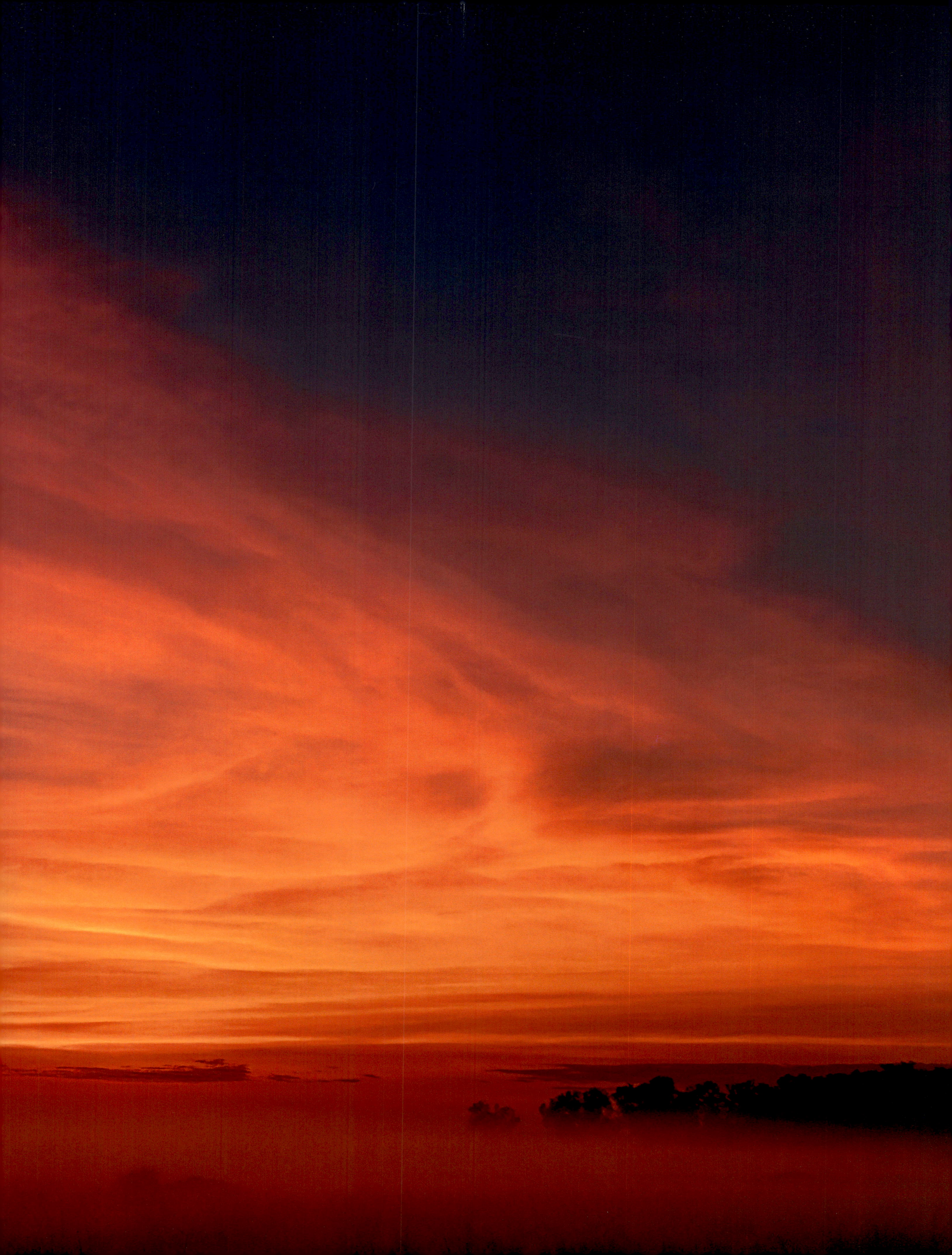

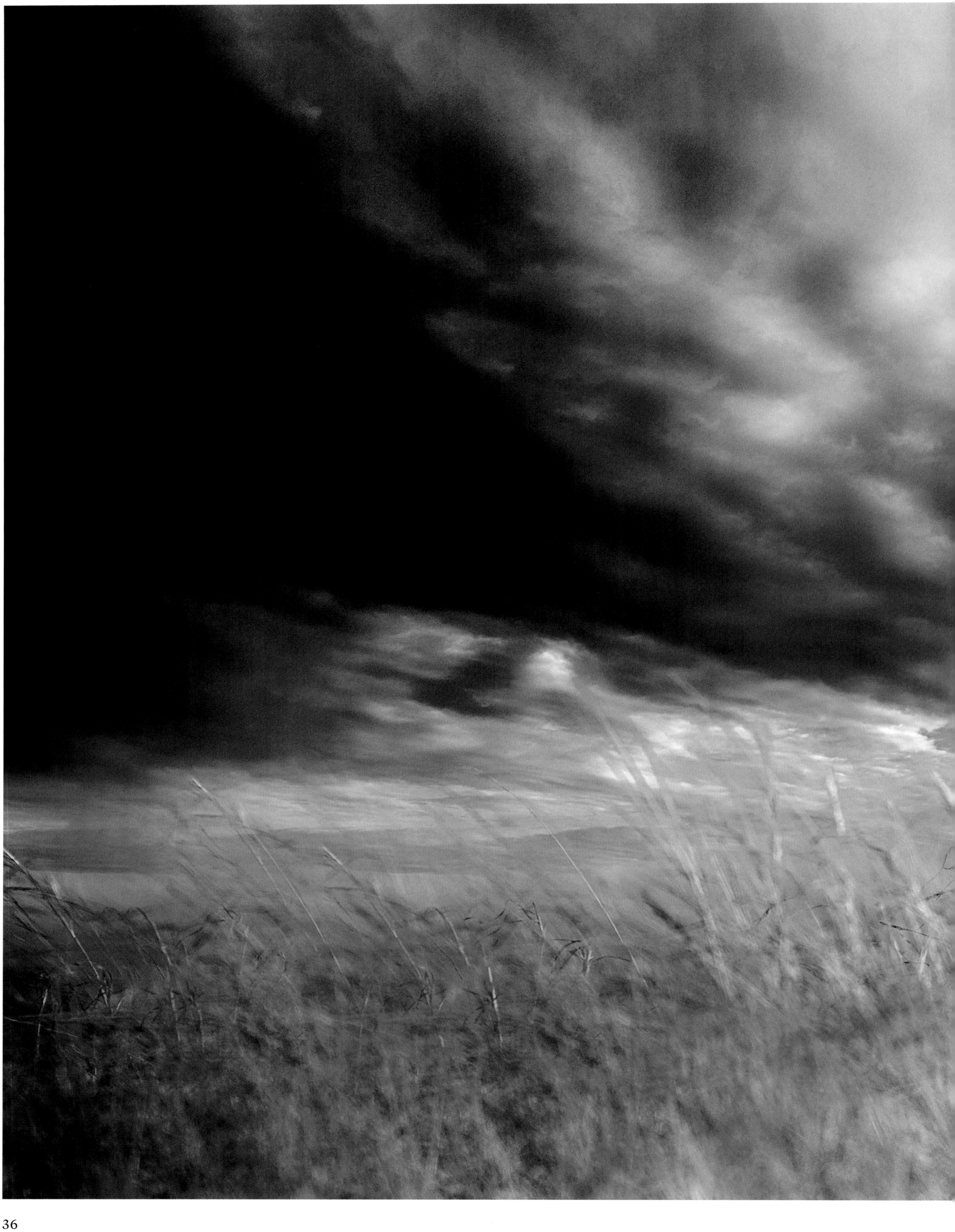

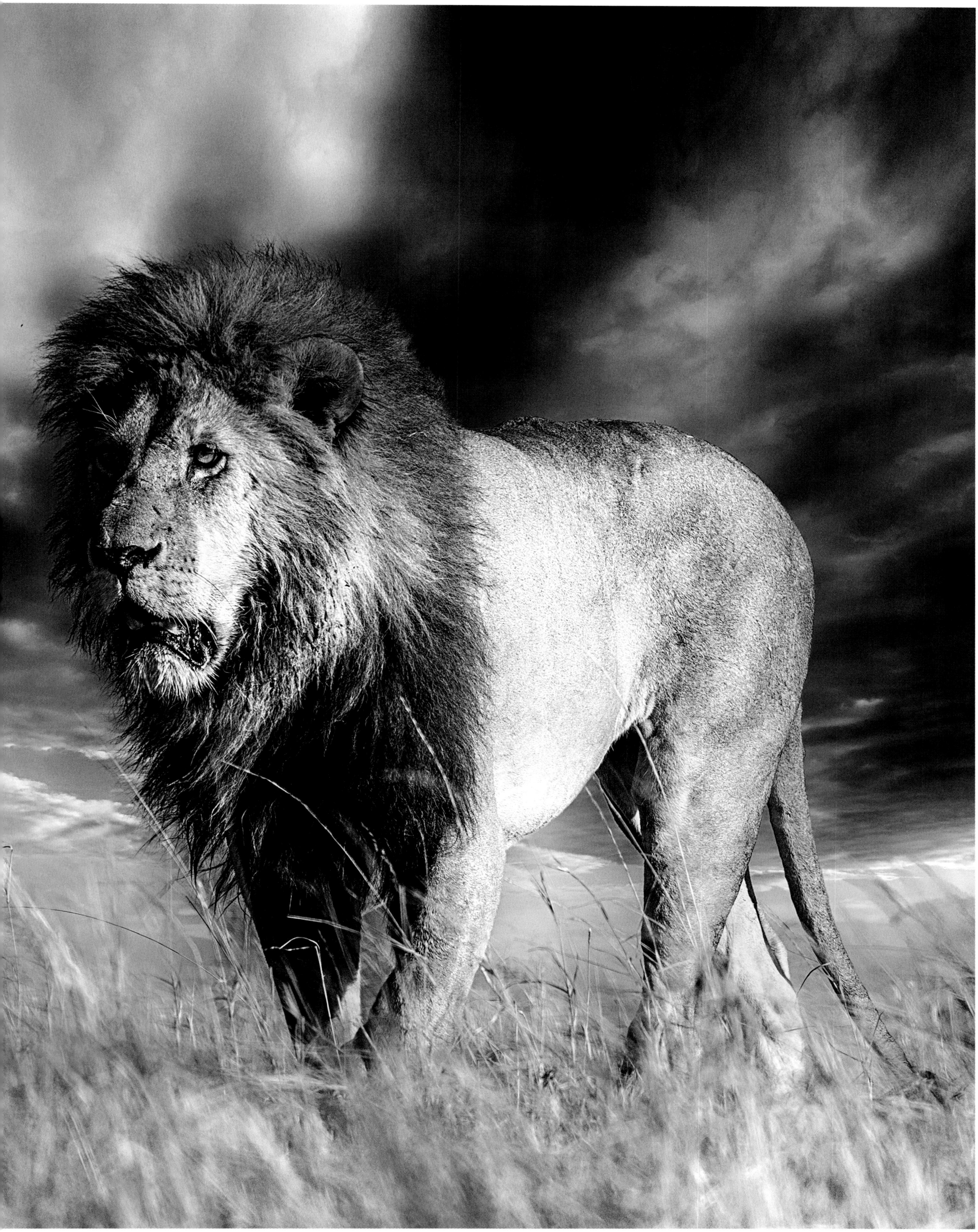

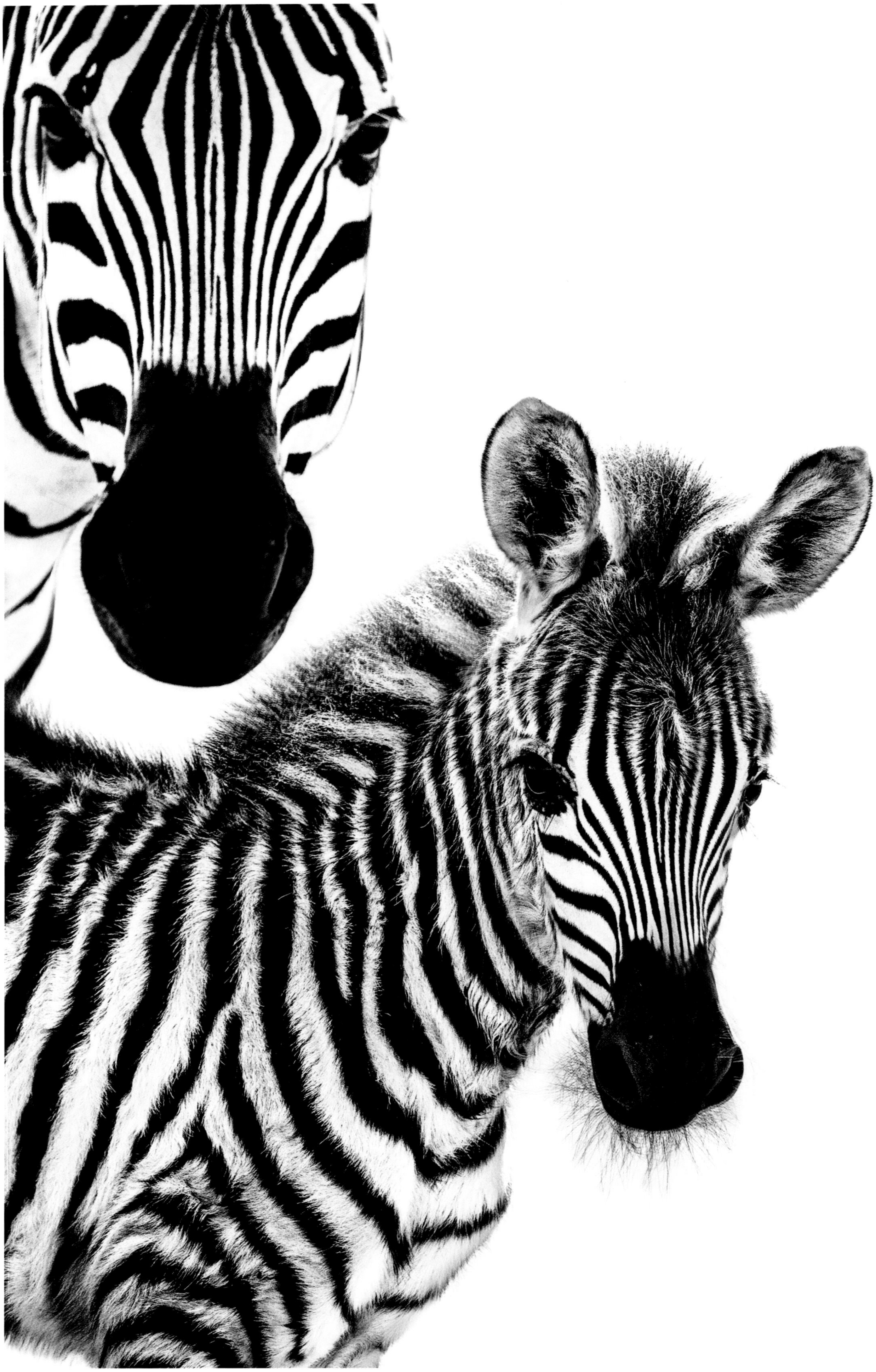

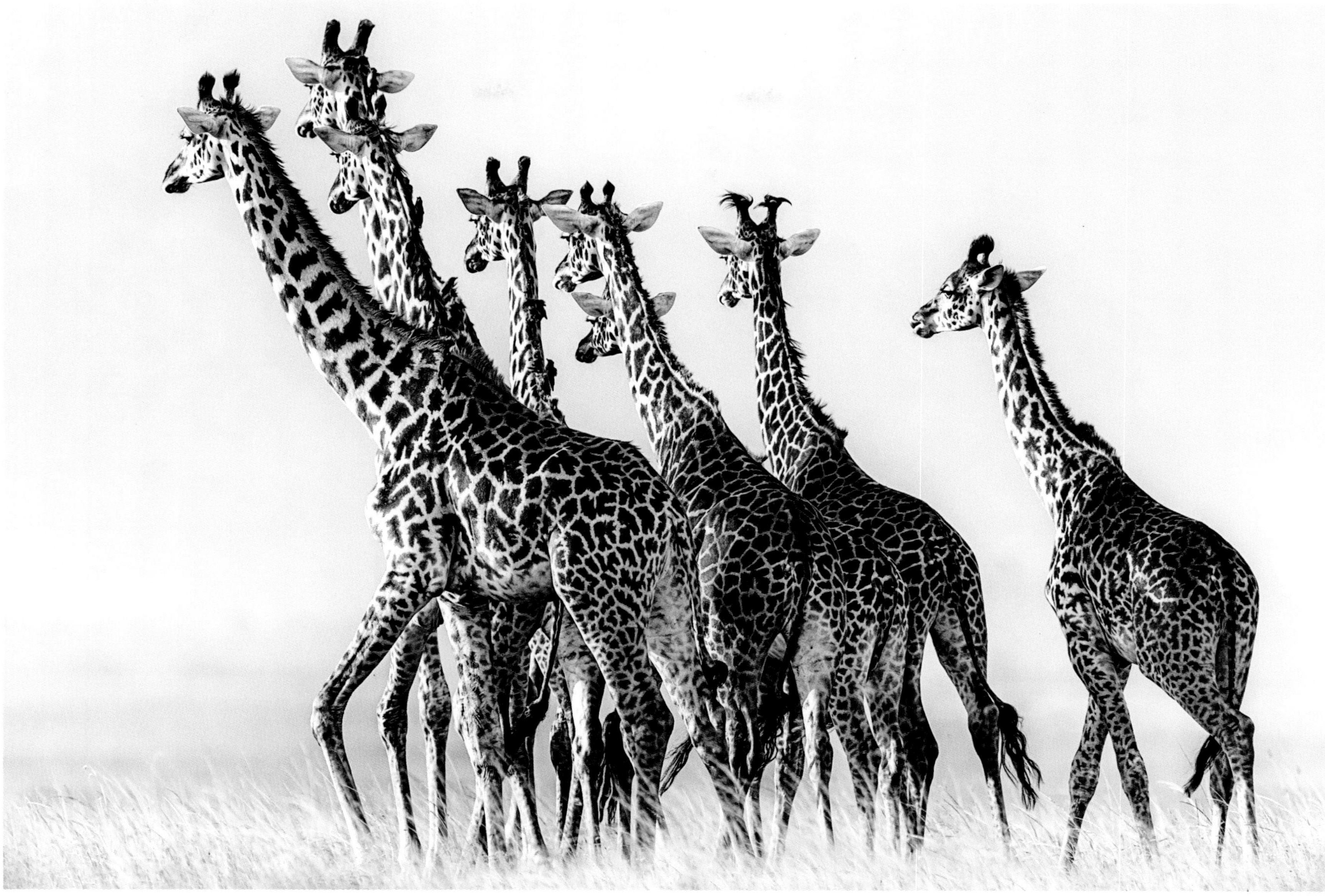

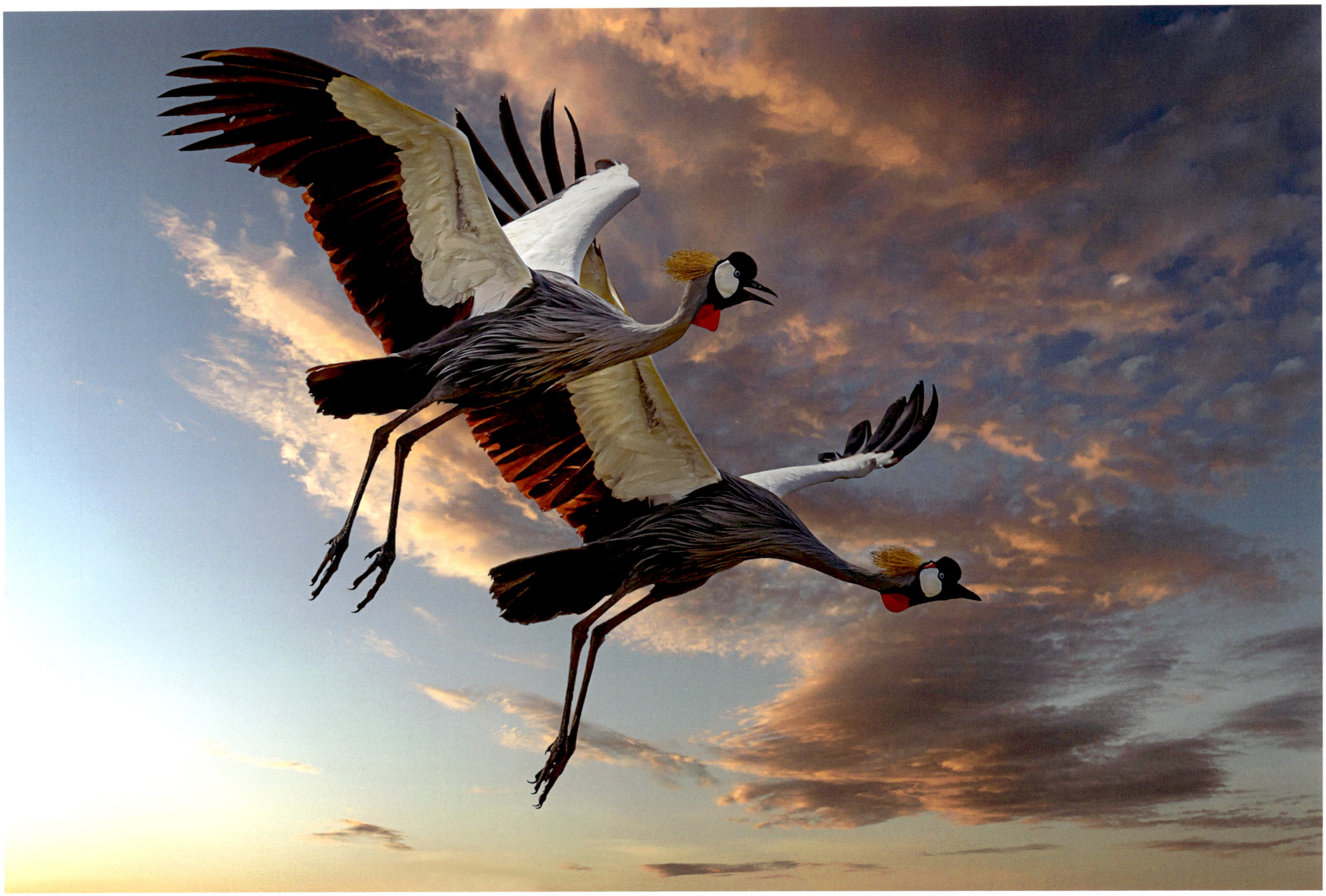

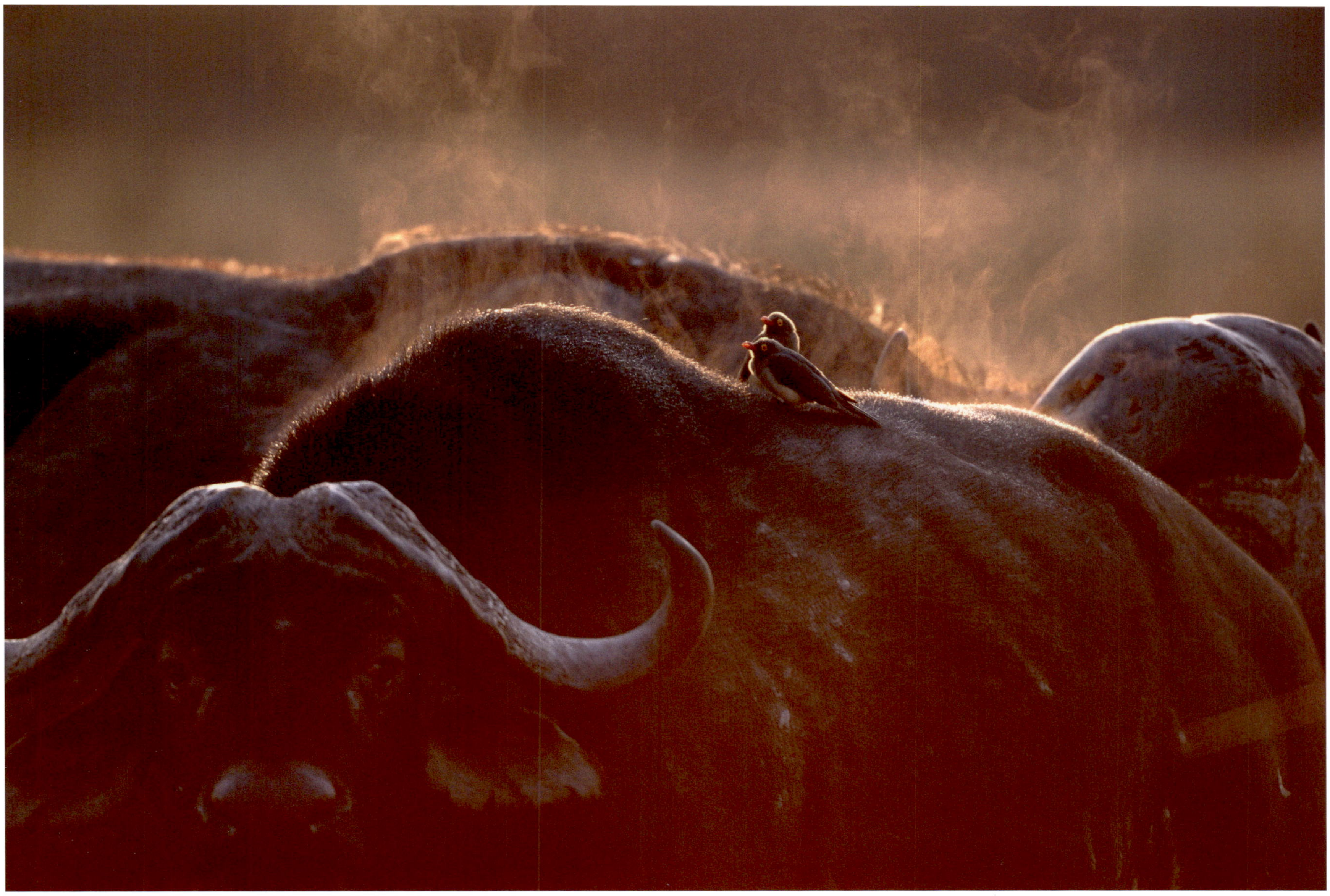

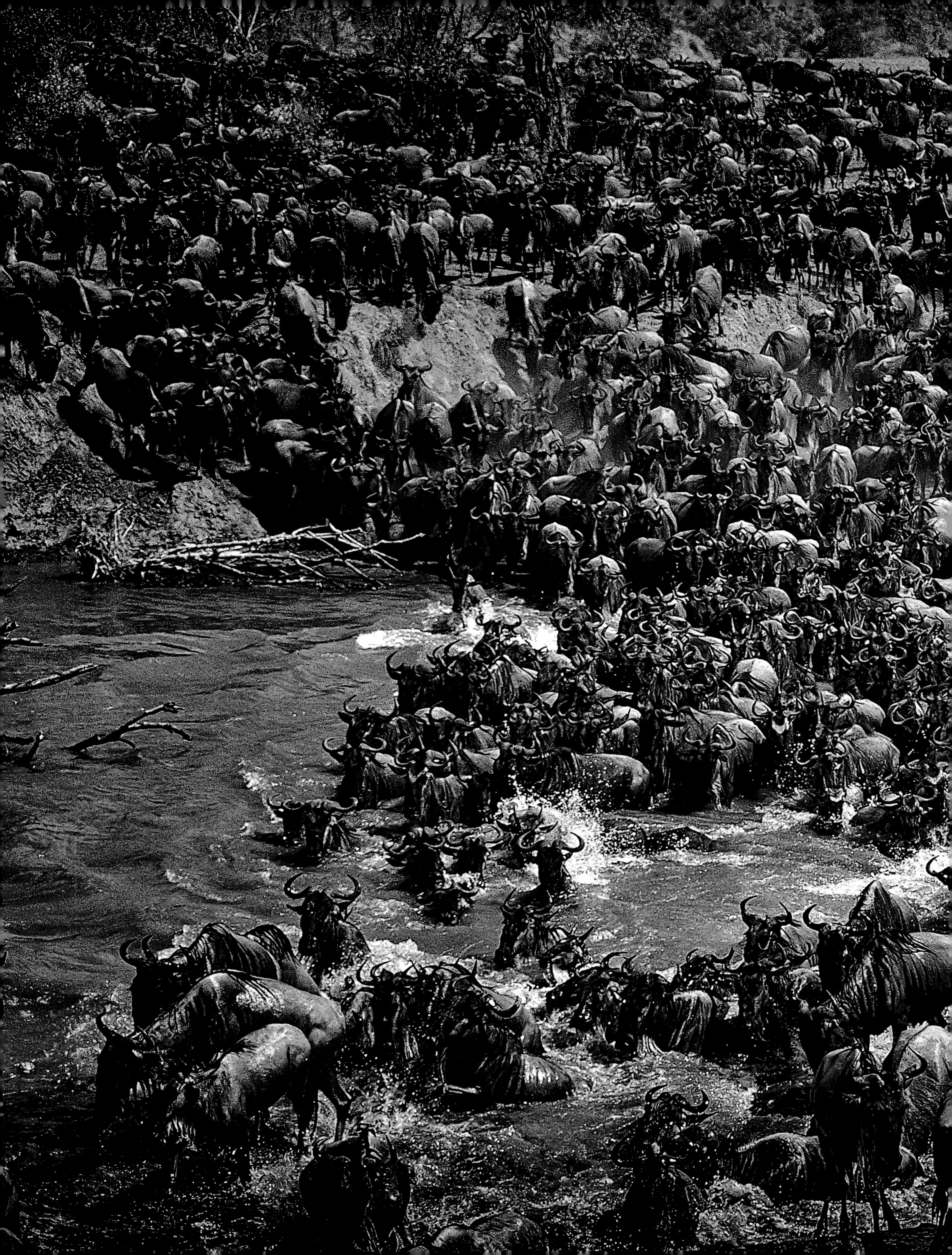

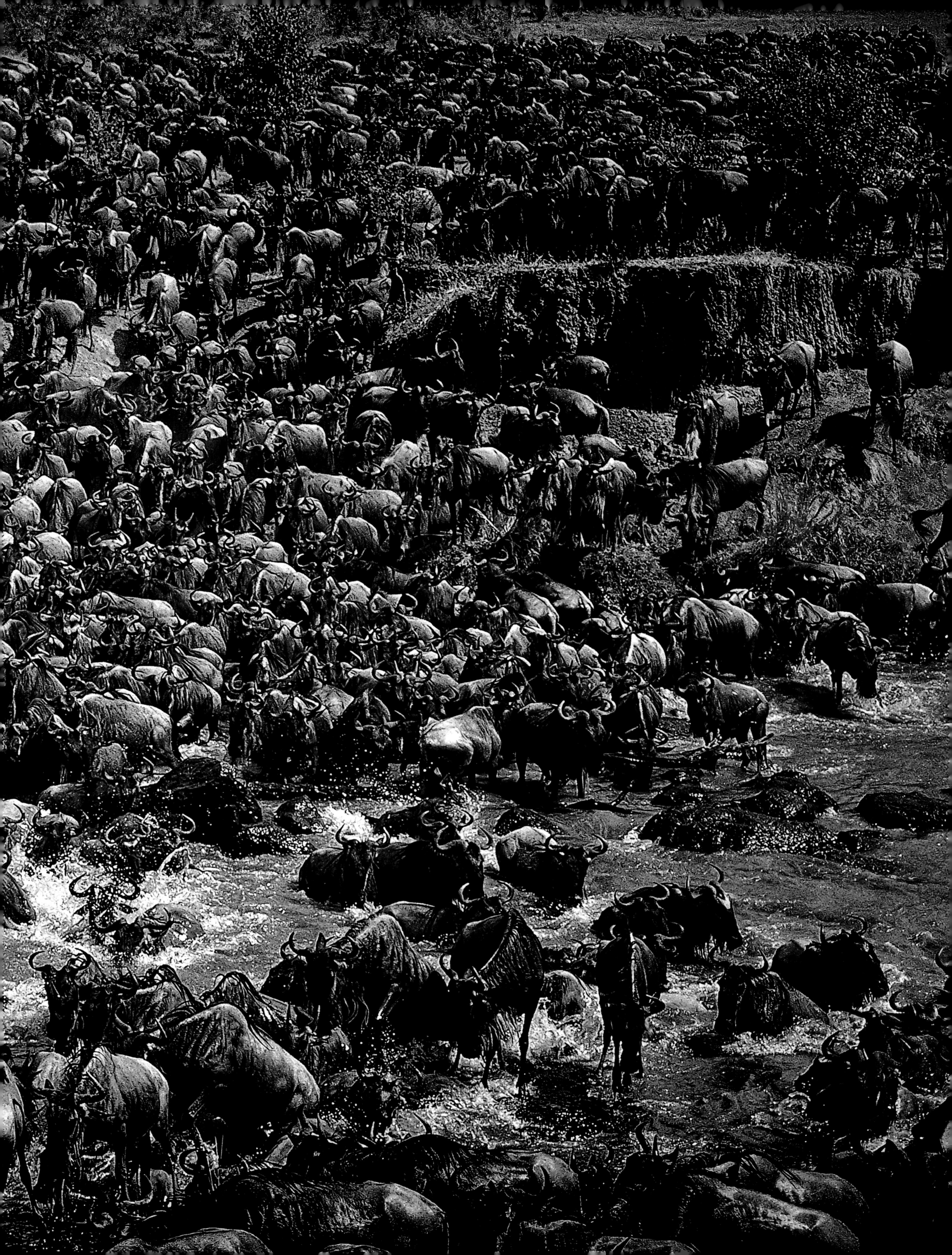

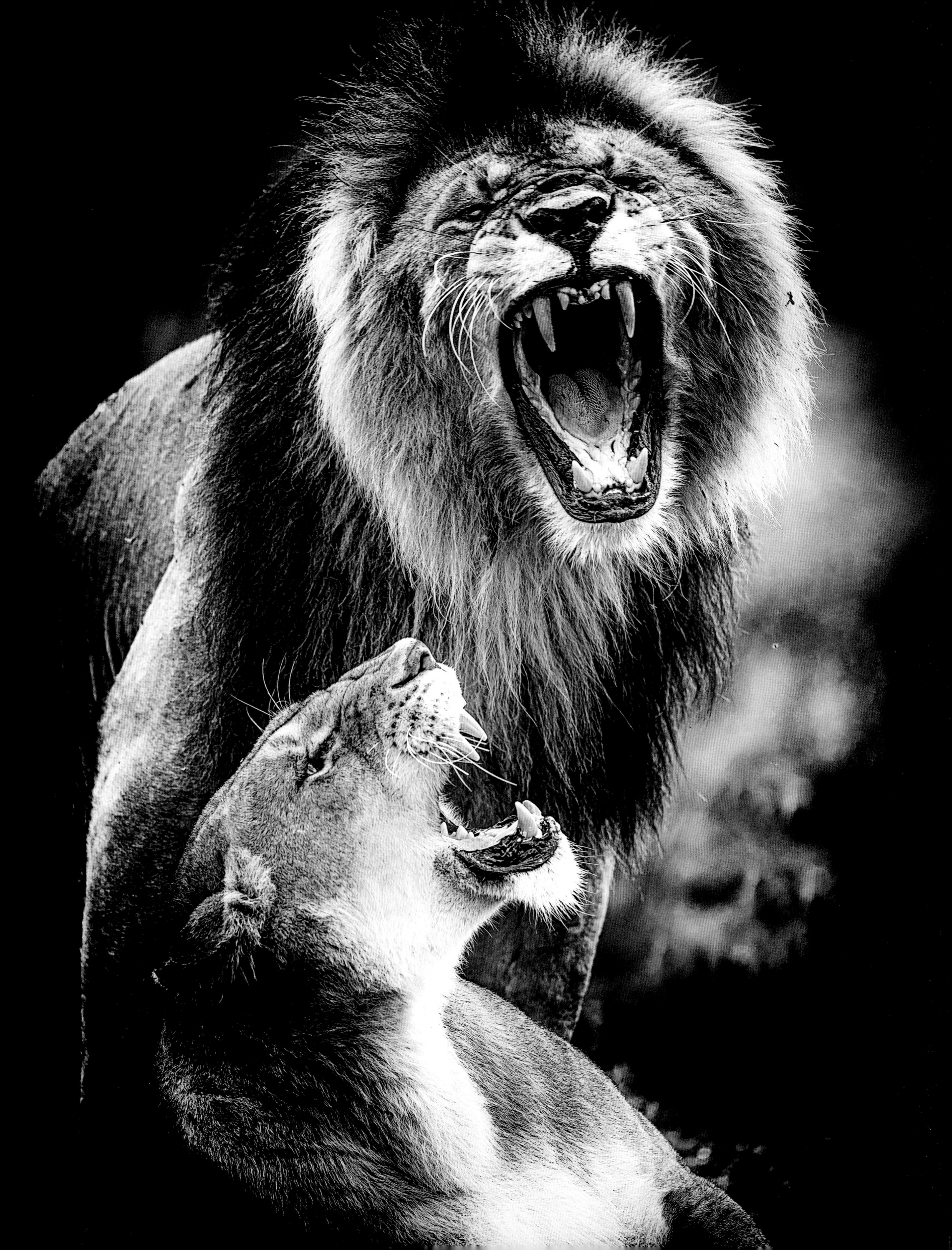

Chapter One

SAVANNAS OF OUR BIRTH

To witness that calm rhythm of life revives our worn souls and recaptures a feeling of belonging to the natural world. No one can return from the Serengeti unchanged, for tawny lions will forever prowl our memory and great herds throng our imagination.

— Dr George B Schaller

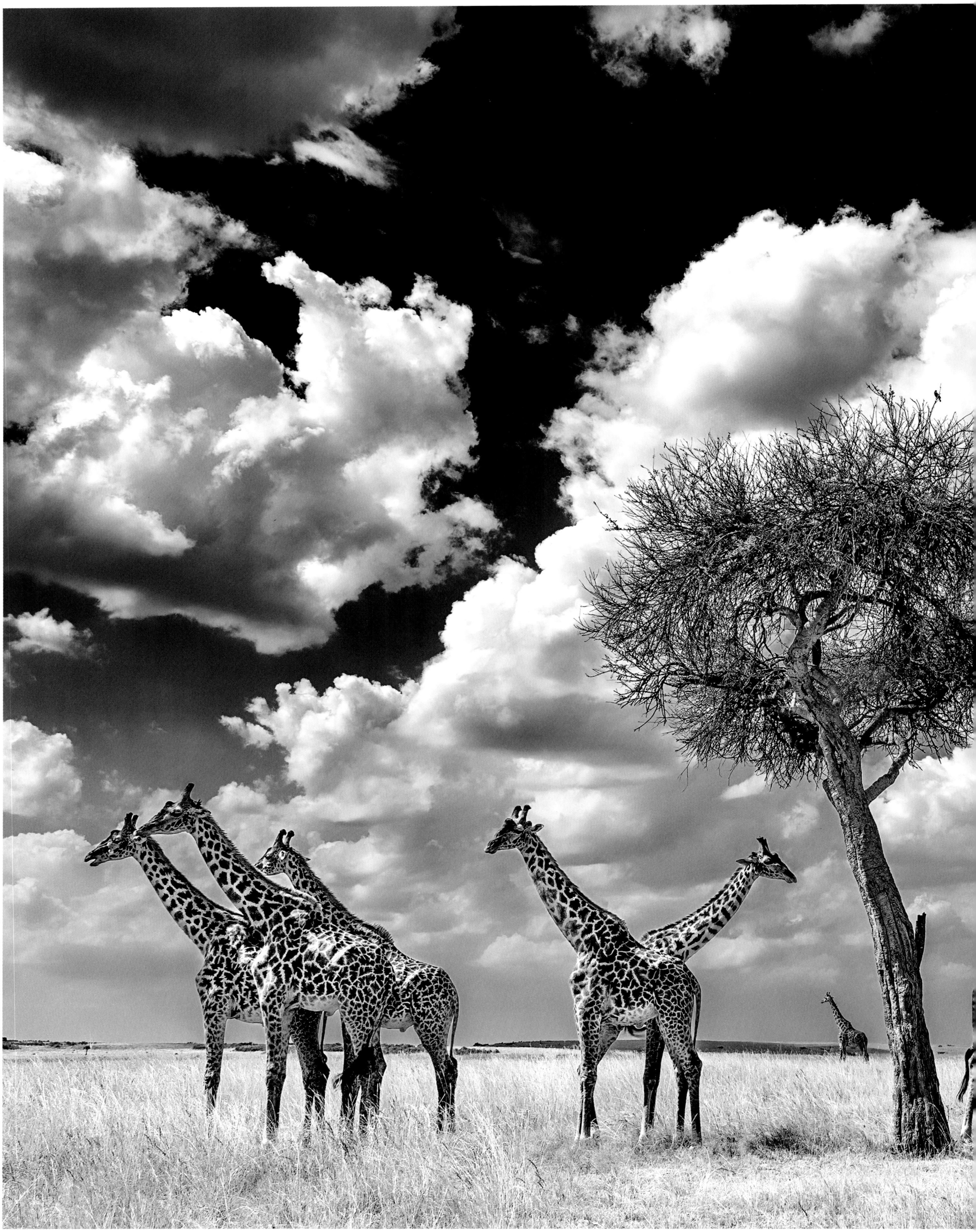

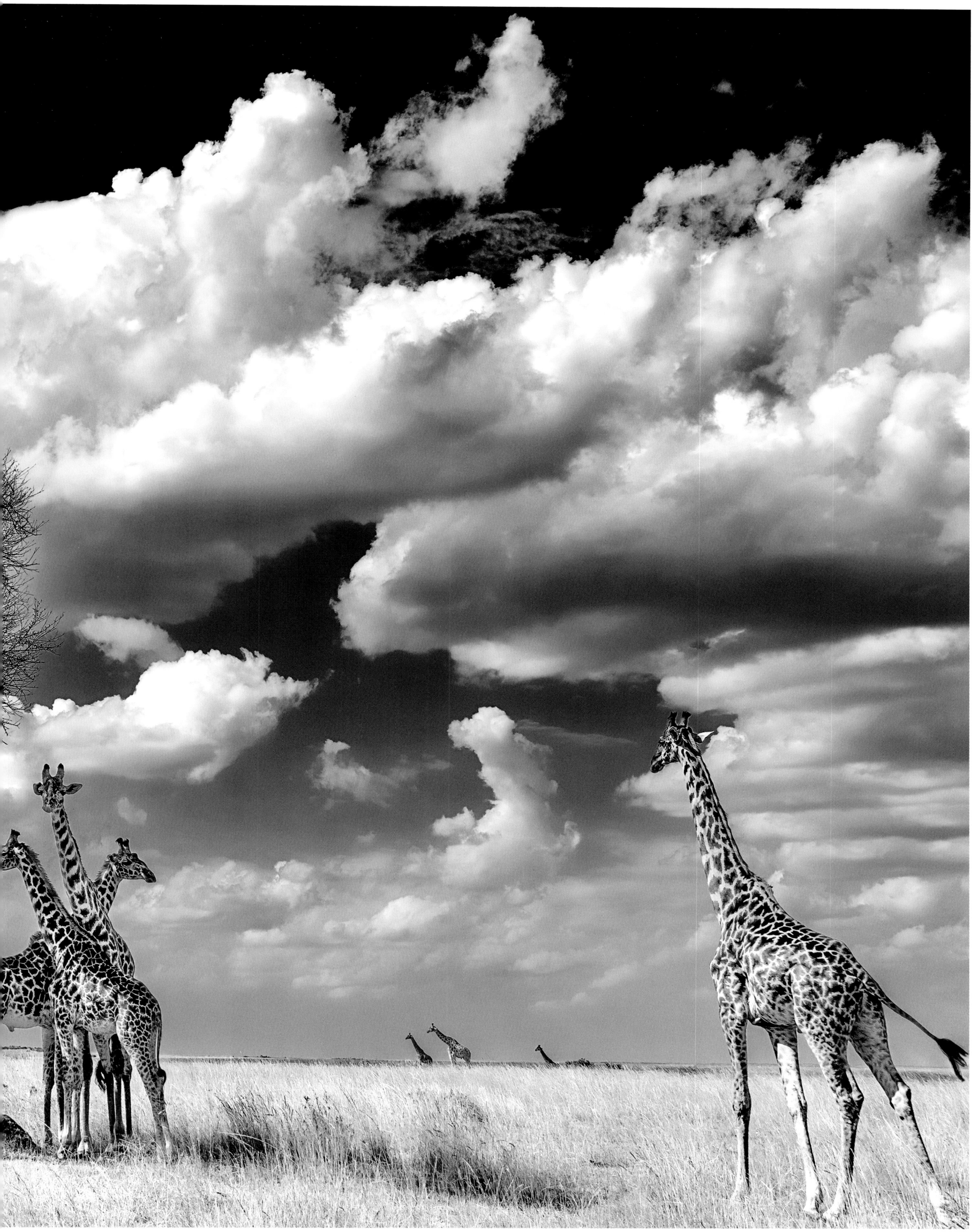

01

Savannas

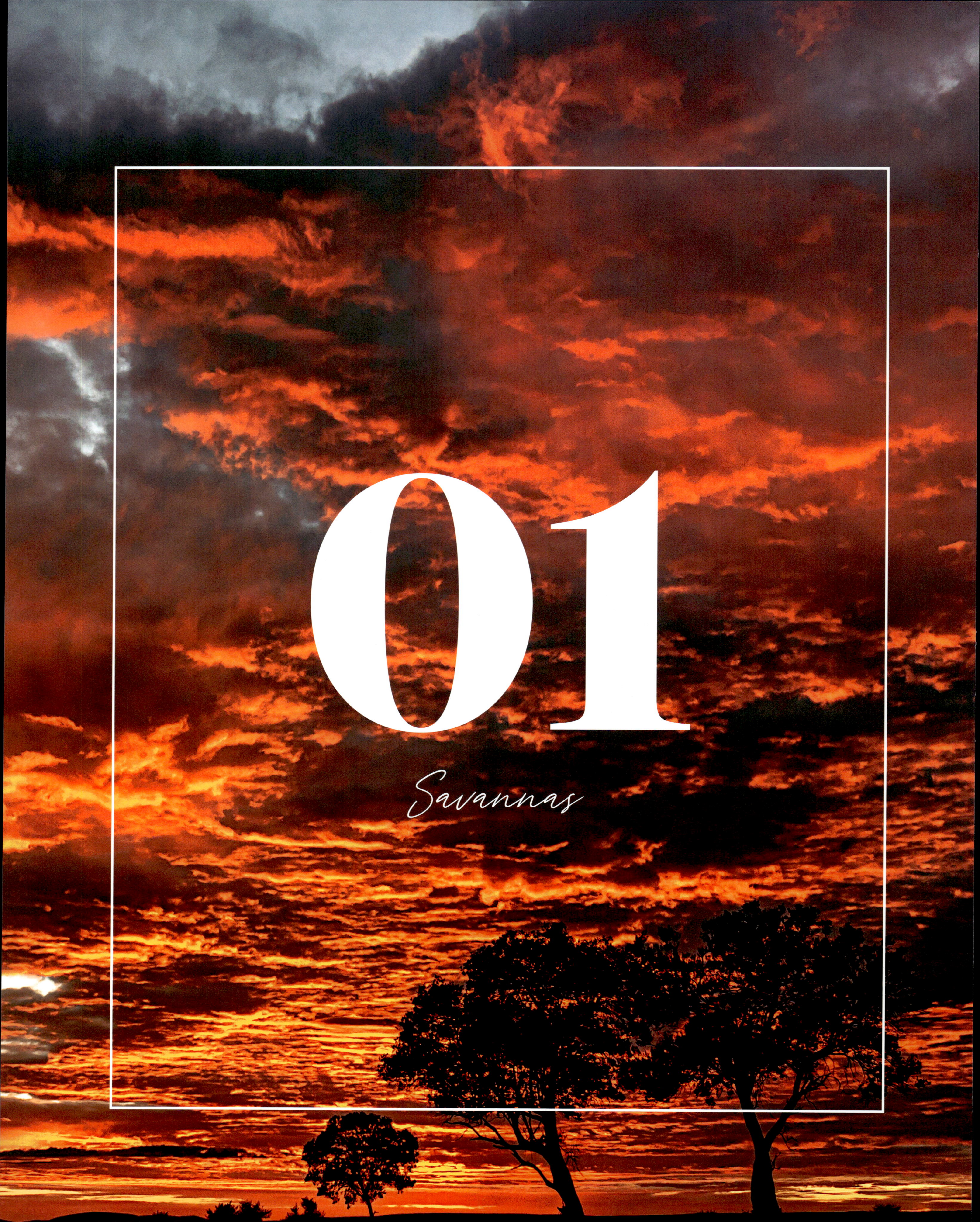

The pulsating sound of a lion's roar is so primal that it reaches back in time to the first stirrings of human consciousness, a familiar element in the complex web of life that defined and patterned our existence for millennia, both as predator and as prey. The primate in us feels the spine-tingling fear of the darkness where big cats move softly on padded paws as they stalk their prey. To the Maasai herdsmen who still share the savanna grasslands of East Africa with lions and leopards, the call of the wild speaks of an uneasy accommodation between pastoralist and predator, between people of the daylight and wild denizens of the night.

There is a place in Tanzania that the Maasai call *sirenget*. The word means 'the land that runs on forever', a land of endless space. To the outside world the *sirenget* is familiar as the Serengeti National Park which, together with the Maasai Mara National Reserve in Kenya, is the last place on Earth where you can still see a semblance of animal life as it existed before our ancestors first stepped out into the grasslands. This is a kingdom of predators where the mighty lion dominates the landscape with its tawny presence. There are 3,000 lions, who knows how many leopards – 1,000, perhaps – 250 cheetahs, more than 5,000 spotted hyenas and a handful of endangered African wild dogs. Today we can only gaze in awe at the vibrancy of the Mara-Serengeti and the manner in which it adjusts to drought or deluge, feast or famine, sustaining all life within its boundaries, an ingenious collaboration between soil and water, herbivore and carnivore.

At the heart of the Mara-Serengeti ecosystem is a strange-looking creature known as the white-bearded wildebeest or gnu, a veritable lawn mower of an antelope that prefers short green grass with a high leaf-to-stem ratio. Gathered in their hundreds of thousands on the Serengeti's short grass plains during the rainy season of November through May, the wildebeest hordes are a thing of wonder, an animal nation on the move, a lowing, grunting life force driven by their endless search for grass and water. Odd they may seem to human eyes, but the design of the wildebeest has been perfected over eons into a masterpiece of survival. The herds never tarry too long in any one part of their range, nurturing the soil with glistening piles of dung and jets of urine, their saliva prompting cell division in the grasses they depend on. All the other animals in the Serengeti are in some way conditioned by the wildebeest's presence: a veritable Noah's Ark boasting thousands of elephants and buffaloes, hundreds of thousands of gazelles, 200,000 zebras, all adding a dazzling presence to the wildebeest multitude that for nearly half a century has remained relatively stable at around 1.2 million animals.

We know from archaeological evidence that the Serengeti has been occupied by cattle people for thousands of years, though the red-robed Maasai herdsmen are relative newcomers. The Maa-speaking people originated in the lower Nile valley in what is now South Sudan, migrating south during the 15th century and arriving in what are now northern Kenya and central Tanzania between the 17th and late 18th century. They were feared as fighters and cattle-rustlers, their warrior caste distinguished by their long plaited hair smeared with cow fat and red ochre. They had no concept of land ownership; instead, they followed the bounty of the rains and displaced the agricultural tribes as they went. Nothing, it seemed – not even the surrender of some of the best of their pastures to the colonial authorities in 1904 – could loosen their attachment to their colourful cultural traditions.

As we grapple with the repercussions of the Covid-19 pandemic and how distanced we have become from nature, it is instructive to examine events that occurred in this region in the late 19th century. In 1841, a viral epidemic of livestock called rinderpest was introduced to Africa when a ship filled with infected animals from Russia offloaded its cargo at Alexandria in Egypt. Rinderpest is thought to date back to 3000 BC and is closely related to measles and canine distemper. It affects ruminants (not horses, donkeys or goats) and occurs naturally in Asia, with immunity acquired if an animal survives its first year. Transmission is through direct contact, drinking contaminated water or by air, with symptoms including fever, oral lesions and diarrhoea, and morality up to 100 per cent in populations where there is no immunity.

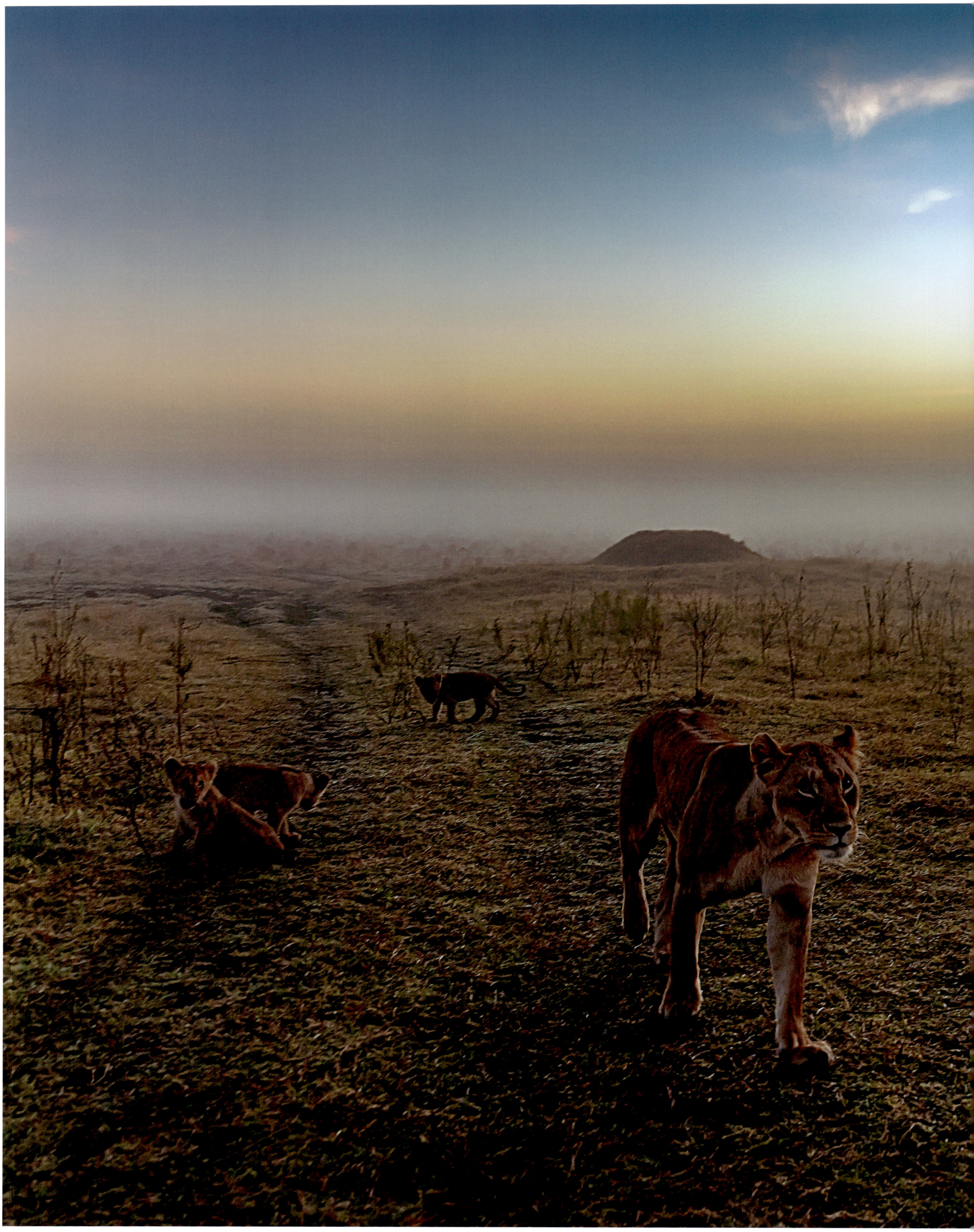

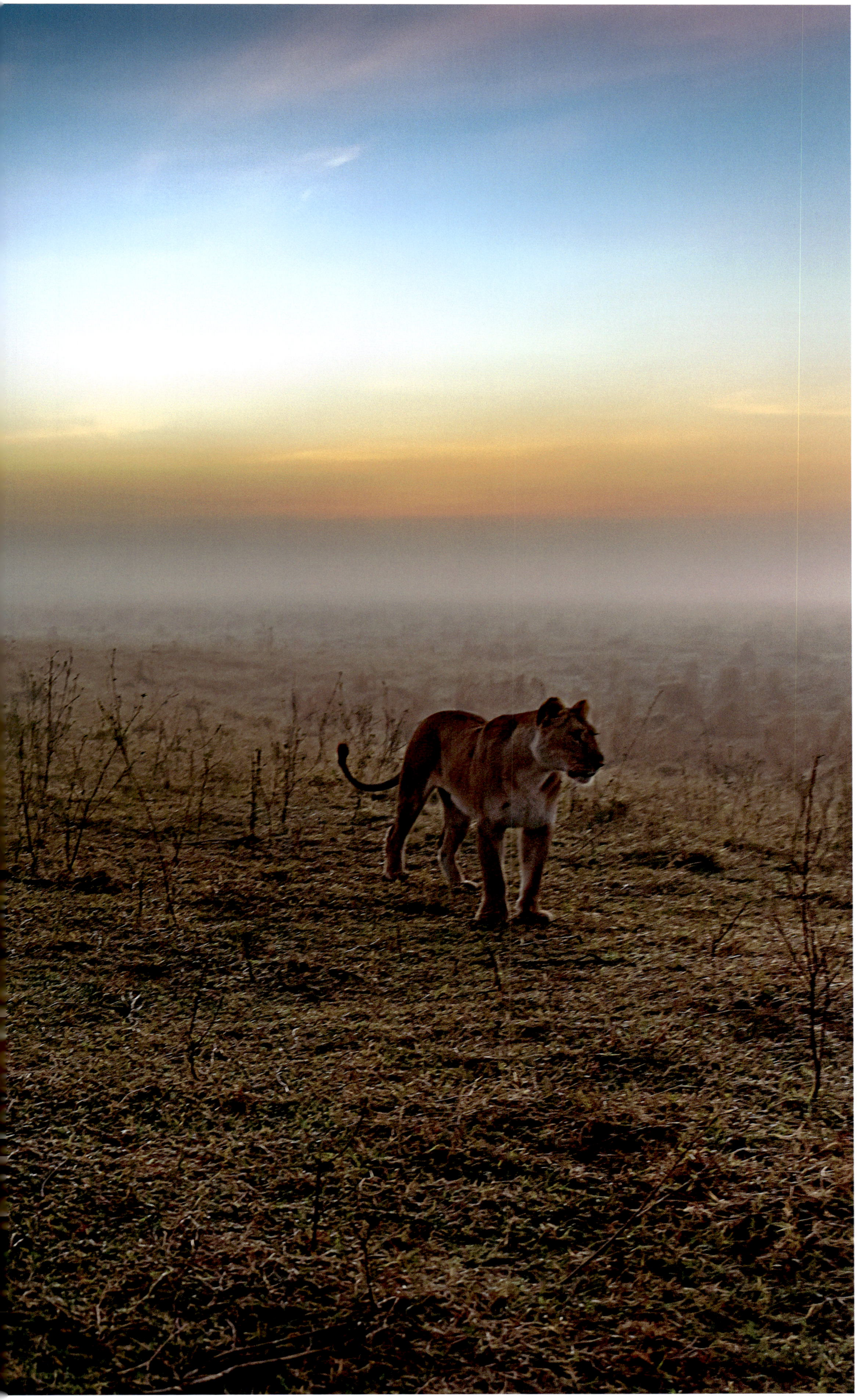

During the 1880s and early 1890s, rinderpest spread like a raging bushfire from the Horn of Africa south through the continent. Within two years, 90 per cent of the cattle, buffalo and wildebeest in East and Southern Africa had died; other large antelope, gazelles and wart hogs were also affected. In its wake came famine and smallpox. The Maasai nation was hardest hit, with two-thirds of its population perishing. Smallpox became endemic and the Maasai spoke of these times as Emutai or 'wipe-out', with survivors scavenging among the vultures and dogs for scraps from the carcasses of their cattle. One commentator noted that 'these events broke the backbone of the economies of many of the most prosperous and advanced communities, undermined established authority and state structures, and altered the political contracts between peoples. It initiated the breakdown of a long-established ecological balance, placing nature again at an advantage.' Such sentiments hint at a potentially disastrous man-against-nature mindset, the need for civilisation to conquer the wilderness in the name of progress and for a cash economy to prosper.

The loss of grazing animals and a reduced human population were to have a dramatic effect on the landscape of sub-Saharan Africa. Acacia seedlings repopulated the grasslands with a blanket of bush – ideal tsetse fly country. In some areas these biting flies transmit the trypanosomic parasite, causing a form of sleeping sickness that can kill cattle and making the habitat unsuitable for livestock grazing. Consequently, the tsetse has long been considered the conservationist's friend, helping to protect large tracts of bush from development.

Today we can only gaze in awe at the vibrancy of the Mara-Serengeti and the manner in which it adjusts to drought or deluge, feast or famine, sustaining all life within its boundaries, an ingenious collaboration between soil and water, herbivore and carnivore.

Historically the Maasai Mara and the northern extension of the Serengeti National Park were much more densely wooded than they are today: aerial photographs from the 1940s show the area swathed in a blanket of thornbush. But nothing stays the same. Elephants and fire have proved a potent force for change by opening up the woodlands, the landscape oscillating between bush and grasslands, favouring different species at different stages in the ebb and flow characteristic of natural environments.

In the late 1950s, there were around 200,000 wildebeest in the Serengeti and none in the Maasai Mara, their numbers kept in check by periodic outbreaks of rinderpest. A rigorous inoculation programme of all livestock across the Mara-Serengeti resulted in 1962 being the last year the disease was detected in wildebeest and 1963 the last year in buffalo. This led to an explosion in the wildebeest population. By 1971, it had grown to nearly 700,000 and five years later reached 1.2 million. But we have seen how quickly things can change, how one event can prove the tipping point in destabilising the intricate workings of natural systems, and how humans and their domestic animals are often involved. In the 1980s, the Mara-Serengeti's vulnerable wild dog population was struck down by outbreaks of rabies and canine distemper contracted from domestic dogs roaming semi-wild with pastoralists. All eight known packs in the area were wiped out. Then in 1994, the lion population lost a thousand lions (one-third of the population) when canine distemper struck, exacerbated by the debilitating effect of tick disease acquired from feeding on heavily infested buffalo carcasses. Domestic dogs were once again the likely source of the distemper outbreak. Microscopic pathogens, invisible to the naked eye, are capable of bringing both the mighty lion and the human being to their knees.

Though pastoralism has been an integral part of these savannas for hundreds of years, the old ways are dying. Maasailand in Kenya has been subdivided into individual plots averaging 40–60 hectares. Now the pastoralists are shackled to a fixed abode, their loaf-shaped dwellings fashioned from wattle and plastered with cow dung replaced by tin-roofed huts and a patchwork of permanent settlements. As fences are erected and wild animal migration routes shut off, it signals the death knell for traditional pastoralism and the free movement of wildlife. This is borne out by Kenya's Loita wildebeest migration, which has dwindled from around 120,000 animals in the 1970s and '80s to fewer than 20,000 today. The animals' wet-season dispersal area on the Loita Plains to the east of the Maasai Mara has been ploughed up into commercial wheat farms, making Narok County both the breadbasket of Kenya and home to Kenya's premier tourist destination. Fortunately the Mara's 14 wildlife conservancies – the first of which was established in 1992 – provide valuable buffer zones around parts of the reserve. Big cats feel safe in these areas thanks to the relationship forged between Maasai landowners and tourism partners, and leopard and cheetah sightings are particularly good.

While the wildebeest migration is the largest and most spectacular mammal migration on Earth today, it pales by comparison with an earlier great migration. Prior to 1800, it is estimated that up to 50 million bison roamed the prairies of North America. Wolves, bears and occasionally cougars preyed on young, old or sick individuals, helping to keep the herds healthy. The bison were at the heart of the culture of the Plains Indians, who hunted them for meat and fashioned tents, robes, bedding and rugs from their hides, with their dried dung proving excellent fuel, burning with very little smoke. In 1830, however, a ruthless campaign was unleashed, aided and abetted by the government and executed by settlers. By 1884, only 335 bison remained and the people of a once-proud indigenous nation were reduced to helpless bystanders, corralled into reservations that represented a fraction of their traditional tribal lands.

Our species' ability to change entire landscapes is unrivalled. Other animals conform to nature – they collaborate with their environment – whereas we set the terms and conditions for ours. Our technology has enabled us to break free from nature's restraints without acquiring the moral authority to act responsibly in the long-term interests of the planet. Drought, famine, disease and the resultant loss of life – at times on a catastrophic scale – are universal themes that speak to us of a need to re-evaluate our relationship with nature and its wild inhabitants.

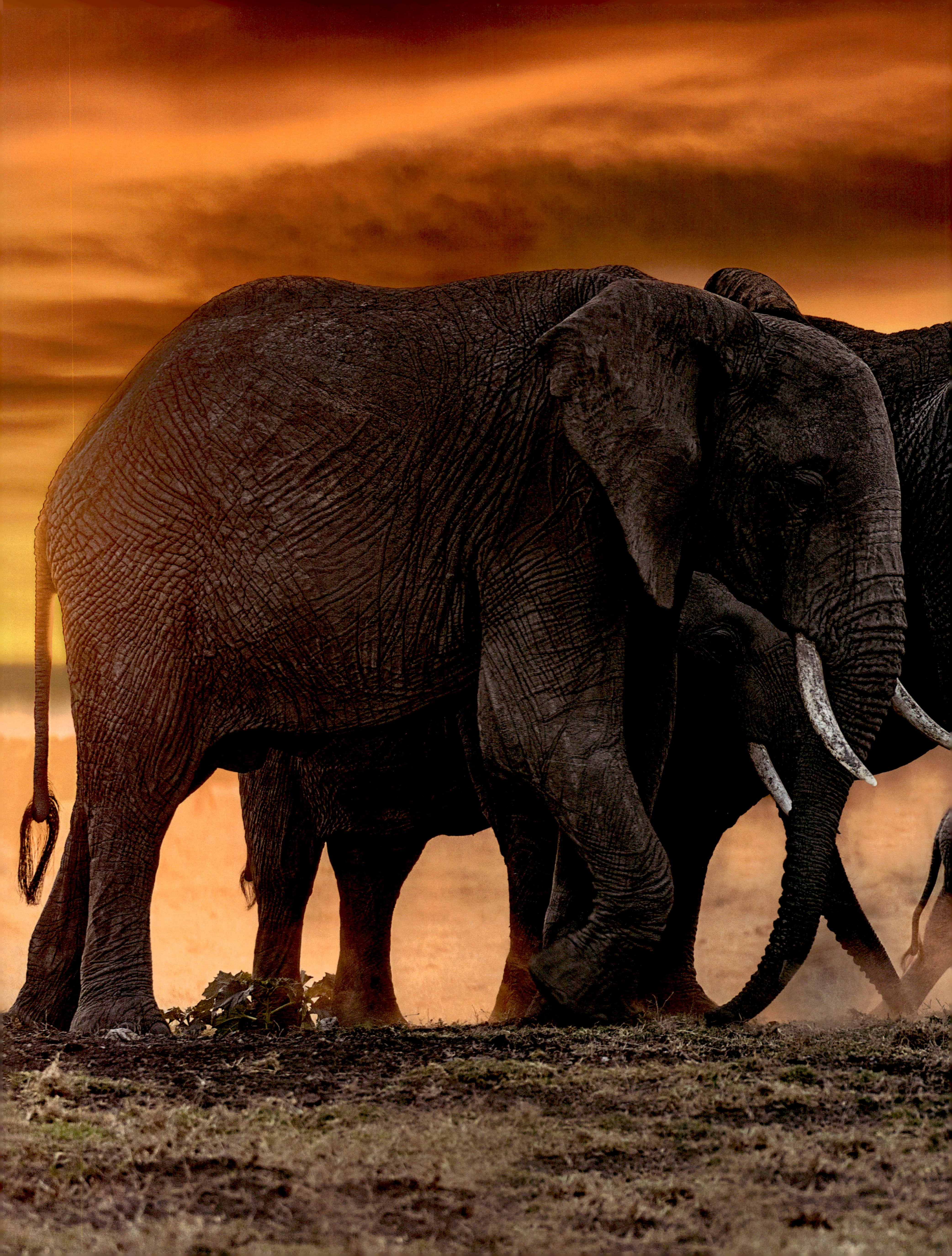

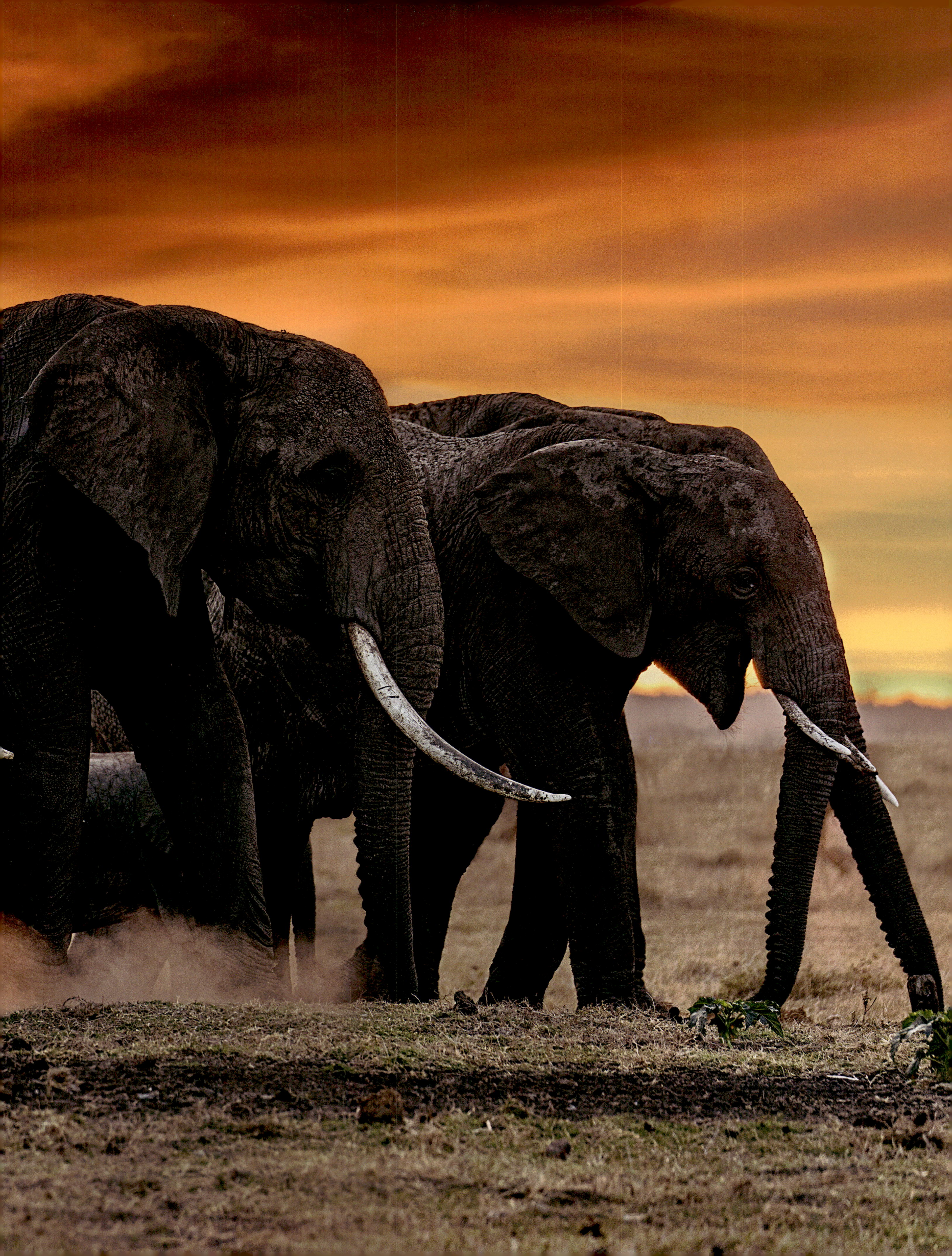

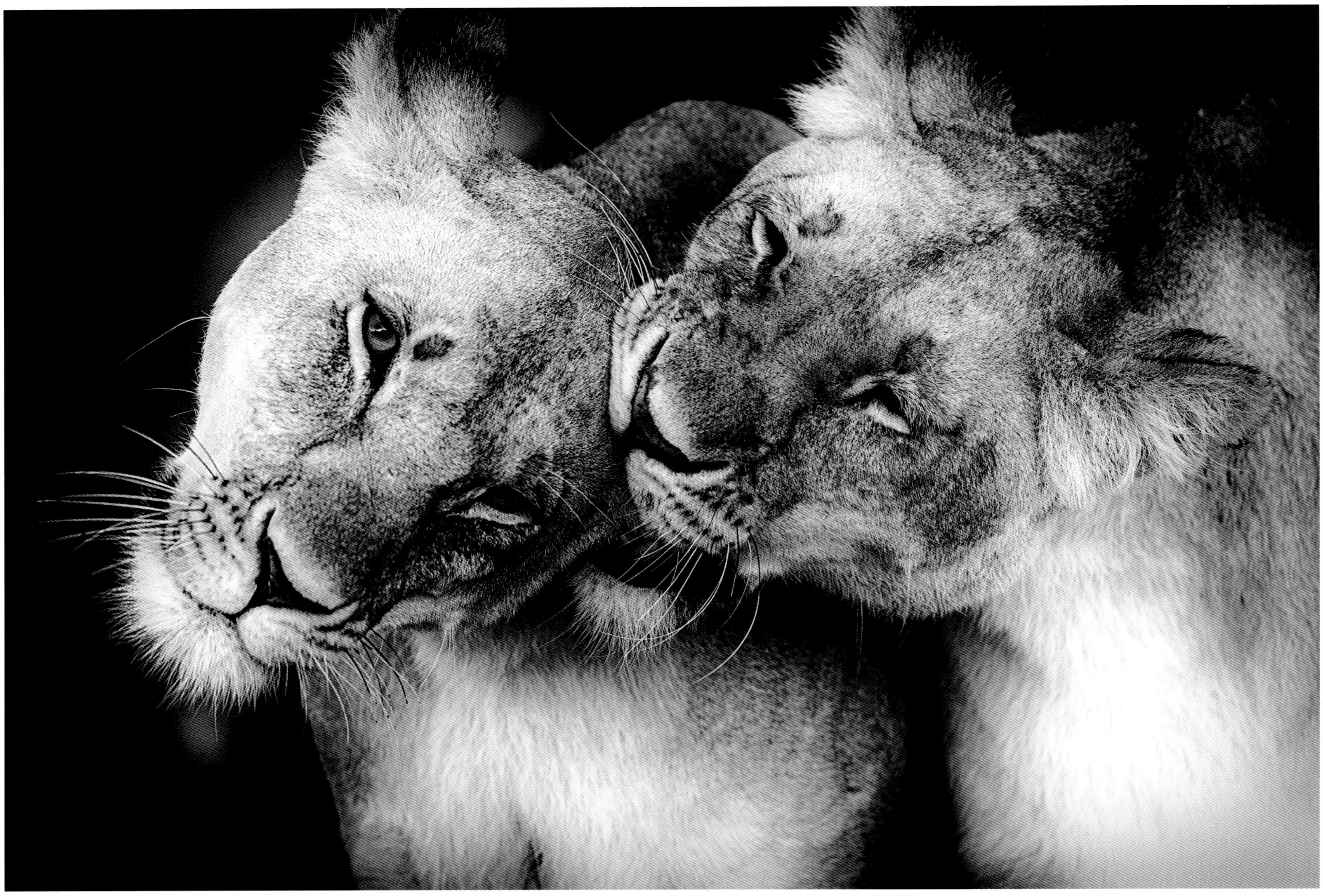

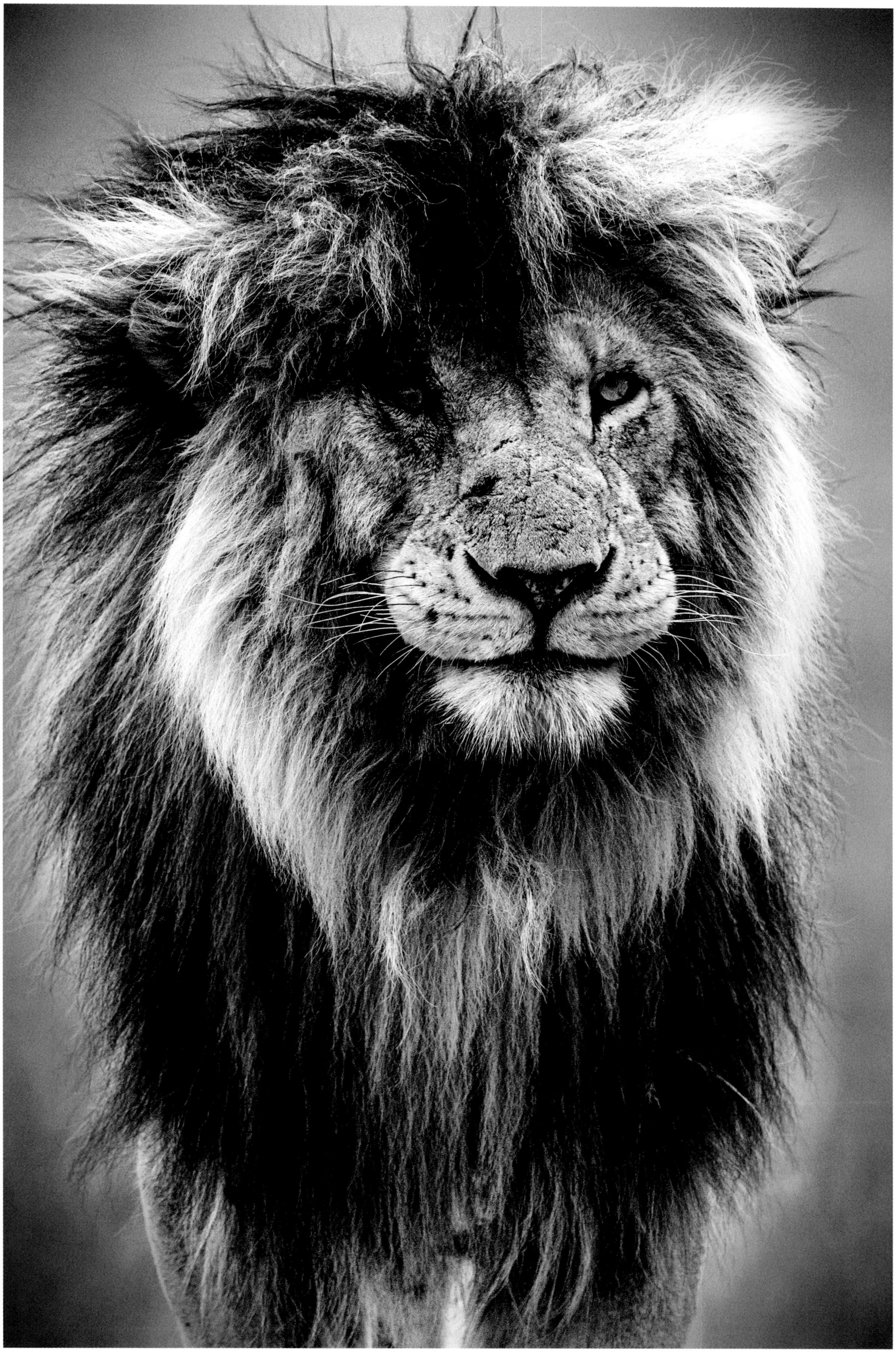

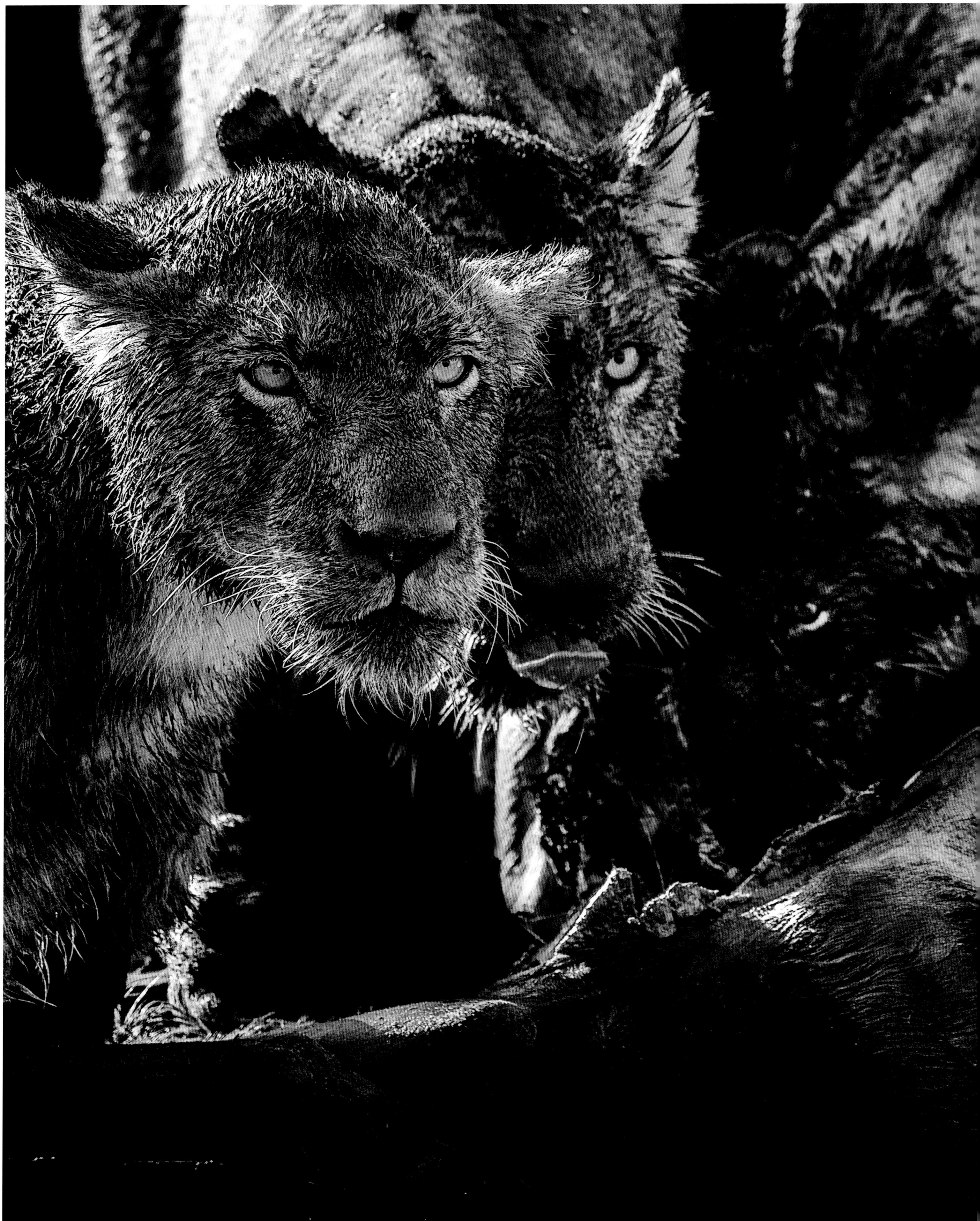

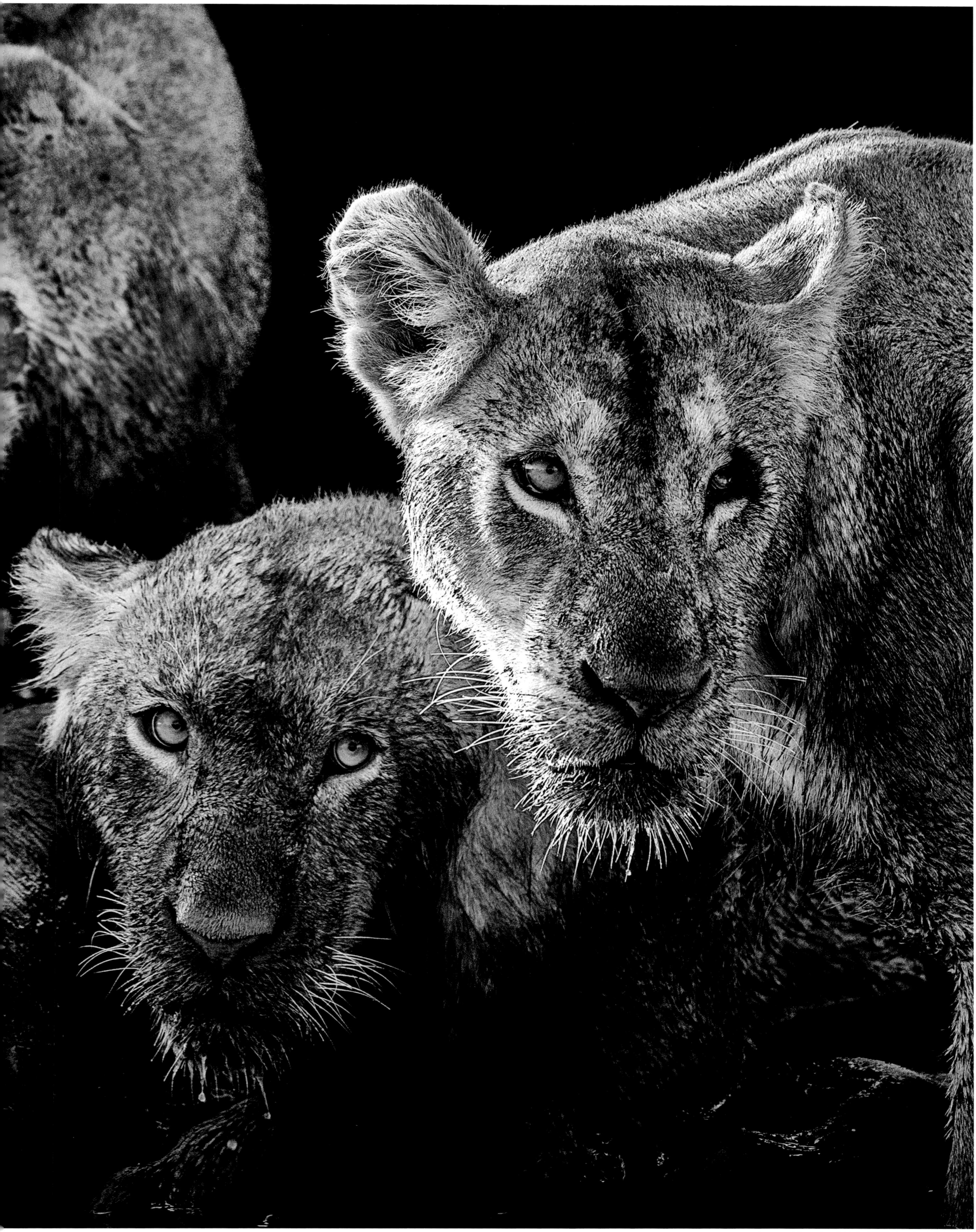

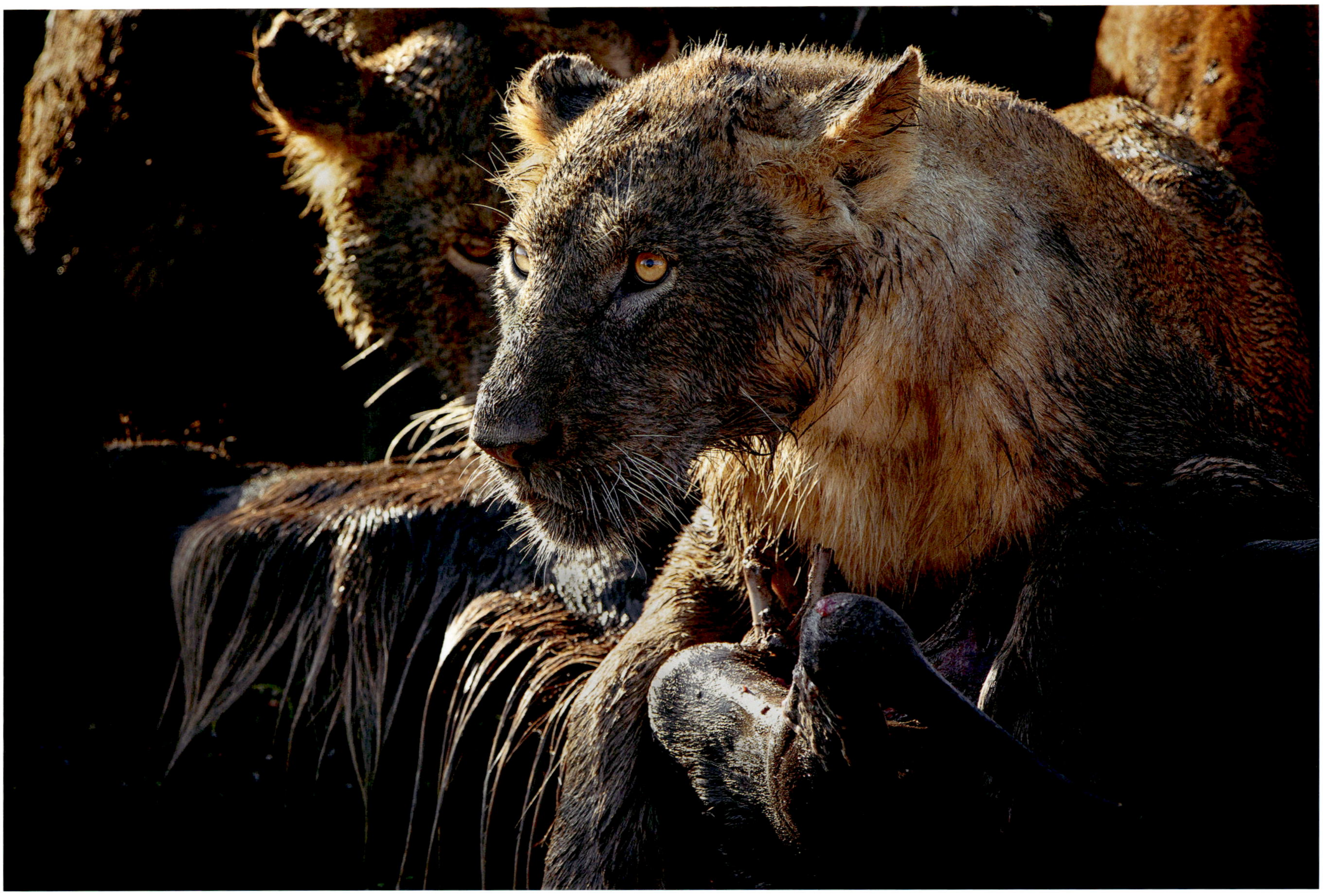

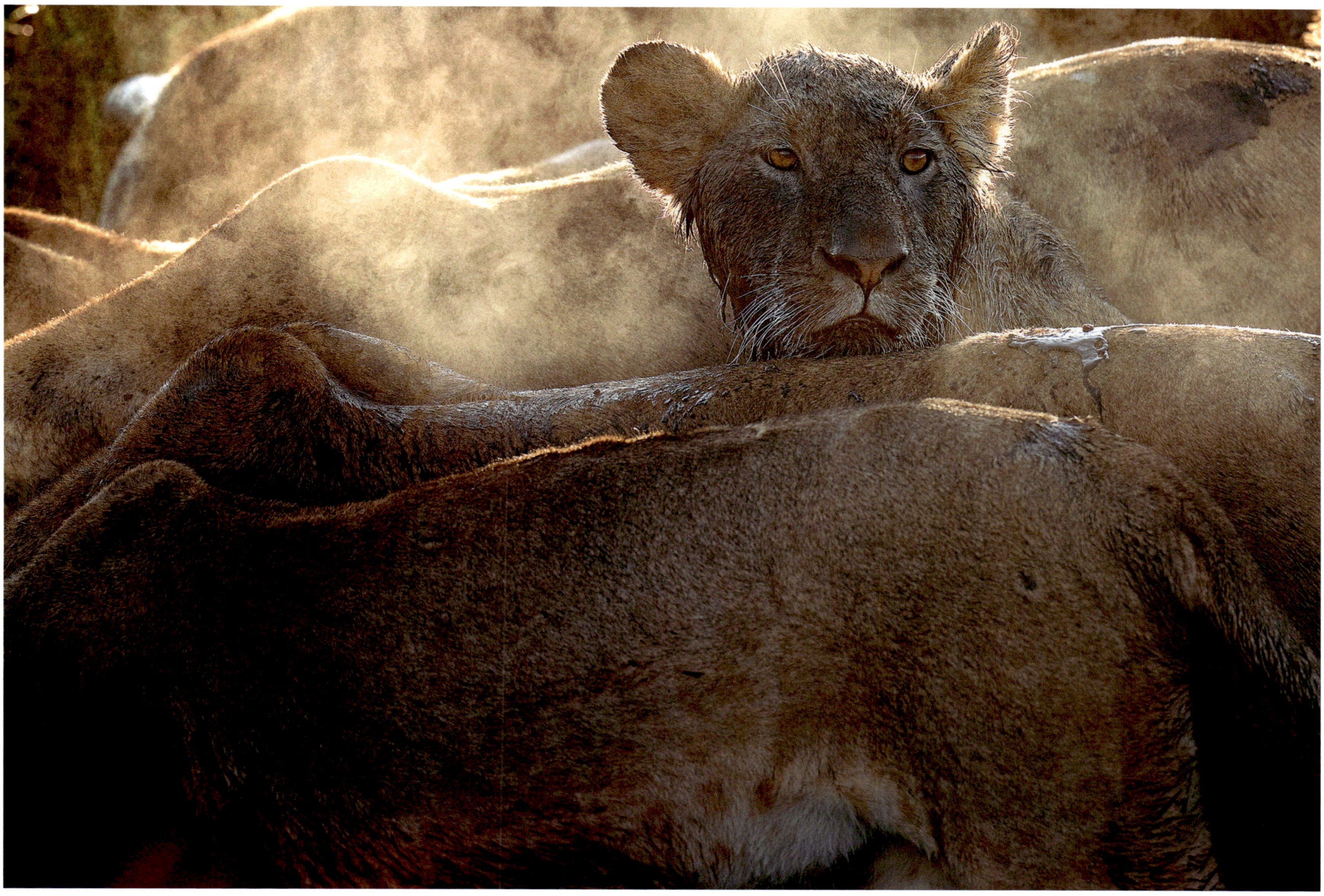

Breathless, we flung us on a windy hill, Laughed in the sun, and kissed the lovely grass.

— *Rupert Brooke*

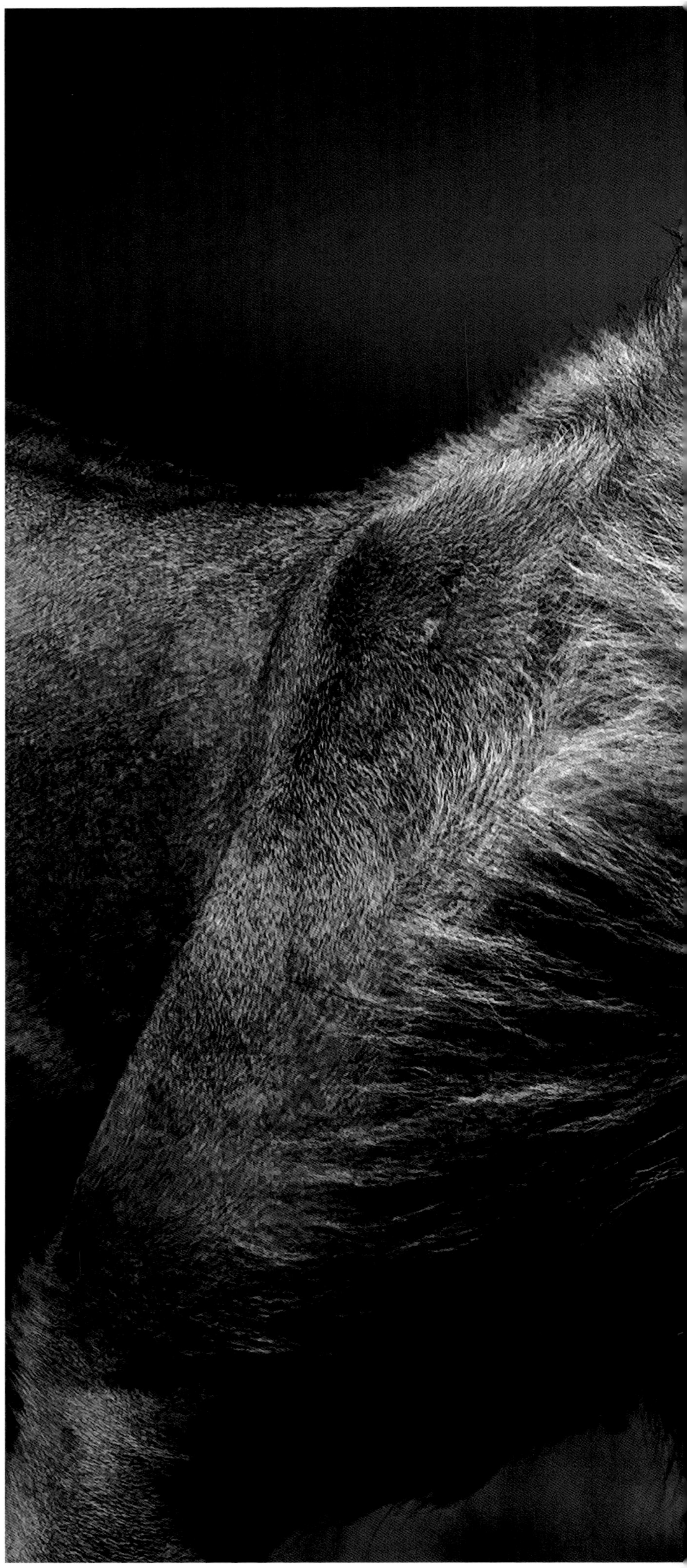

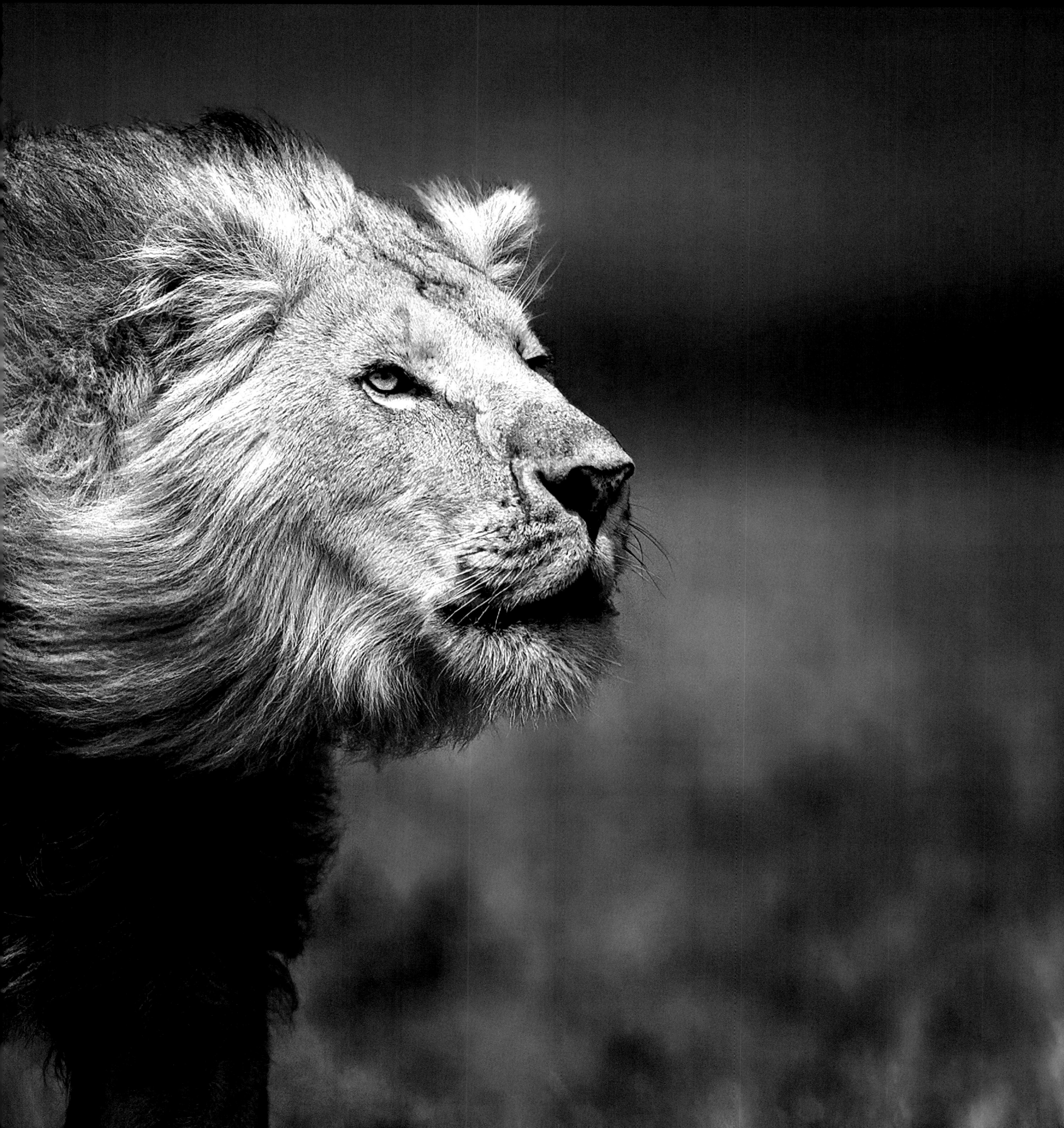

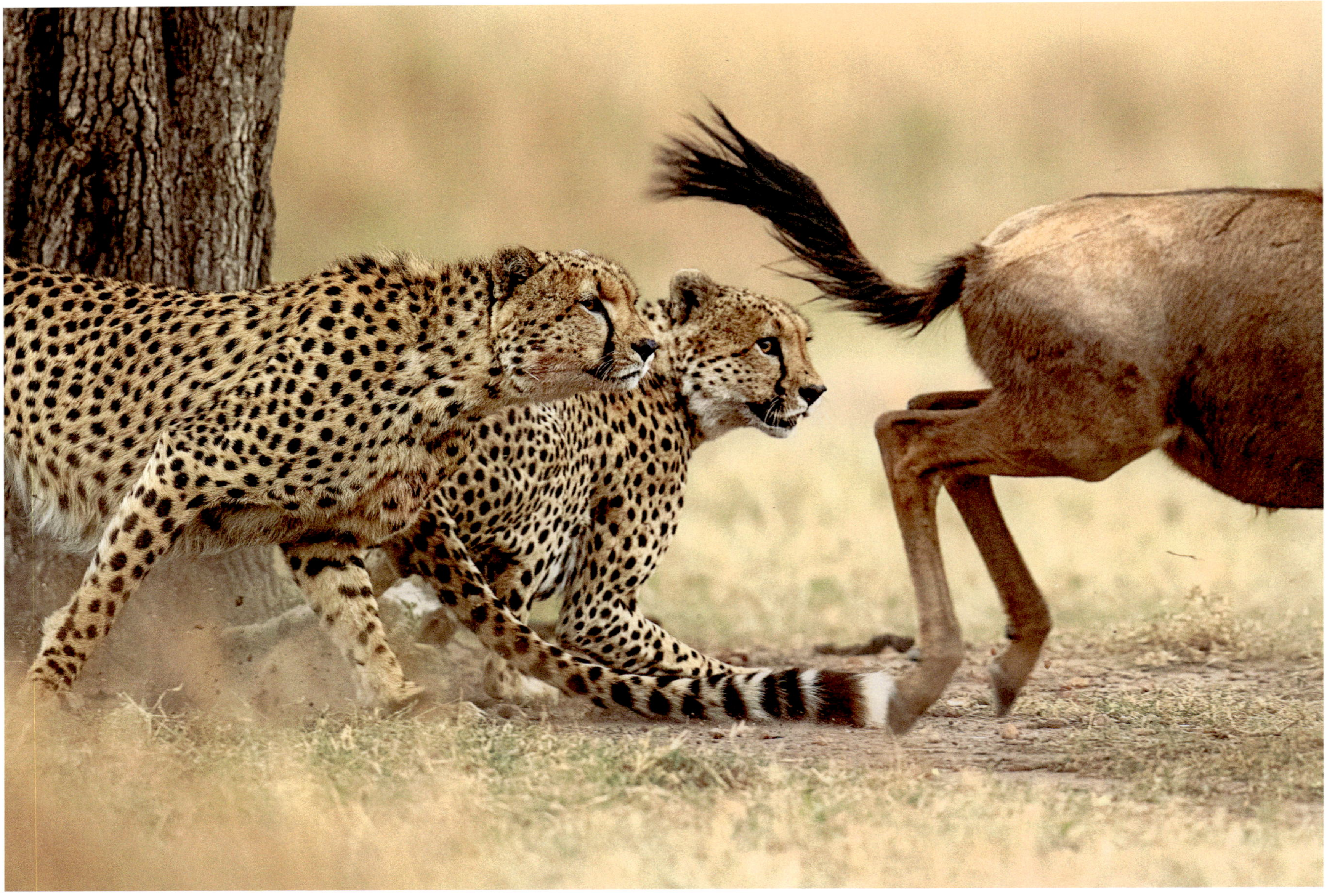

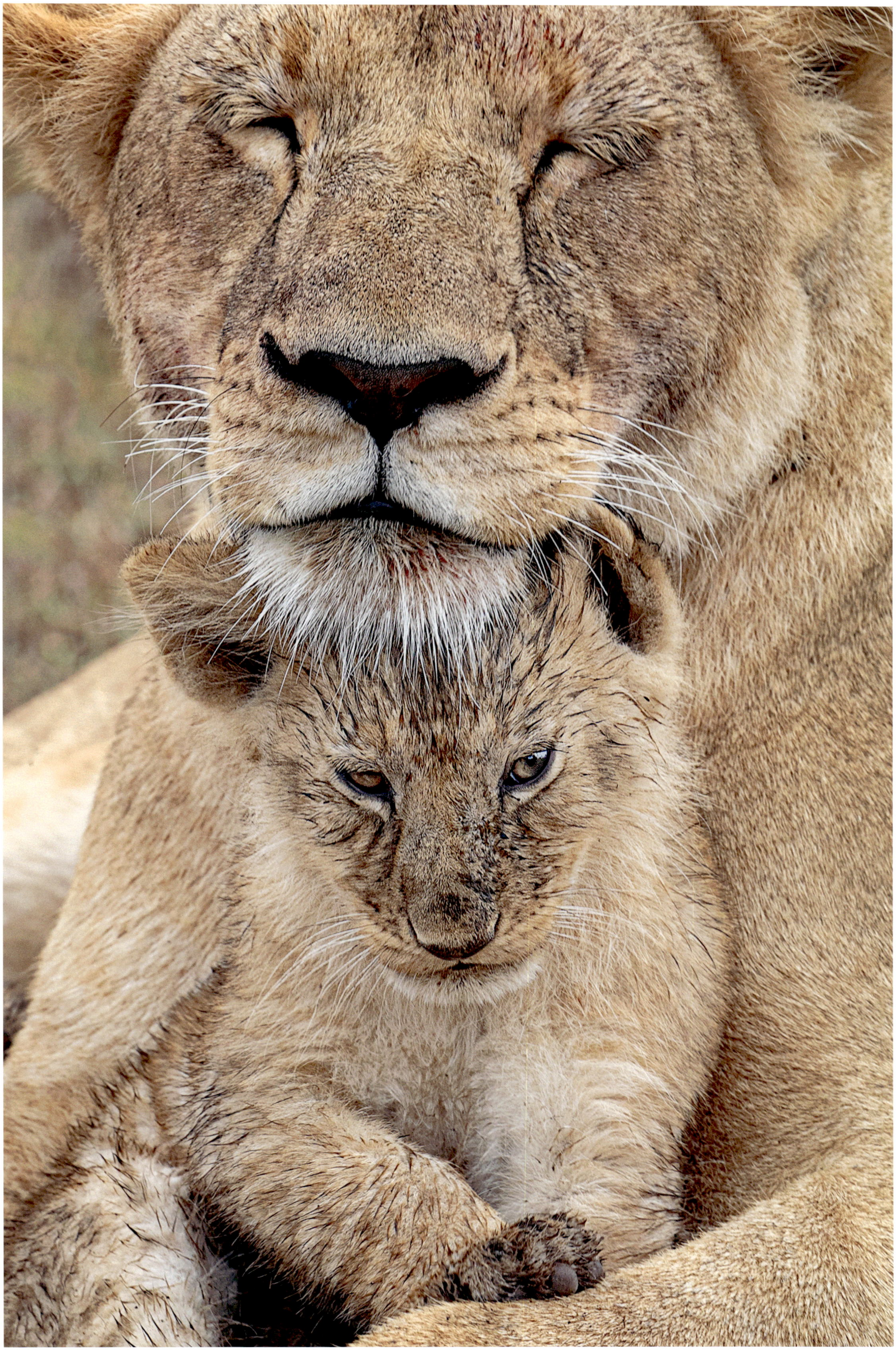

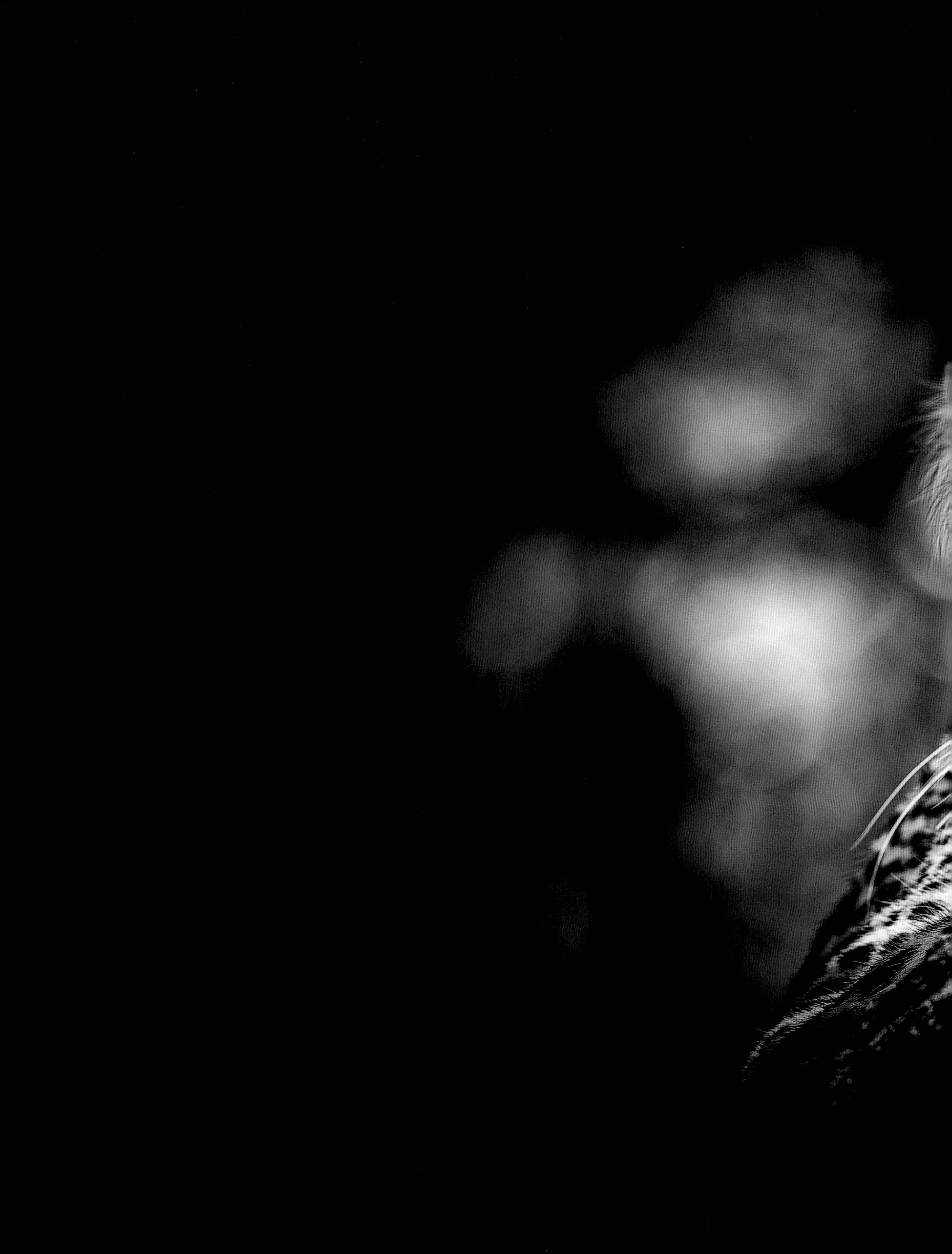

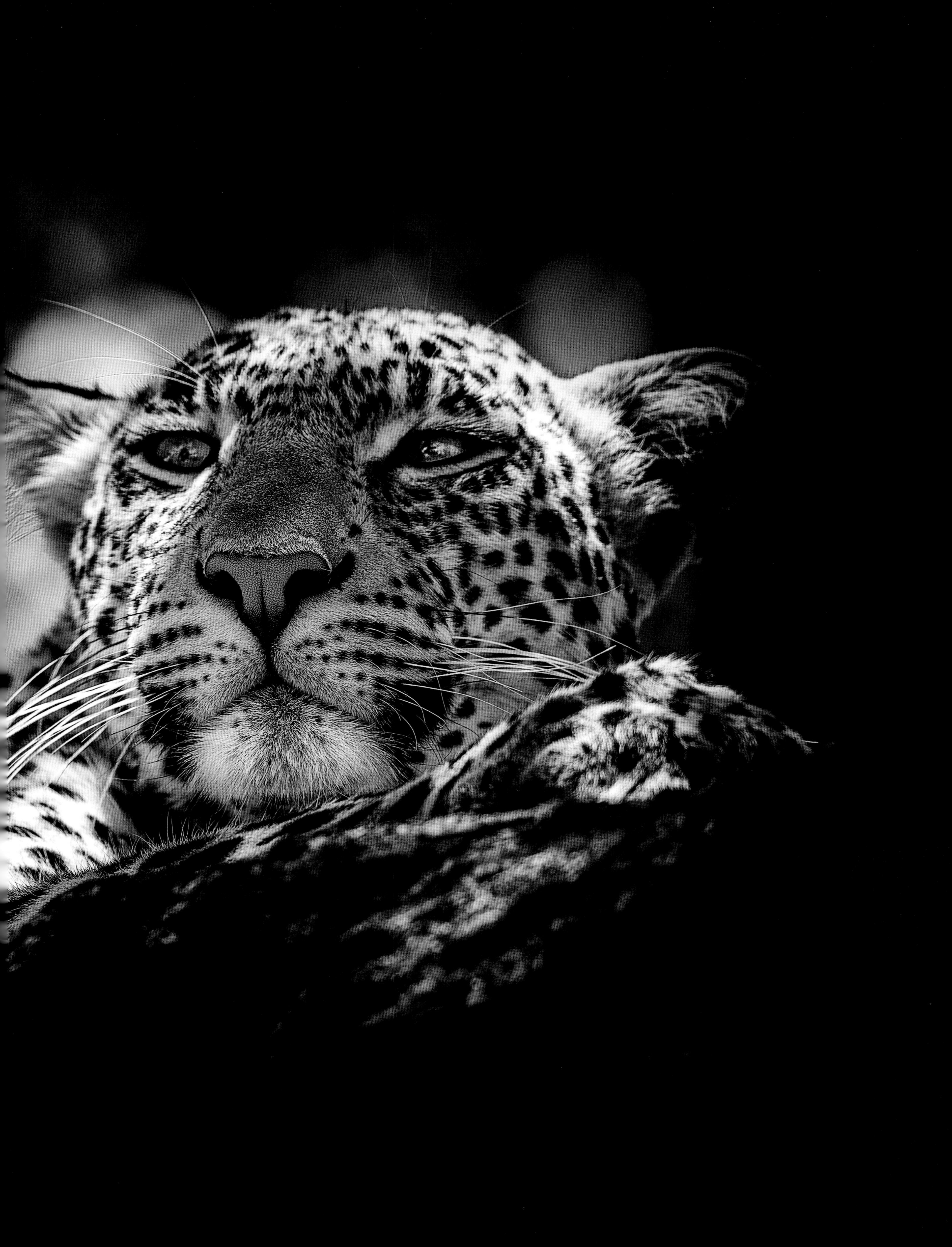

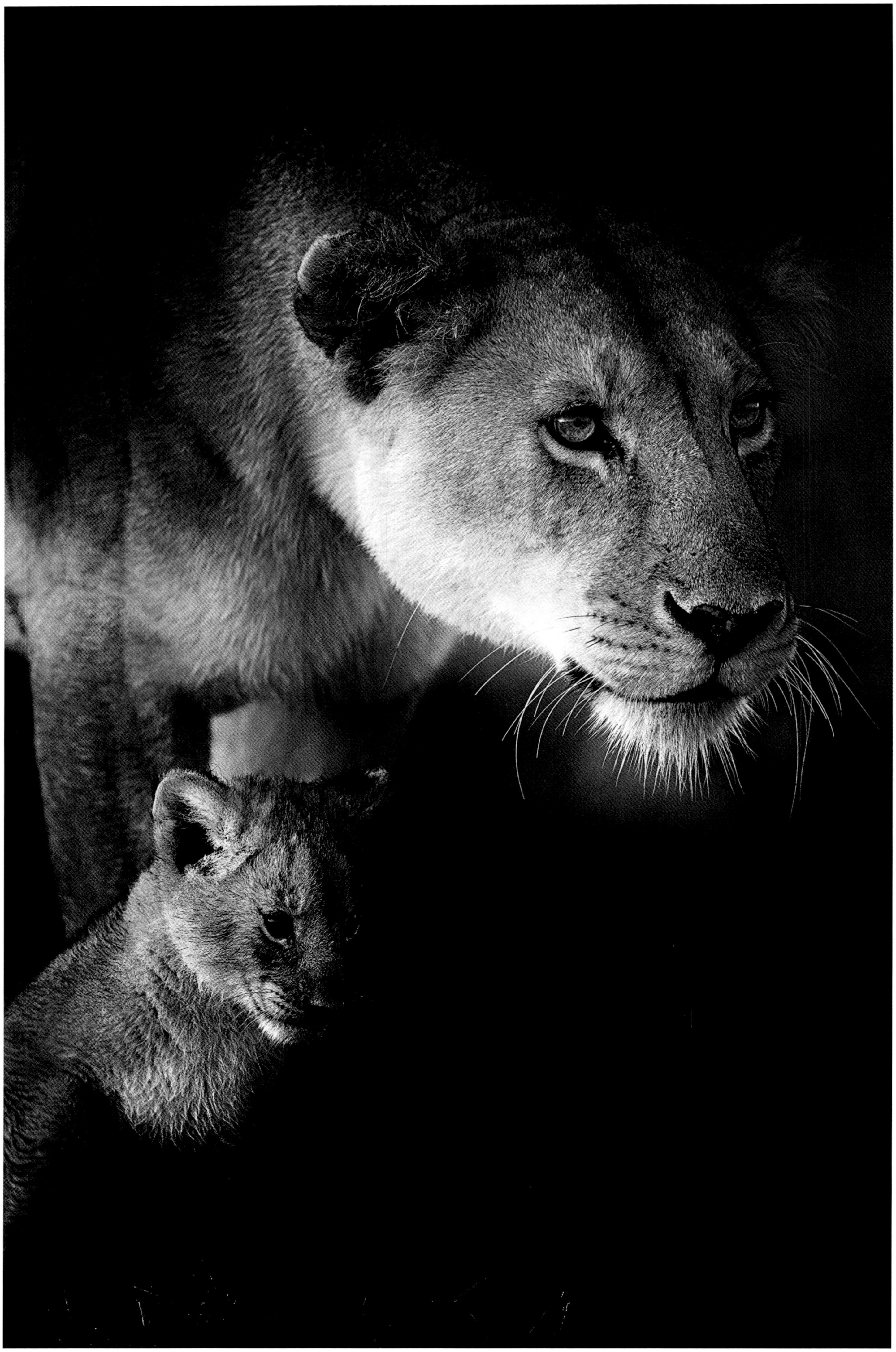

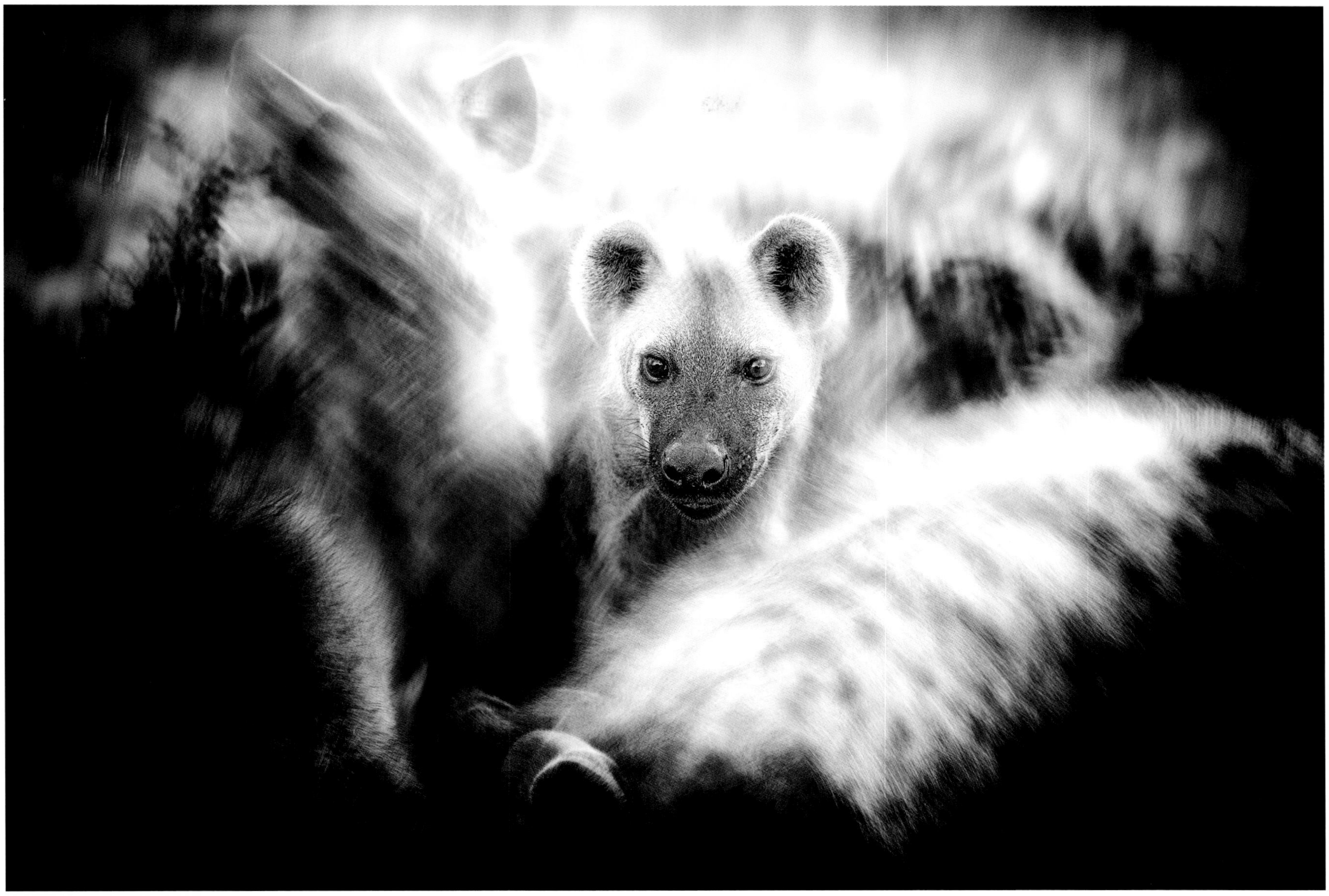

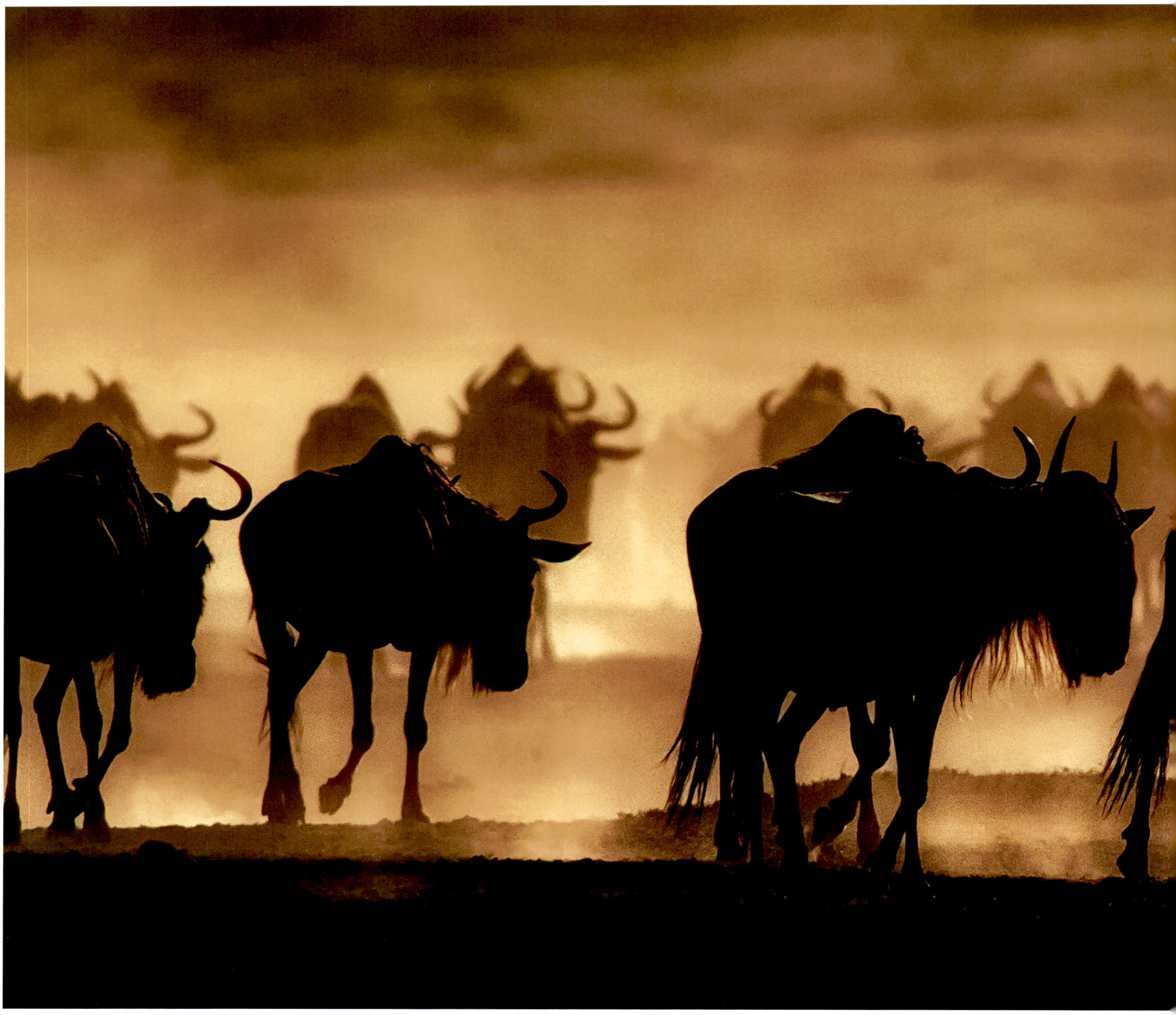

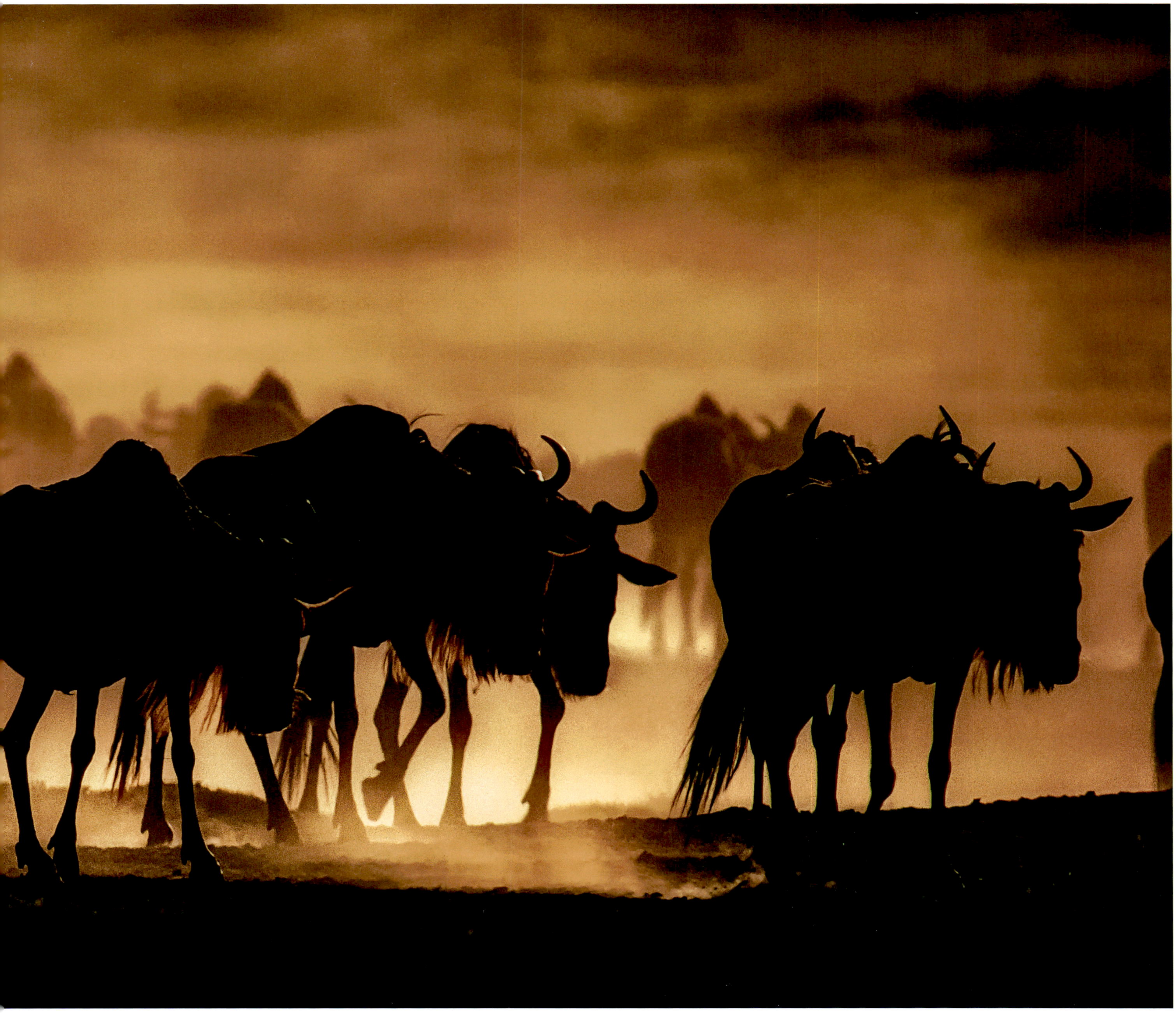

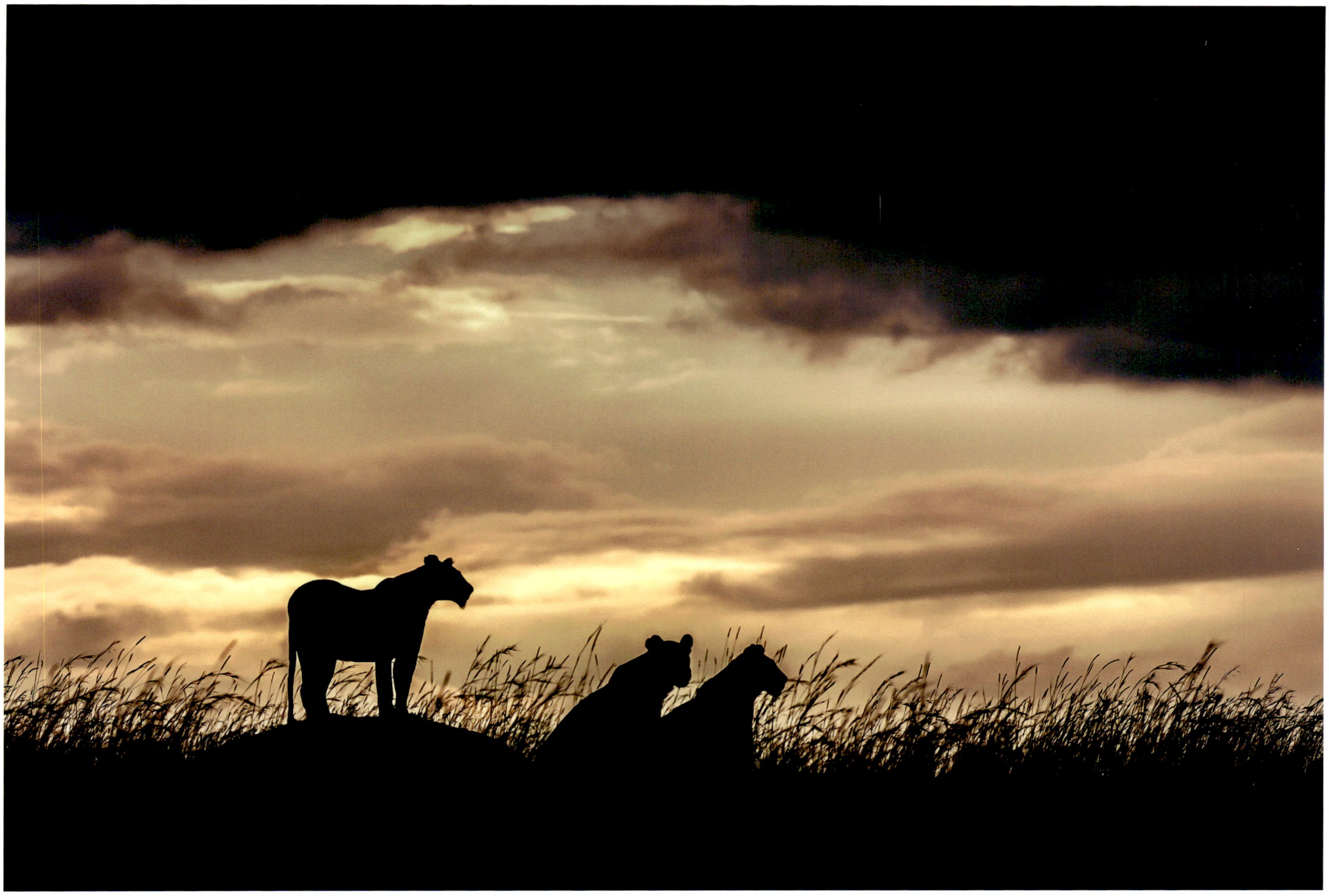

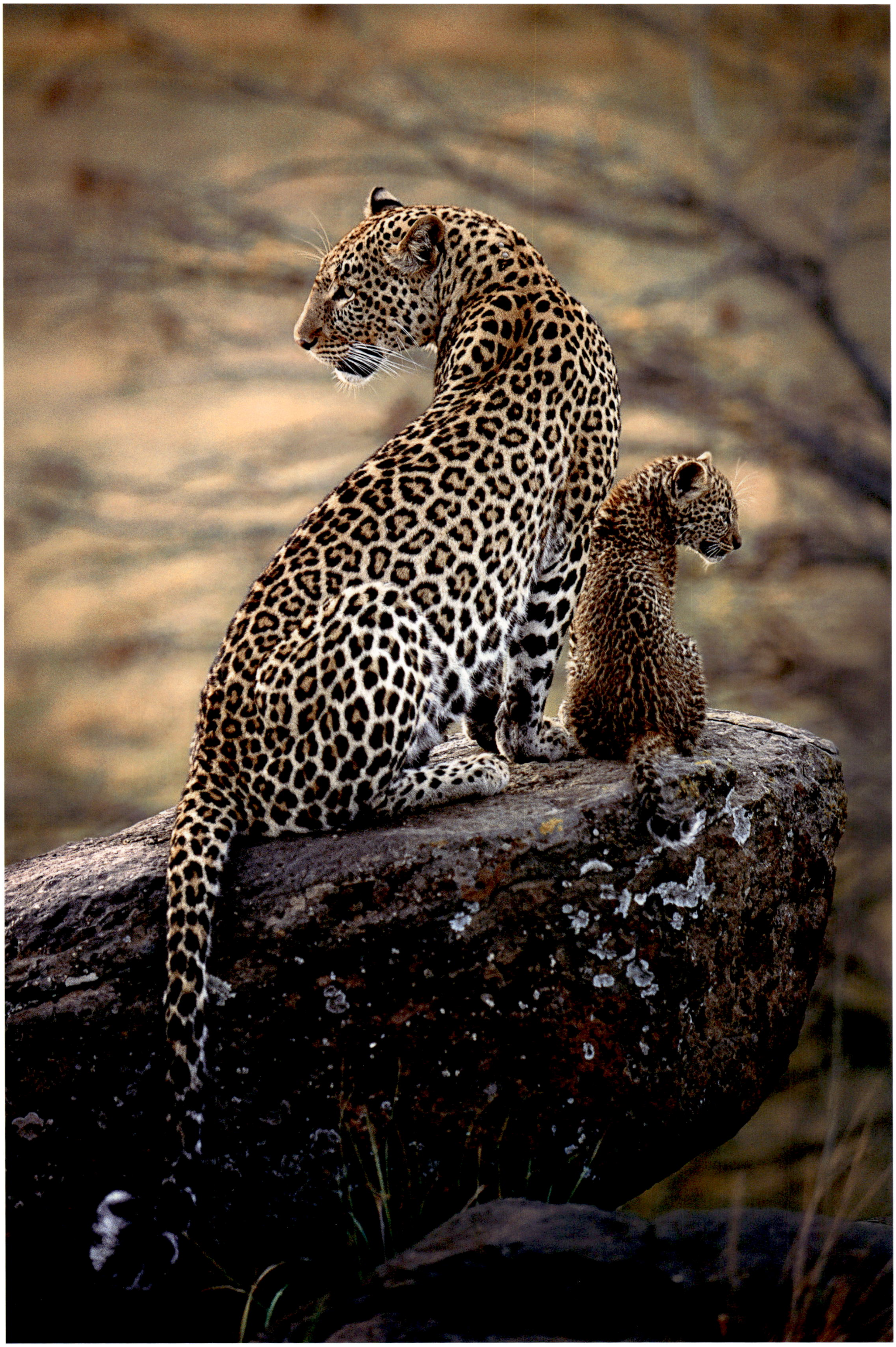

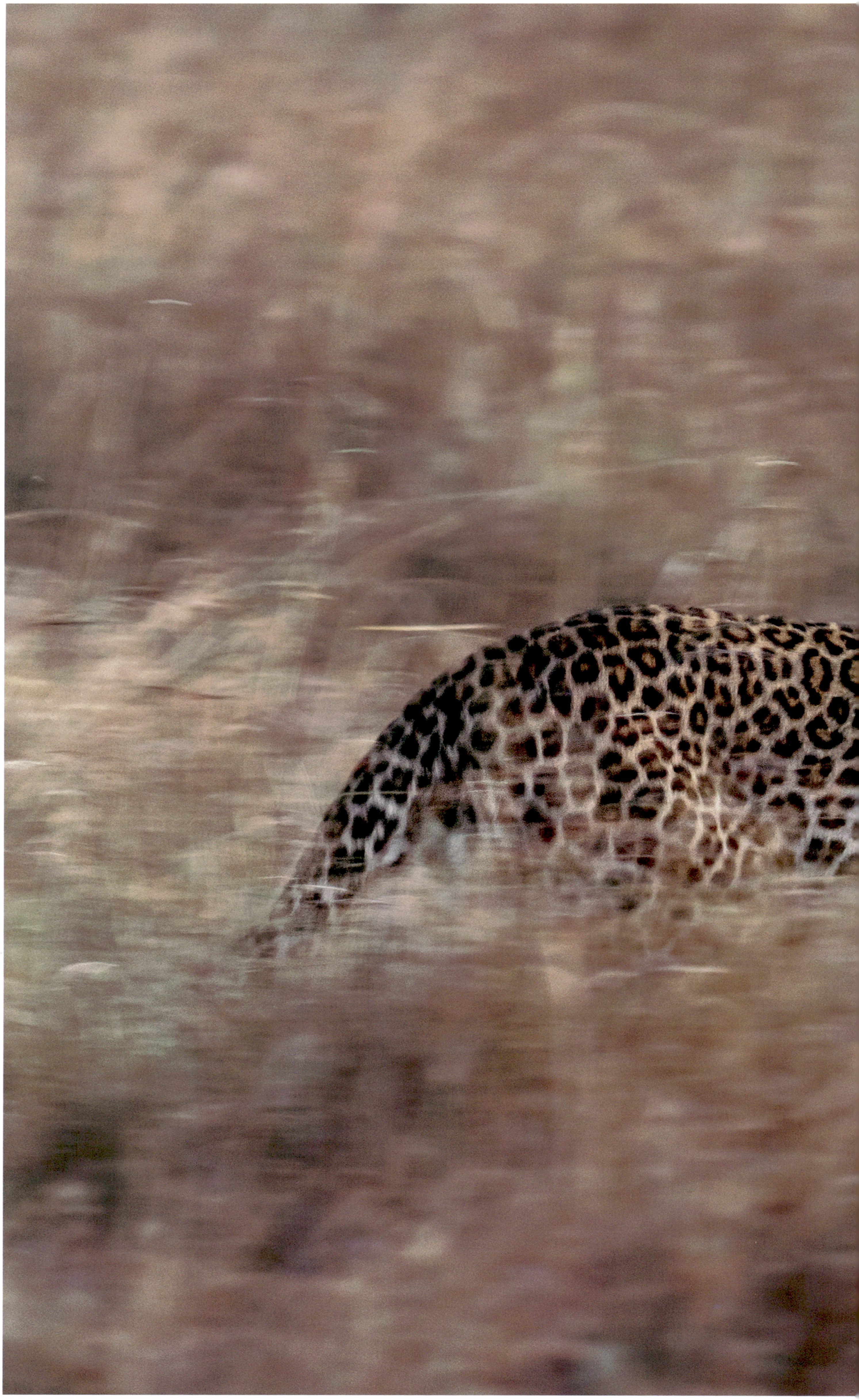

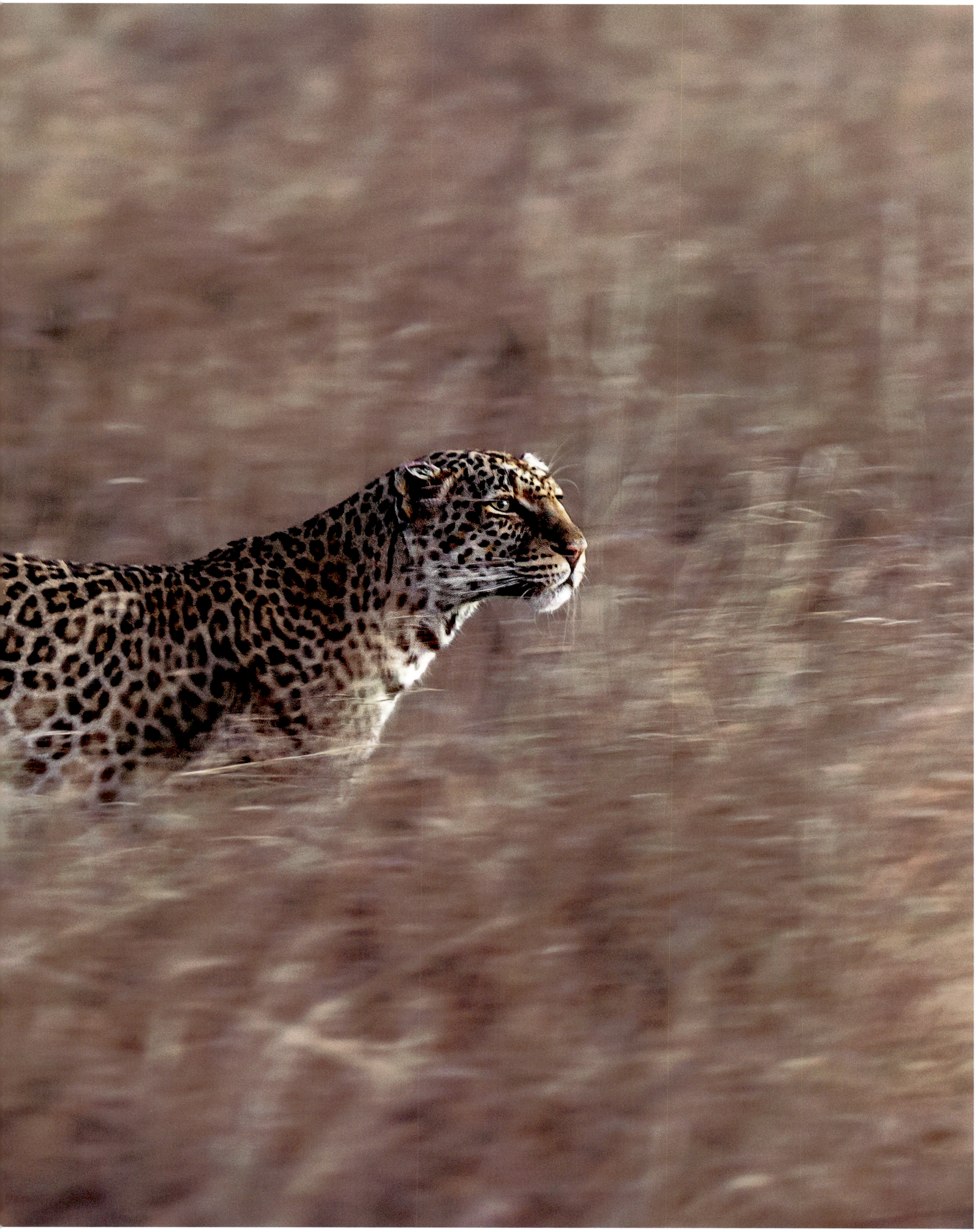

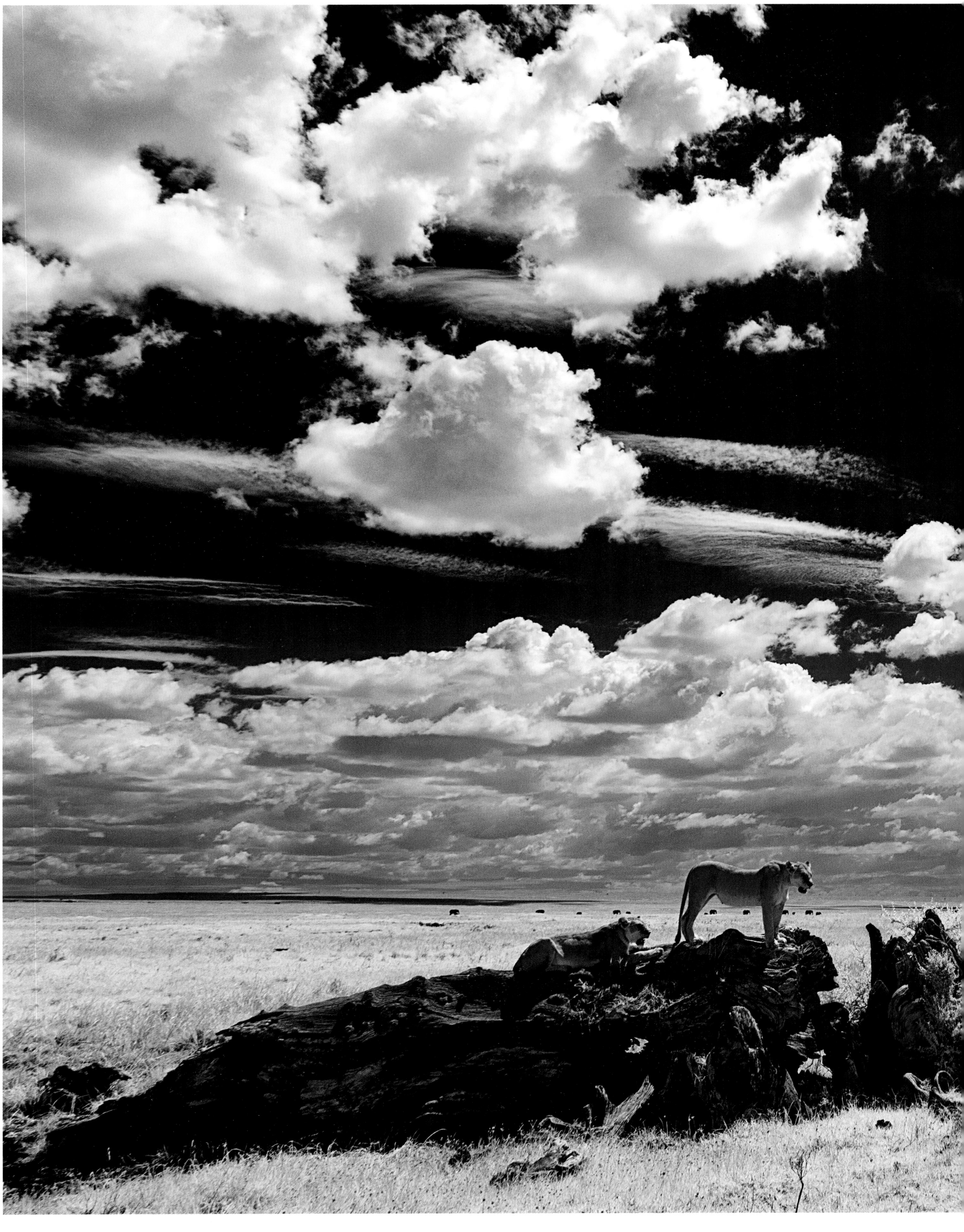

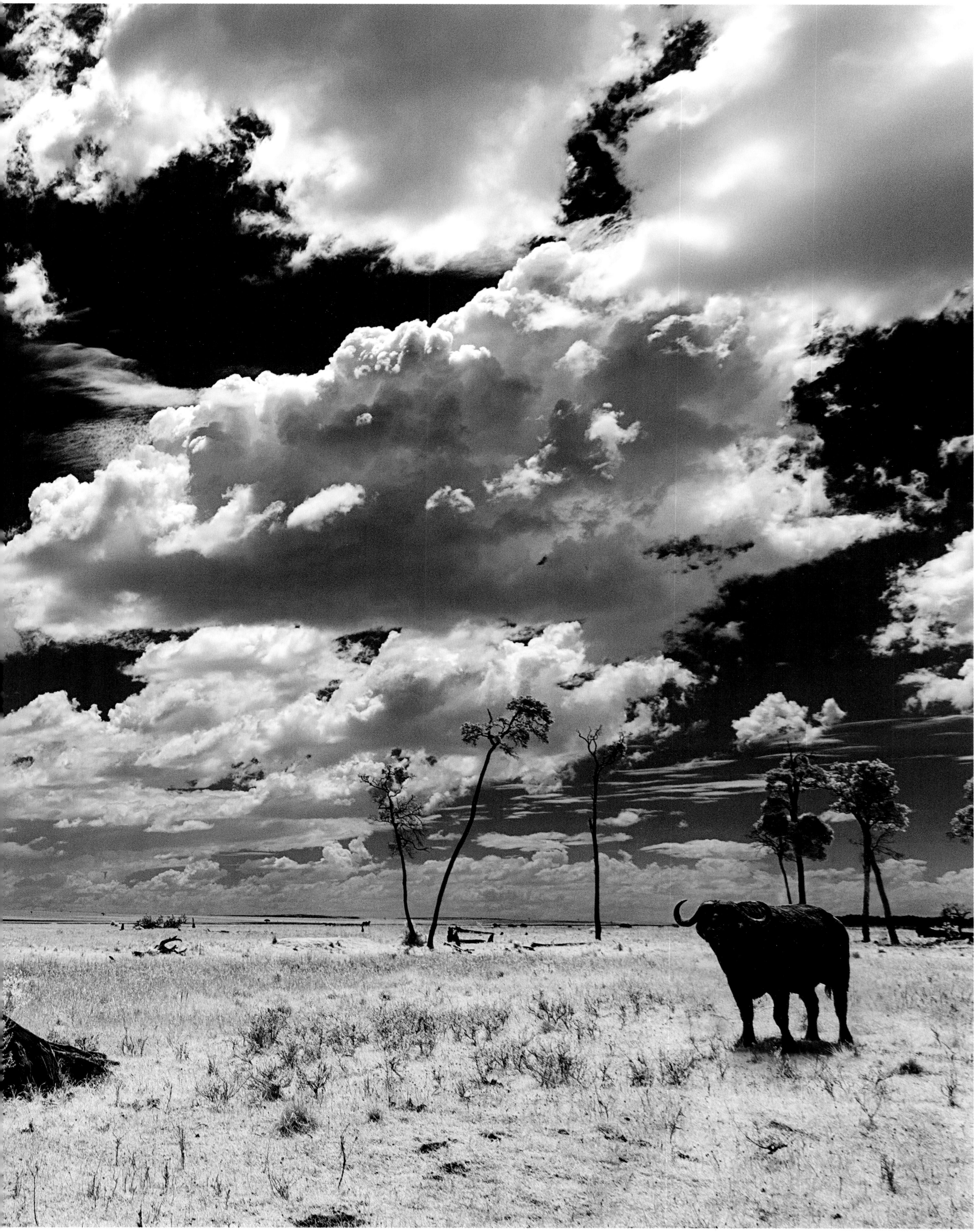

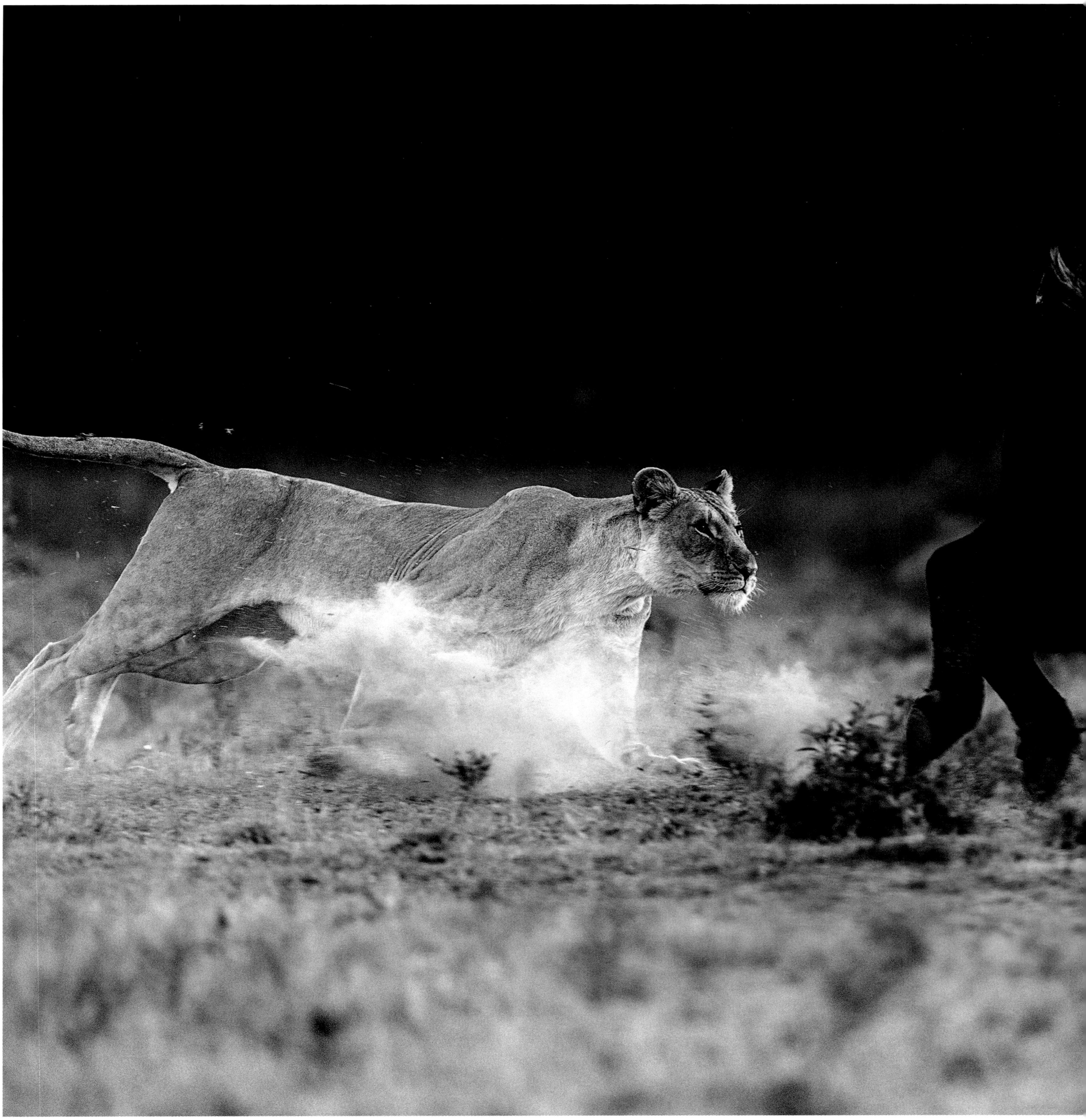

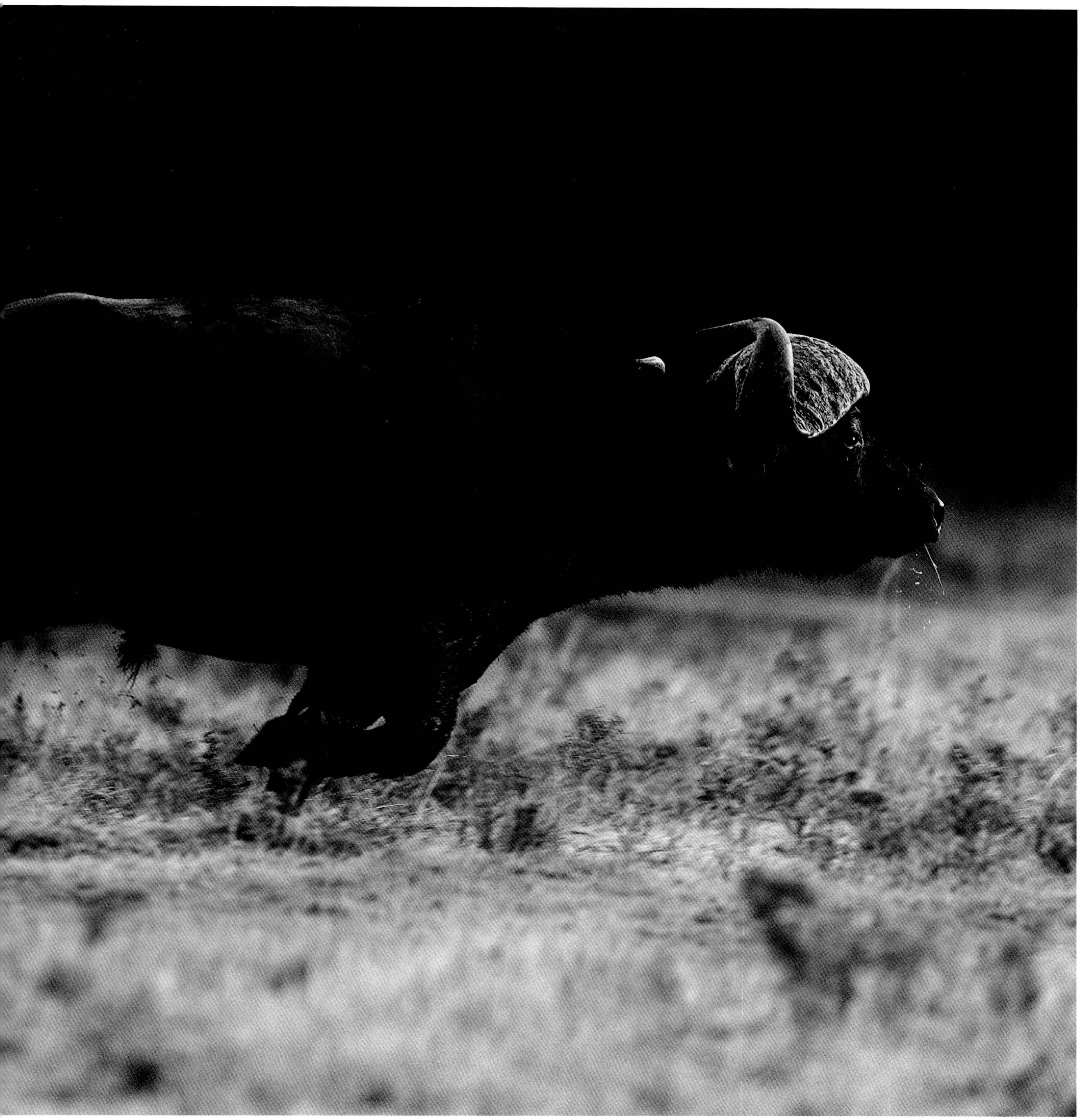

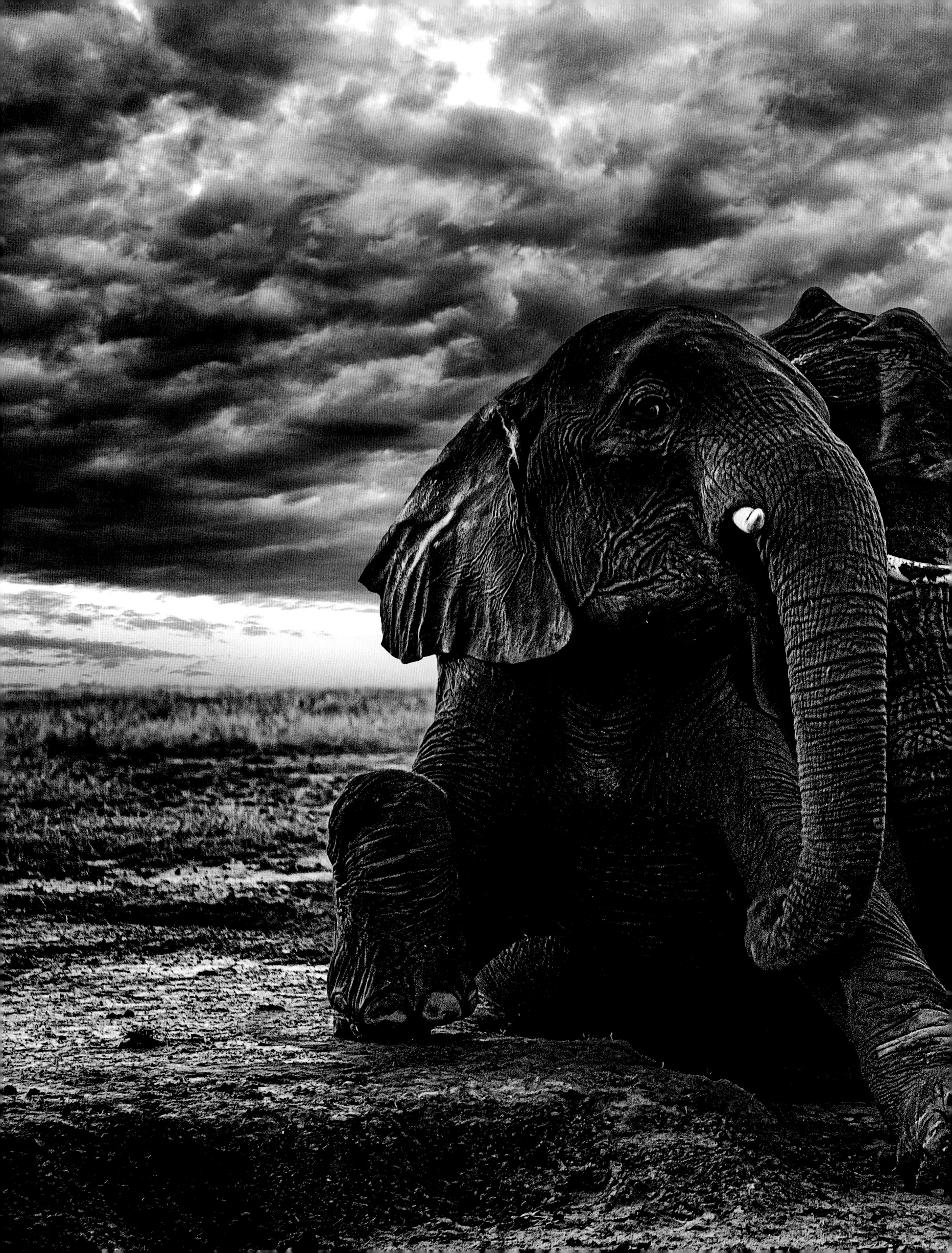

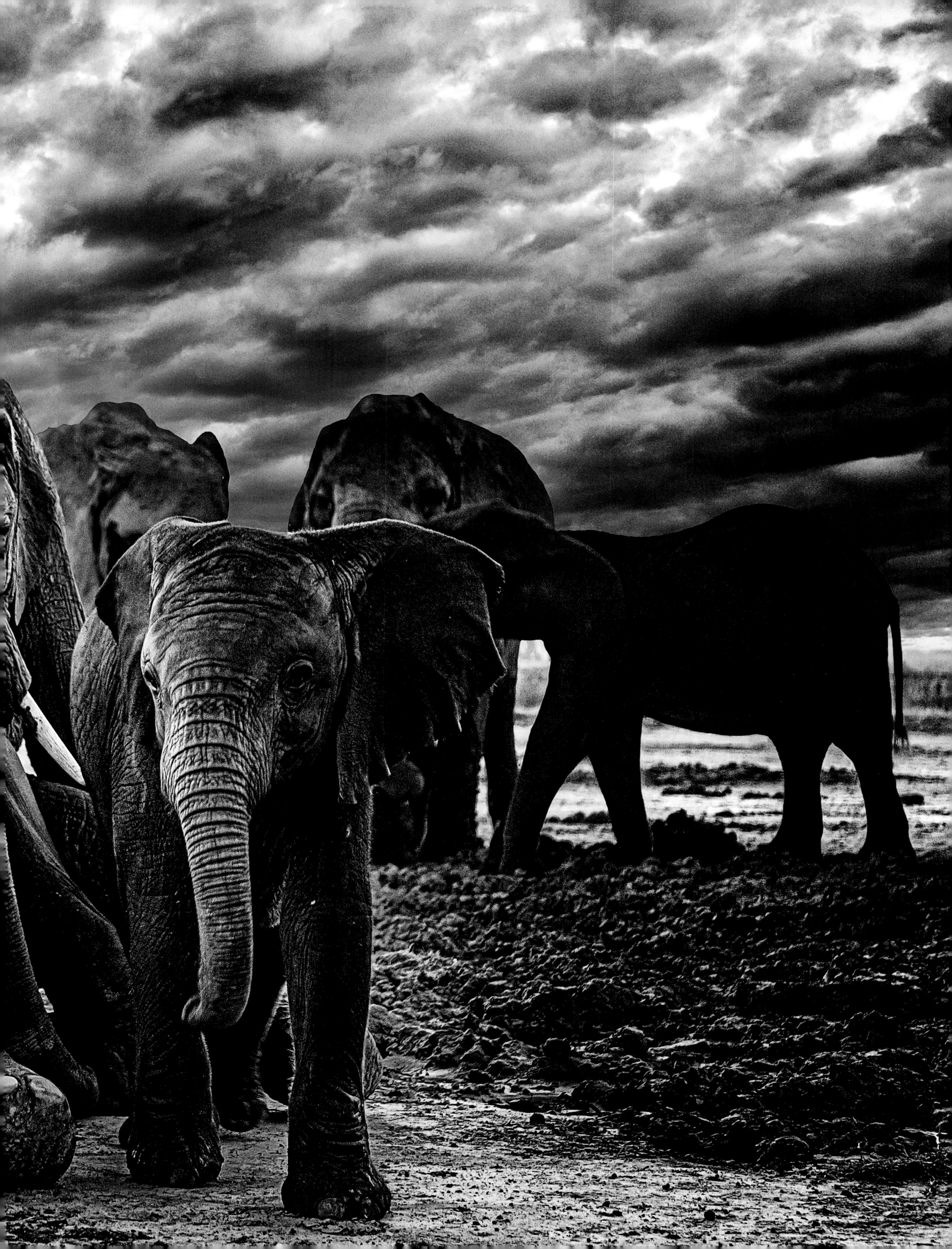

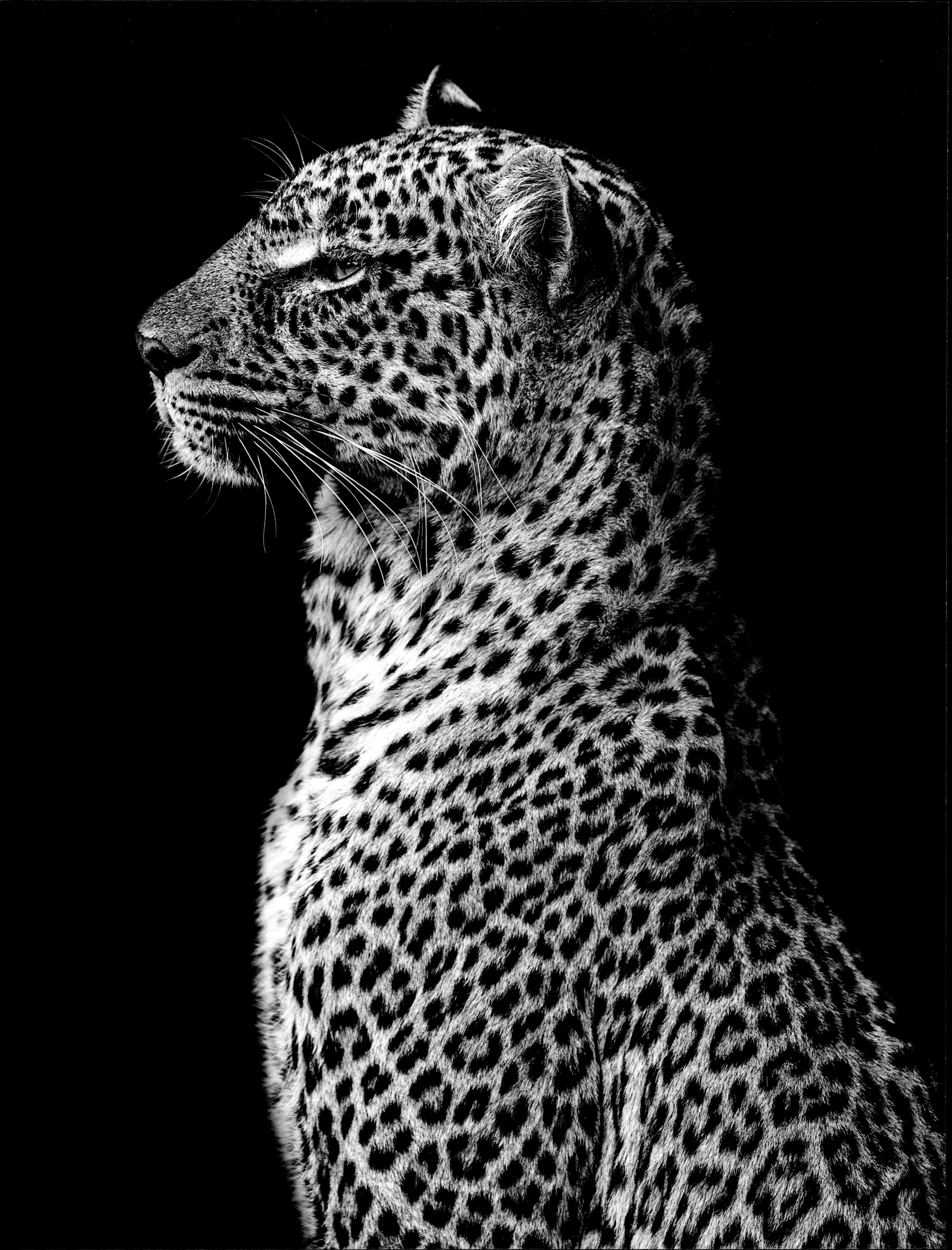

Chapter Two

FOR THE LOVE OF TREES

Trees exhale for us so that we can inhale them to stay alive. Can we ever forget that? Let us love trees with every breath we take until we perish.

— Munia Khan

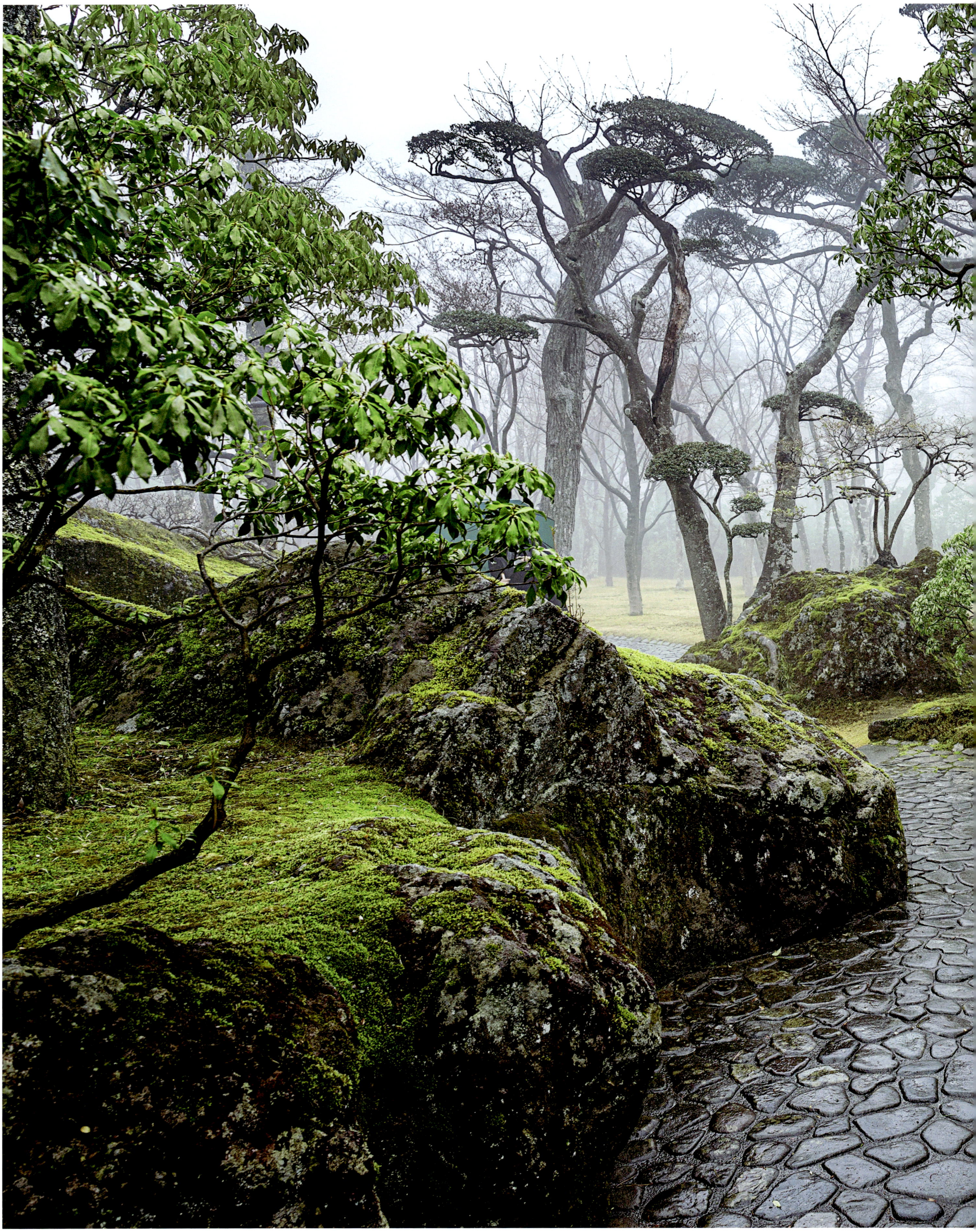

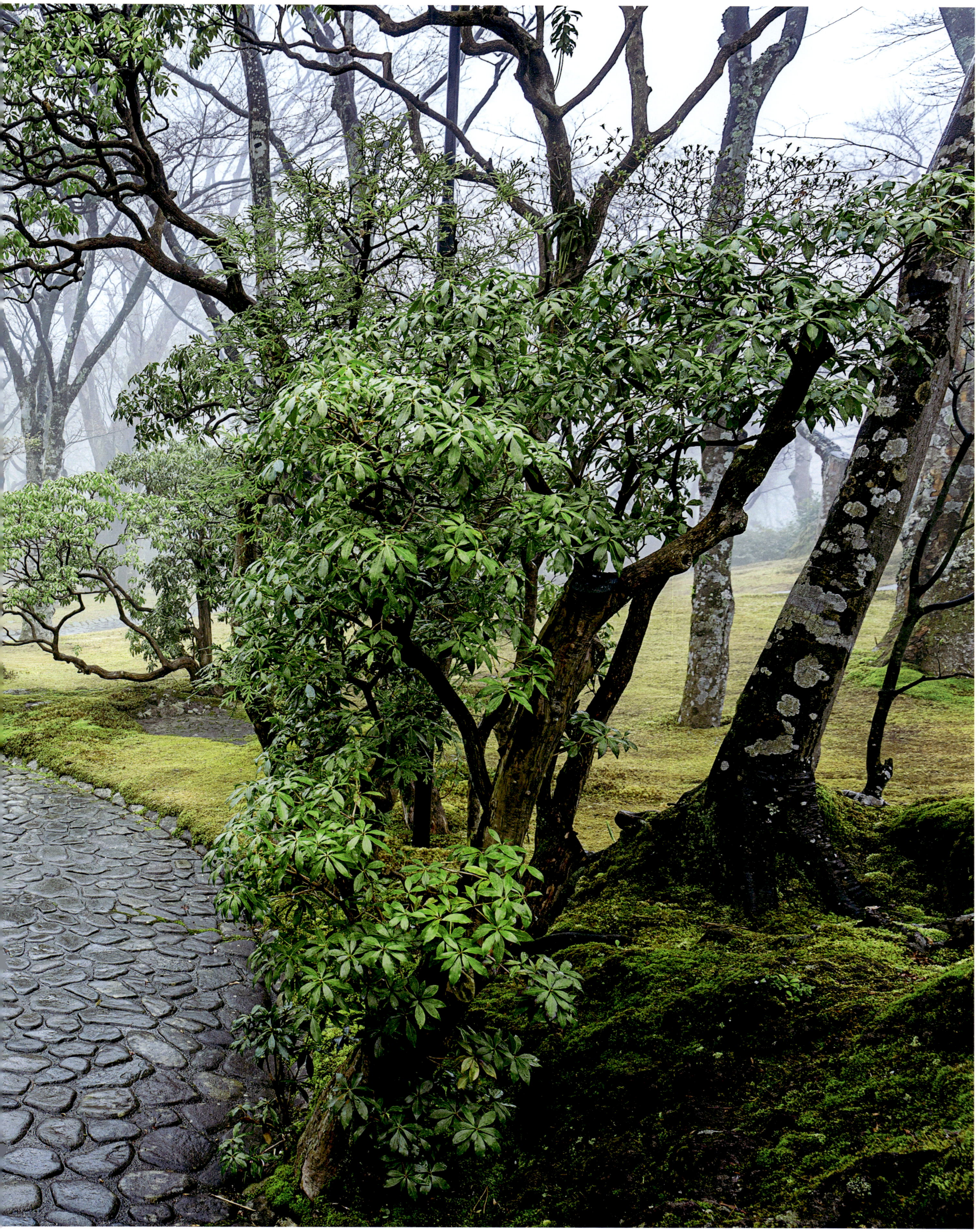

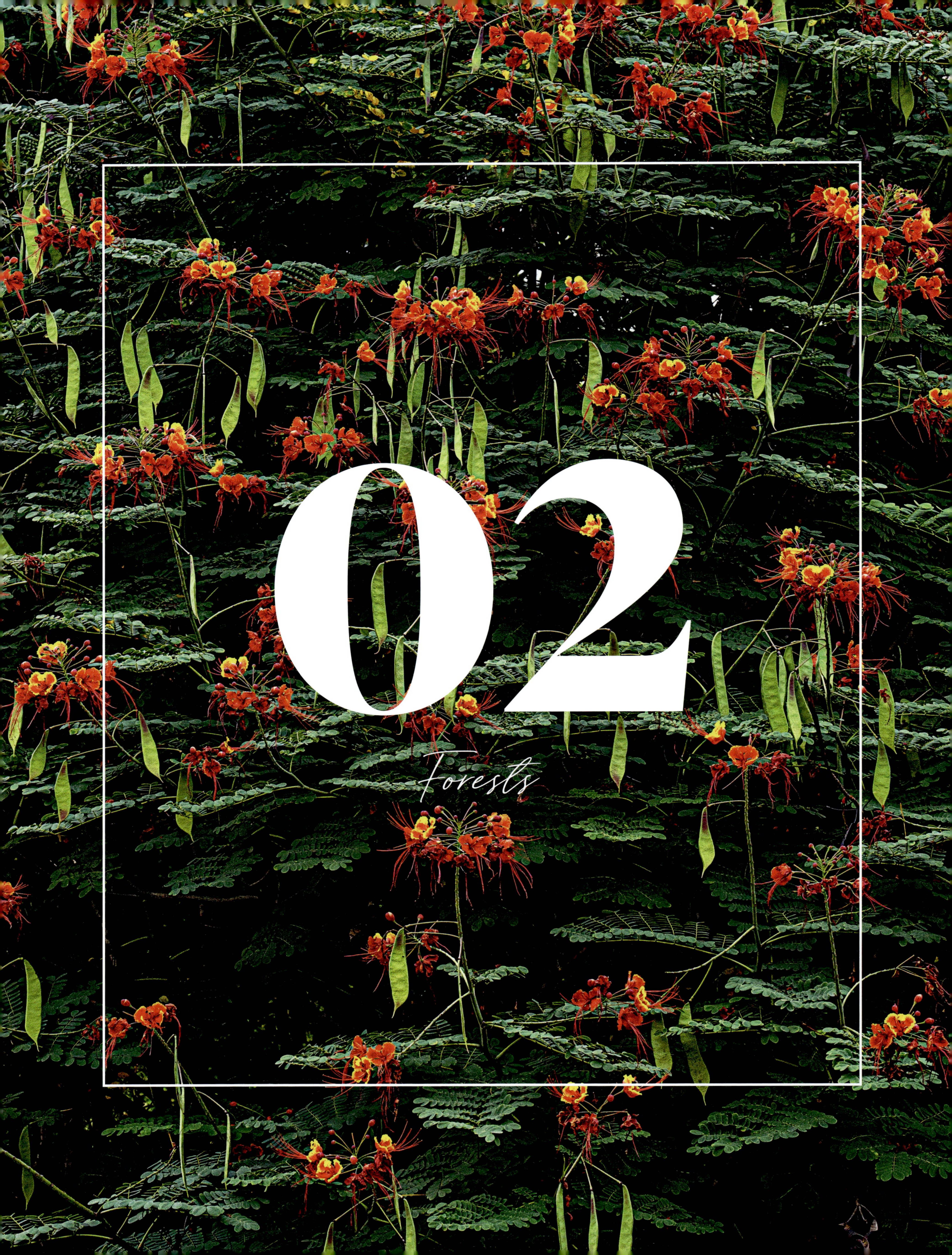

02

Forests

Our planet has lost more than half of its trees since humans first learnt how to wield an axe: we are cutting them down at the rate of about 15 billion a year. The highest losses are among the rainforest communities that are our oldest living ecosystems. Some have survived in their present form for at least 70 million years and while covering just six per cent of the Earth's surface, rainforests are home to more than half of all our plant and animal species, many as yet undiscovered. A 10-square-kilometre plot of forest can contain as many as 1,500 flowering plants, 750 species of trees, 400 species of birds and 150 of butterflies. Rainforests store more carbon than other forests and are irreplaceable habitat for some of the most iconic creatures on the planet from orangutans in Borneo to mountain gorillas in the Virunga Mountains of east-central Africa, tigers in India and jaguars in the Pantanal wetlands of South America. Each one of these charismatic creatures is now endangered, its ancient forest home under threat.

We cannot live without trees, yet barely register they are alive. They are the bedrock of our existence, nourishing the animal kingdom, giants of the natural world whose sheer size fills us with awe. Firmly rooted in the earth, they reach for the sky, feasting on sunlight and converting its energy to organic matter through photosynthesis. They embody growth and the sustainability of life, speaking to us of death and rebirth as witnessed each autumn when the broad leaves of deciduous trees transform into a kaleidoscope of reds and oranges, browns and yellows, parading a theatre of colours before cascading to the ground, showering the earth with leaf litter. The mulch fertilises the soil, nourishing the roots of those same trees to produce a crop of fresh green leaves in the never-ending cycle of renewal.

Author Judith Crews reminds us in *Forest and Tree Symbolism in Folklore* of how trees and forests retain an air of mystery. Trees are the visible face of Mother Earth, bearers of fruits and beverages, reservoirs for water, the source of traditional medicines, building blocks for houses and stockades, containers for storing and transporting goods. In many African cultures certain groves of trees are sacred and untouchable, the abode of spirits or souls, links to ancestors, a means to communicate with the gods, places where councils of elders gather to sit and talk on matters of gravitas, soothed by the trees' shady and immovable presence. Likewise stately fig trees and mammoth baobabs (some dating back more than 2,000 years) are potent symbols of wisdom and authority.

The Mbuti, a group of hunter-gatherers living in the Ituri rainforest in the Democratic Republic of the Congo, imbibe a deep sense of spirituality and symbolism from the darkened world of the tropics. Vanessa Drake Moraga, writing in 1996 in *An Eternity of Forest – Paintings by Mbuti Women*, illuminates how the forest embodies Mother Nature, the womb (ndu), the giver of life. It is a twilight world of buzzing insects, ant trails and tangled vines that thrive in humidity akin to that of a sauna. The Mbuti consider themselves children of the forest and celebrate its powerful imagery in their beautifully painted bark cloths, prepared by men from the inner bark of trees and embellished by women with abstract motifs. These intricate paintings are rich in meaning and are worn as ritual dress for festivals and rites of passage: circumcision, marriage, burial. The bark cloths capture the essence of the Mbuti's forest existence, a vibrant world teeming with life, infused with sound, shape and motion. Song and dance evoke the wonder and bounty of the forest with the mimetic 'elephant hunt' and 'honey-bee' dances giving thanks for the food of the forest, honouring the hunt.

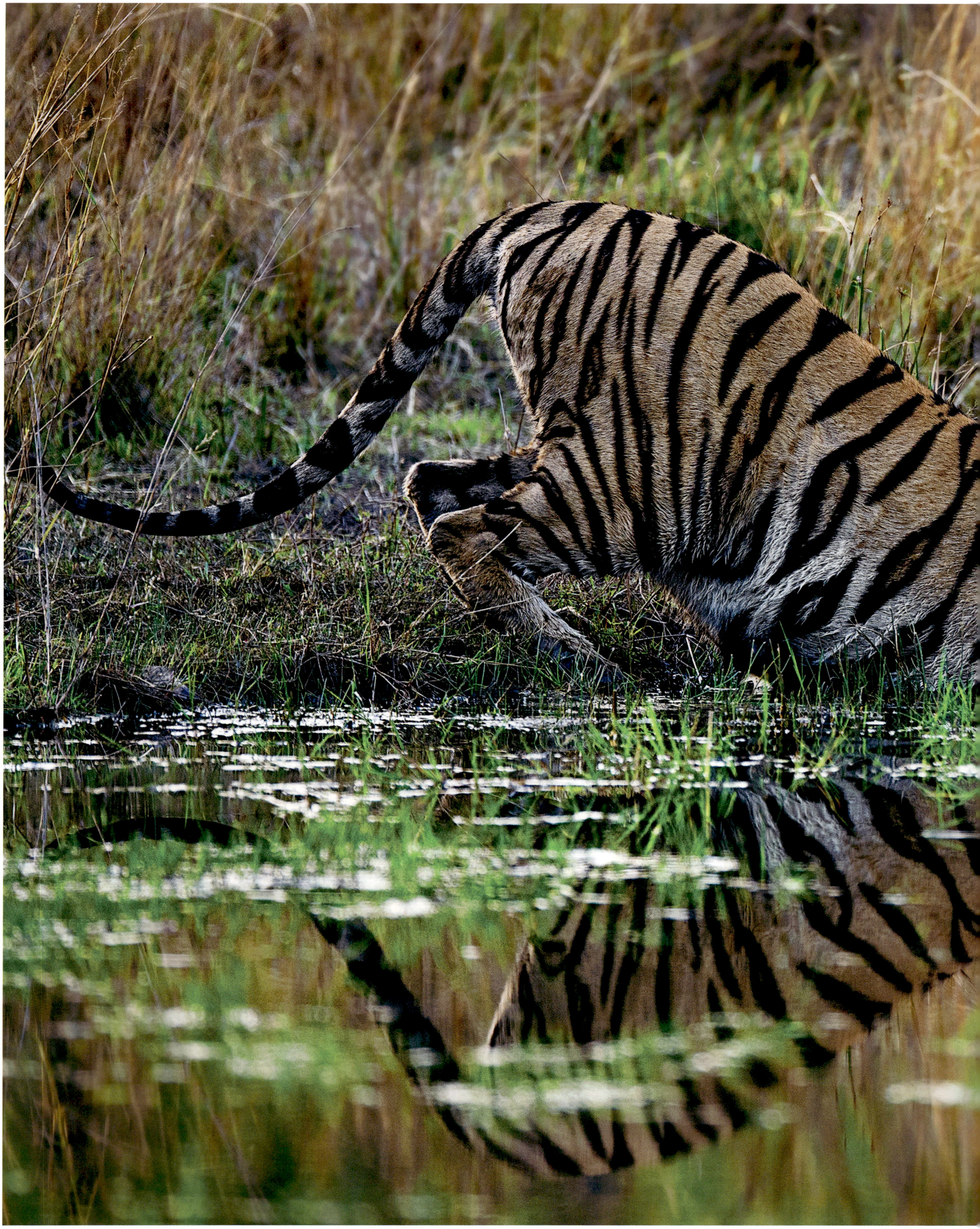

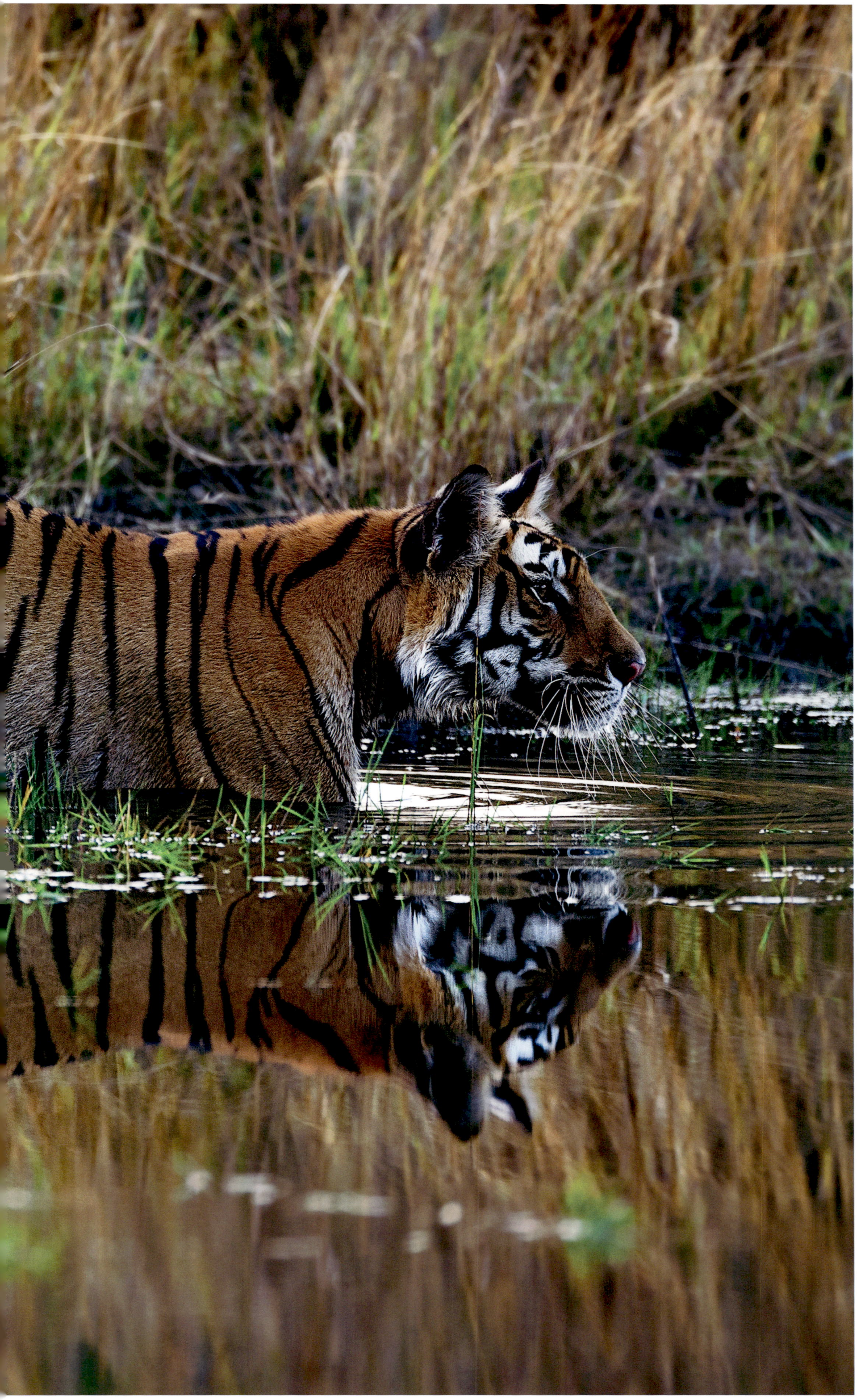

Visual 'silences' in the bark-cloth designs mirror the Mbuti concepts of sound and silence. Some of their most valued songs are without words, sung to awaken the forest and make it rejoice through the beauty of the sound alone. It is not a lack of sound but an absence of noise (*akami*) that creates silence or quiet (*ekimi*). Noise to the Mbuti is conflict; it jars on the soul, while sound has spiritual and magical properties, providing a means of heightened communication with other people and with the forest itself.

The sound of silence: what a wonderful thought in times of such intense urban noise pollution. There is wisdom to be learnt from people who still live close to nature that can help reawaken the sense of something sacred in our hearts. Just as the bison provided for the spiritual and bodily sustenance of the Plains Indians, and cattle fulfilled a similar role in Maasai culture – cattle as a gift from God – the rainforests create meaning and purpose in the lives of the Mbuti people as well as providing food. The bison, cow and forest each forged a powerful covenant with the land for these very different human societies defined by a deep respect for nature.

Forests offer each one of us a sense of renewal, a place to retire for insight and inspiration, somewhere to communicate with the inner self that sages throughout eternity have responded to. A walk among trees can quieten and calm the mind, allowing us to reconnect with our deepest being and reflect on our pathway – the purpose of our life. This is not pure fantasy. Japanese researchers have shown how therapeutic a walk in the woods can be, lowering blood pressure, boosting the immune system and releasing natural chemicals that reduce feelings of aggression, frustration and anxiety. Tree bathing, as it is known, acts through aromatic substances exuded by trees, some of which have been extracted and bottled by the wellness industry to soothe the stressed and weary. How much more energising, though, to take a walk through a wooded glade and soak up nature's miraculous tonic first hand.

Today's biosphere reserves, world heritage sites and other protected areas echo our ancient relationship with trees as we strive to conserve our dwindling forests and the indigenous societies for whom they are still home. But we must remain vigilant. Since 2006, some of Africa's oldest, largest and most revered baobab trees have abruptly died, wholly or in part: victims, it appears, of climate change. Nine of the 13 oldest baobabs – estimated at from 1,100 to 2,500 years old – have gone, or at least their oldest parts have collapsed and died, providing a timely reminder of our impact on the planet.

Of all the creatures evoking the spirit of the forests and jungles, none is more potent than the tiger. The largest and most powerful of the world's 38 species of wild cat is celebrated in coats of arms and national flags across Asia, the inspiration for sages, storytellers, artists and craftspeople: in Chinese culture, the four stripes on the tiger's forehead were believed to form the character Wang (王), designating it the king of all animals. The cult of the tiger is an ancient one, marking it out as a creature of the spirit world, a symbol of courage and inner strength, guardian against evil spirits. Tigers and dragons have often been depicted together, polar opposites balancing the universal forces of yin and yang, the female and male energies that form the seeds from which all creation evolved. The tiger embodies yang energy, the masculine force, corresponding with the sun, the summer season and fire, its exquisite coat markings, supple power and elegance mirroring everything we admire in nature.

One of the best places to see wild tigers is Ranthambore National Park in the desert state of Rajasthan in India. The park is a wonderland of ancient ruined palaces set among shimmering lakes resplendent with birdlife. The tiger's mighty visage is imprinted on your mind as you scan the hillsides and meadows, desperate to match your imagination with the reality of this god-like creature, a striped resident of the sunlight and shadows, the merest hint of black and gold merging with the long dry grass. The aura of the tiger holds you in its spell.

**Tyger Tyger burning bright
In the forests of the night,
What immortal hand or eye
Could frame thy fearful symmetry**

**In what distant deeps or skies
Burnt the fire of thine eyes
On what wings dare he aspire
What the hand, dare seize the fire**

— *William Blake*

At home in the Maasai Mara in Kenya, Angie and I have come to know many of the lions, leopards and cheetahs as intimately as we know some of our human friends. We identify with them in a very personal way. We care about their lives. The same is true of Ranthambhore's tigers, epitomised by Machali, Lady of the Lakes. Machali was our first tiger, a young female glimpsed as she ghosted past our vehicle while we were filming in 1997 and destined to become the most visible and photographed of all the 45 tigers living in the park until she died in August 2016 at the age of 17. Today, her legacy continues: some of her daughters still roam her old haunts in India's most beautiful and alluring tiger reserve.

Charismatic creatures such as Machali help remind the world what we stand to lose when the last tiger ceases to roar. When you look into the golden eyes of a wild tiger, you recognise the life force that breathes in all of us. The great striped cat is the key, the pivotal reason for protecting India's forest reserves. Without tigers, these last wild landscapes will be stripped of their grass and trees, quarried for their stone and sand by a human tidal wave that threatens to reduce sanctuaries such as these to little more than islands surrounded by a sea of people. The country's tourist industry needs its iconic tigers to draw the crowds, in the same way that the Maasai Mara needs its lions.

The magnitude of the challenge is not to be underestimated. In 1900, more than 100,000 tigers roamed the planet. Today they have lost an estimated 95 per cent of their historical range. Their survival rests on preserving wildlife corridors linking far-flung reserves to ensure the genetic viability of the population. There is reason for hope. When India's Prime Minister Indira Gandhi launched Project Tiger in 1973, there were nine tiger reserves in the country. Today there are 50. The subcontinent is now home to nearly 3,000 tigers, a third more than four years ago. Promising as this is, though, there are fewer than 4,000 tigers remaining in the world's 13 tiger-range countries: India, Bangladesh, Bhutan, Cambodia, China, Indonesia, Lao PDR, Malaysia, Myanmar, Nepal, Russia, Thailand and Vietnam.

Meanwhile, vast numbers of tigers are kept as exotic pets or bred for products in tiger farms around the world, with 5,000 captive tigers in the US alone. Of these, only six per cent are in accredited zoos and facilities, while the trade in tiger bone and skins has accelerated to the point that a tiger is worth more than US$ 50,000. Every part of the animal is coveted as a cure-all, with its magnificent skin worn as a status symbol in Tibet and China. The use of tiger body parts in Traditional Chinese Medicine dates back over a thousand years. The calcium and protein of tiger bone is believed to act as an anti-inflammatory, while its strength is said to revitalise and ease the symptoms of chronic ailments. Despite there being no scientific evidence for any such powers, throughout Asia and in Chinatowns across Europe and North America Chinese doctors prescribe tiger-bone wine to fortify the body; among the elite, tiger-penis soup is drunk as an aphrodisiac. The teeth are ground to powder to treat fevers, claws to treat insomnia and those spellbinding 30-centimetre-long whiskers used to treat toothache. These ancient spiritual tenets evolved when the world's population was small. Amplified by the prodigious increase in our numbers, they are now helping to bring about the tiger's downfall.

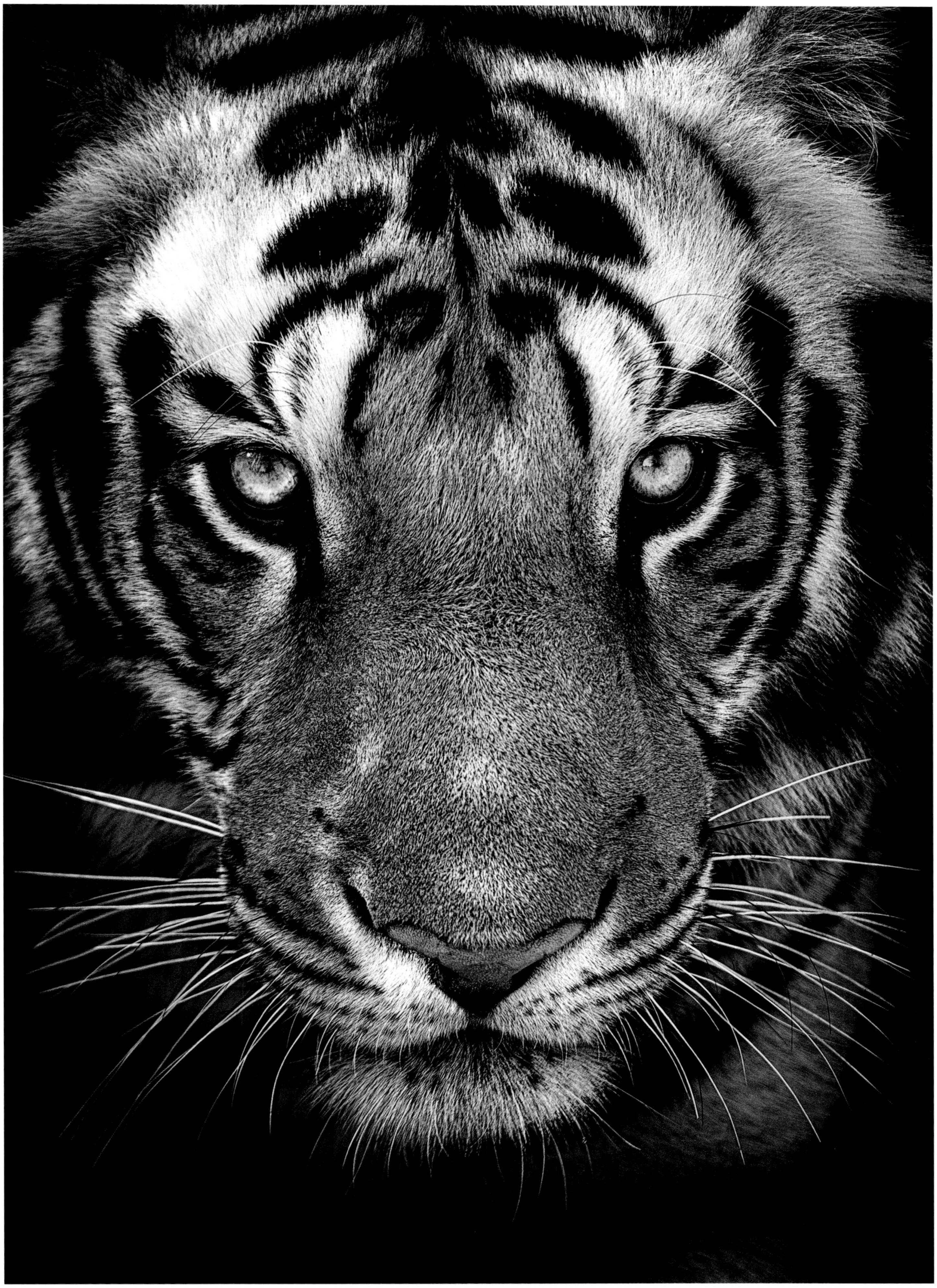

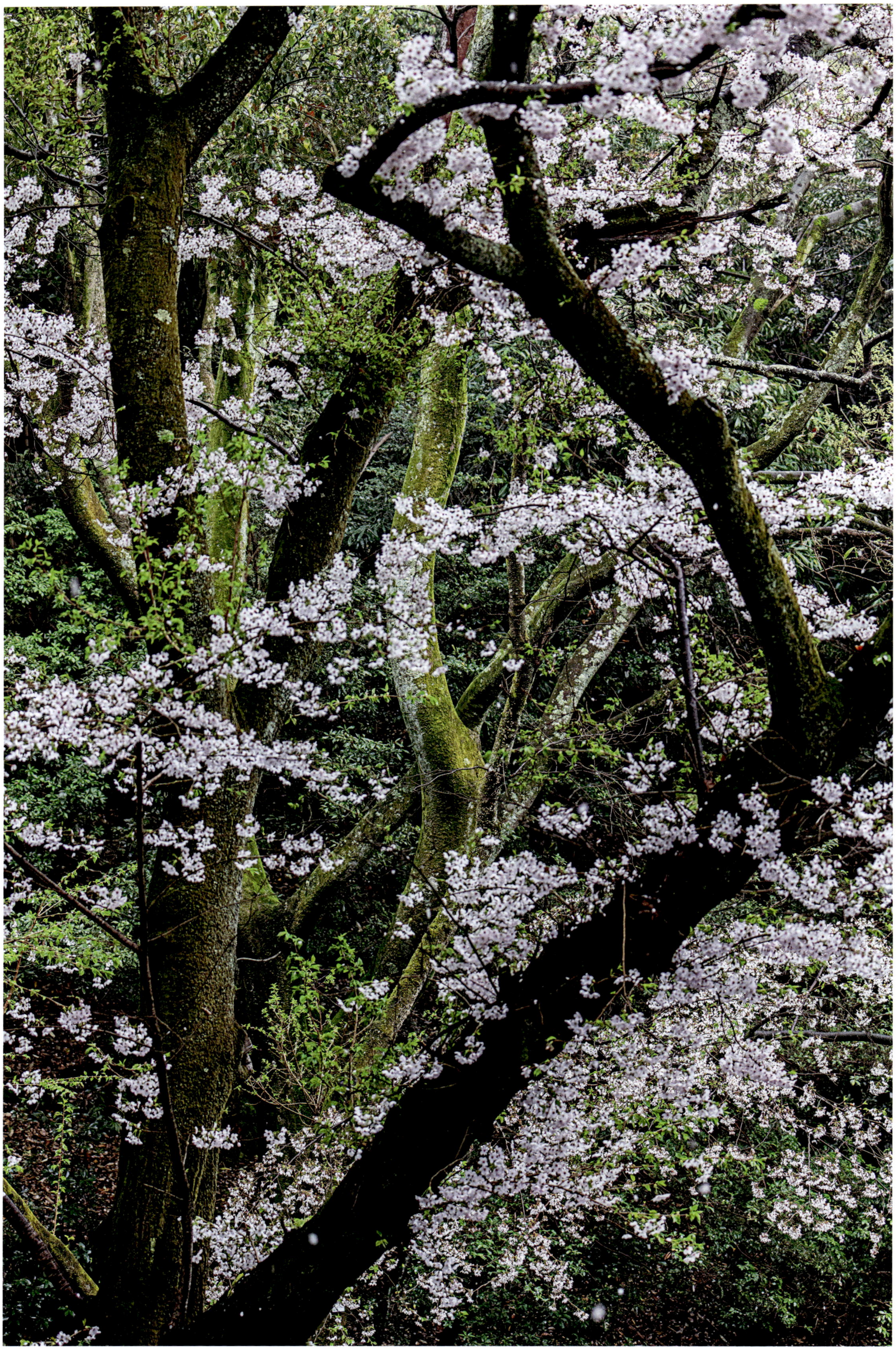

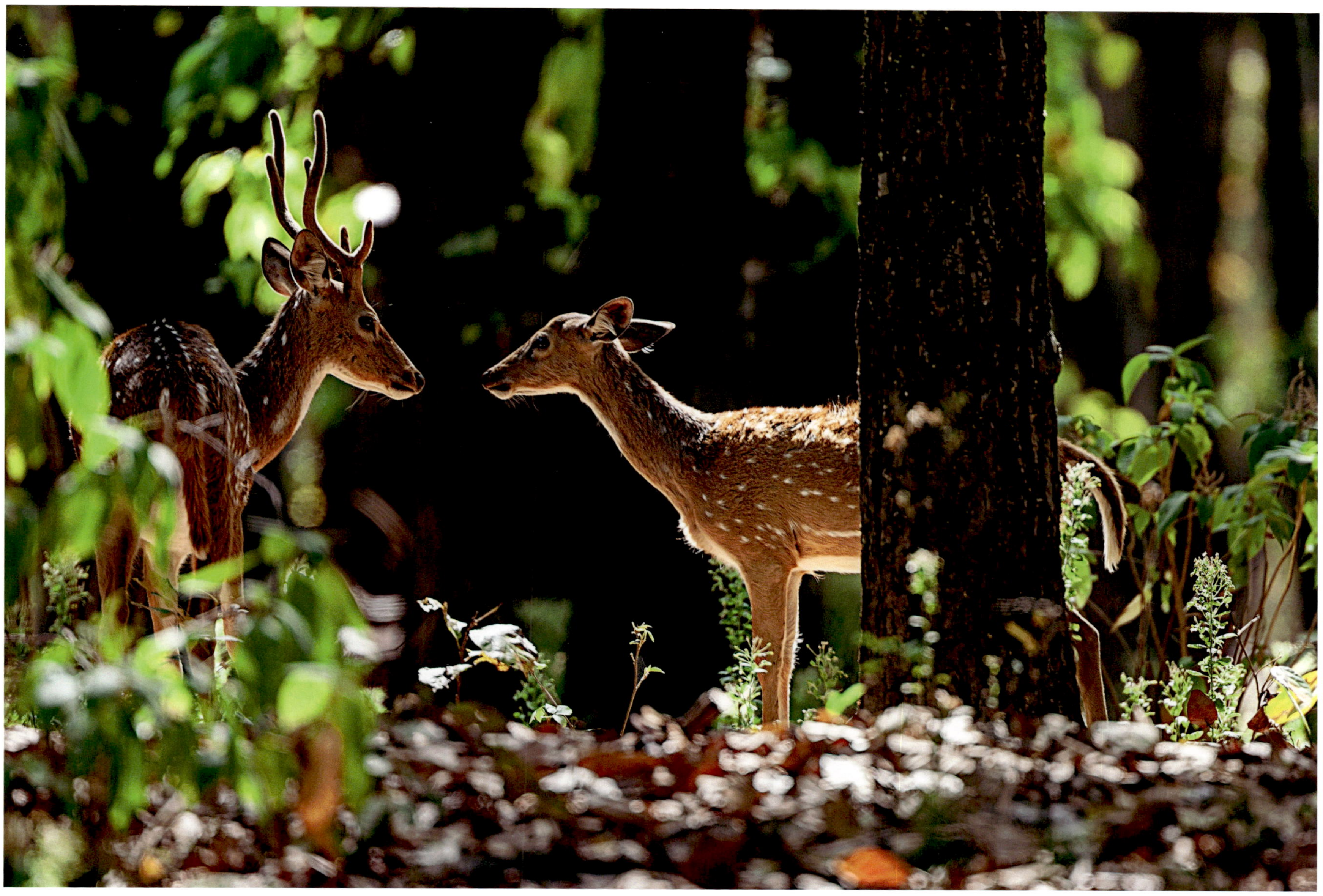

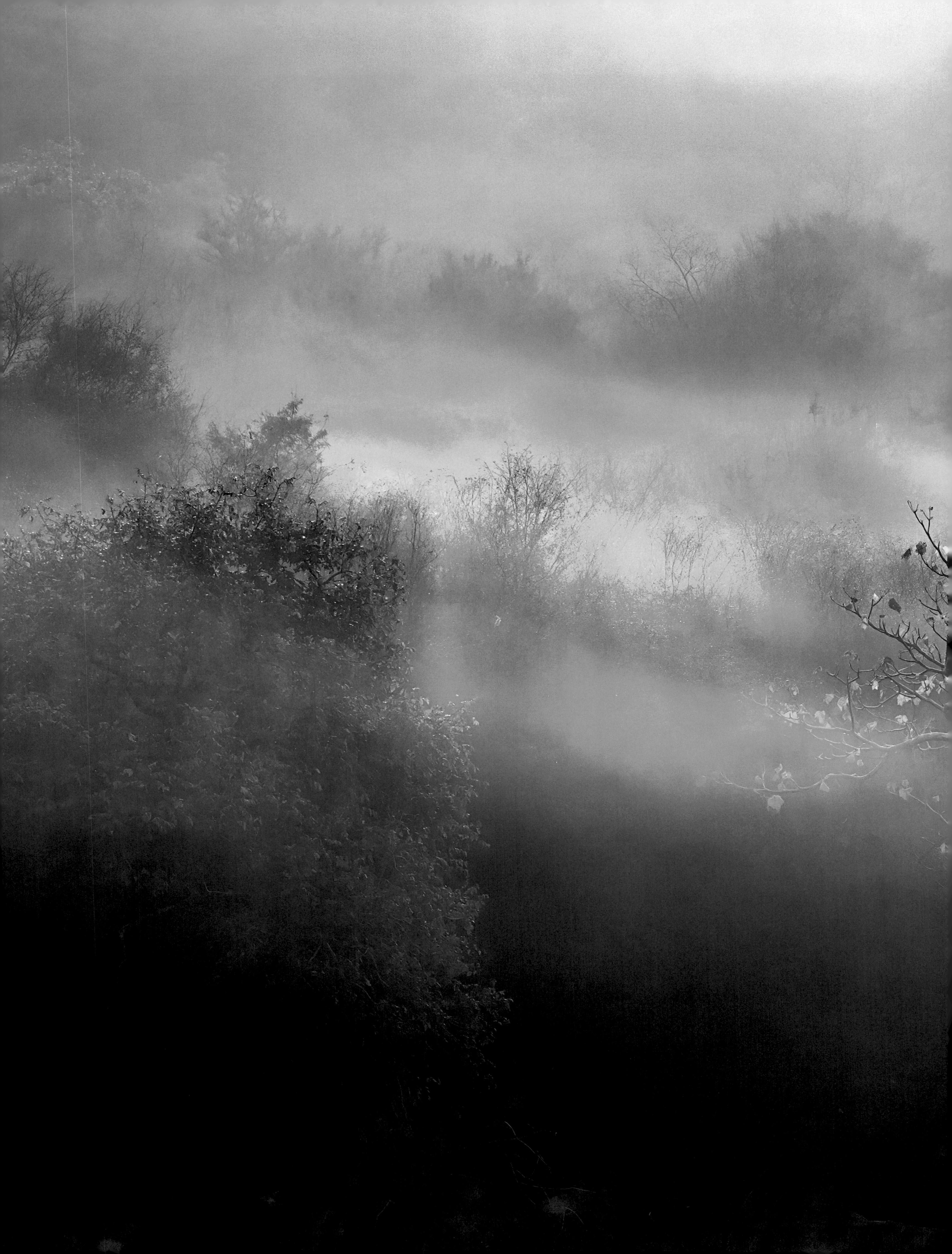

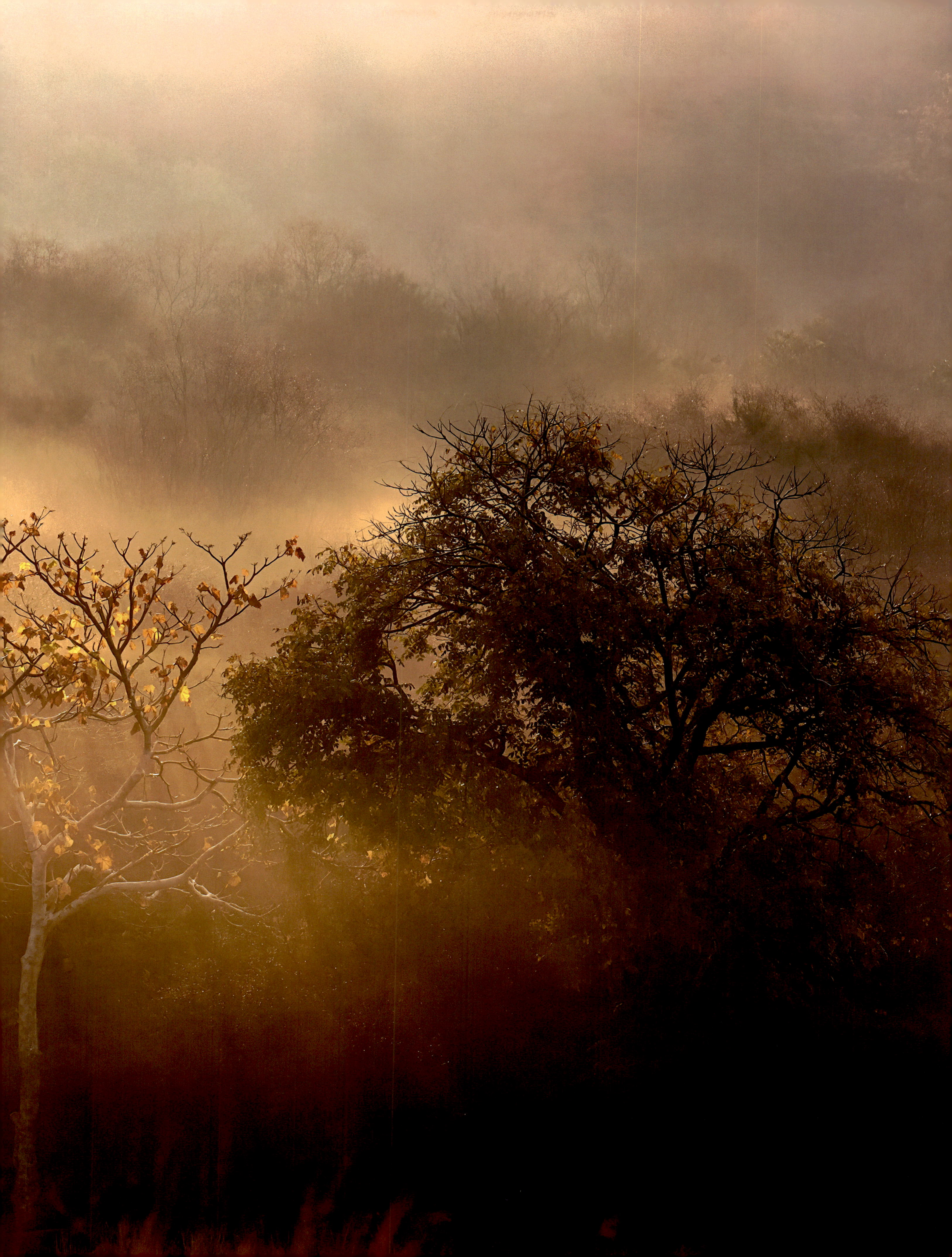

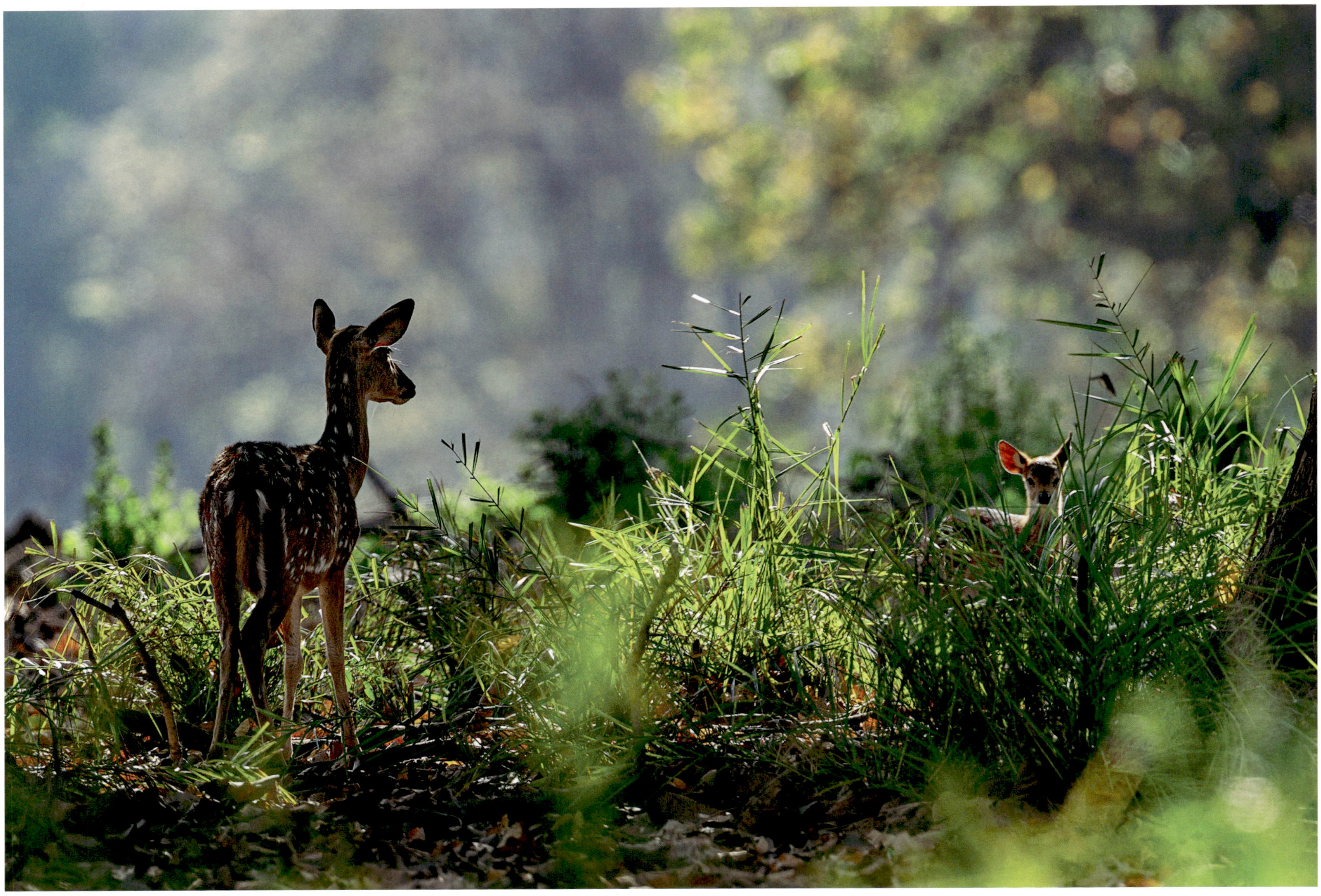

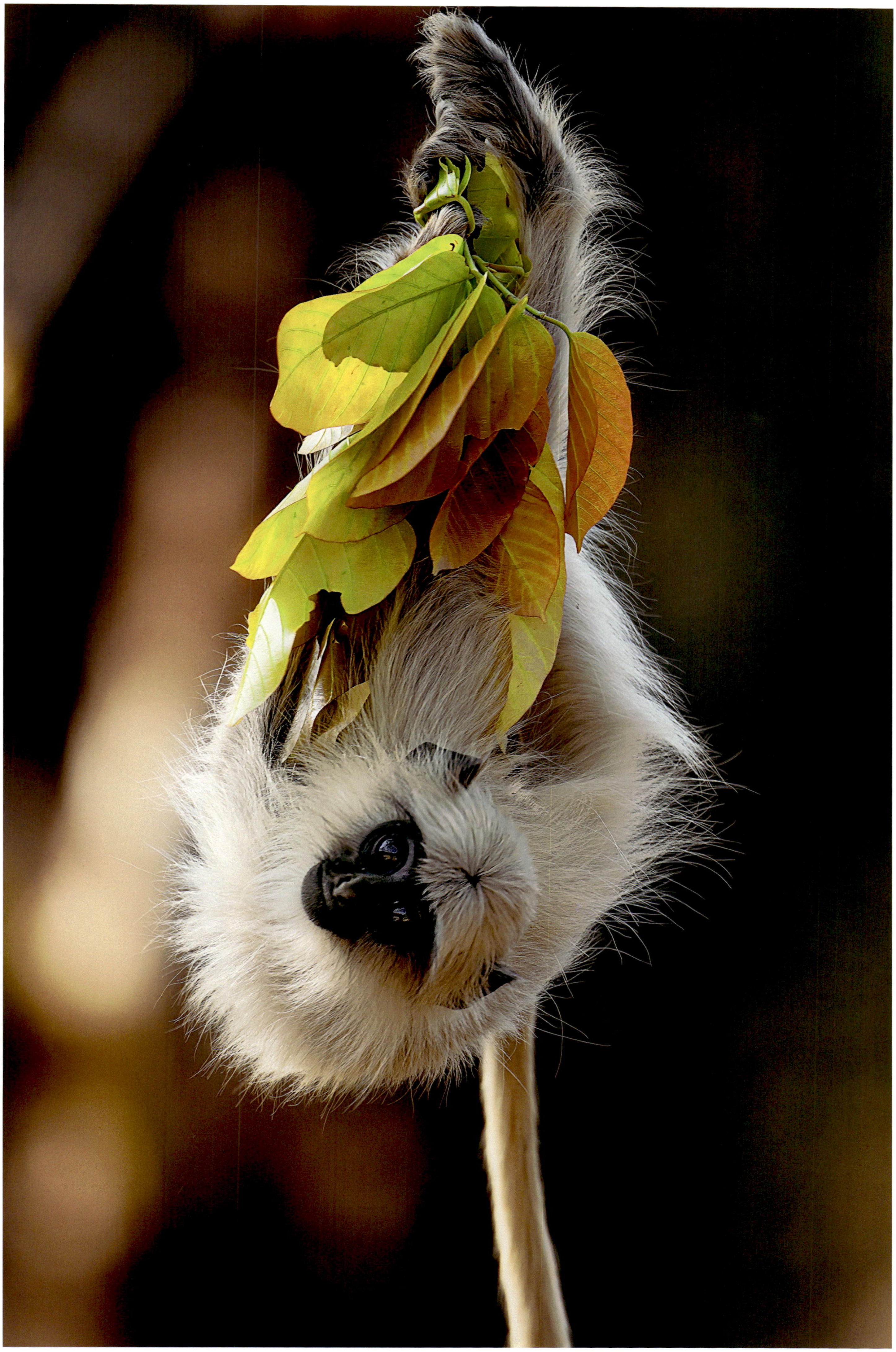

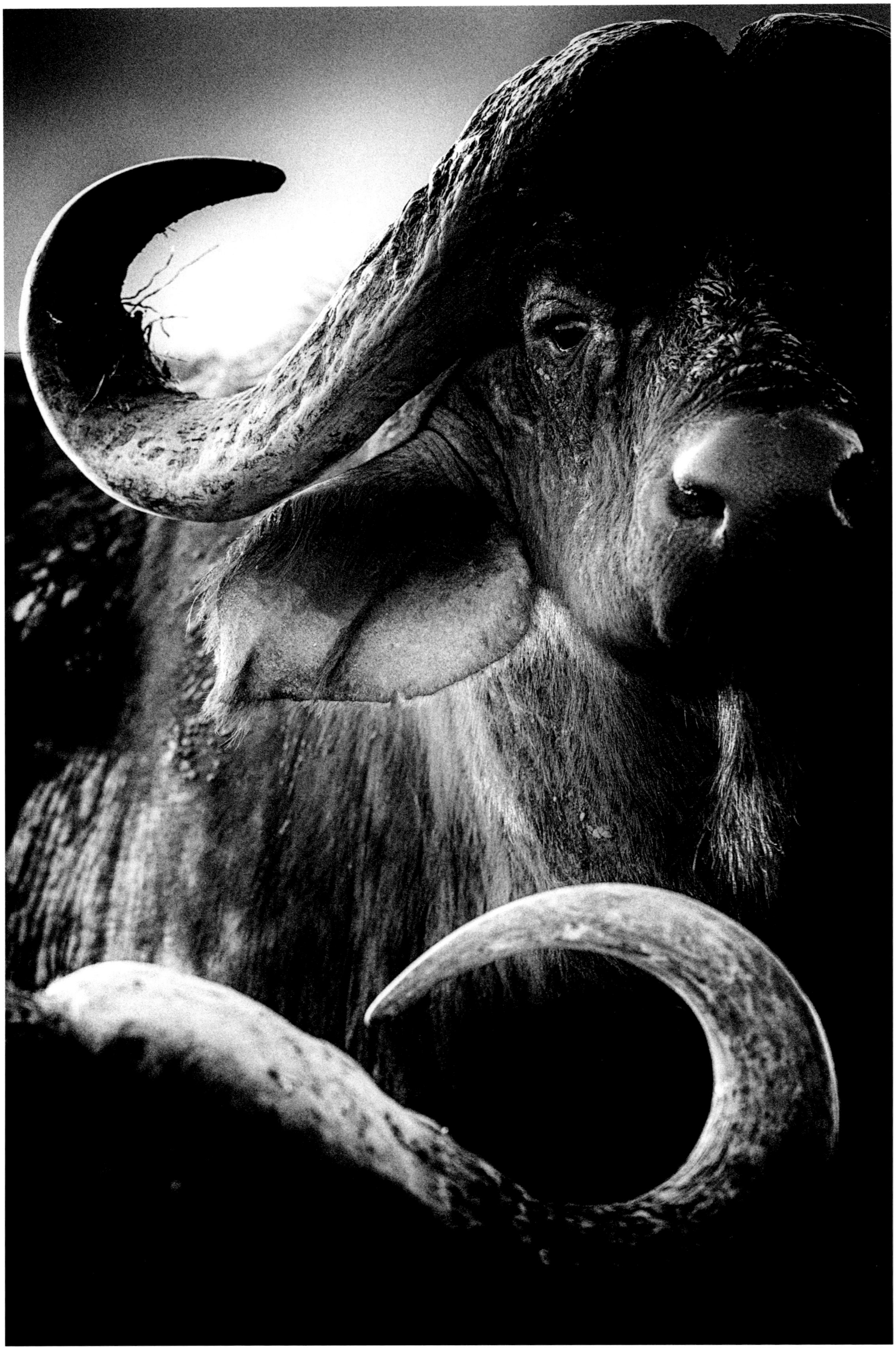

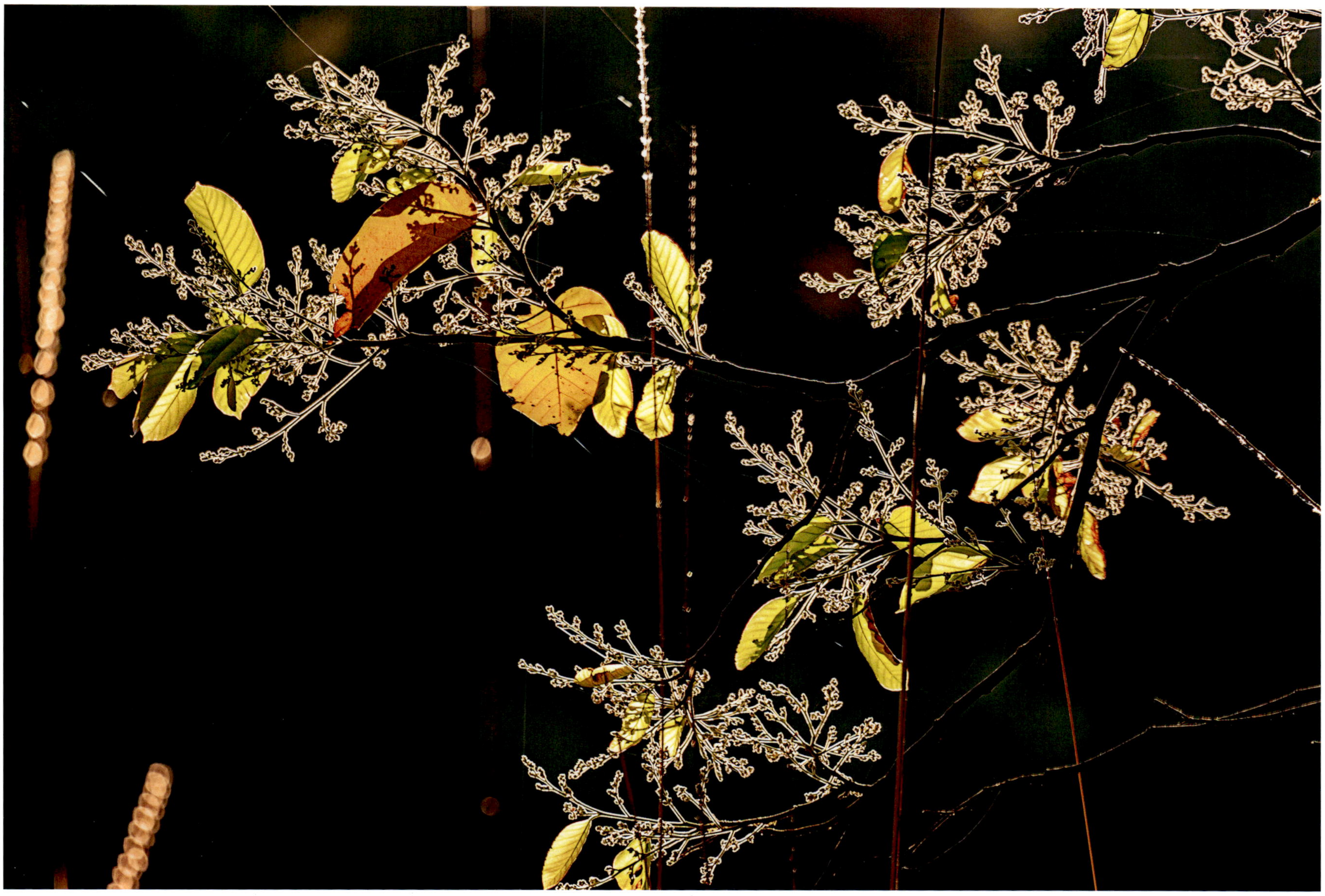

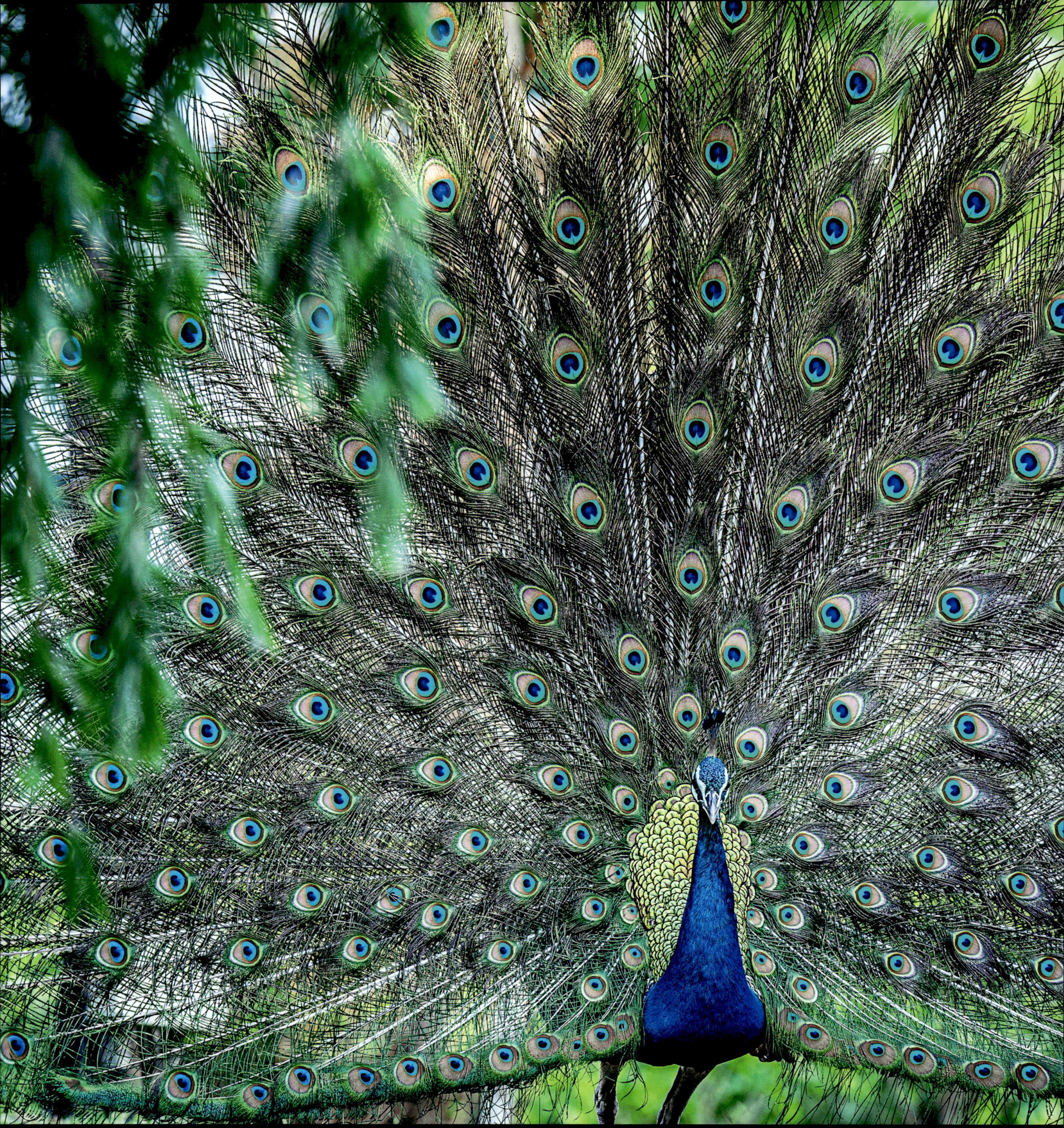

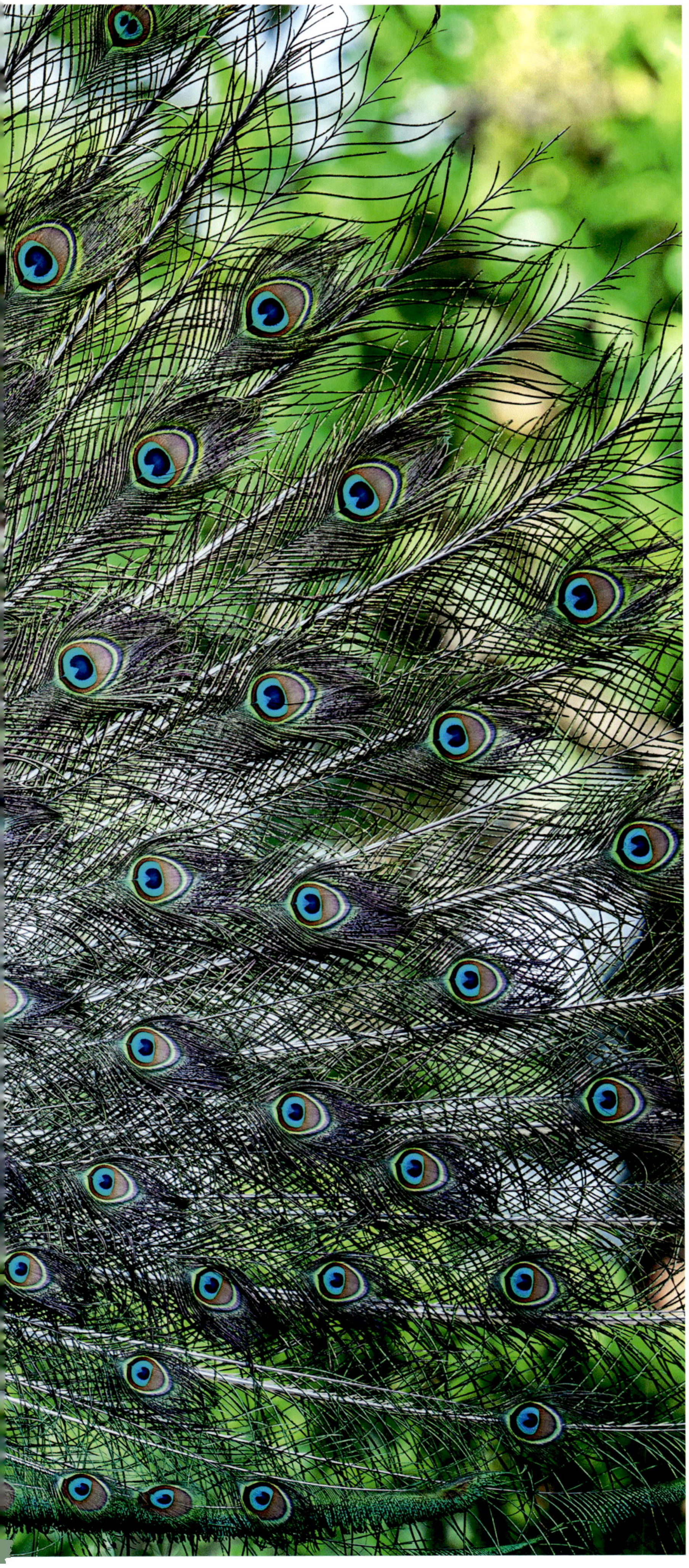

In wilderness, I sense the miracle of life, and behind it, our scientific accomplishments fade to trivia.

— *Charles Lindbergh*

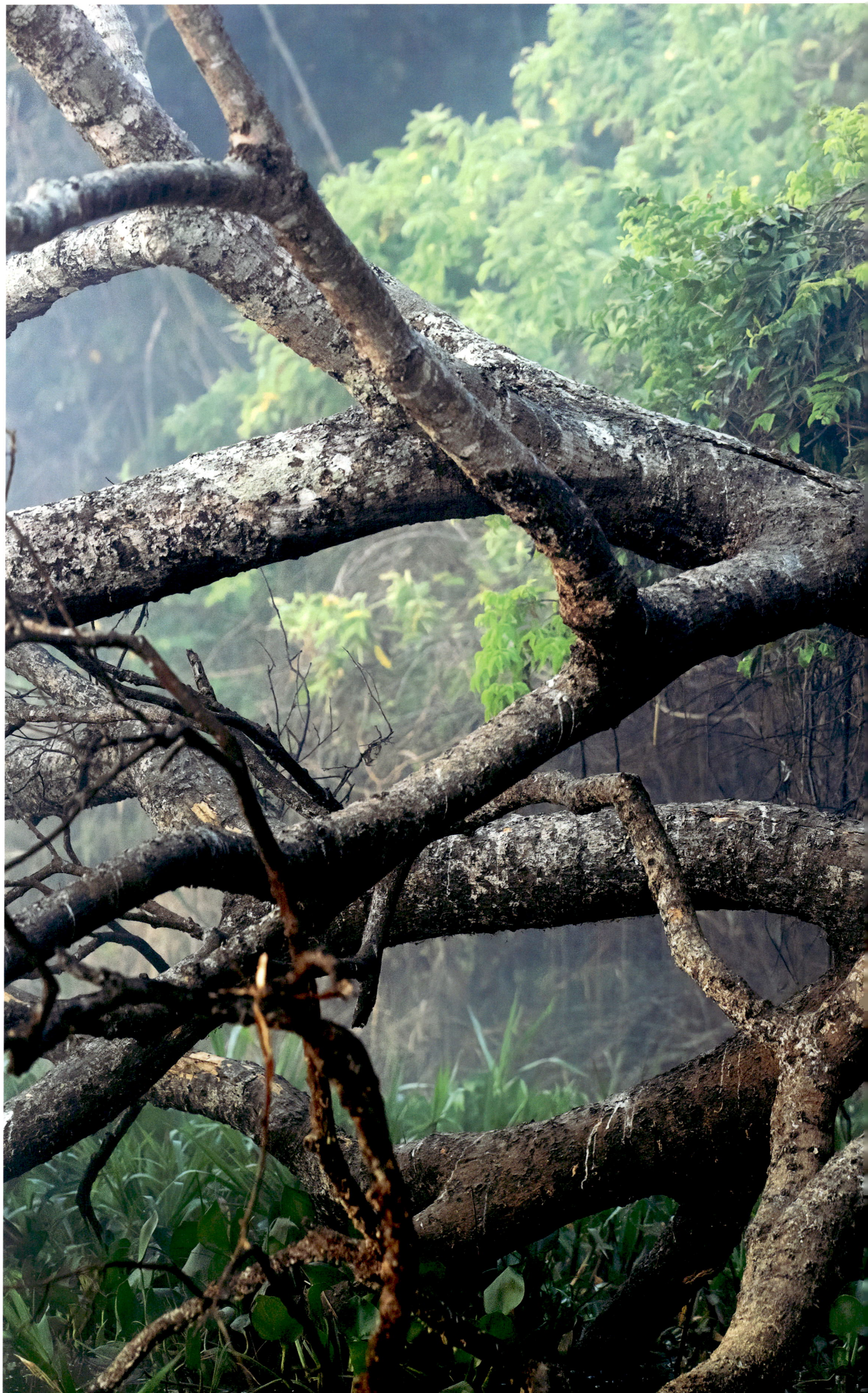

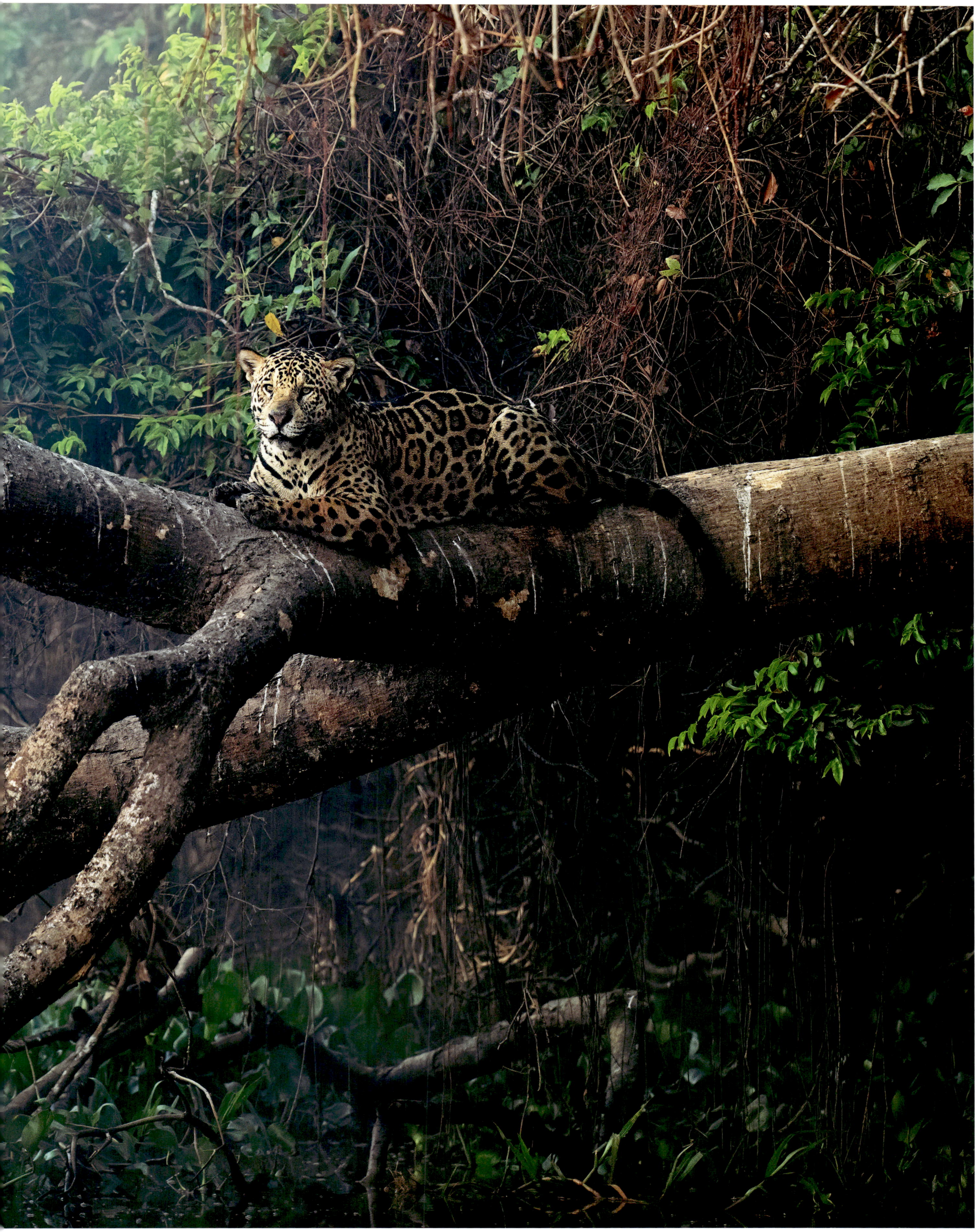

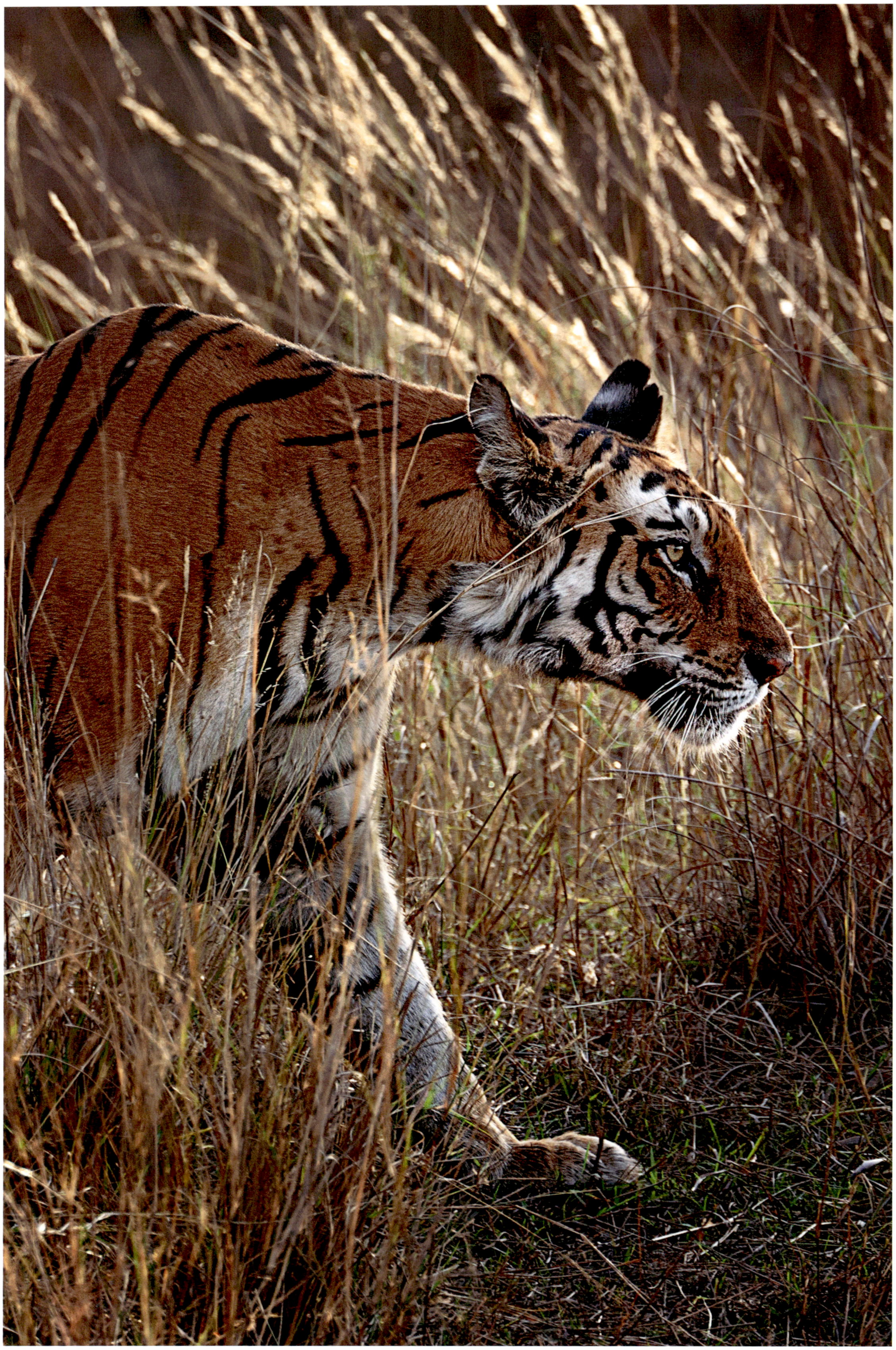

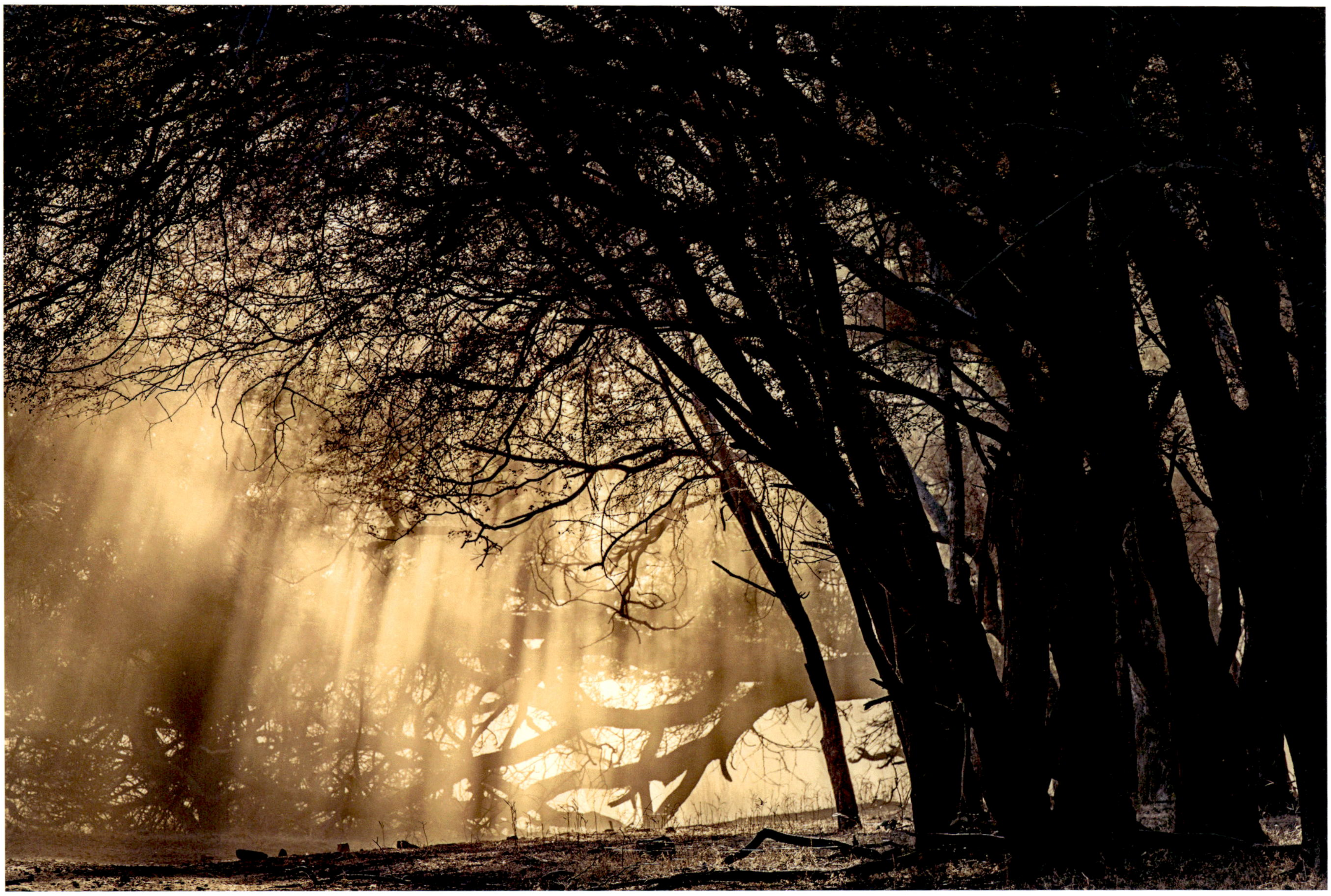

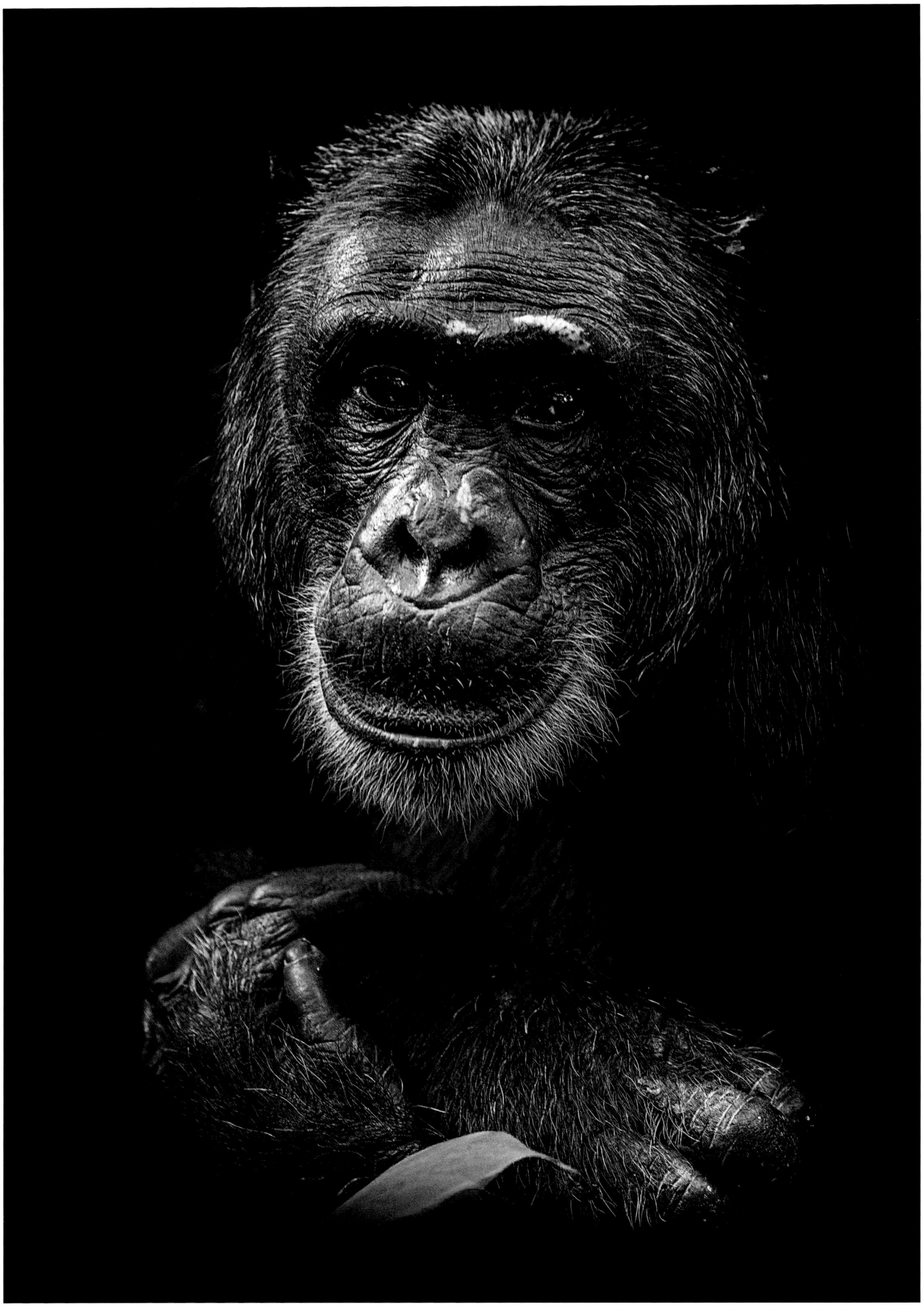

Come to the woods, for here is rest. There is no repose like that of the green deep woods.

—John Muir

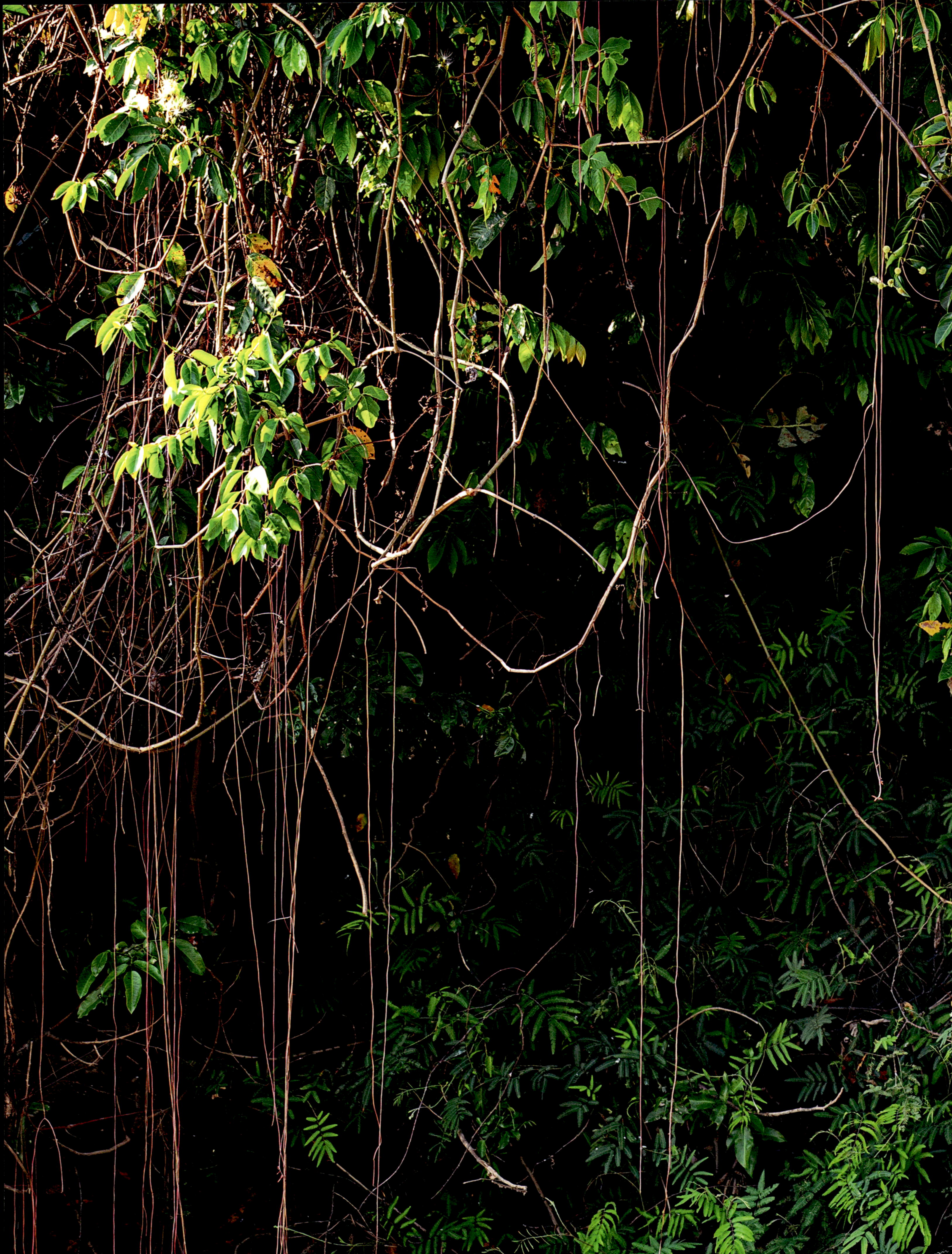

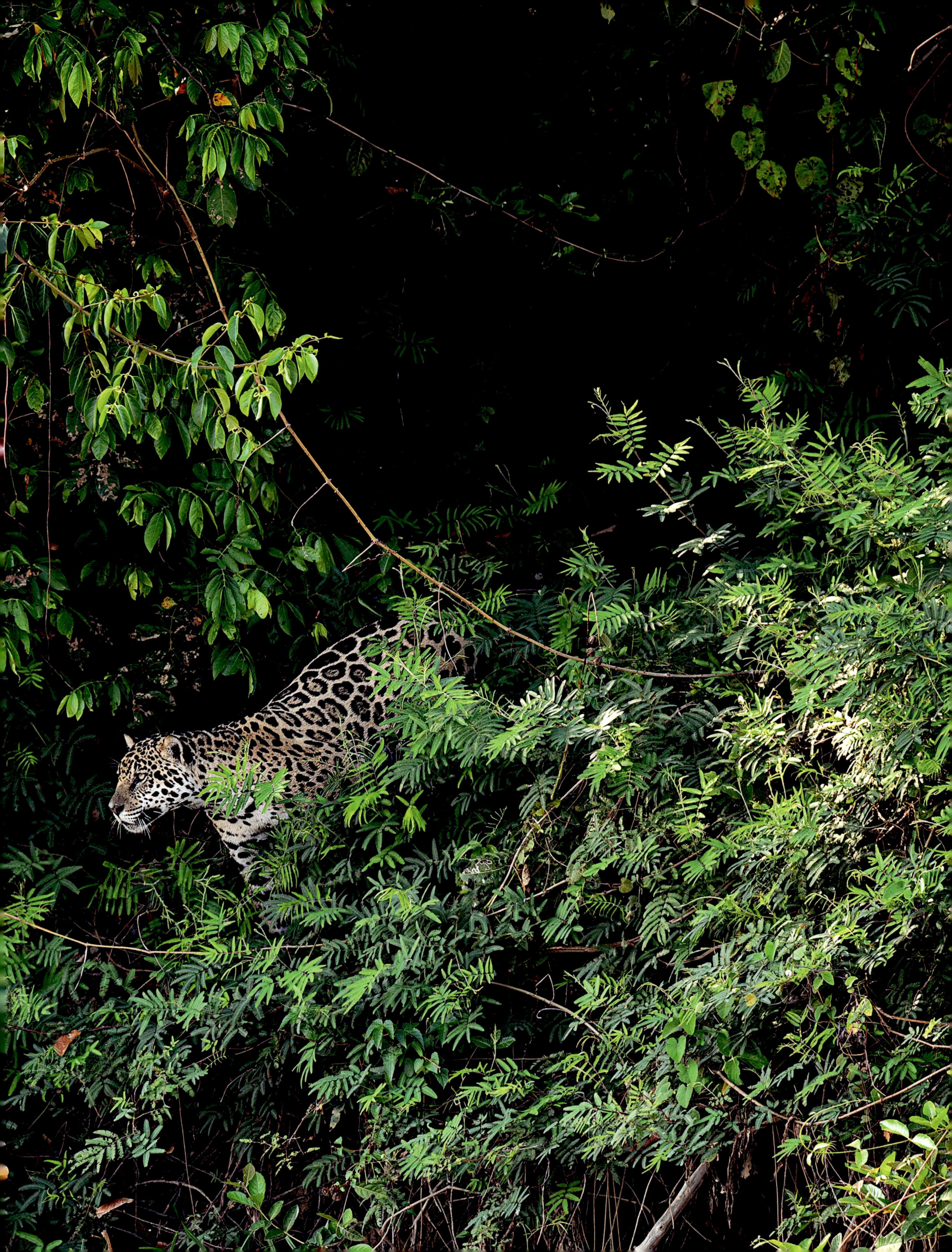

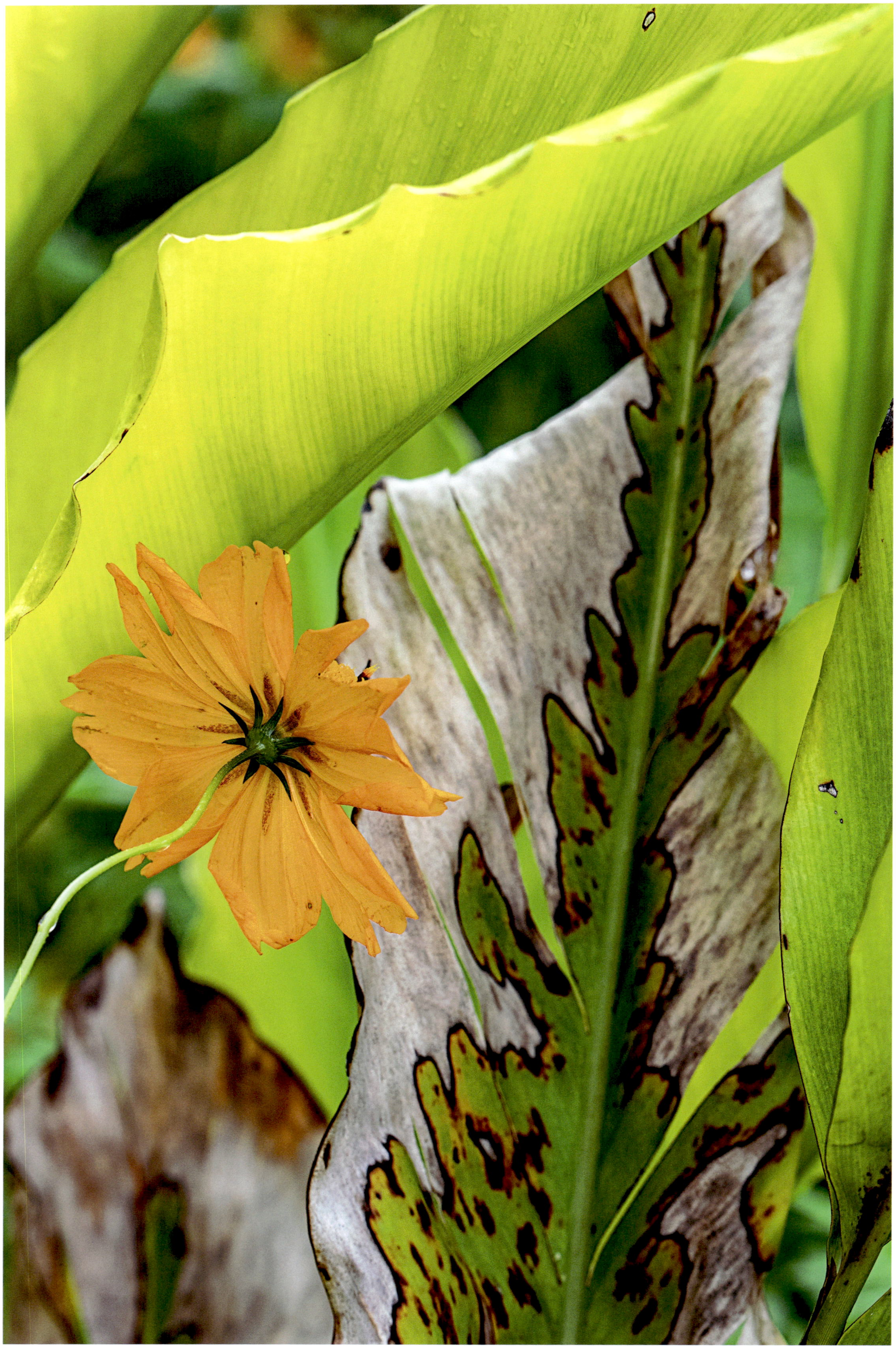

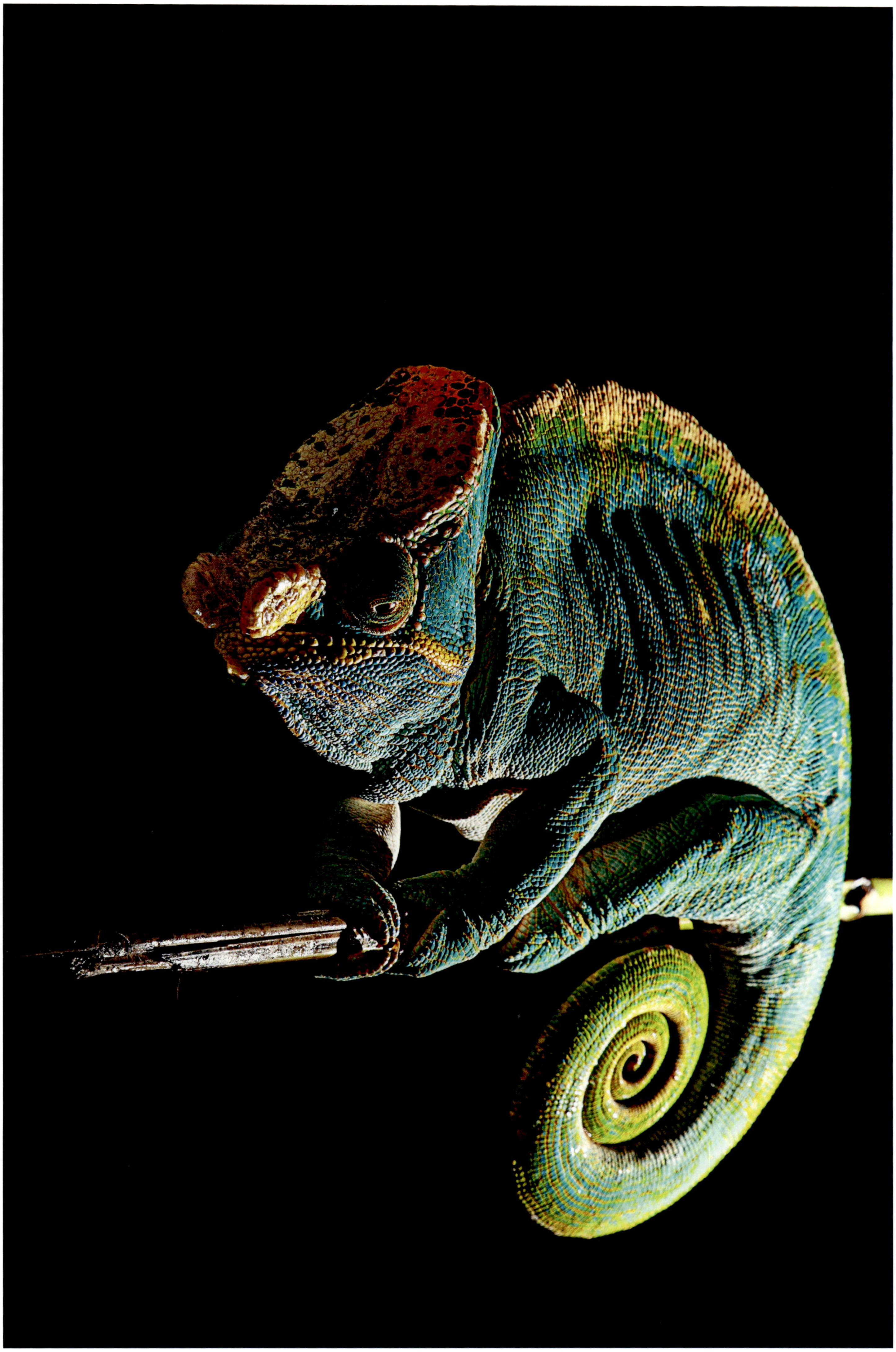

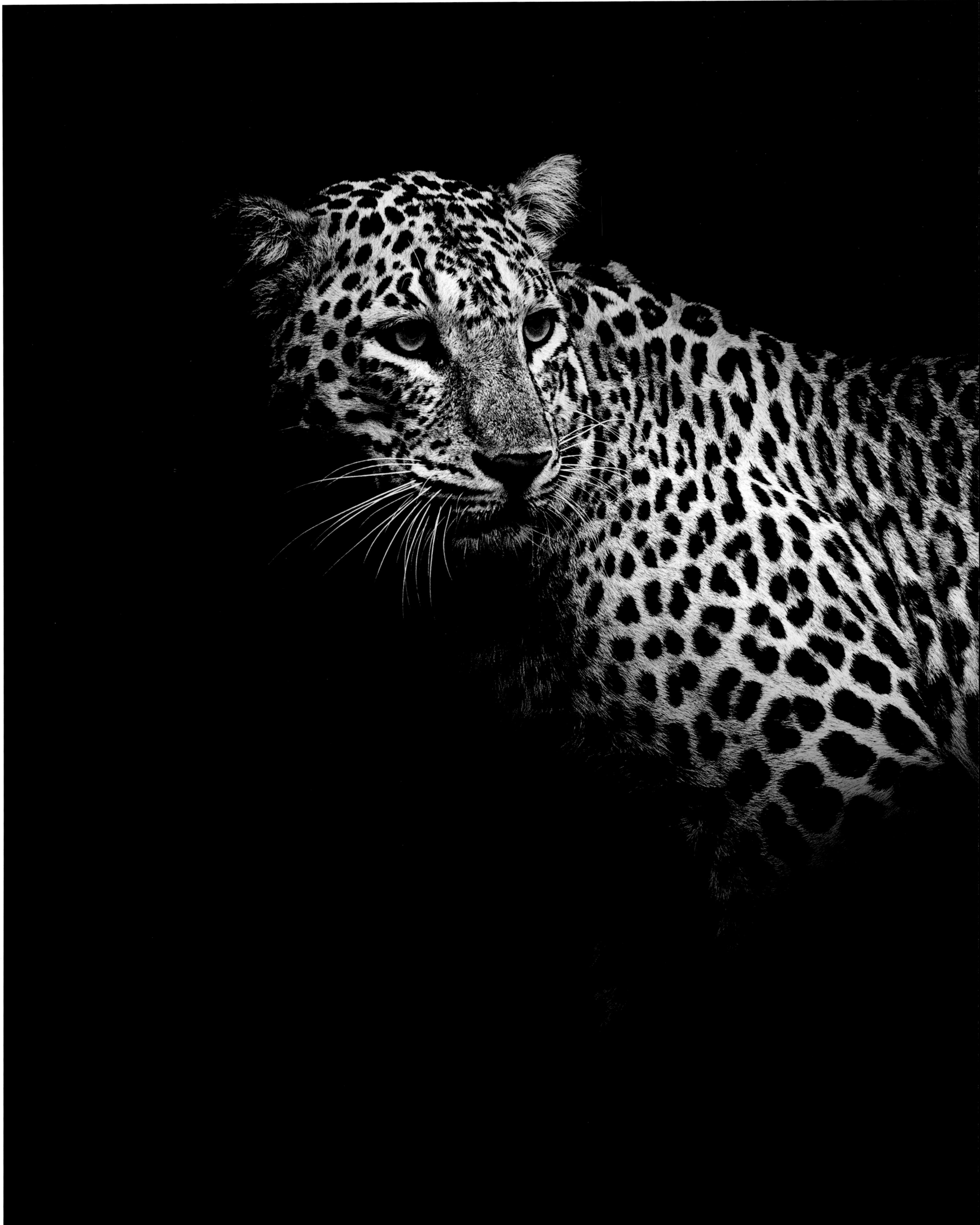

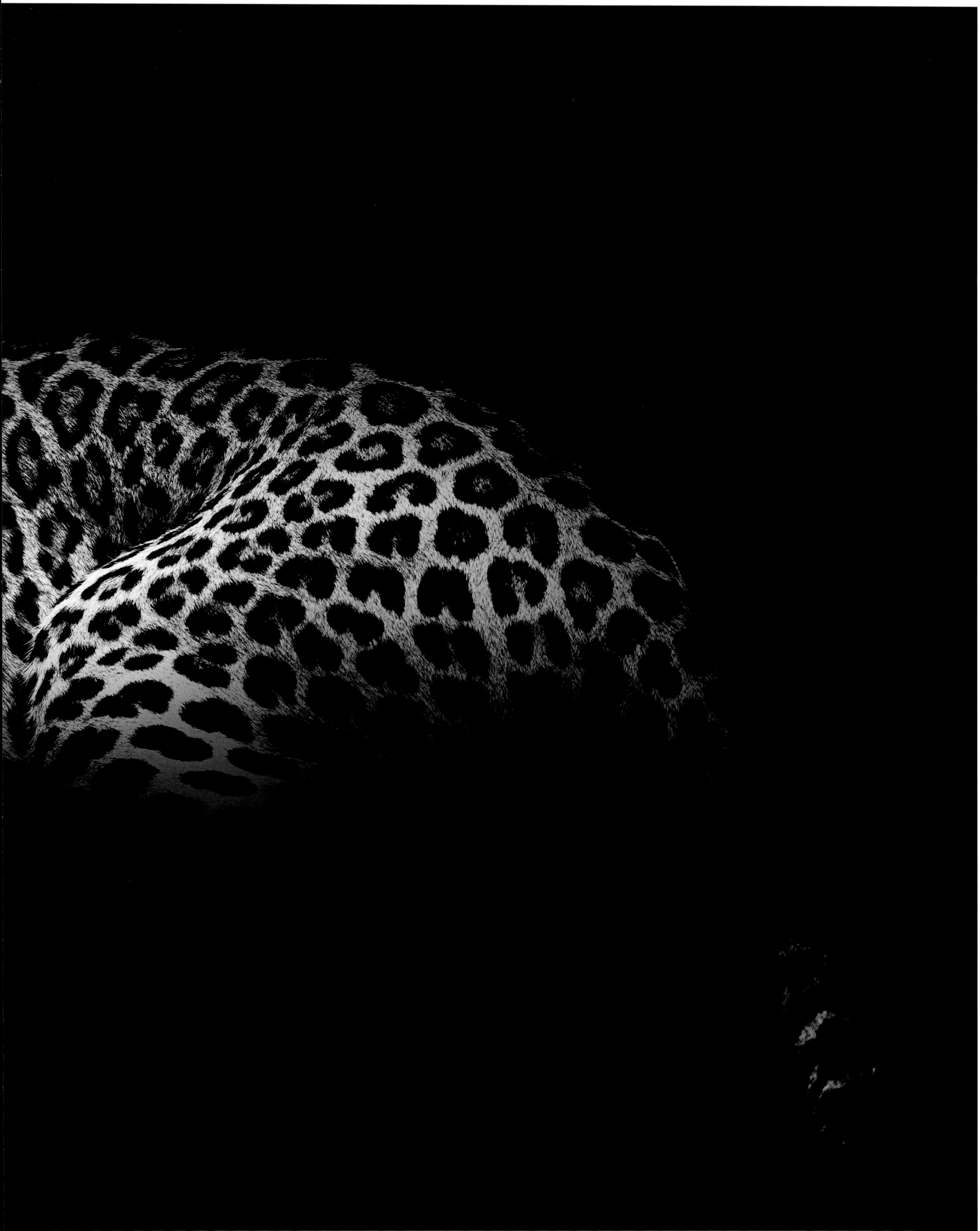

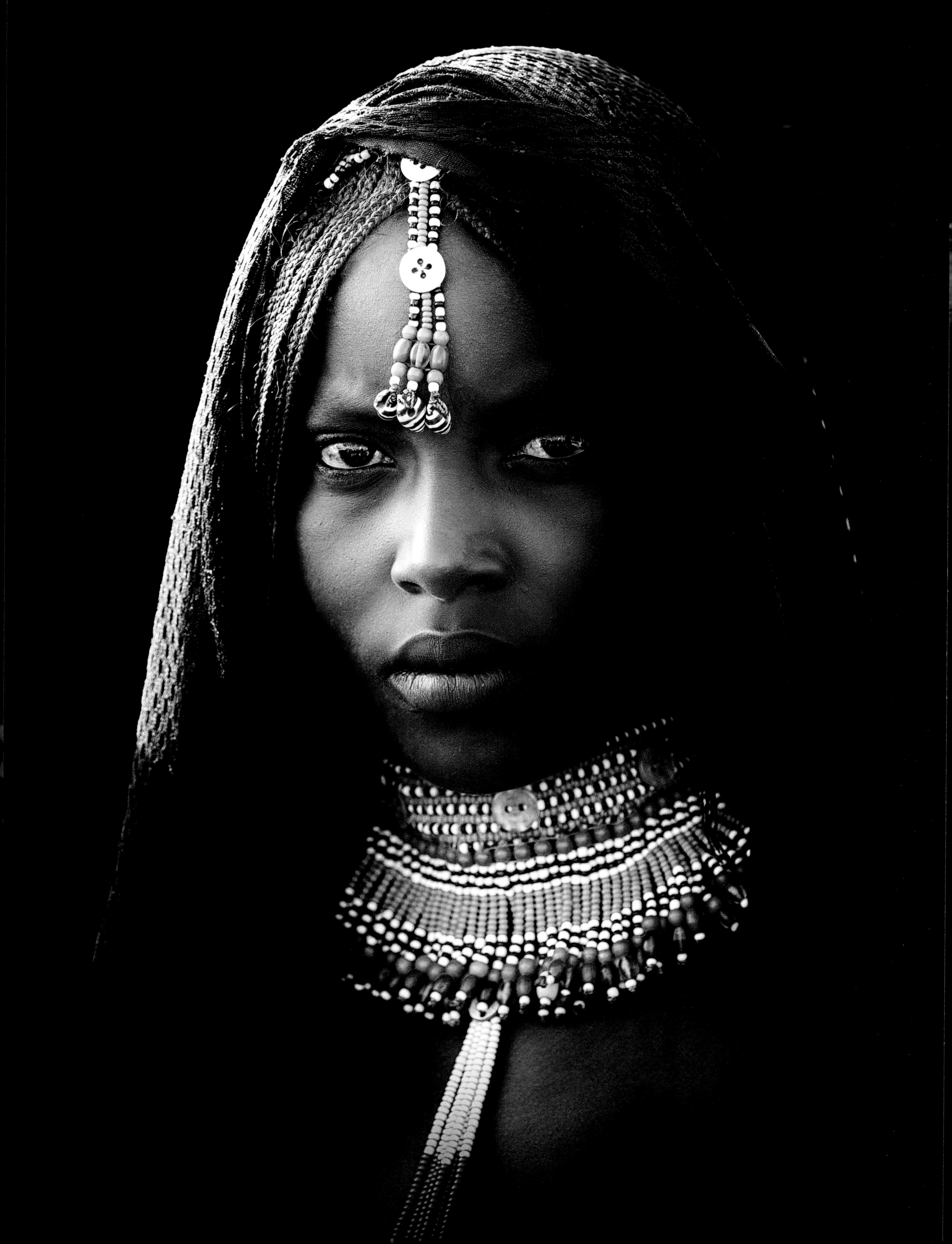

Chapter Three

GRAINS OF SAND

I will fill myself with the desert and the sky. I will be stone and stars, unchanging and strong and safe. The desert is complete; it is spare and alone, but perfect in its solitude. I will be the desert.

— Kiersten White

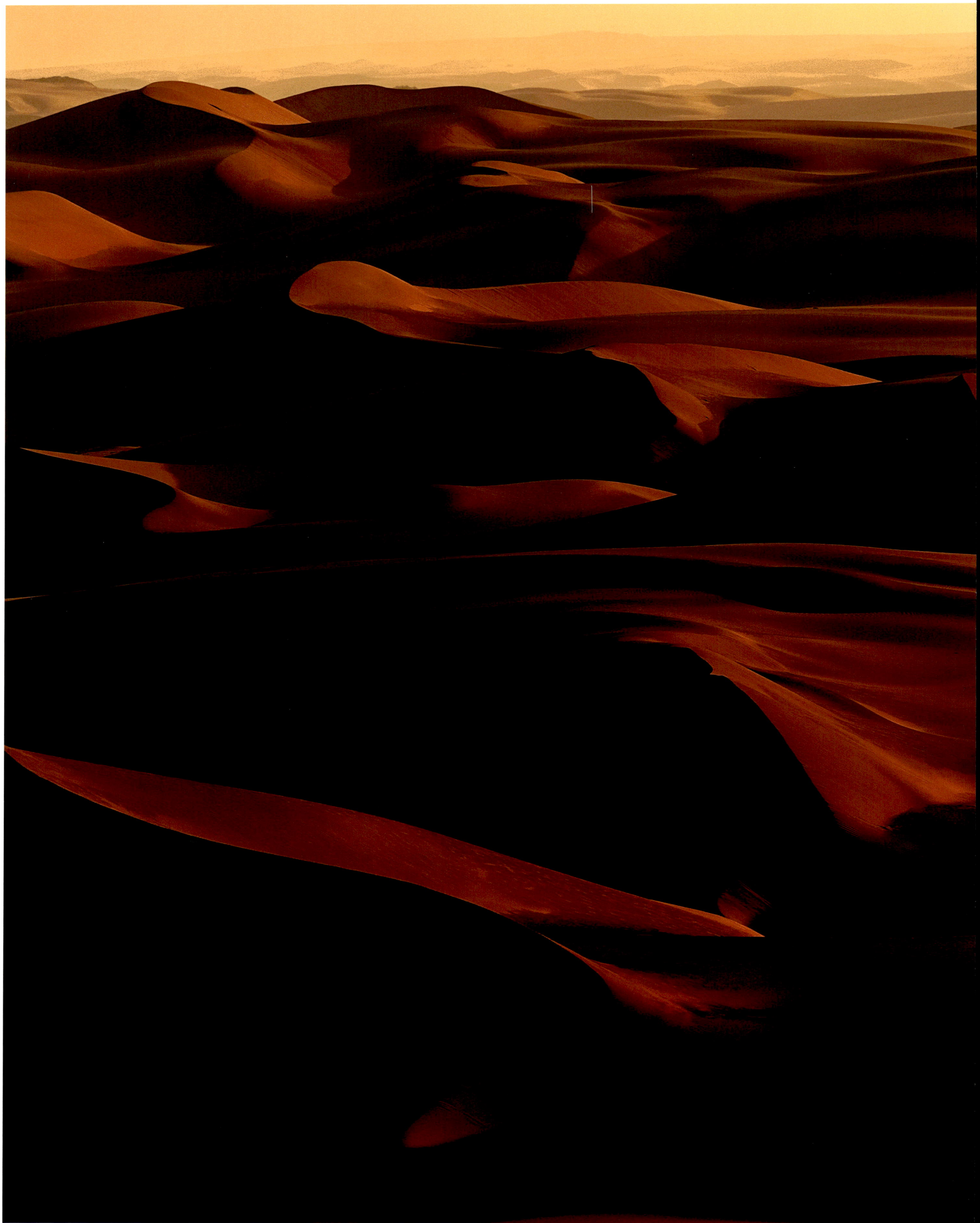

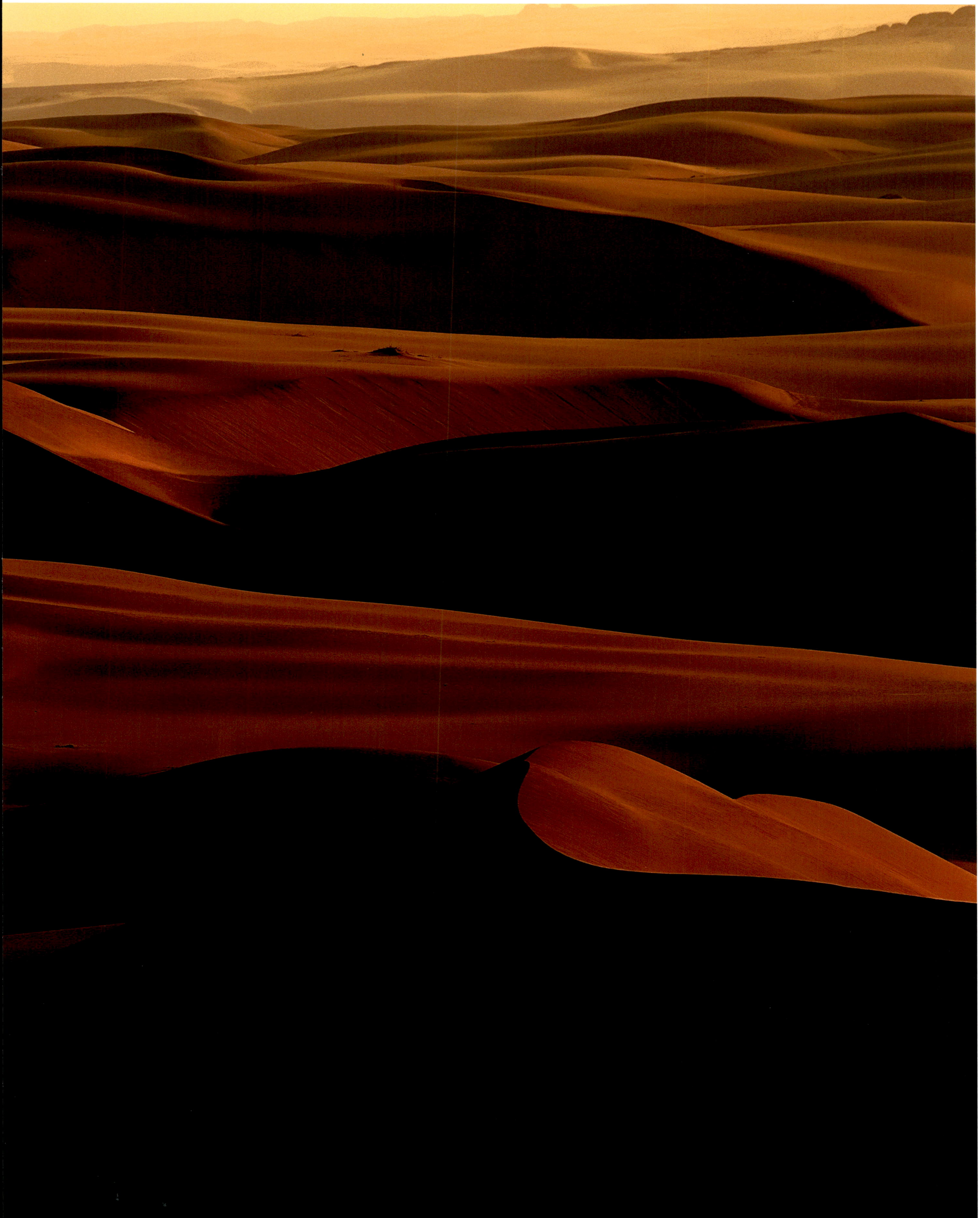

03

Deserts

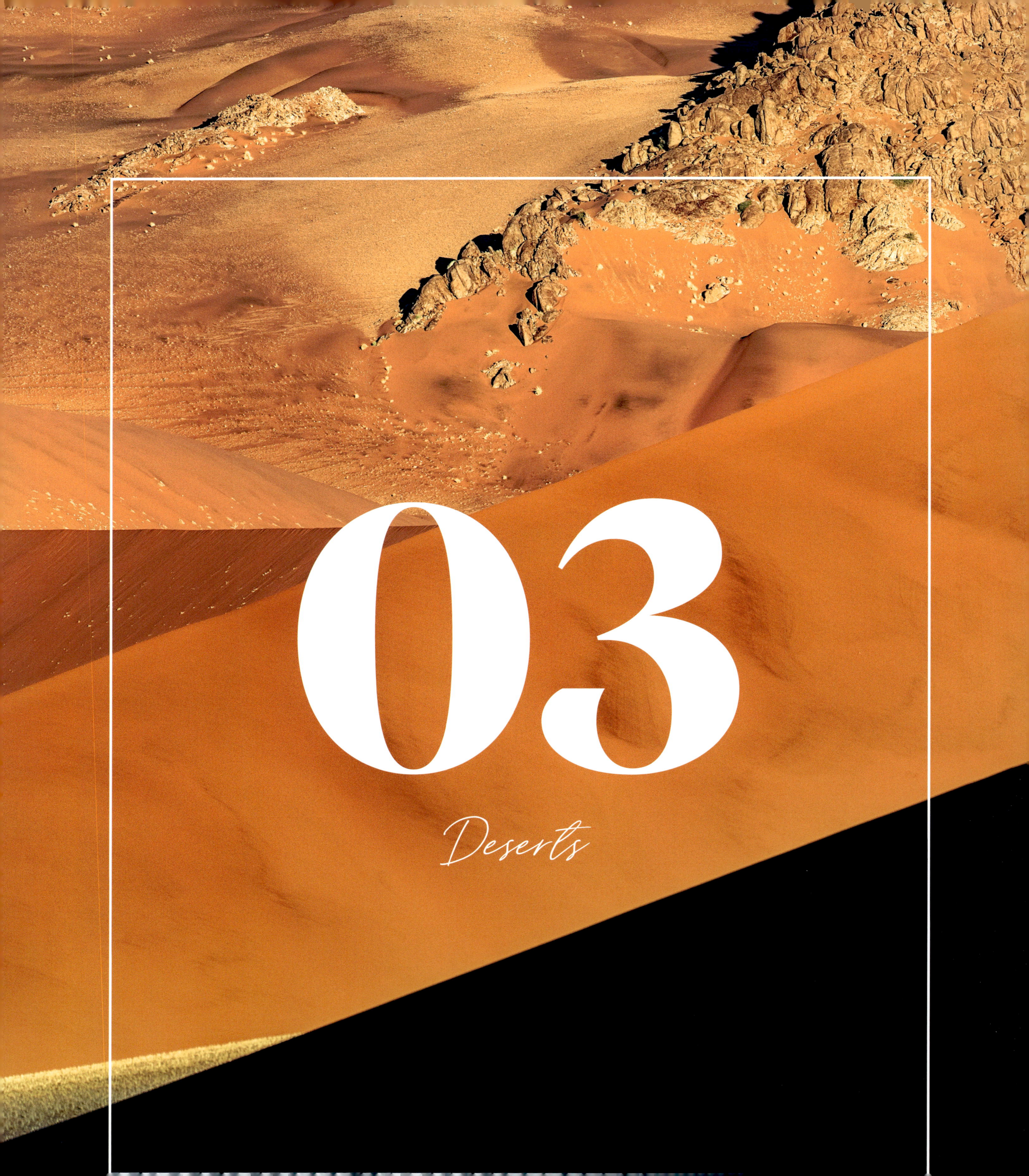

The desert is a state of mind as much as a place. The desert doesn't care for reputations, for who you are or where you come from. Prophets of old were drawn to its inner quiet; sages and poets still seek solitude in nature to cleanse the mind and the spirit. Harsh and remote deserts come in many guises: coastal as in the Namib; cold like the Arctic and Antarctic; hot and dry as the Sahara; and semi-arid as exemplified by parts of Greenland. The Sahara, at 4,800 kilometres long and 1,800 kilometres wide, is one of the harshest environments on Earth, covering a third of the African continent.

Though such austere and inaccessible regions may seem to have little value for humans, deserts are vitally important to the planetary ecosystem, and their dry conditions promote the formation and concentration of important minerals. Gypsum, borates, nitrates, potassium and other salts are all found in deserts, which also hold 75 per cent of the planet's known oil reserves. Deserts cover approximately one-third of the world's dry land and are among the most fragile and endangered of its biomes.

Our ancestors' journeys out of Africa would eventually take them to every corner of the Earth, with our species, Homo sapiens, dispersing within Africa roughly 300,000 years ago. Anatomically, modern humans descend from a population of Homo sapiens that migrated from East Africa no later than 70,000 years ago, spreading along the southern coast of Asia and into Oceania by about 50,000 years ago. In those times the Sahara was grassy and lush, offering an exit route favourable to overland travel year round.

Deserts have been a way of life for many different peoples able to find sufficient food to support hunter-gathering communities such as the Bushmen of the Kalahari and Australian aborigines. Others, such as the Bedouin of Oman, still roam the deep deserts of the planet with their dromedary camels, herding goats and sheep, although their lifestyle is more semi-nomadic and dependent on their knowledge of the location of water, using animal skins as tents for shelter, and relying on the milk, bones and meat of their treasured animals for sustenance. Angie and I visited Oman in 2007 to work with the Willis family on their film about the critically endangered Arabian leopard (of which there are probably fewer than a hundred left in the wild). Camping out in the Jabal Samhan Mountains, one of the last refuges of this subspecies of leopard, is a never-to-be-forgotten experience. Nightfall is a hauntingly beautiful time, made sharper by the chill air that wells up in clouds of mist at sunrise. We strained our ears for the haunting repetitive grunting roar of a leopard, but if there were any near they stayed silent. Next morning we searched the narrow game trails frequented by the leopards, tracing the places where they most often leave scrape marks and scats to let other leopards know their whereabouts: ideal places for film-makers and researchers to set camera traps. Somehow the leopards find enough to survive on, though the sparsity of large herbivores is reflected in the smaller size of these big cats, with males weighing around 30 kilograms and females 20 kilograms – half the size of their African counterparts.

We spent time with Hadi Musalam al Hickmani, son of a family of camel herders who for centuries have plied their trade in these mountains and know every nuance of the area. Seeing camels trekking over red and yellow dunes transforms them into a thing of beauty and fascination; the definitive ships of the desert. A few days later we experienced the thrill of traditional Bedouin camel races, marvelling at the skill of the riders as they clung like limpets to the rump of their mounts, thundering over the sand to the delight of the villagers, while filling us with a sense of wonder at these ancient rituals involving humans and their livestock.

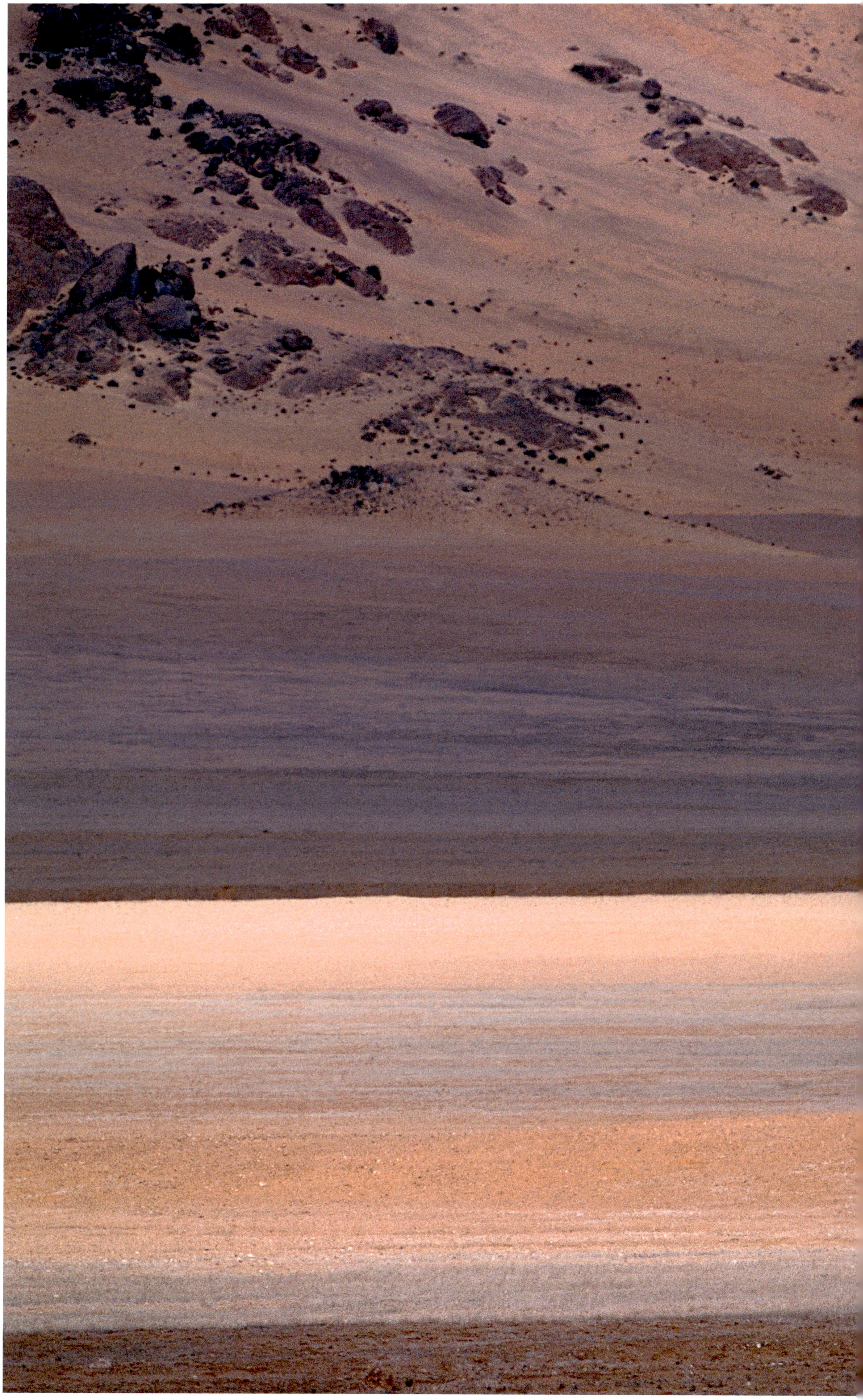

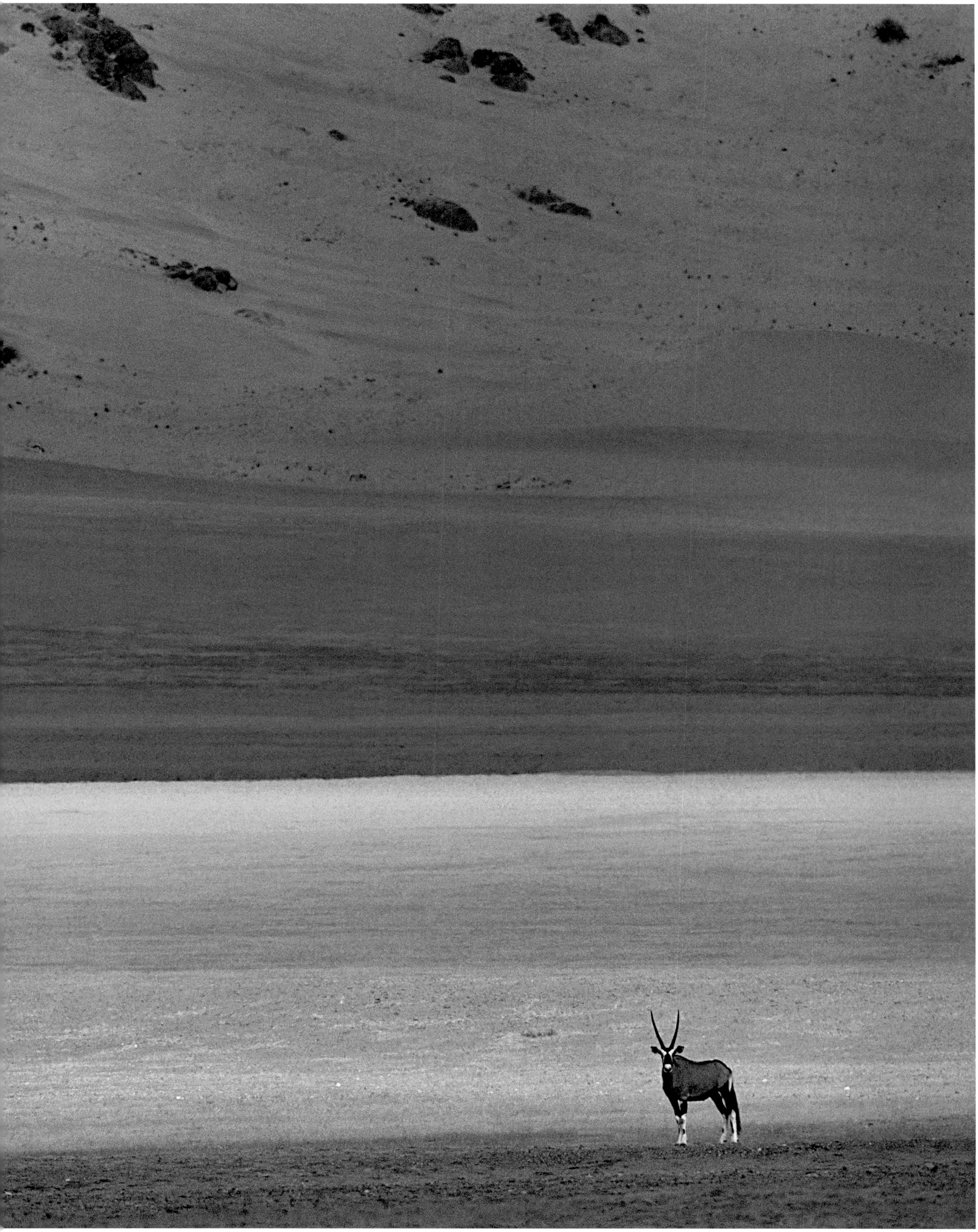

Among all the desert states, Namibia stands out. The name Namib comes from the Nama for 'open space' and at 55 million years, it is the world's oldest desert, running the entire length of the country's Atlantic coastline. It is home to perhaps 80–90 desert-adapted lions and just a hundred desert-adapted elephants (including only 18 males) that wander vast distances to find sufficient food. This is a land like no other. The air is so crisp and clear that you see with a new clarity, teasing out every nuance and detail of the mountain ranges, the rutted bark and twisted shapes of camelthorn trees, revelling in the glory of backlit ash-blonde grass at dawn and dusk, the golden hour when colours are so intense, so vivid and saturated that they stun the senses. A safari here is a spiritual experience, the chance to rediscover the joy of being alive, to absorb the wonder of nature.

For lions, leopards and cheetahs it means moving at night, relying on the blood and body fluids of their prey to replenish water requirements. Elephants depend on the wisdom and knowledge of the matriarchs – the oldest females in the family herds – that have survived long enough to know the best places to find food and to dig for water. All around, a tapestry of animal tracks bears silent testimony to those that have passed by earlier. Dominating the landscape are the scimitar-horned oryx, known here as gemsbok. These majestic antelopes pose statuesque atop the rocky hillsides, seeking cooler air during the stifling heat of midday. Ever since our first visit to Namibia 20 years ago, Angie and I have found ourselves beguiled by these emblems of the desert, steadfast survivors of the dunes, distant specks of life among a sea of whispering grass.

You cannot fail to be struck by the resoluteness of nature in a land like this. It is as if someone had torched the living elements from the earth.

At the Namib's southern reaches is a place called Sossusvlei, which boasts the highest dunes in the world. Knife-edged mountains of red sand soar 300 metres into the bluest skies on Earth. You cannot fail to be struck by the resoluteness of nature in a land like this. It is as if someone had torched the living elements from the earth. Each morning clouds of mist roll in from the ocean, replenishing the moisture in these thirsty lands. There are tenebroid beetles that perform handstands among the dunes to capture the droplets of water, allowing it to run down into their mouths. Side-winding adders bury themselves up to their watchful reptilian eyeballs as they wait for prey to pass close enough for a lightning strike. Shovel-snouted lizards barely touch the red-hot sand as they skim over it at more than 90 centimetres per second; when resting they carefully lift their feet away from the 70° Celsius surface to keep from overheating.

Sundowners at Dune Valley, close to where we were camped at Serra Cafema Lodge, revealed an ocean of sand spread before our eyes, enriching the senses as the sun shimmered and died behind the distant mountains. We drove back to camp in silence, the sky a star-spangled splendour, inky black in colour, punctured by millions of tiny flickering lights. In such a sparsely populated land as Namibia (fewer than two million inhabitants in an area appreciably larger than France or Texas), there is a greater sense of connection to Mother Earth. It is the first country in the world to enshrine the protection of its environment within its constitution. Here you can still feel the visceral bond between humans and Earth, a place to remember that art, whether painted, sculpted or photographed, has its genesis in nature. Let it be the source of your inspiration.

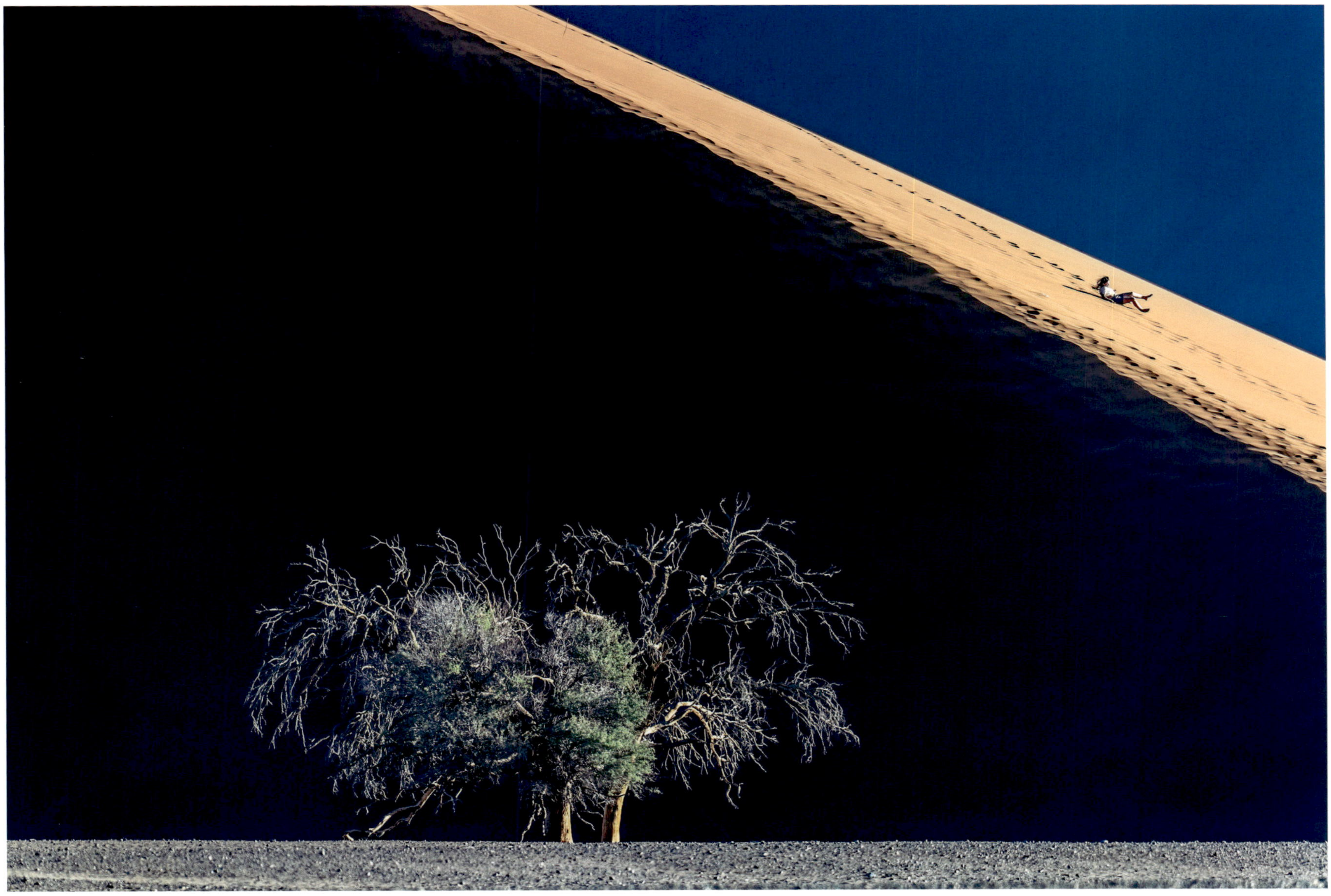

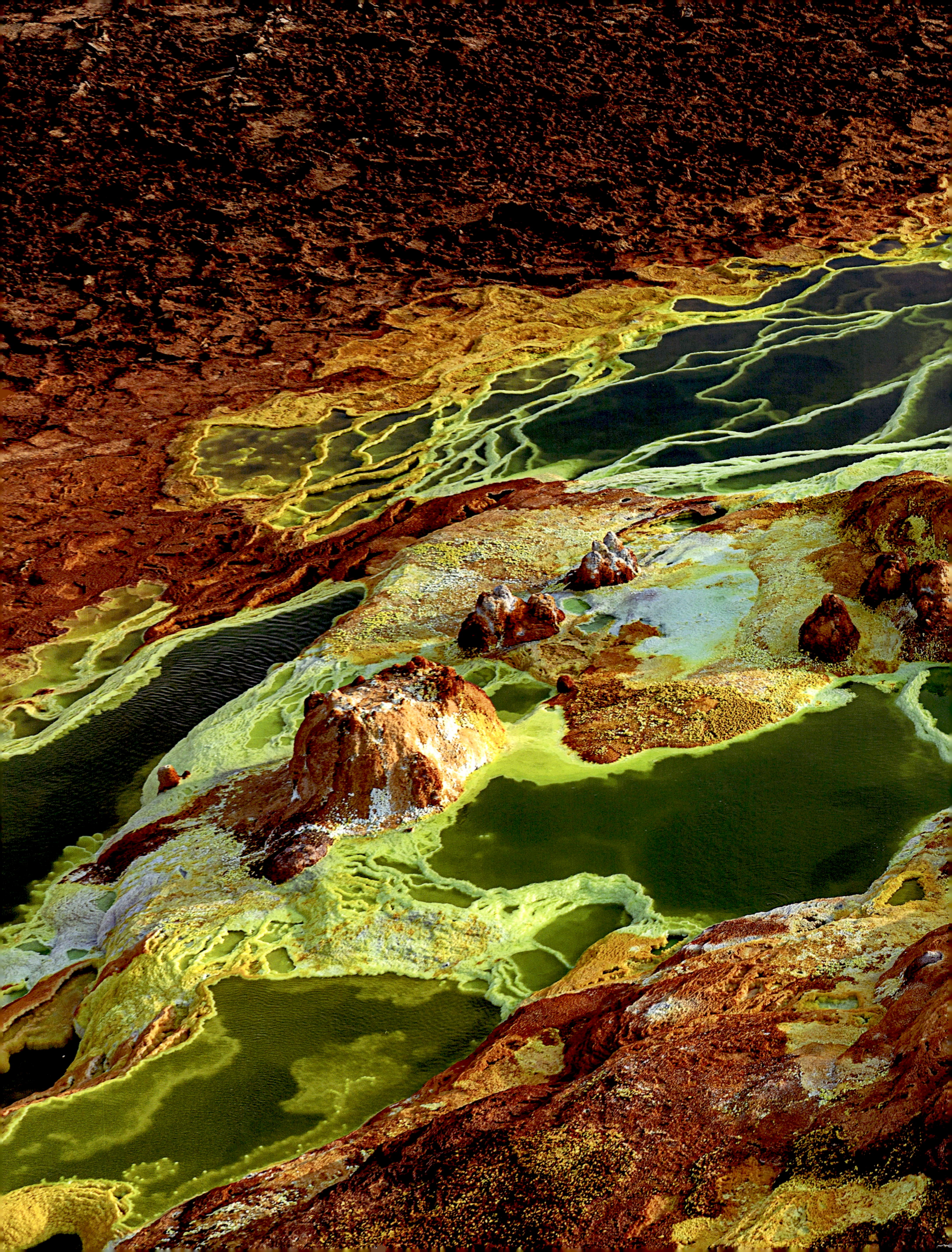

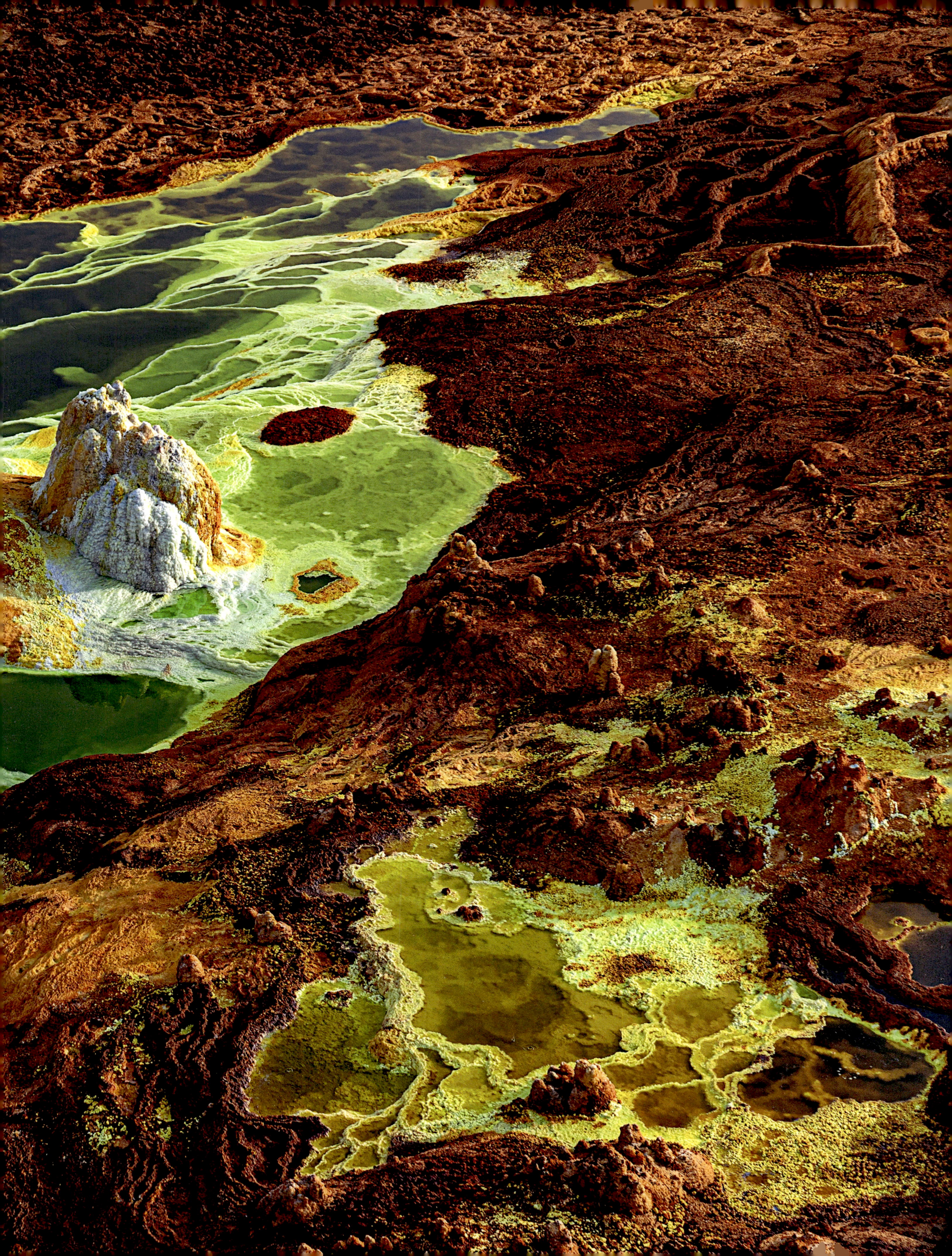

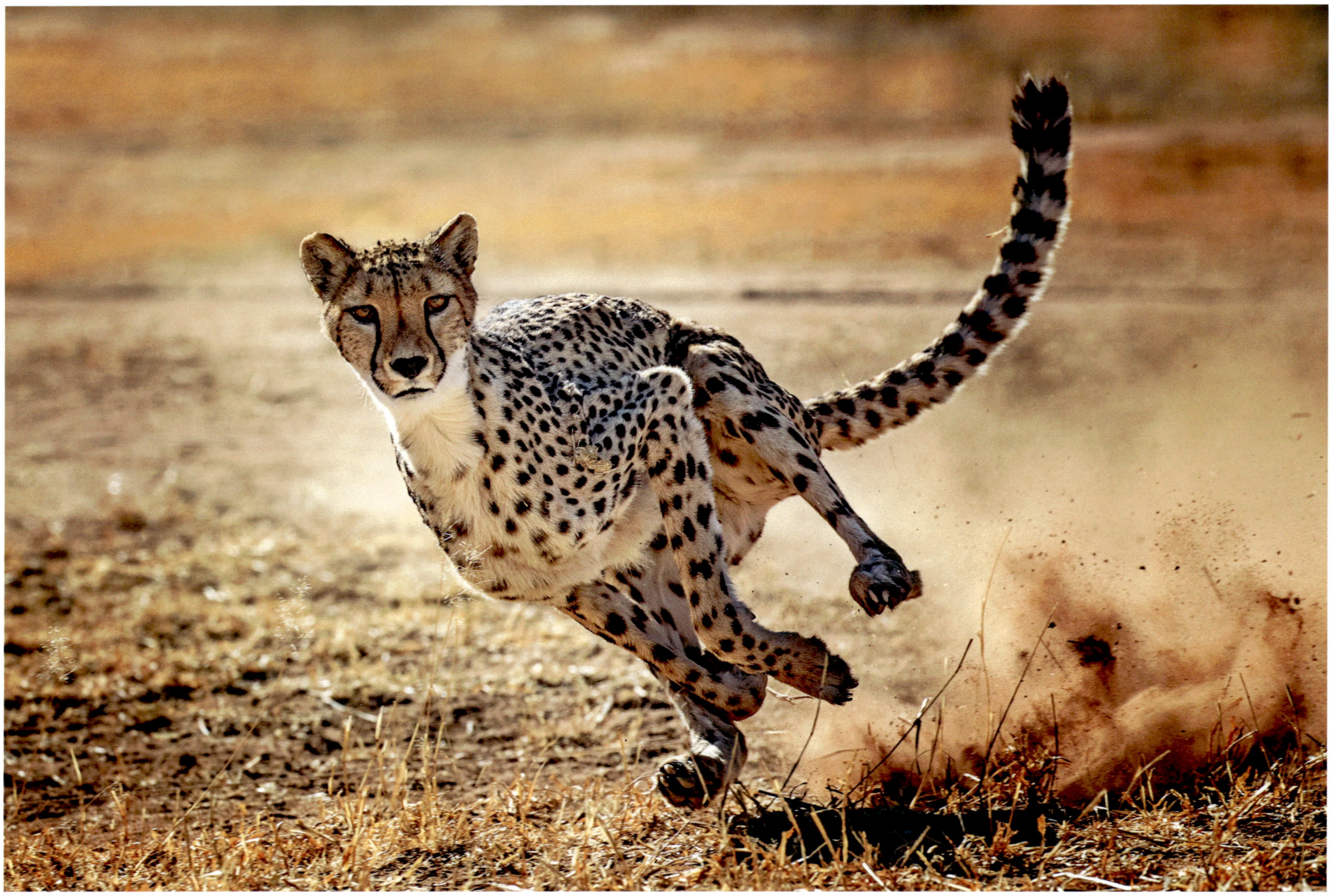

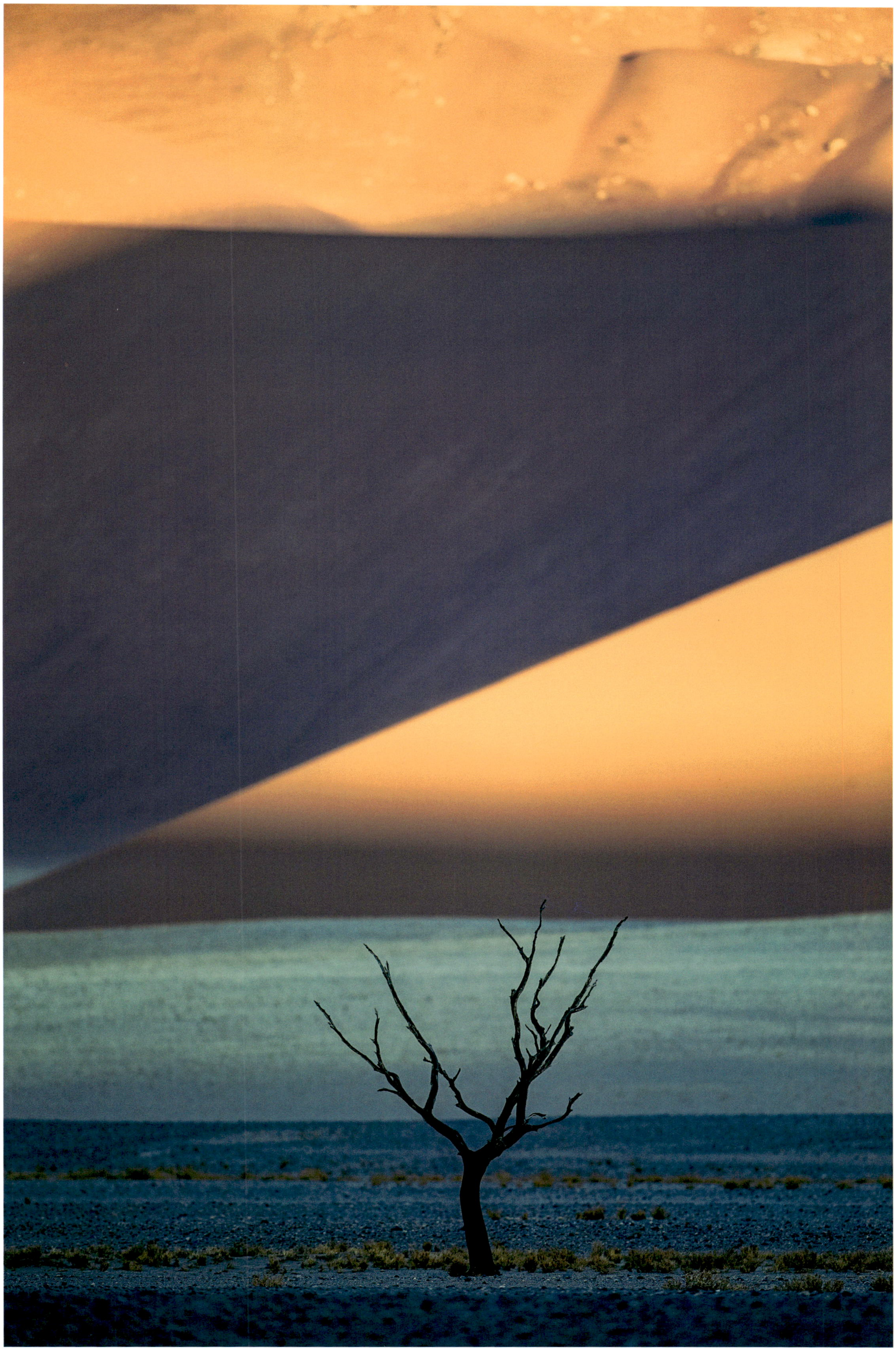

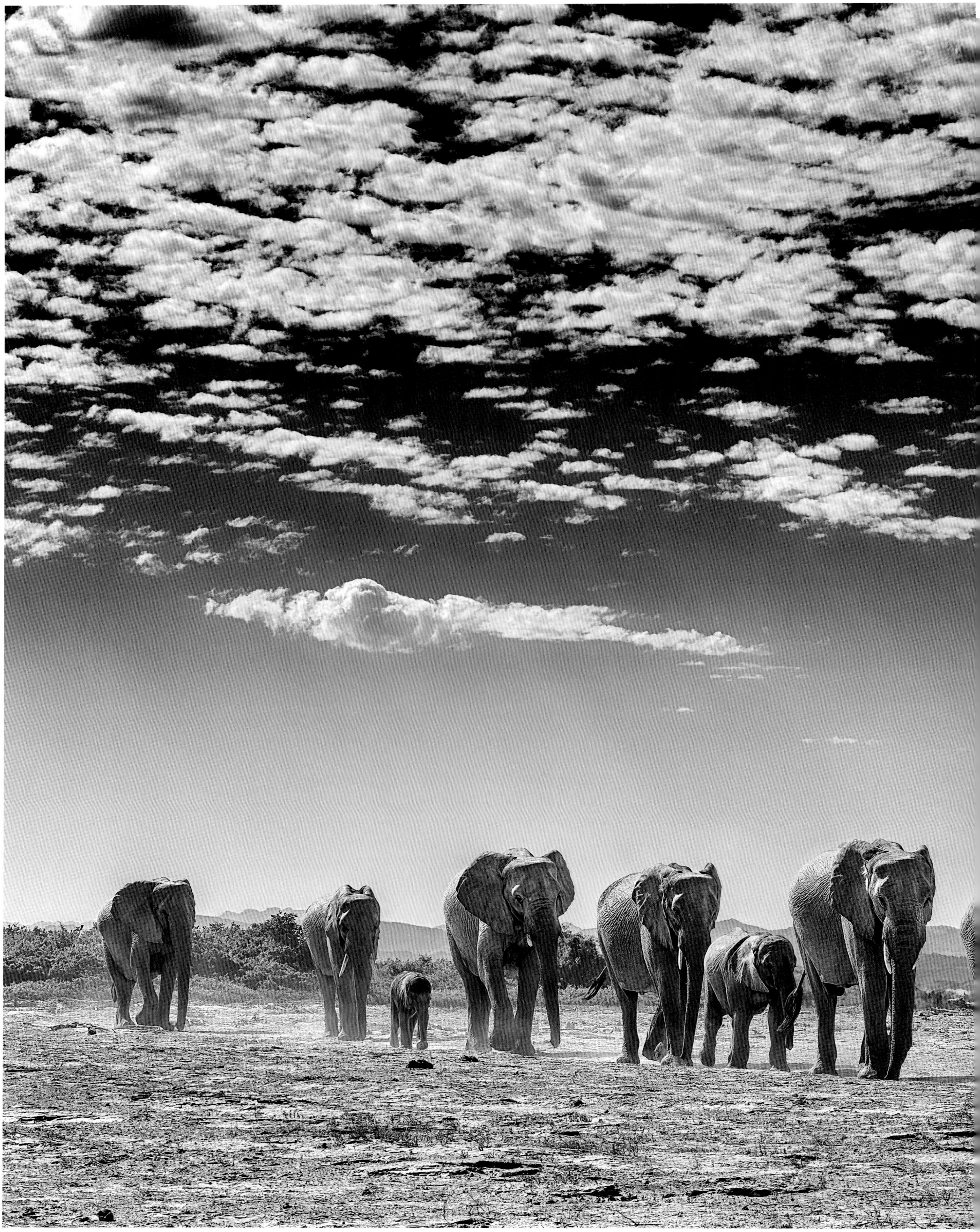

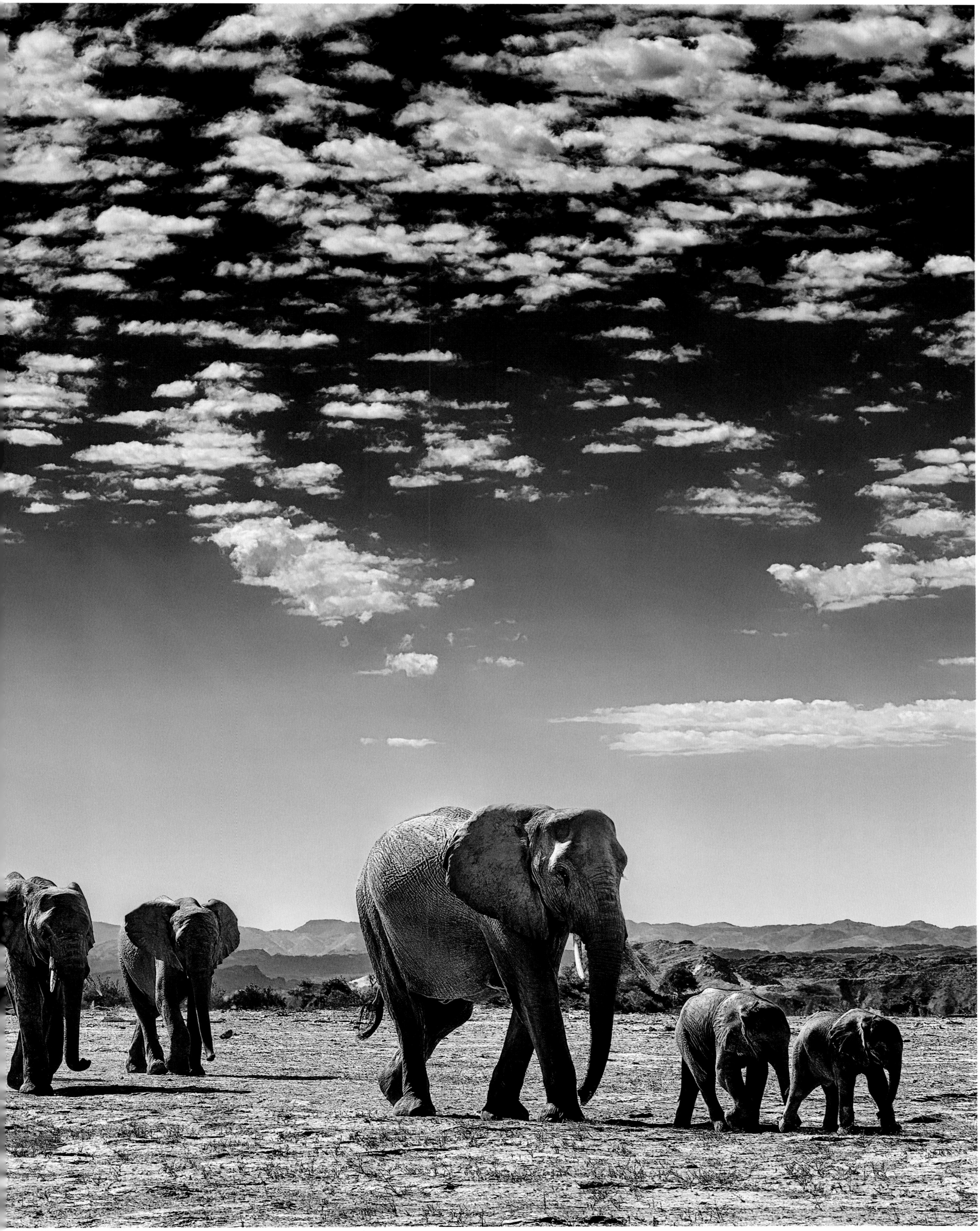

By discovering nature, you discover yourself.

— *Maxime Lagacé*

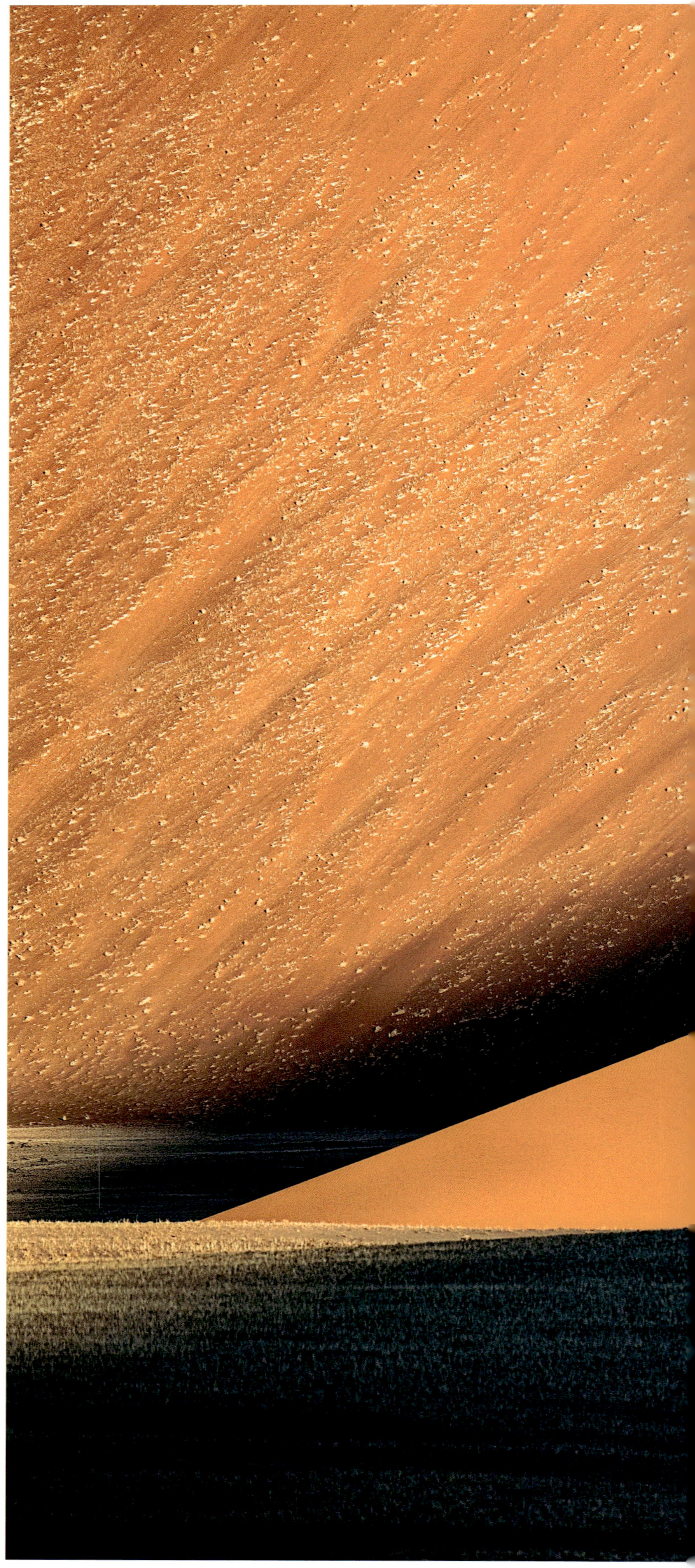

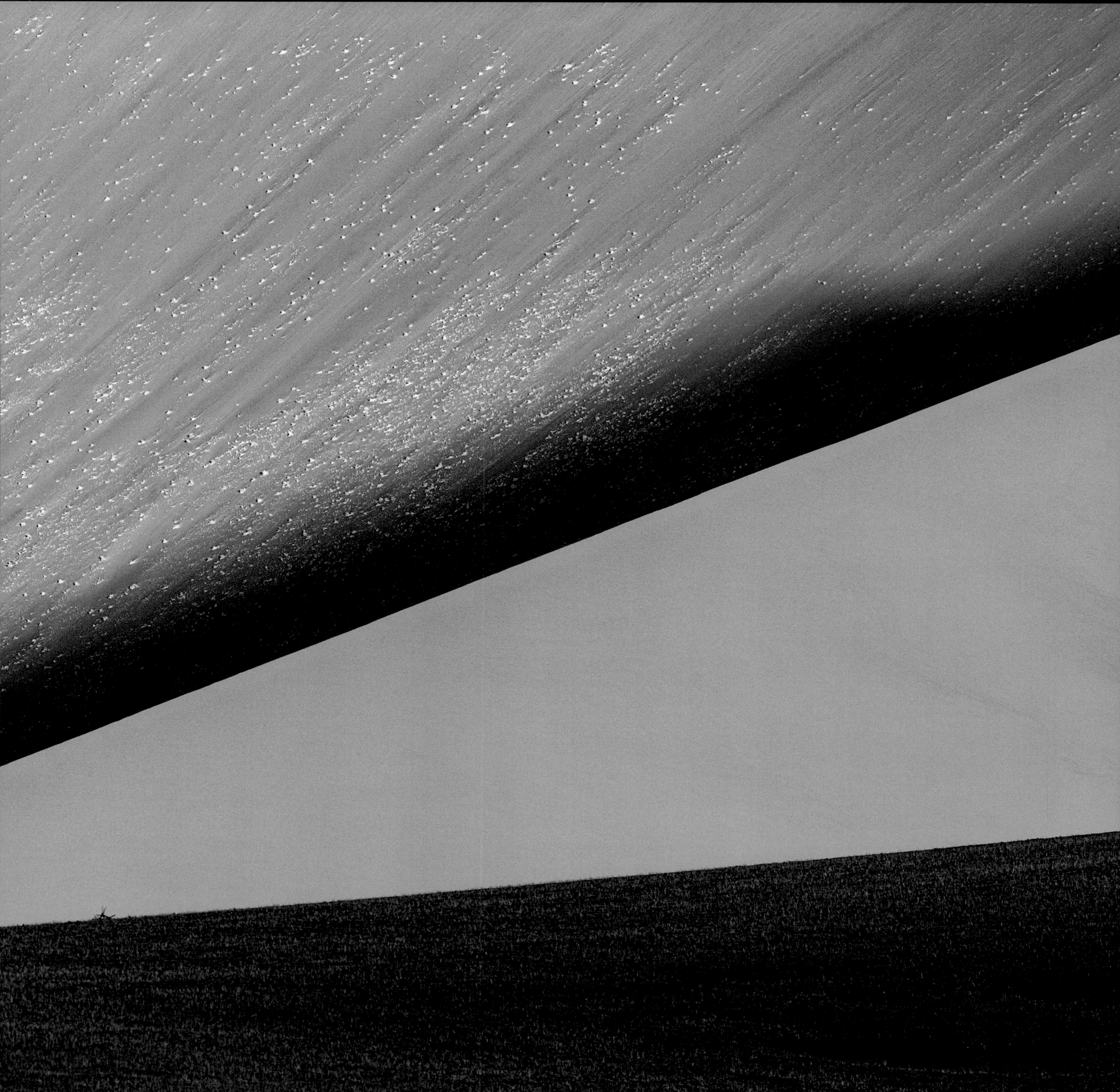

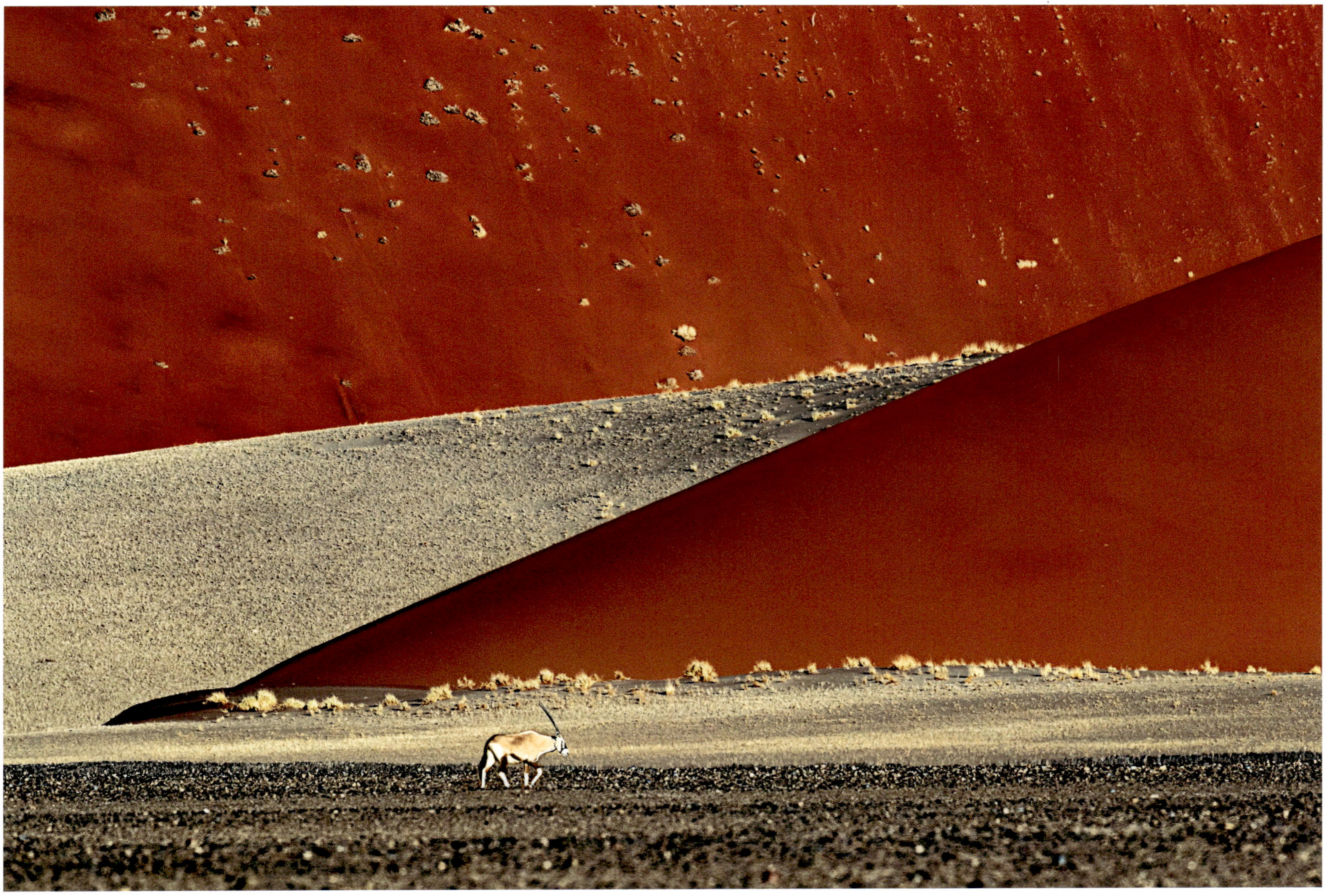

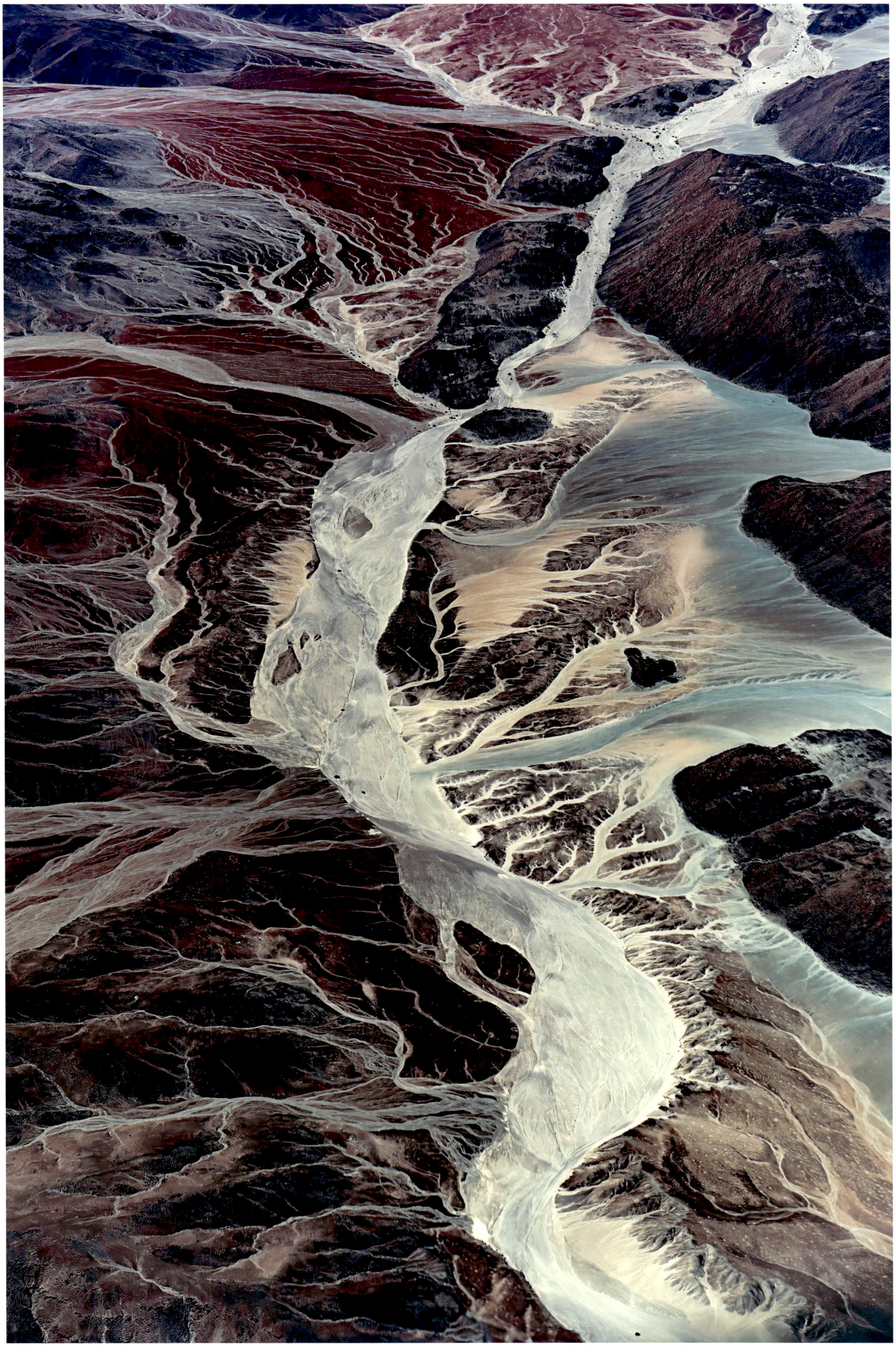

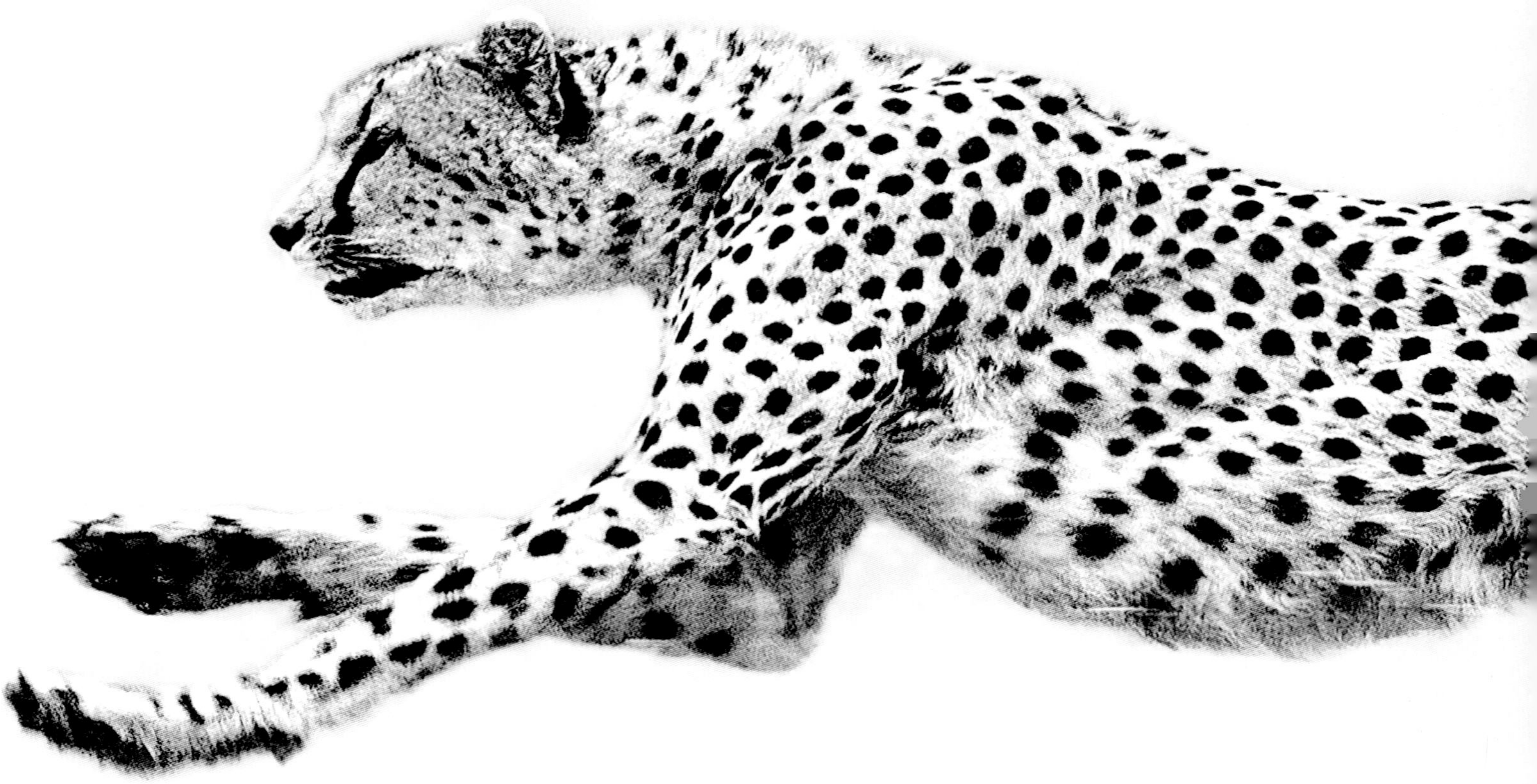

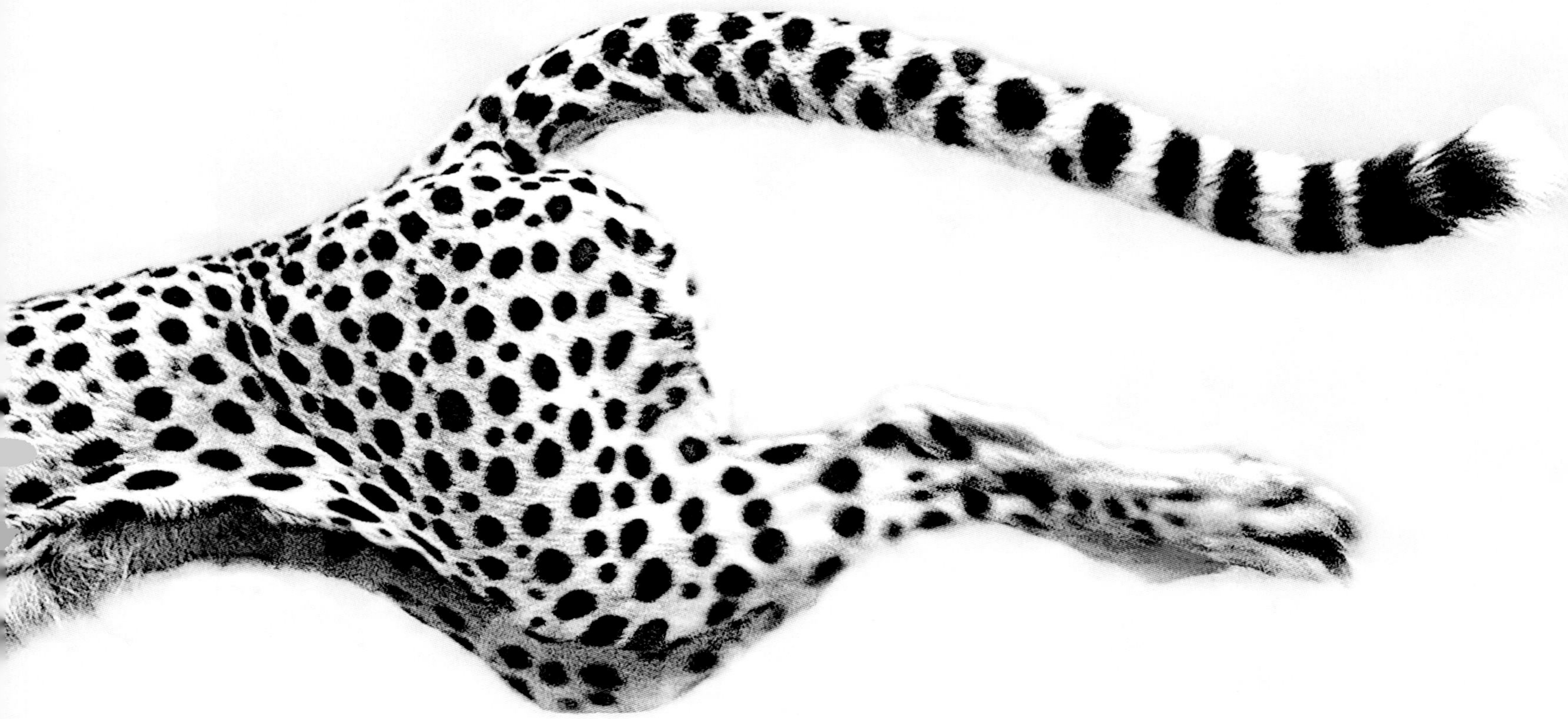

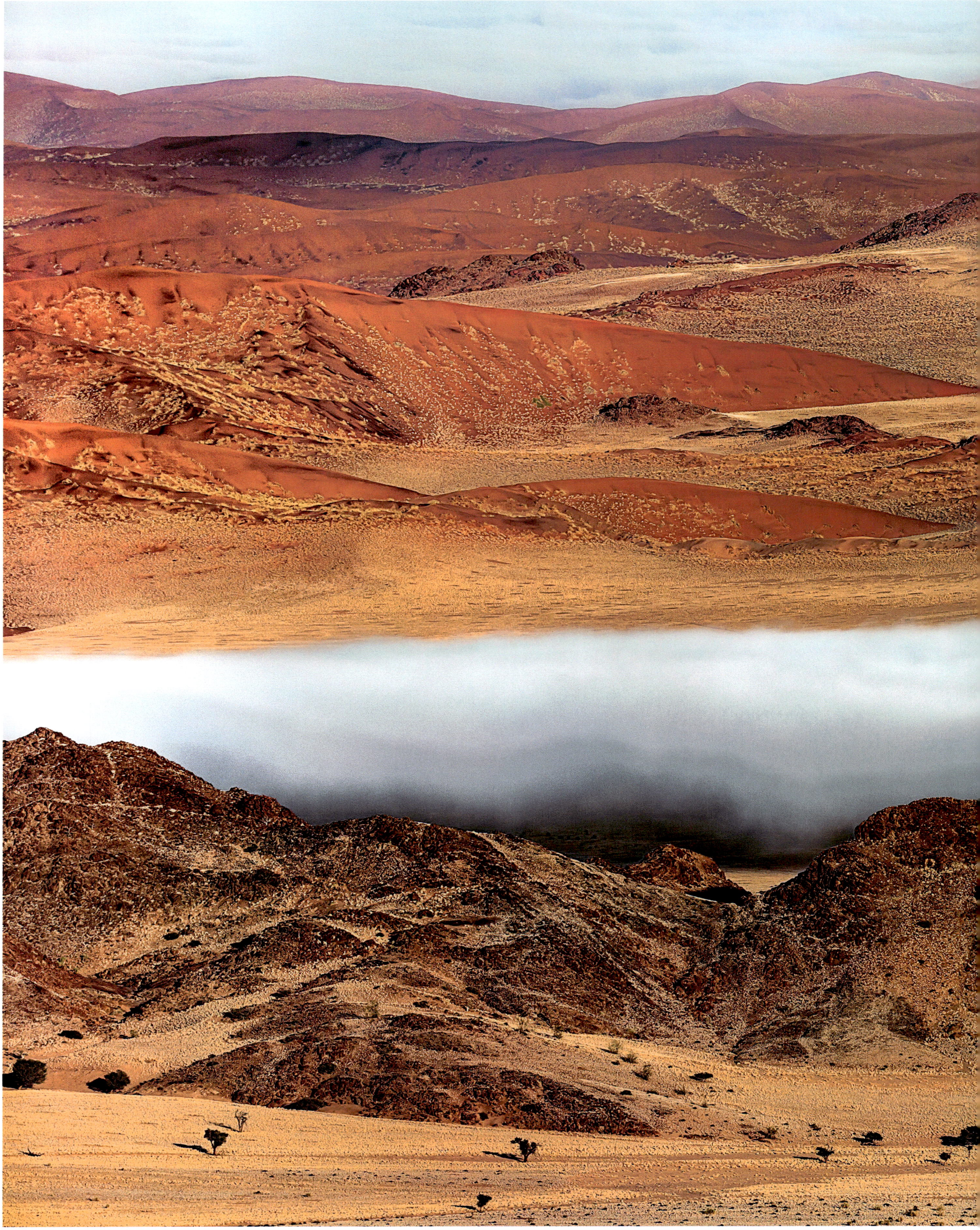

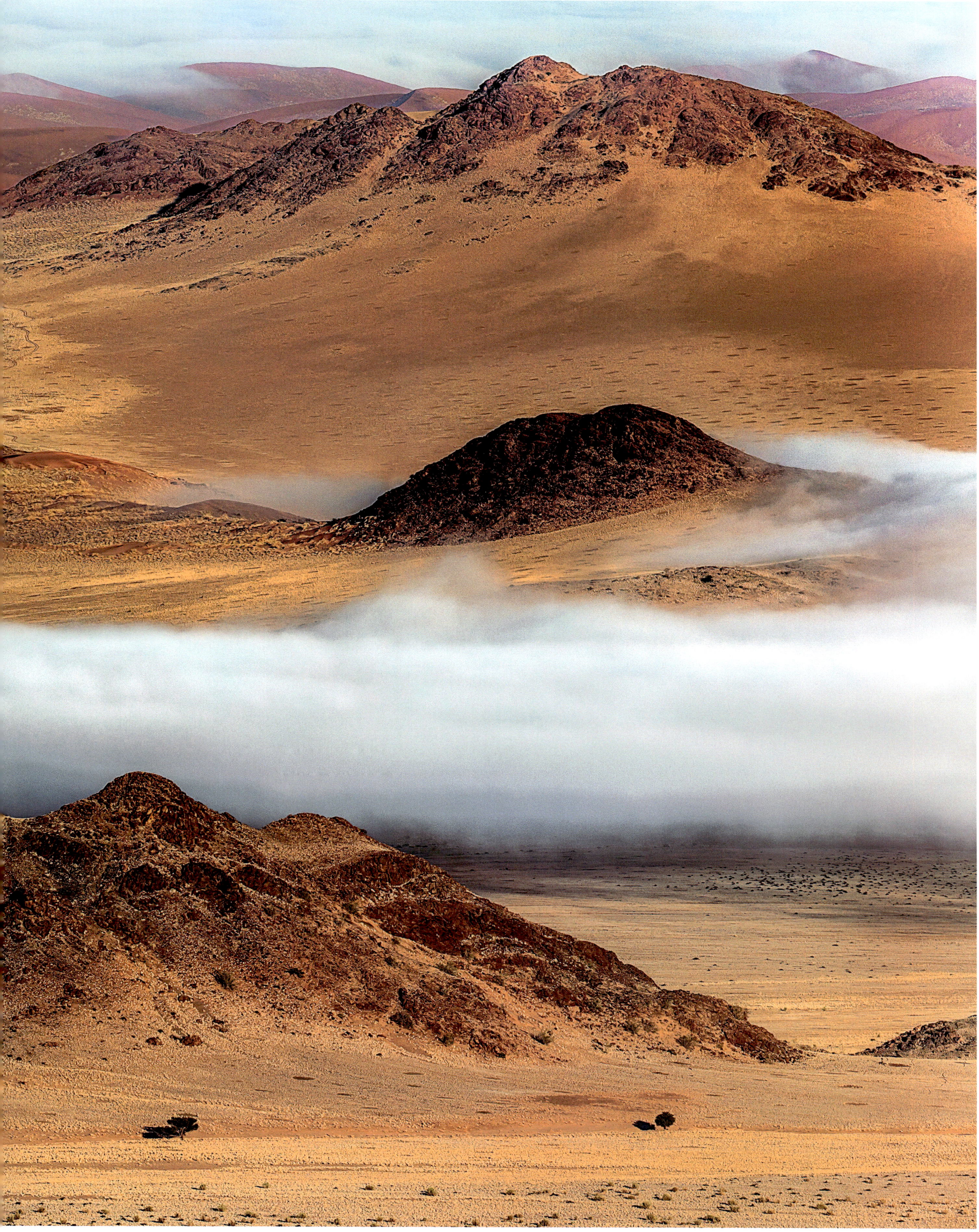

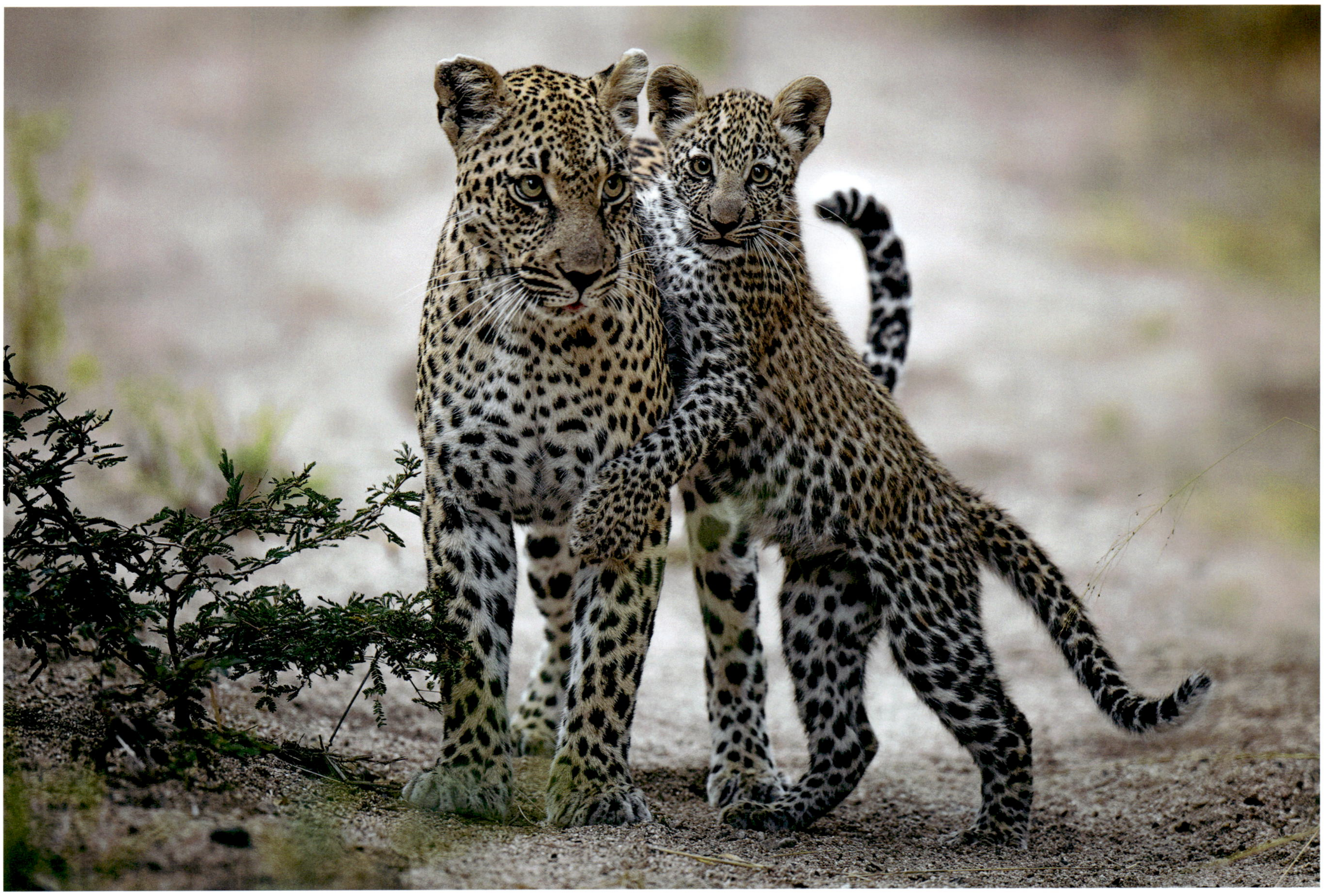

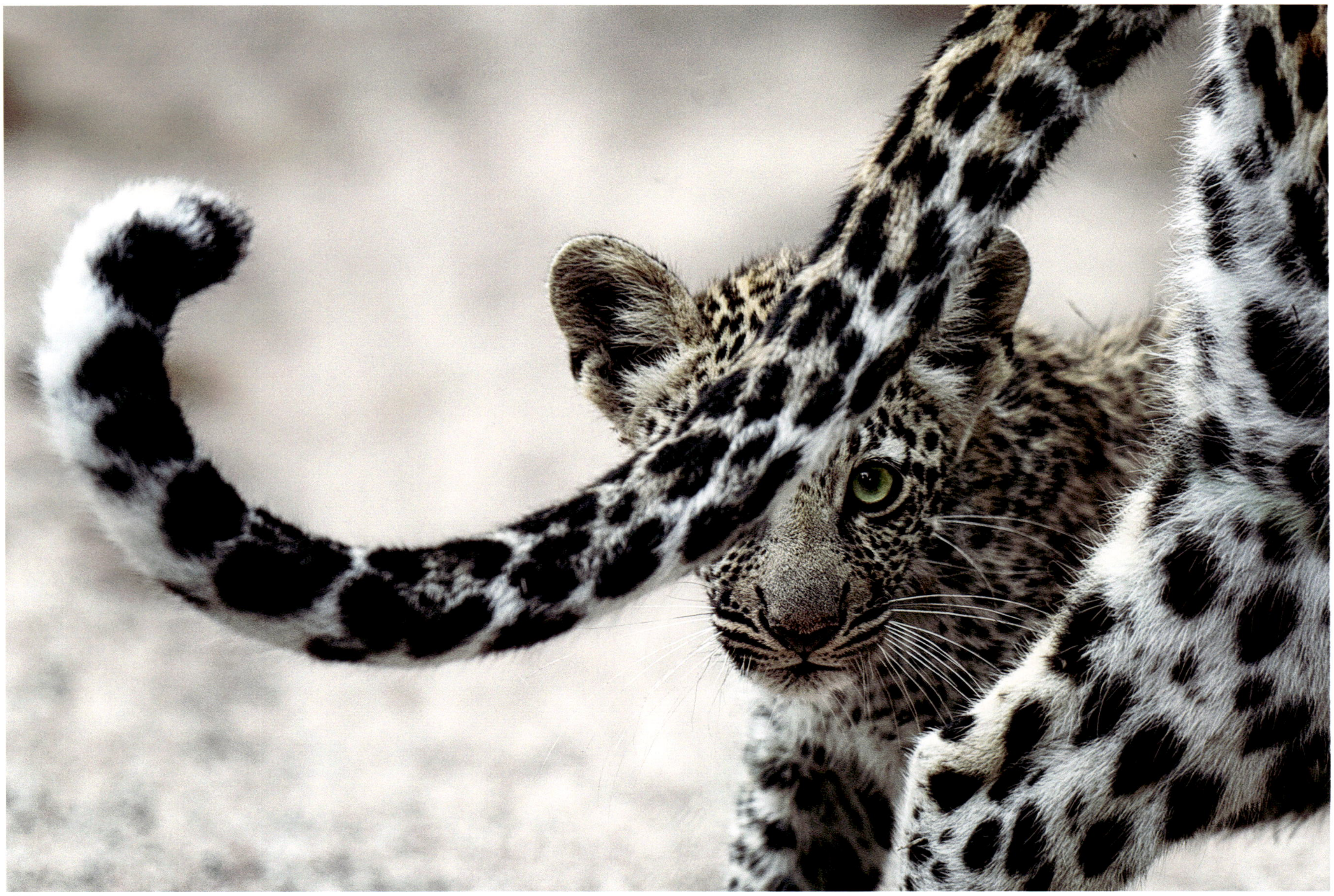

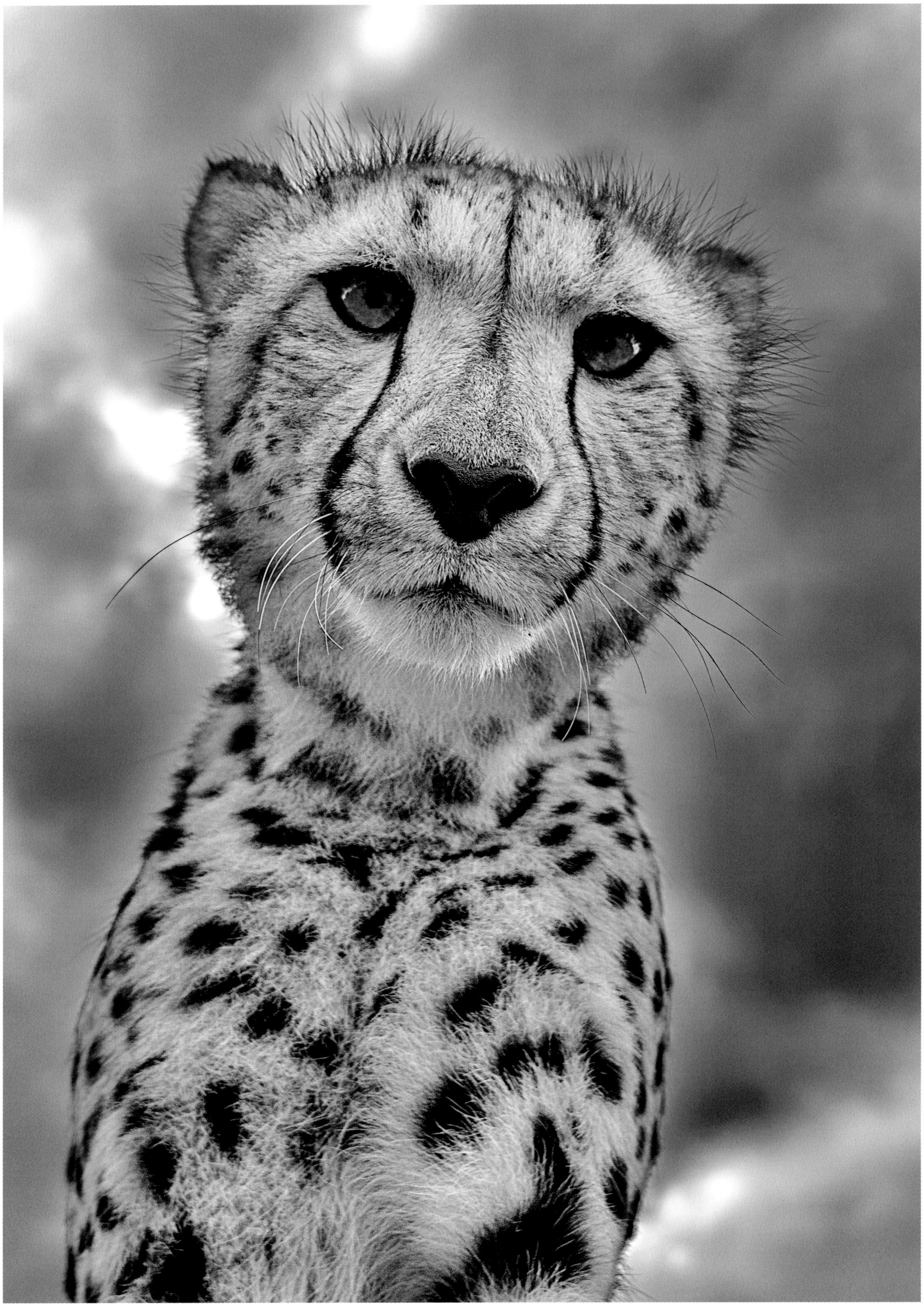

To see a world in
a grain of sand,
And a heaven in
a wild flower,
Hold infinity in the
palm of your hand,
And eternity in an hour.

— *William Blake*

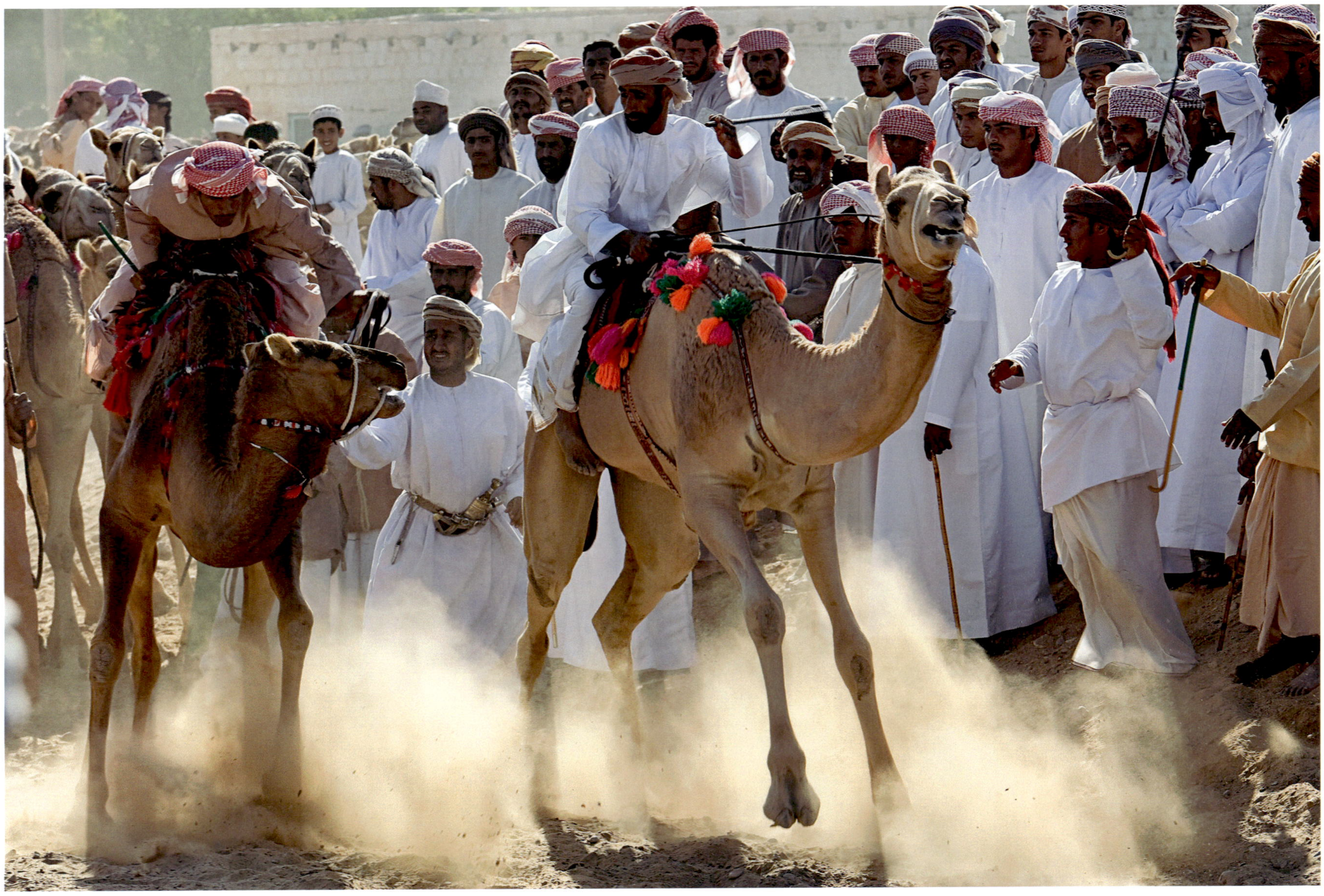

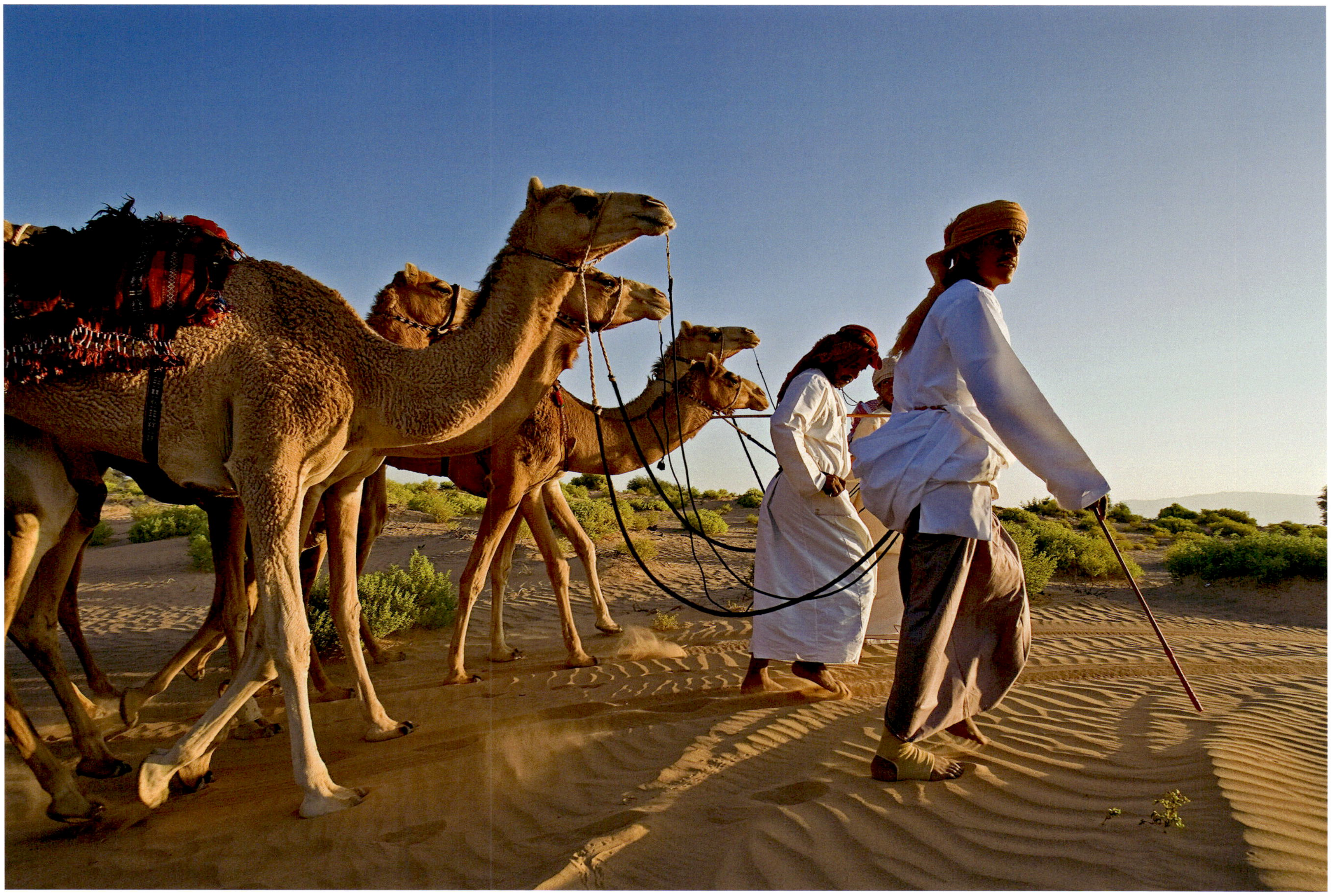

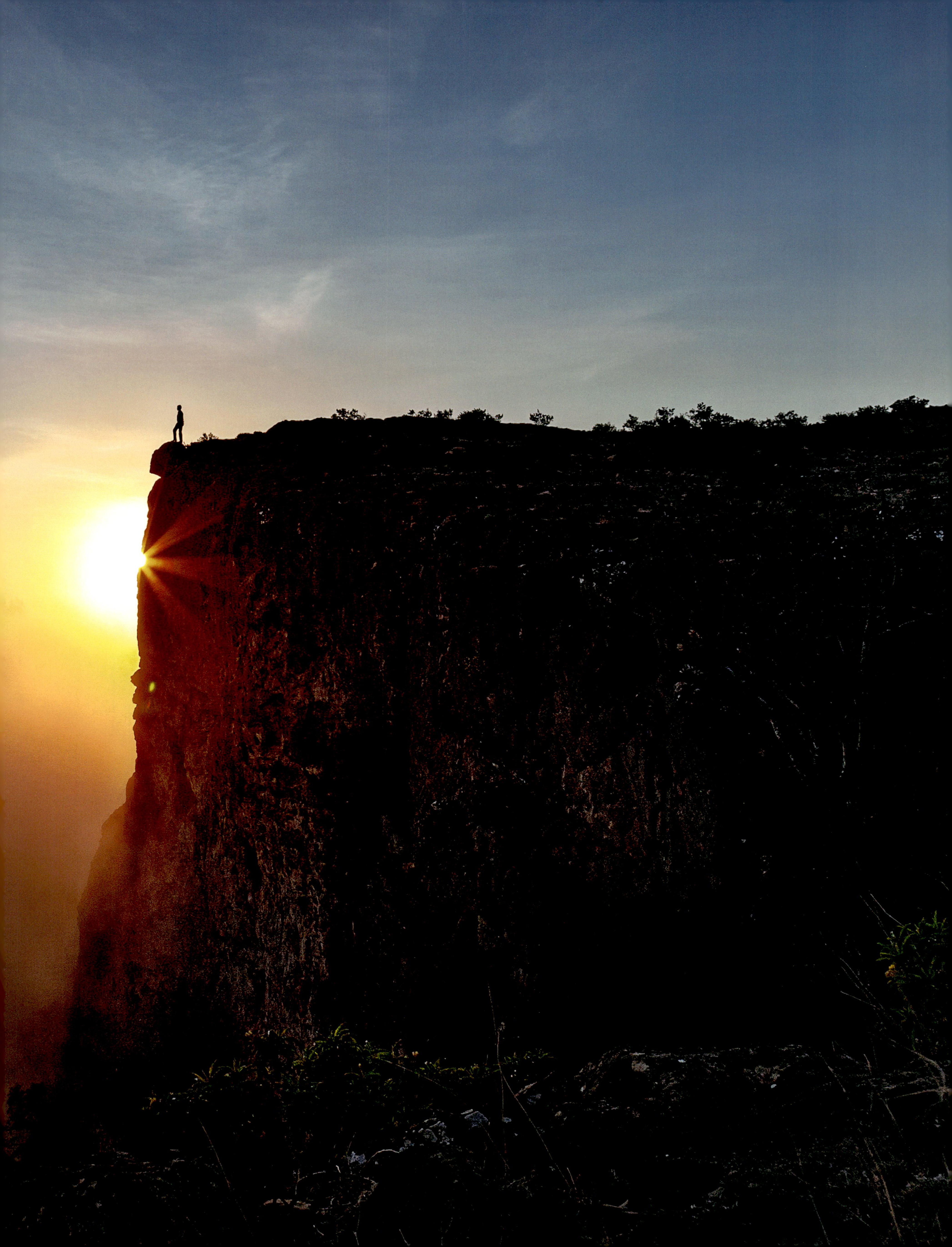

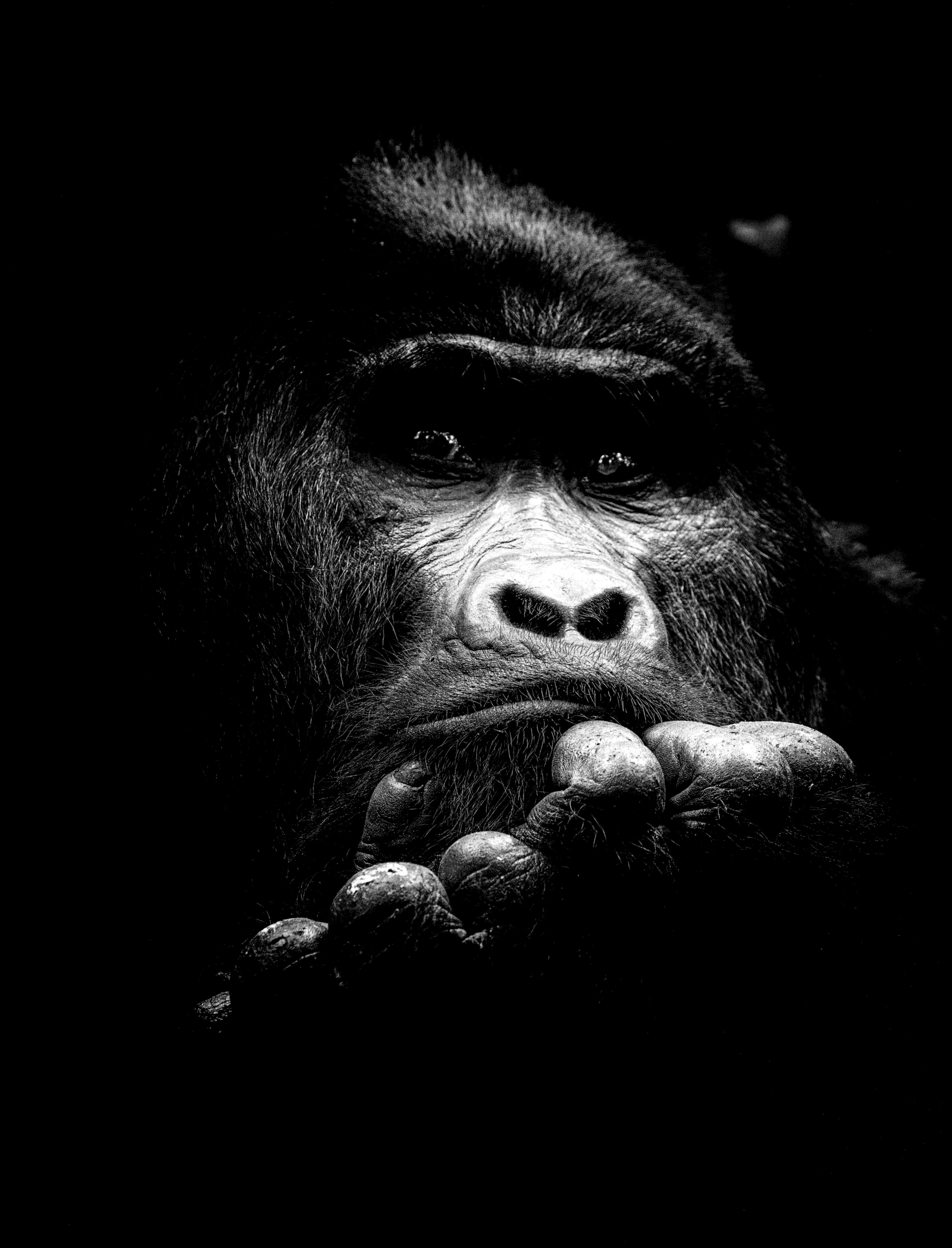

Chapter Four

STONES OF SILENCE

Thousands of tired, nerve-shaken, over-civilised people are beginning to find out that going to the mountains is going home; that wildness is a necessity.

— John Muir

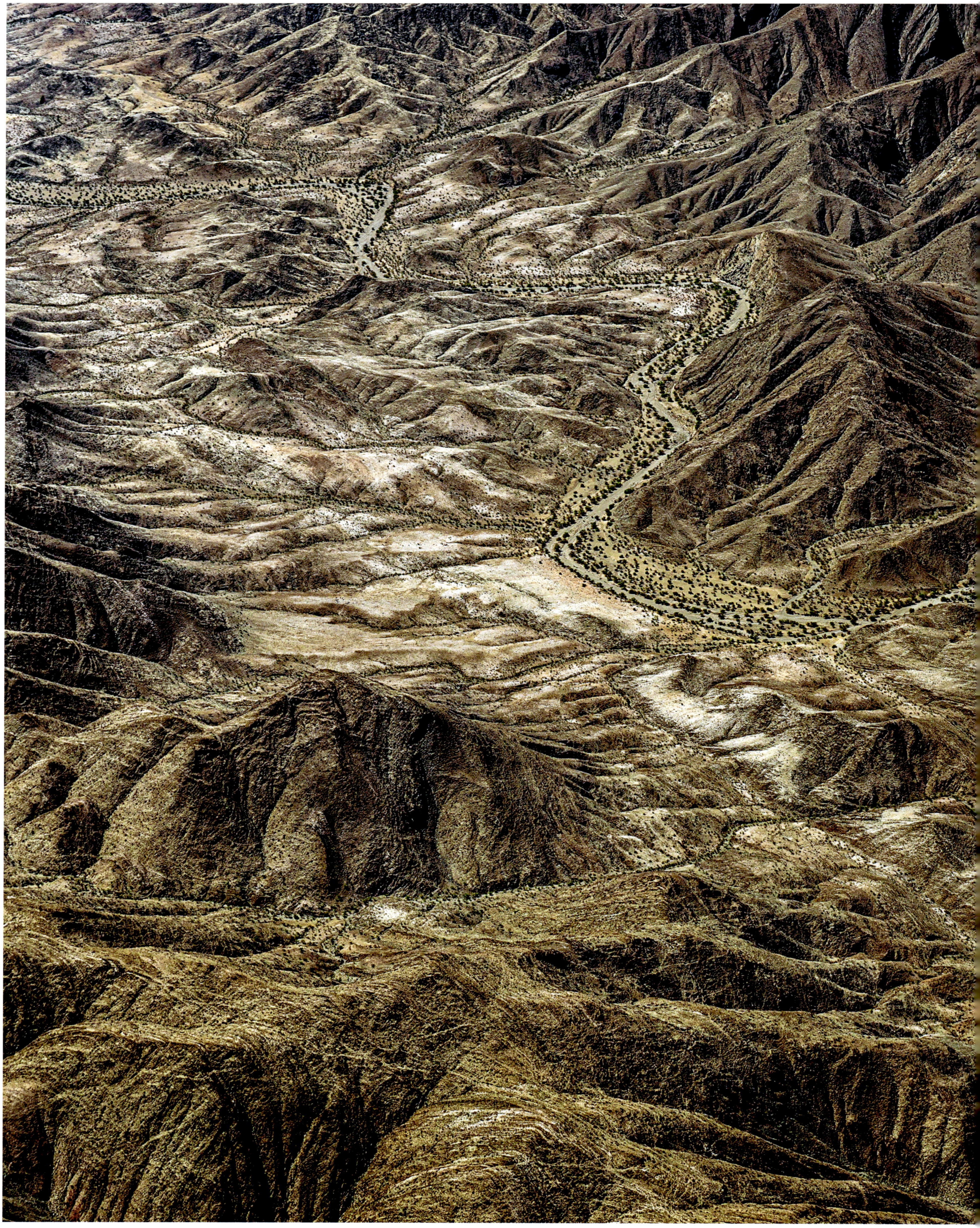

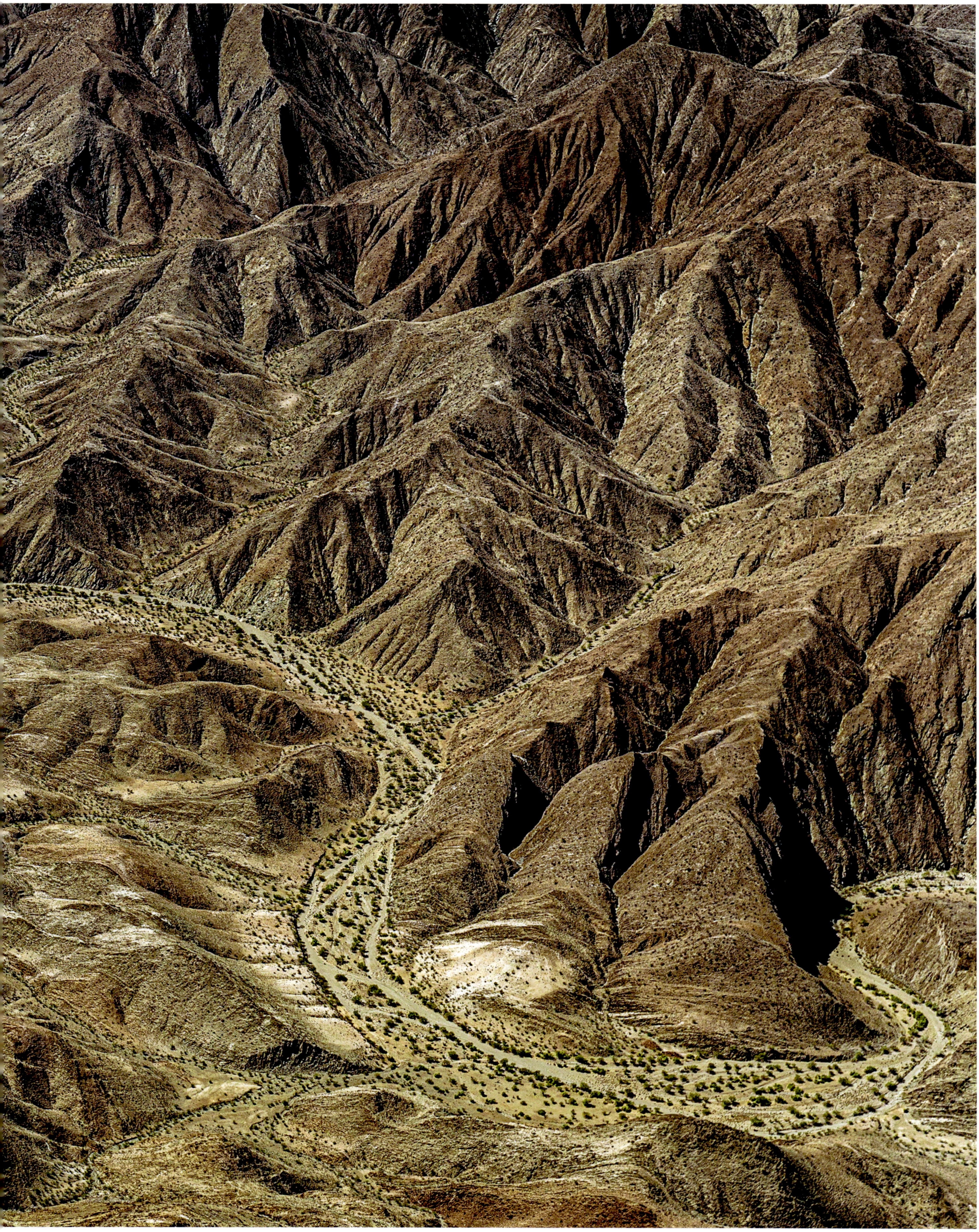

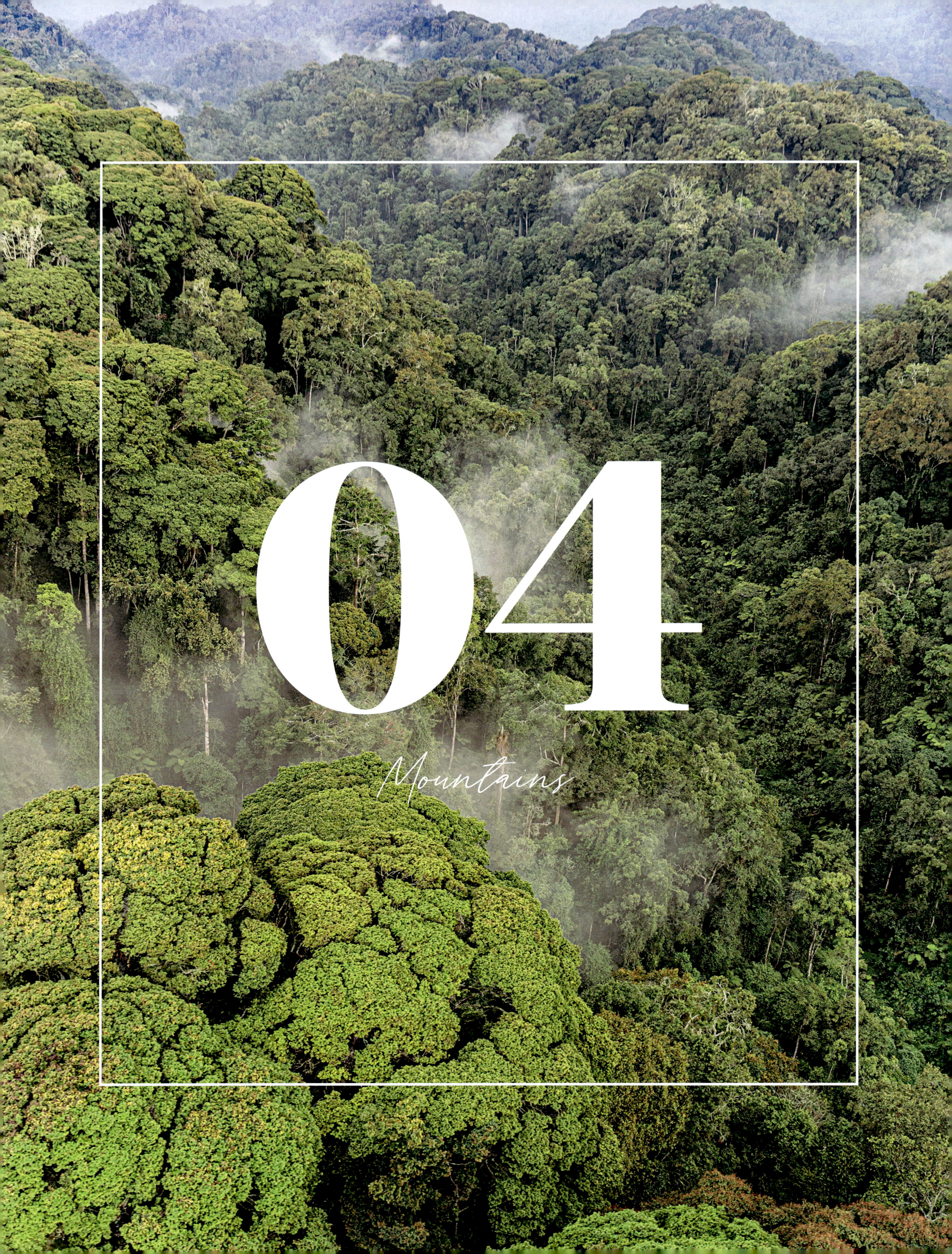

04

Mountains

Remote and inaccessible, mountains tower above the valleys and plateaus where most of humanity seeks shelter, their rocky peaks emerging out of the mist like islands floating above the clouds. For early travellers, mountains' brooding and daunting profile made them places to be avoided rather than embraced, the setting for harsh winters, violent winds and lashing rainfall, home to avalanches, floods and rockfalls. Yet, there is a benevolent aspect to these most imposing of natural monuments that symbolises eternity, evoking the stillness and solitude which religious practitioners have always sought, witnessed by the temples and places of worship erected along their stark facades, somewhere pilgrims trek to pay their respects, the site of revelations and miracles, staircase to the gods.

Mountains may look lifeless and immovable, but they are the water towers of the world, providing fresh water to half of the planet's population. They are a major influence on regional and global climates, support irrigation, industry, domestic use and hydropower, and are home to 50 per cent of all global biodiversity hotspots. The widespread retreat of glaciers that has been observed from polar to tropical regions in recent decades makes mountains highly sensitive barometers of climate change.

Several mountains are considered sacred. The Maasai of Tanzania named the active volcano in East Africa's Great Rift Valley Ol Doinyo Lengai, the 'mountain of God'. They believe their Supreme God Enkai chose its very tip as home and from time to time, they climb to the top bearing offerings and prayers to enhance fertility and cure disease for themselves and their precious livestock; they feel his presence but have never seen him and there are no depictions of him.

Both Angie and I have climbed another of Tanzania's landmark volcanoes, Mount Kilimanjaro; its snow-capped peak and the sight of elephants wandering the plains in its shadow make it one of the world's most photographed natural features. Kili is the highest single free-standing mountain on Earth, rising 5,895 metres above sea level. You don't have to be a mountaineer to climb Kili, but it does remind you of our natural inclination to challenge ourselves. Edmund Hillary, who on 29 May 1953 with Norbert Tenzing became the first to climb Mount Everest, the tallest mountain in the world, said, 'It's not the mountain we conquer, but ourselves,' while the Italian Reinhold Messner – widely considered the greatest climber of all time – captured the beguiling nature of mountaineering perfectly when he said, 'I am sure that the real key for understanding climbing is the coming back. It means if you are really in difficult places ... and you come back, you feel that you got again a chance for life. You are reborn. And only in this moment, you understand deeply that life is the biggest gift we have.'

Angie and I had always dreamt of making a pilgrimage to the mountain kingdom of Bhutan. Flying there from India on a clear day, you might glimpse the snowcapped peak of Mount Everest situated on the crest of the Great Himalayas, on the border between Nepal and Tibet. It rises like a white obelisk, just one of many breathtaking peaks erupting into the sky. This is a view with effects beyond words, a transcendent moment of pure elation painted in earth-brown and white. Experiences such as this evoke feelings of wonder, even ecstasy, embodying the sheer intensity of living, a sense of being at one with the world. As a child, Angie remembers being regaled with stories of this legendary Kingdom of the Thunder Dragon, mesmerised by black and white photographs of towering mountains and sparkling rivers, dense stands of oak and pine trees; an ancient land with a Buddhist culture and a tantalising hint of mystery. Just 320 kilometres in length and barely 160 kilometres in breadth, Bhutan may be small, but what other nation measures the wealth of its people in happiness rather than gross domestic product? The Bhutanese government also lays great emphasis on protecting the environment in a country with more than 75 per cent forest cover. As Karma Tshering, organiser of a world-record tree-planting event in 2015, said, 'Bhutan's young generation wants a clean and green future. We will never compromise on that.'

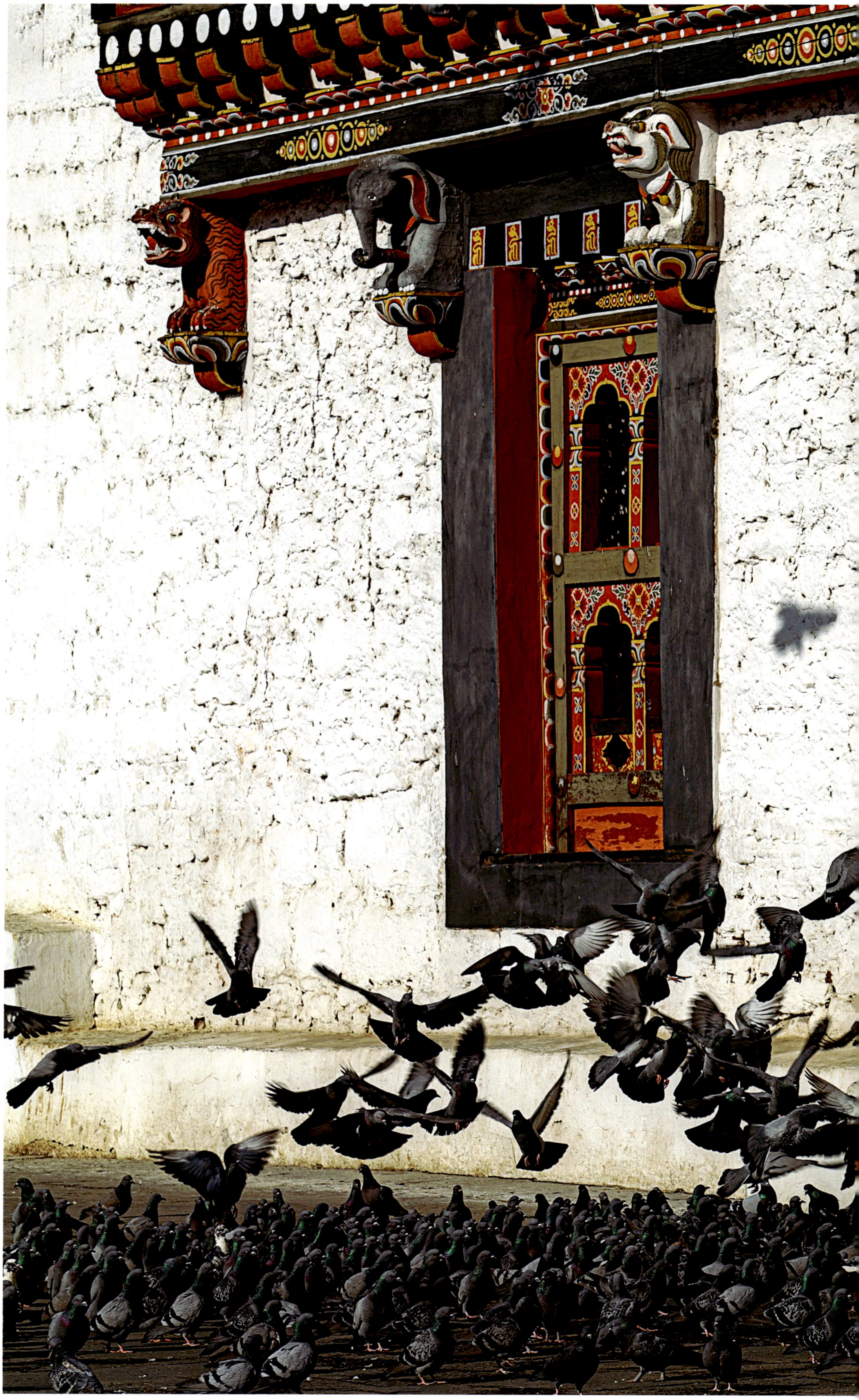

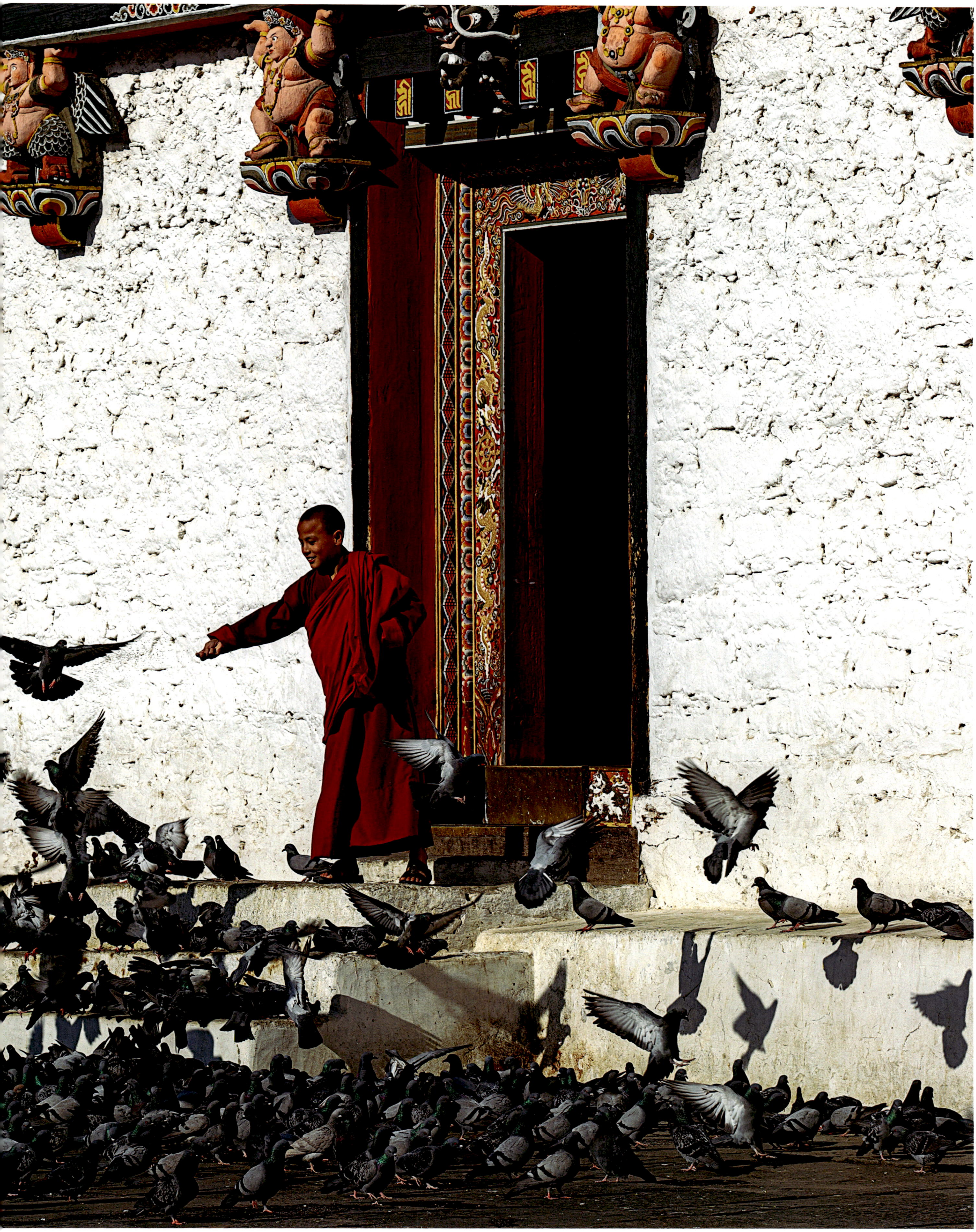

With a population of just 750,000, Bhutan is the perfect place to reflect on life in the fast lane; a chance to step back in time and reorder one's priorities away from the industrialised world: in 2010, barely 27,000 people visited Bhutan. We had timed our visit to coincide with the Paro festival that takes place in March/April each year at the Paro (Rinpung) Dzong, an ancient temple fortress that provides the focal point for the ceremony. Thousands of Bhutanese sit crowded shoulder to shoulder on the white brick terraces that act as an amphitheatre for the dances and processions, peacefully taking in every nuance of the spectacle unfolding in front of them, feasting on chillies, rice, vegetables – and more chillies! Angie has always loved dance and Bhutanese dances reflect the people's deepest fears and most fundamental joy as well as celebrating the life and work of Lord Buddha. The power of myth expressed forcefully through the medium of dance is a universal language, transcending the written and spoken word. The previous evening we had dined with a senior monk or lama whom I now saw praying, his eyes tightly closed in concentration and reverence, facing the Thangka, a wall-sized tapestry depicting the Buddha Guru Rinpoche who introduced Buddhism to Bhutan in the eighth century. He greeted me warmly, then counselled me to be mindful of the sacred nature of what I was so excitedly photographing:

The festival is not meant as entertainment. This is not 'show time'. It is a celebration enacted through the power of song and dance to speak to us of the fears and joys each of us experience in life. If you do not take time to sit and be present to what is happening here, to tame the mind, then you will have lost all sense of meaning inherent in the moment. Your photographs may please the eye, but they won't nourish your inner being. Go sit with Angie. She understands.

We in the West have lost so many of our own ancient rituals, believing erroneously that they are no longer relevant to modern living. Here in Bhutan there is still a sense of being part of something more substantial than the individual. People's belief systems are still intact, helping them to appreciate and revere all of life. As Angie and I travelled across the country, we felt a heightened sense of respect for our surroundings. It had a peculiarly civilising effect, inspiring us to try to achieve a more balanced and considered way of being, to absorb the ethos of Buddhism that believes in stoicism in the face of the vagaries of existence and that all life is sacred.

There is a place in Uganda called Bwindi – the Impenetrable Forest – where the trees grow so tall and dense that in places they shut out the light. The word 'impenetrable' stirs the imagination. This is one of the most primeval and biologically diverse areas on Earth. The richness of the soil and abundance of rainfall allows nature's creativity to run wild. Here the stars and moonlight cast a magic spell, a twilight world of owls and nightjars.

Seen from the air, Bwindi is often wreathed in mist, a blanket of trees and vegetation emerging then vanishing again, nature's abundance overwhelming in its beauty. You catch your breath as the sun breaks through the clouds to reveal a latticework of green erupting like a million broccoli heads, infused with brown and copper tones and flashes of red where flowers celebrate the dawning of a new day. In places, black and white colobus monkeys perch sentinel-like, wise old men of nature with an elevated view of sky and earth and forest. Bwindi is to trees what the savanna is to wildebeest, reminding you that plants make up 83 per cent of the Earth's biomass, while humans are just 0.01 per cent of it. Without plants to capture the energy of sunlight and feed the world, there would be no life.

Bwindi may look remote and inaccessible from the air, but on the ground there is a sense of expectation and discovery. You 'enter' a rainforest, drawing back the veil, transitioning from flat earth and daylight to an area of breathtaking beauty tinged with majesty. This is a timeless place, akin to entering an ancient cathedral with arching wooden beams and timber roof illuminated in places by shafts of light. It is a sacred space of broad-leaved trees, towering buttress-rooted figs and ankle-snagging creepers, teeming with flora and fauna. Sparkling crystal-clear streams ripple and gurgle across rock-strewn channels, creating pathways of light among the forest. By retaining moisture, the forest remains humid and warm, making it the perfect home for the the transboundary Bwindi and Sarambwe (DRC) ecosystem population of 459 mountain gorillas (Gorilla beringei beringei), approximately half the 1,063 mountain gorillas on Earth according to a 2018 survey.

An encounter with any of the great beasts of myth and legend – the lions, bears, wolves and tigers – is a life-changing moment filled with echoes from the past; a timely reminder of our own human frailty and place in nature. A meeting with a 180-kilogram silverback gorilla is of a different order, especially one as mellow and accepting as Rafiki (which means 'friend' in Swahili), the dominant male in the 16-strong Nkuringo group. At 25 years of age and clad in a thick coal-black coat with a broad saddle of silver-grey fur across his back, Rafiki was instantly recognisable. The mighty fur-covered forearms, the power of the naked chest muscles and the massive domed head with flared nostrils and eyes that appeared to see right through you made him a hypnotic mix of power and benevolence. Gazing deep into his hazelnut-brown eyes evoked a sense of recognition that was deeply moving and humbling. The impulse was to get down on your knees and repent for all the cruelty, injustice and suffering we have inflicted on the Earth, to atone for the past. These are the same creatures that were slaughtered by hunters and explorers as recently as 1951 as we clung to the myth of the gorilla as a tyrannical monster-ape, the King Kong of cinema. Gorillas are still prized for their skulls and hands, their flesh consumed as exotic fare at dining tables in Nigeria, New York and London, despite new data confirming that humans and gorillas are about 98 per cent identical on a genetic level.

You enter a rainforest, drawing back the veil, transitioning from flat earth and daylight to an area of breathtaking beauty tinged with majesty.

As if to underline the fragility of life, within days of my writing these words, Rafiki was dead, speared through the abdomen when he charged a group of four poachers in defence of his family. In recent months levels of poaching had increased as tourism to Bwindi and the Virungas dwindled in the face of the Covid-19 pandemic: fewer tourists, less park revenue, less ability to patrol and monitor the gorillas and keep poachers at bay.

governments to partner with international companies with almost unlimited finances to exploit natural resources, even when they are within protected areas – despite the potential long-term damage to conservation imperatives and to the wellbeing of local communities. As with the death of Rafiki, it is evident there are no victories in conservation, only the need to remain forever vigilant on behalf of the natural world.

It is evident that there are no victories in conservation, only the need to remain forever vigilant on behalf of the natural world.

Worryingly, about one-third of the world's protected areas face intense pressure from human activities: buildings, agriculture, roads and night-time lighting. Even national parks are not immune to demands from industry and governments to exploit – rather than protect – their natural resources. Virunga in the Democratic Republic of Congo, the oldest and most diverse park in Africa and a UNESCO World Heritage Site, was at the centre of a bitter controversy in 2012 when it was discovered that the government had given SOCO, a British oil company (now Pharos Energy), permission to conduct seismic testing. Opposition from high-profile international figures and the British government, along with legal mediation, eventually prevailed. Worryingly, the DRC government has since said that one solution would be to de-gazette that part of the park where oil is believed to be economically viable for exploitation. This underlines the desire of many

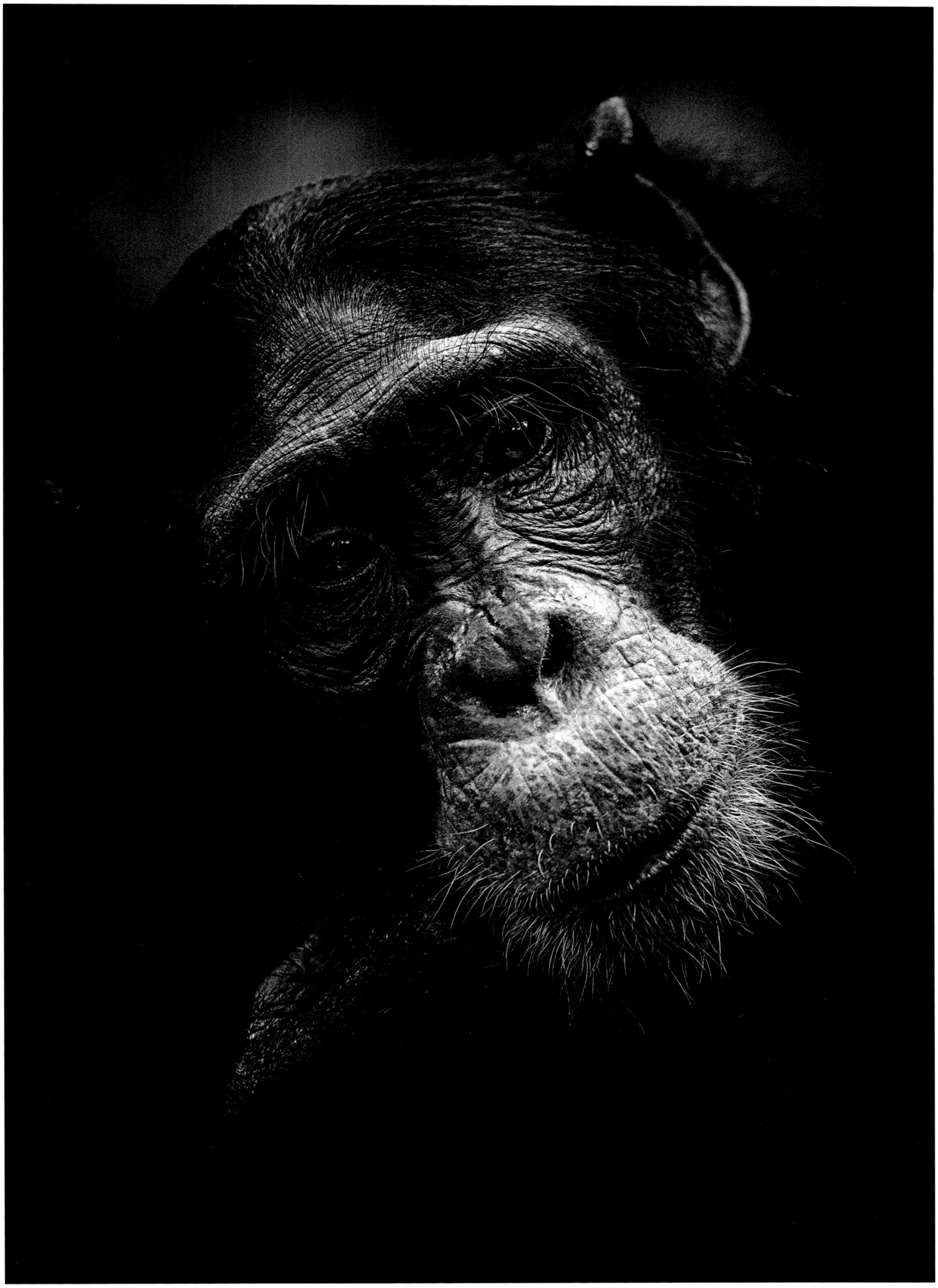

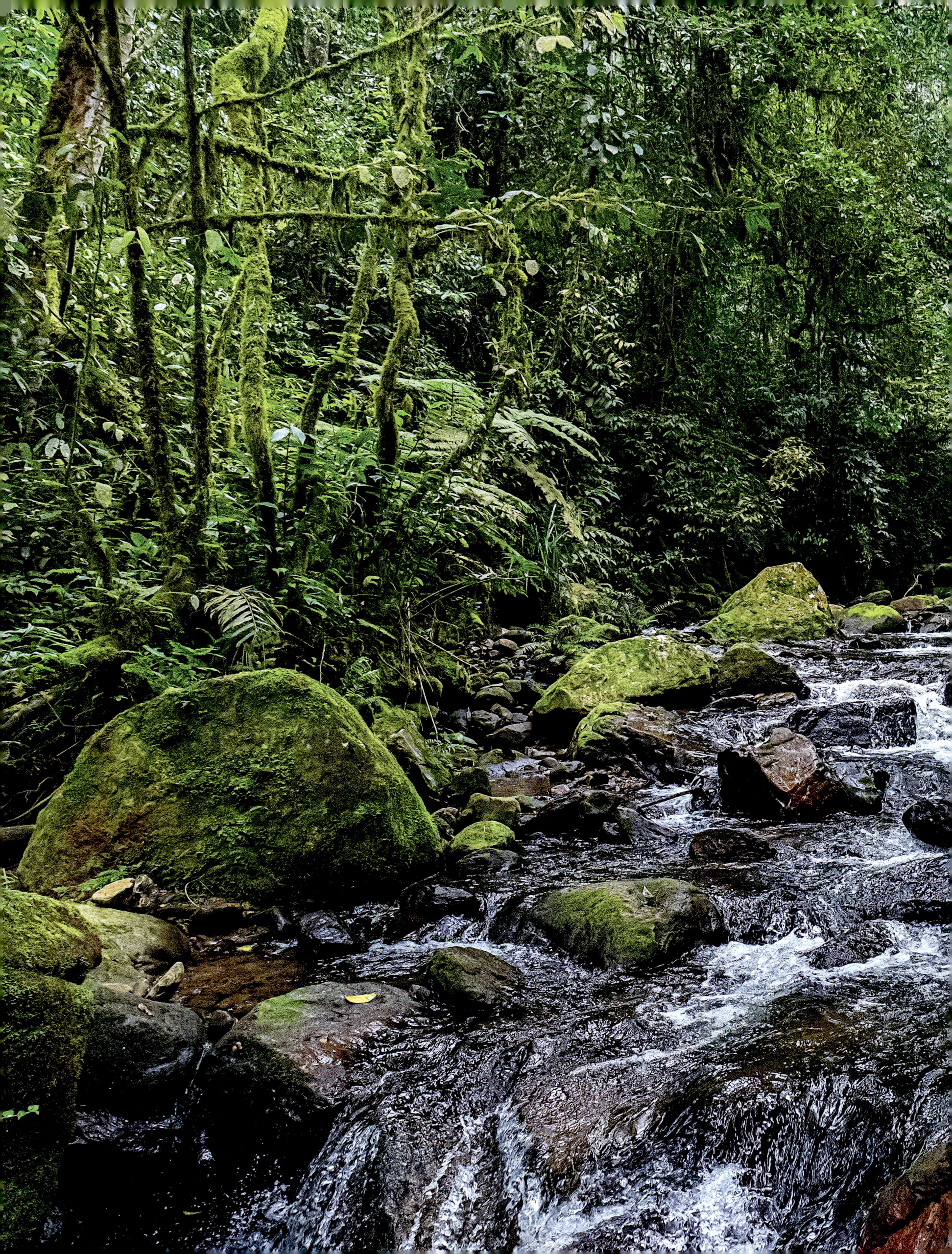

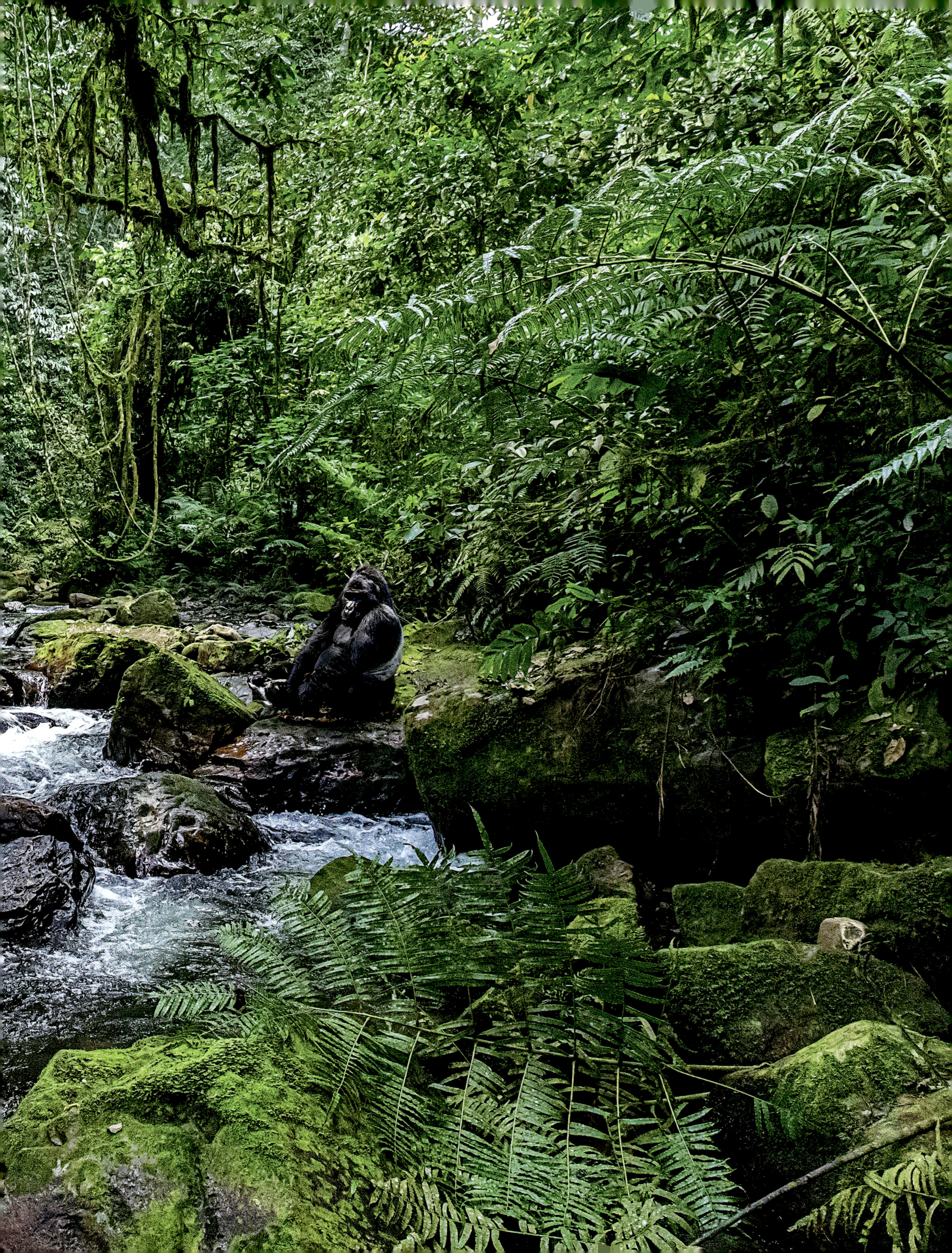

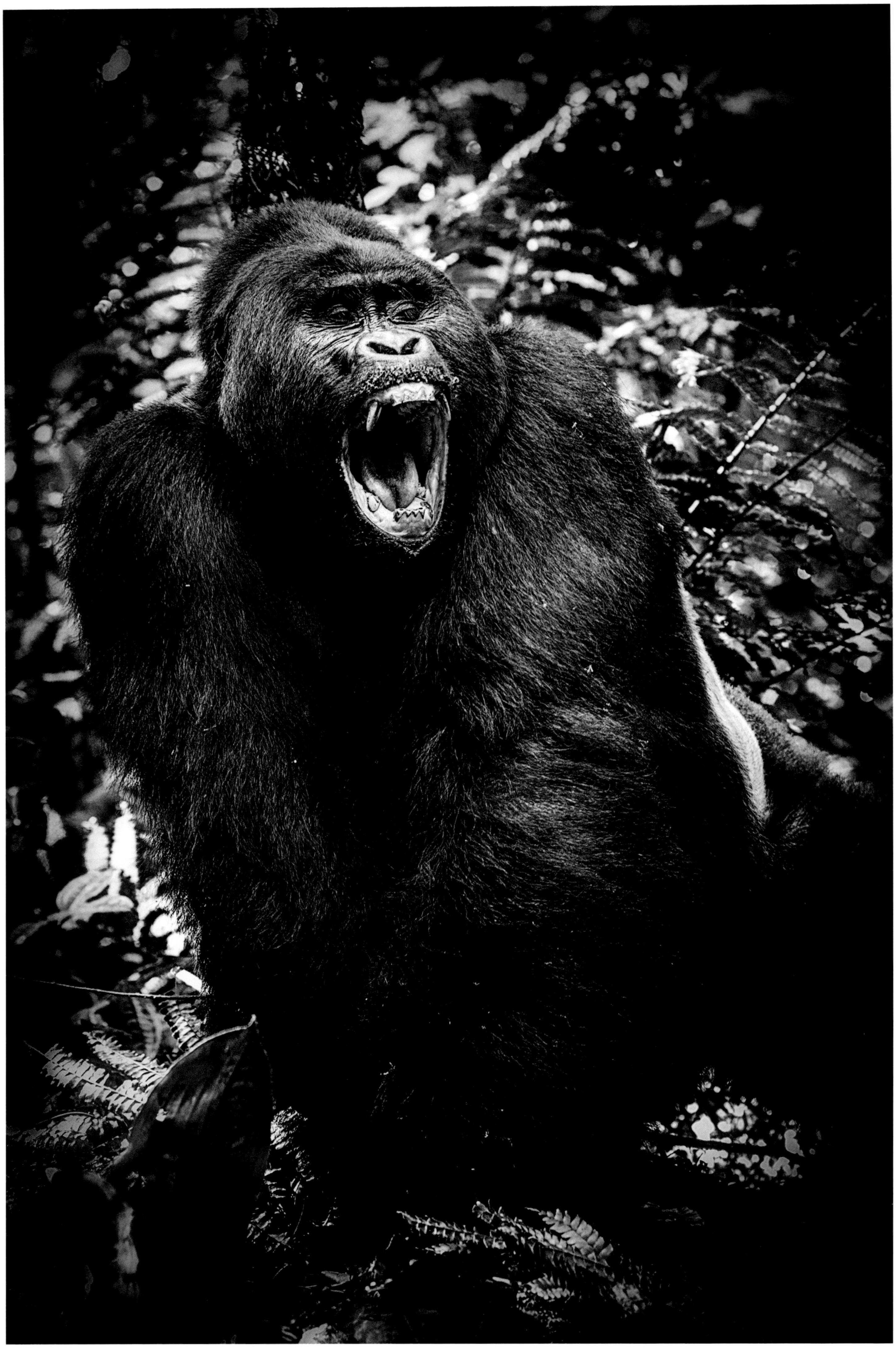

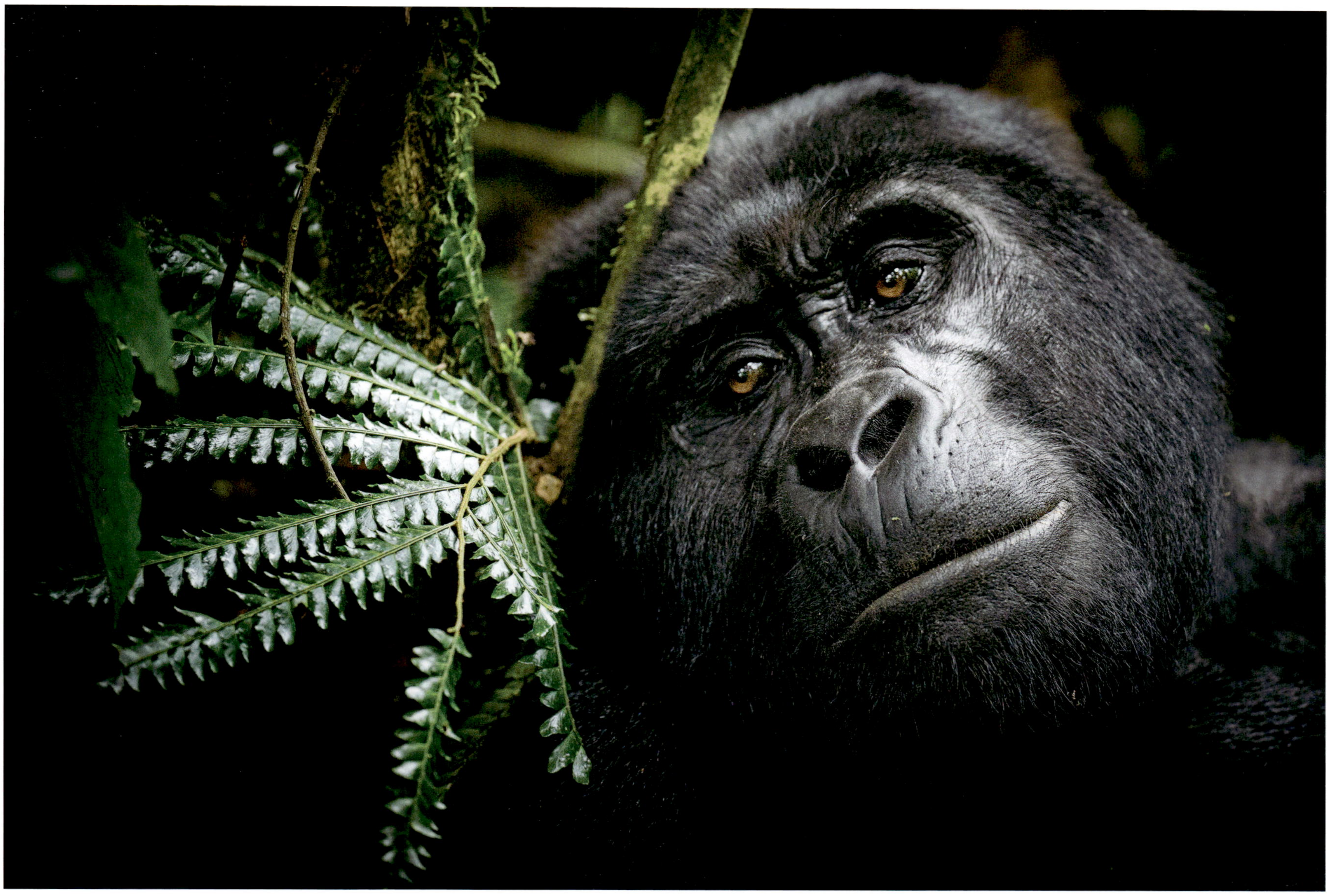

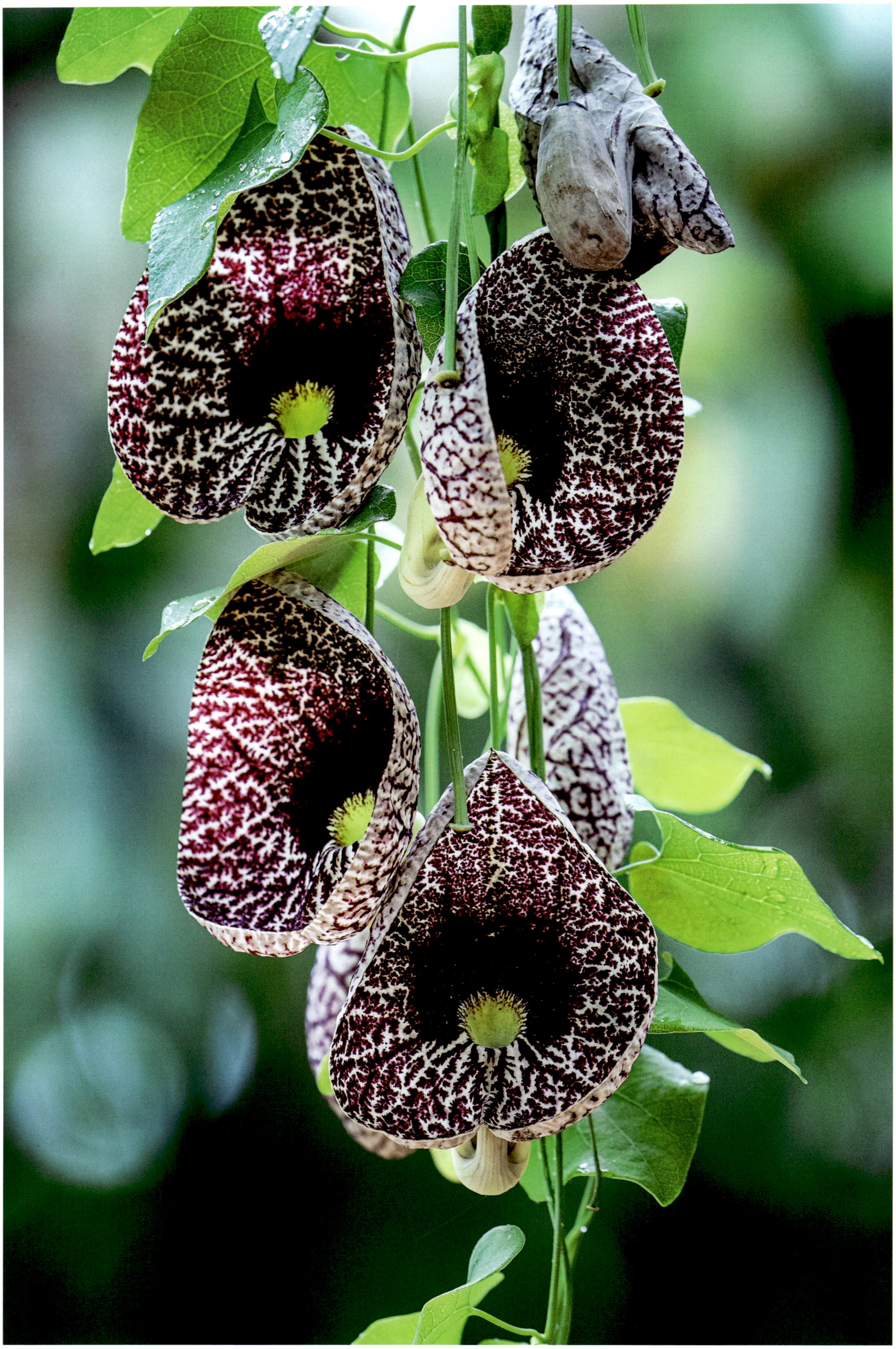

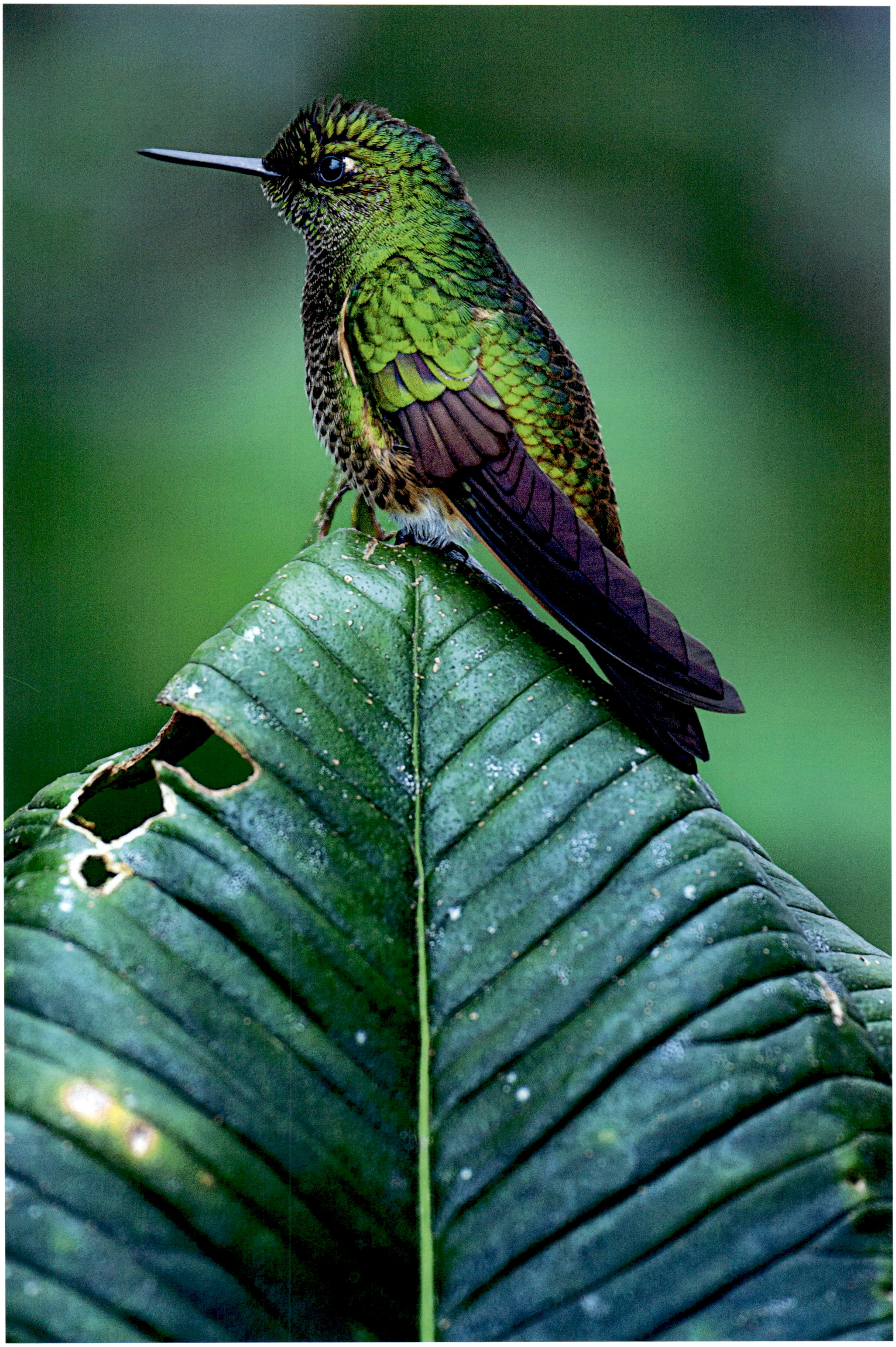

No matter how sophisticated you may be, a large granite mountain cannot be denied – it speaks in silence to the very core of your being.

— *Ansel Adams*

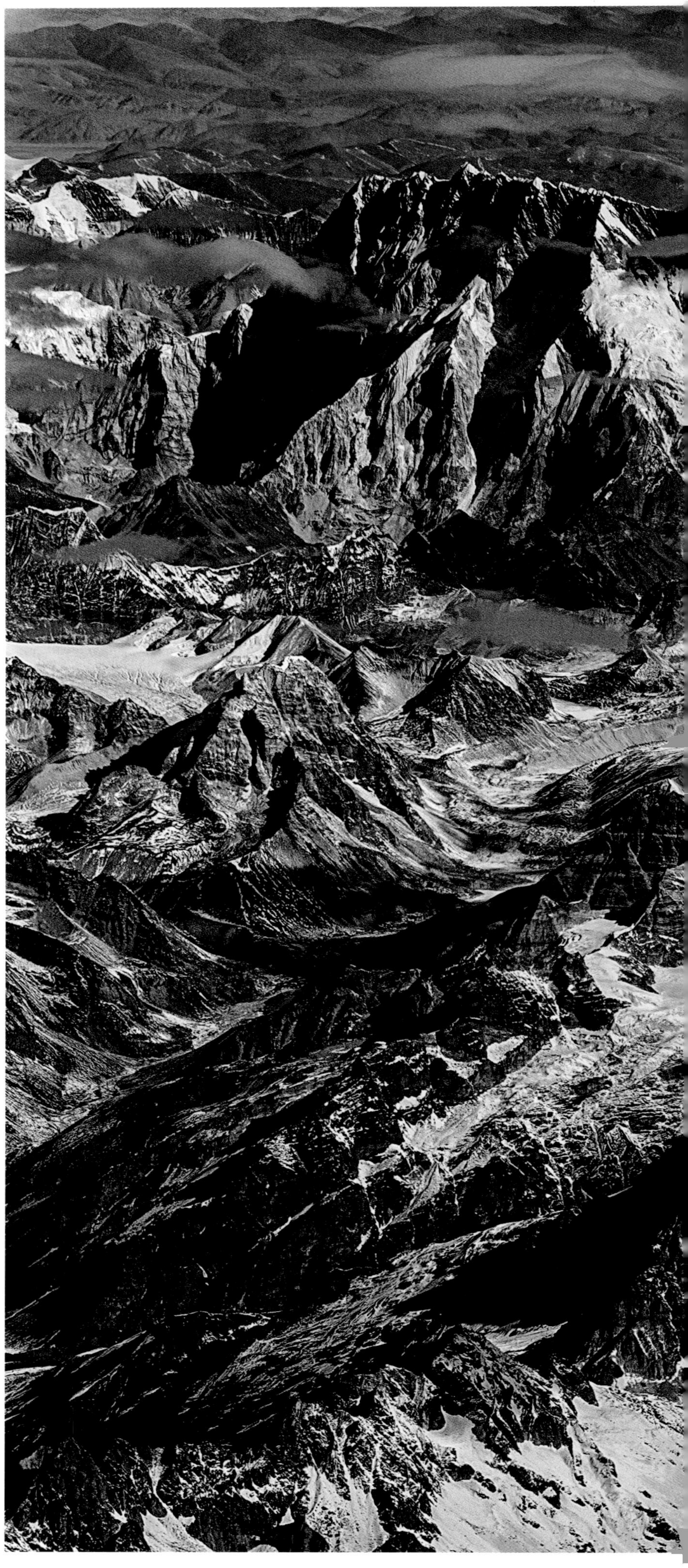

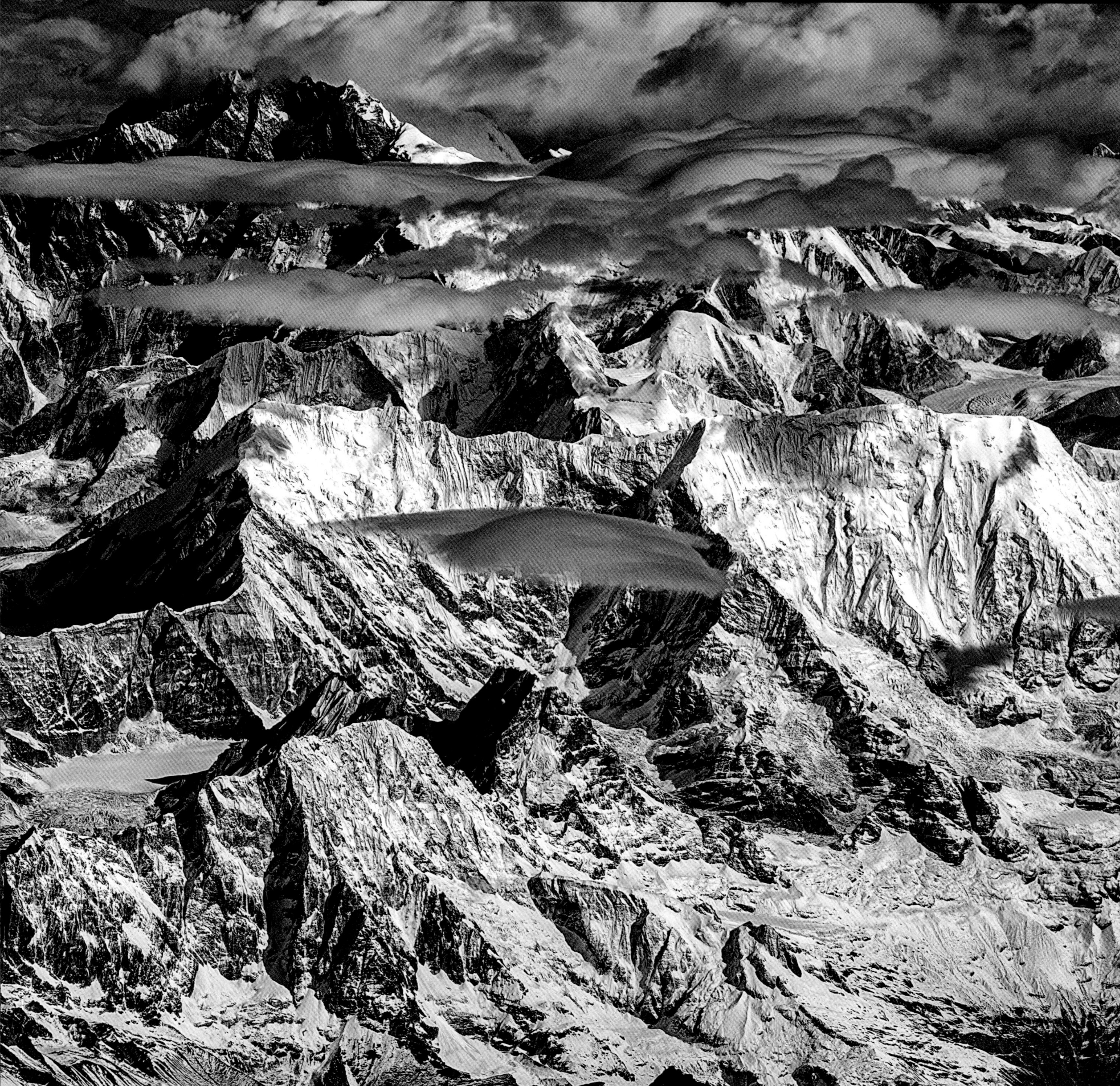

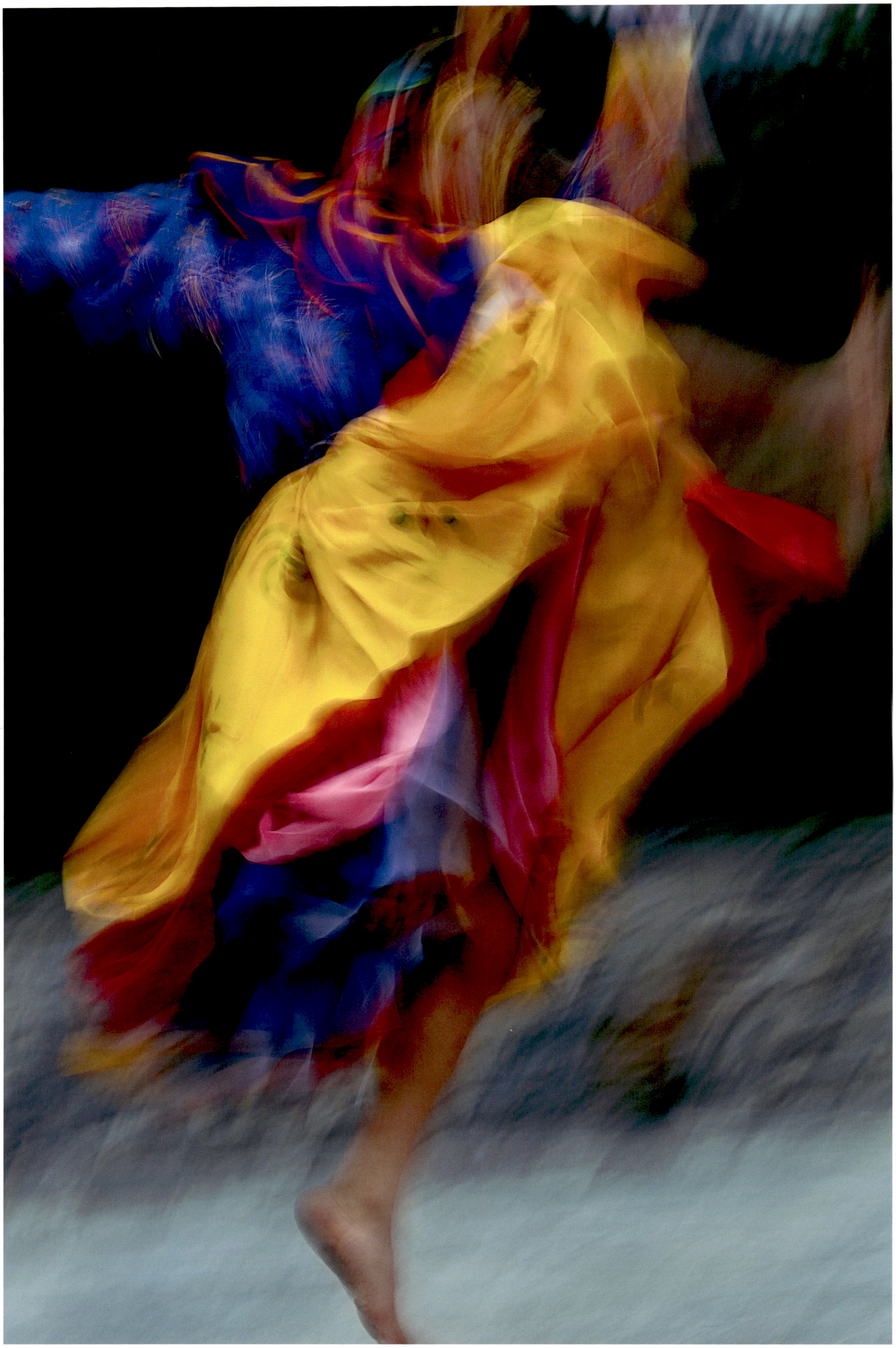

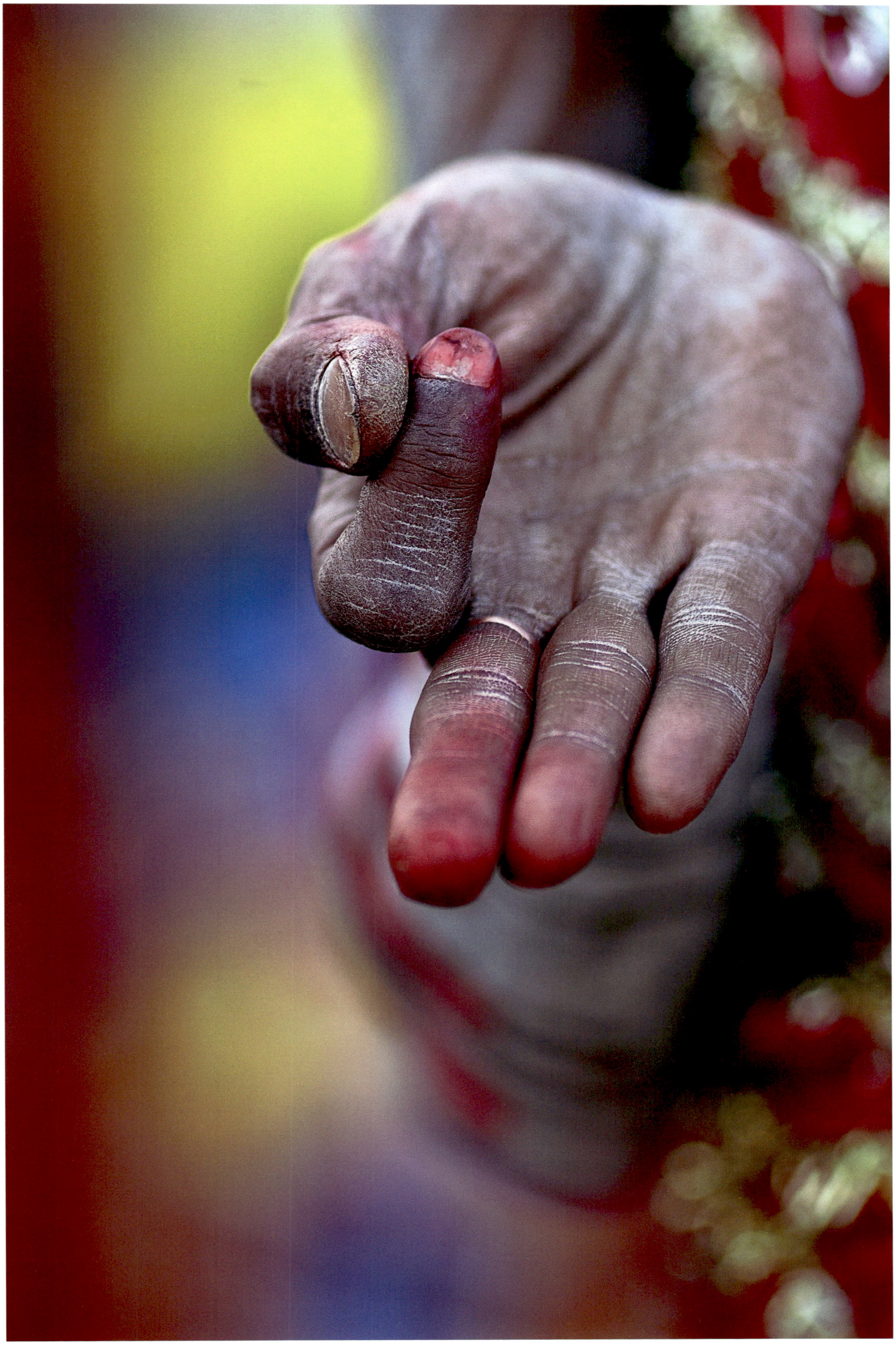

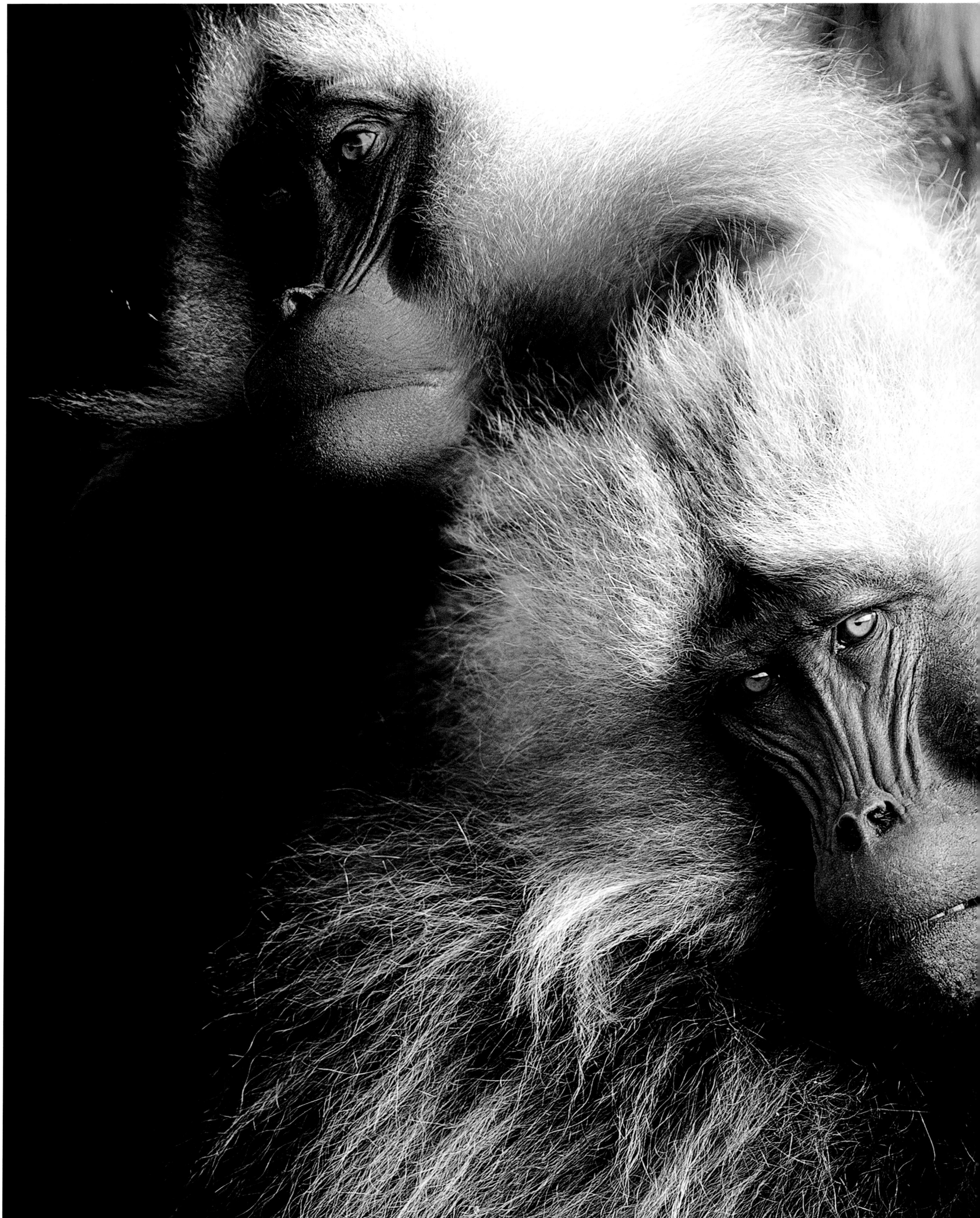

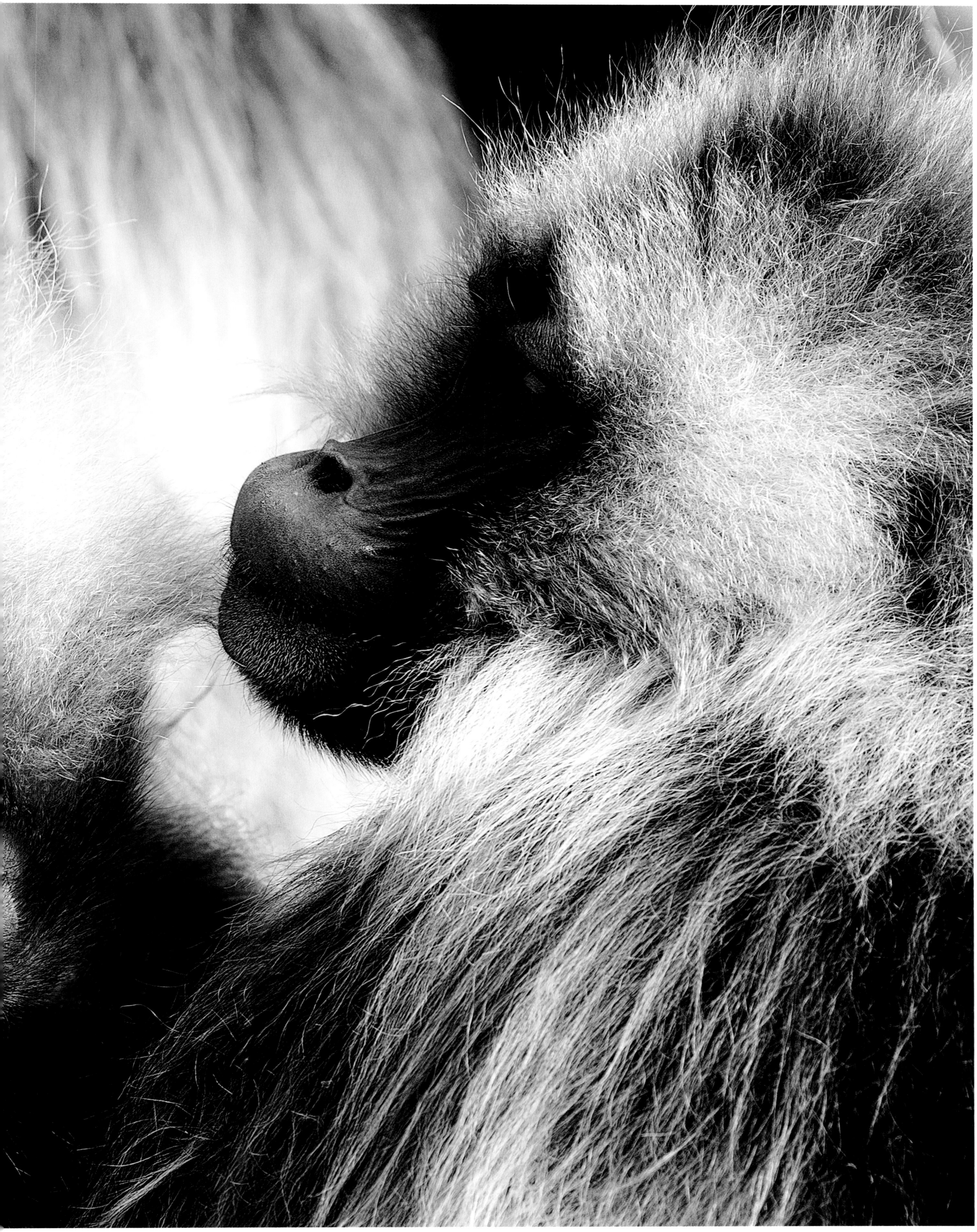

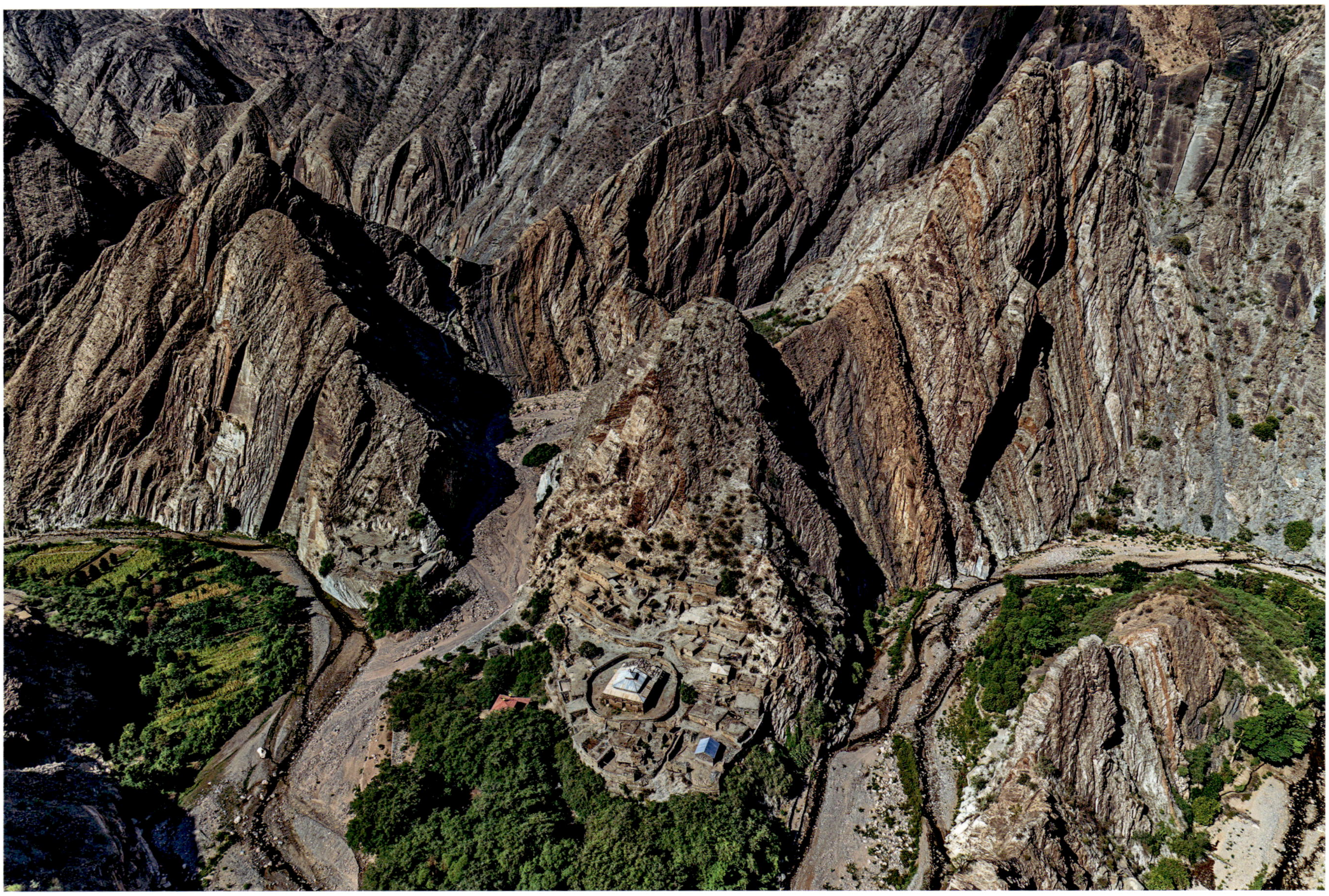

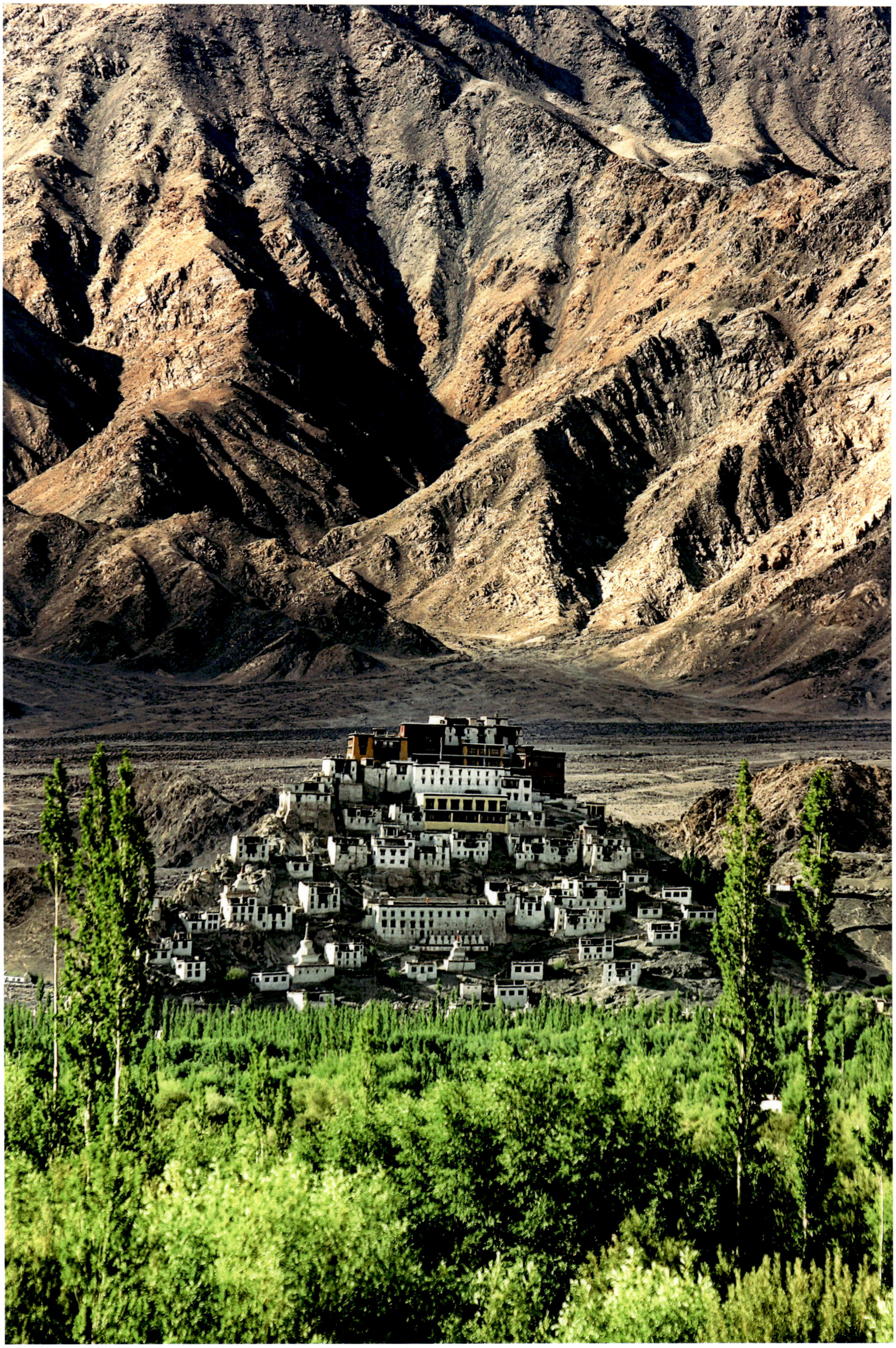

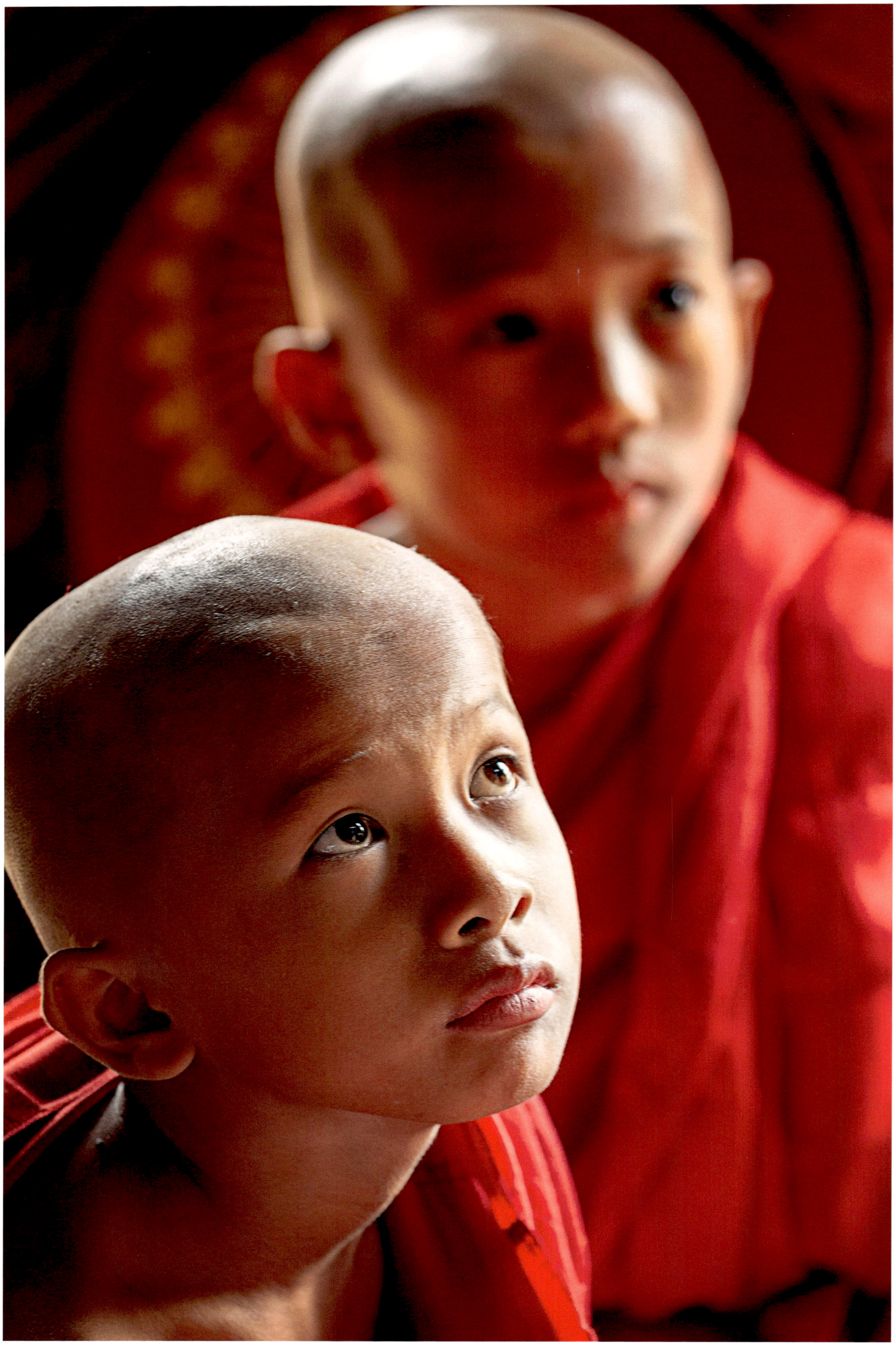

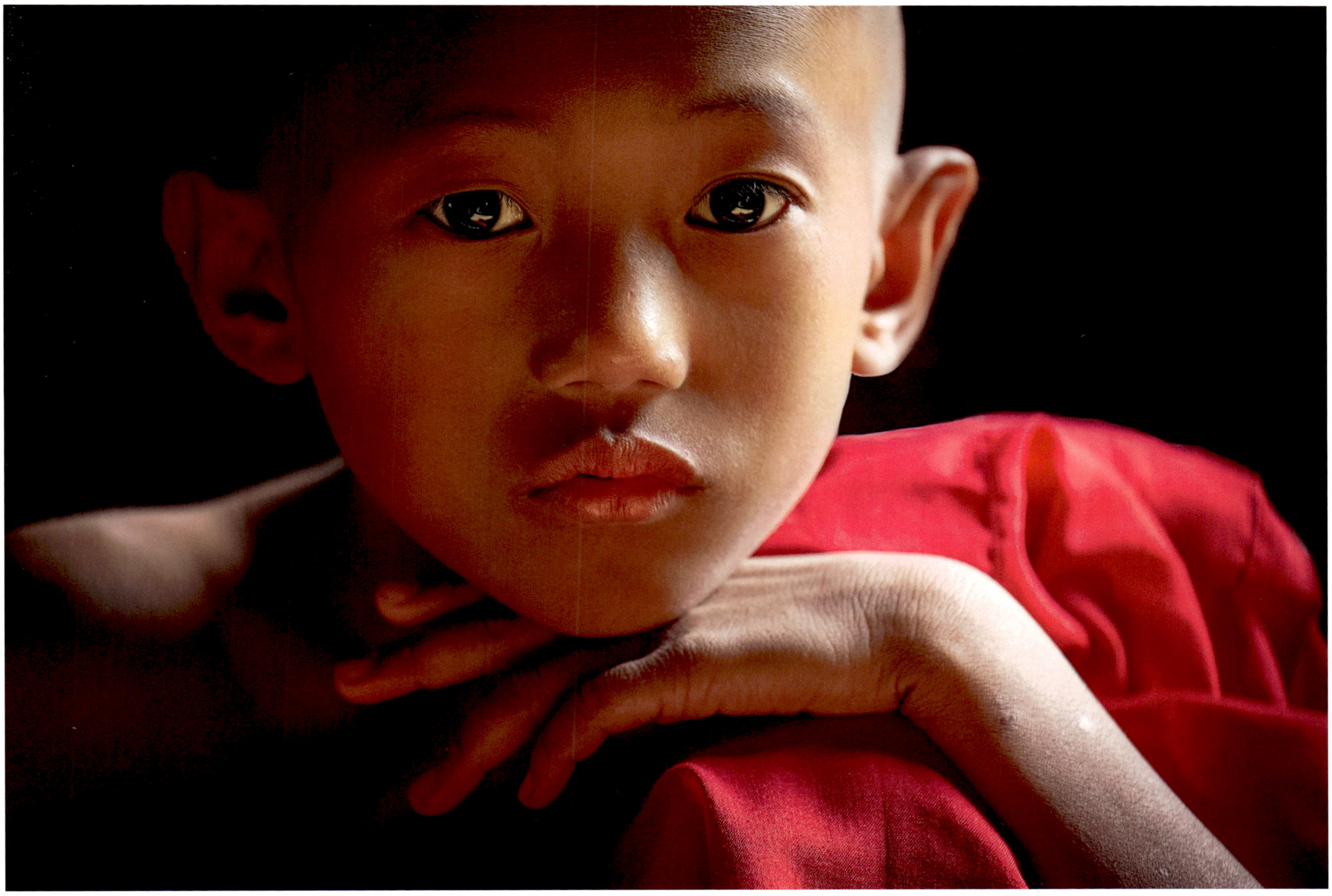

Look at a tree, a flower, a plant. Let your awareness rest upon it. How still they are, how deeply rooted in being. Allow nature to teach you stillness.

— *Eckhardt Tolle*

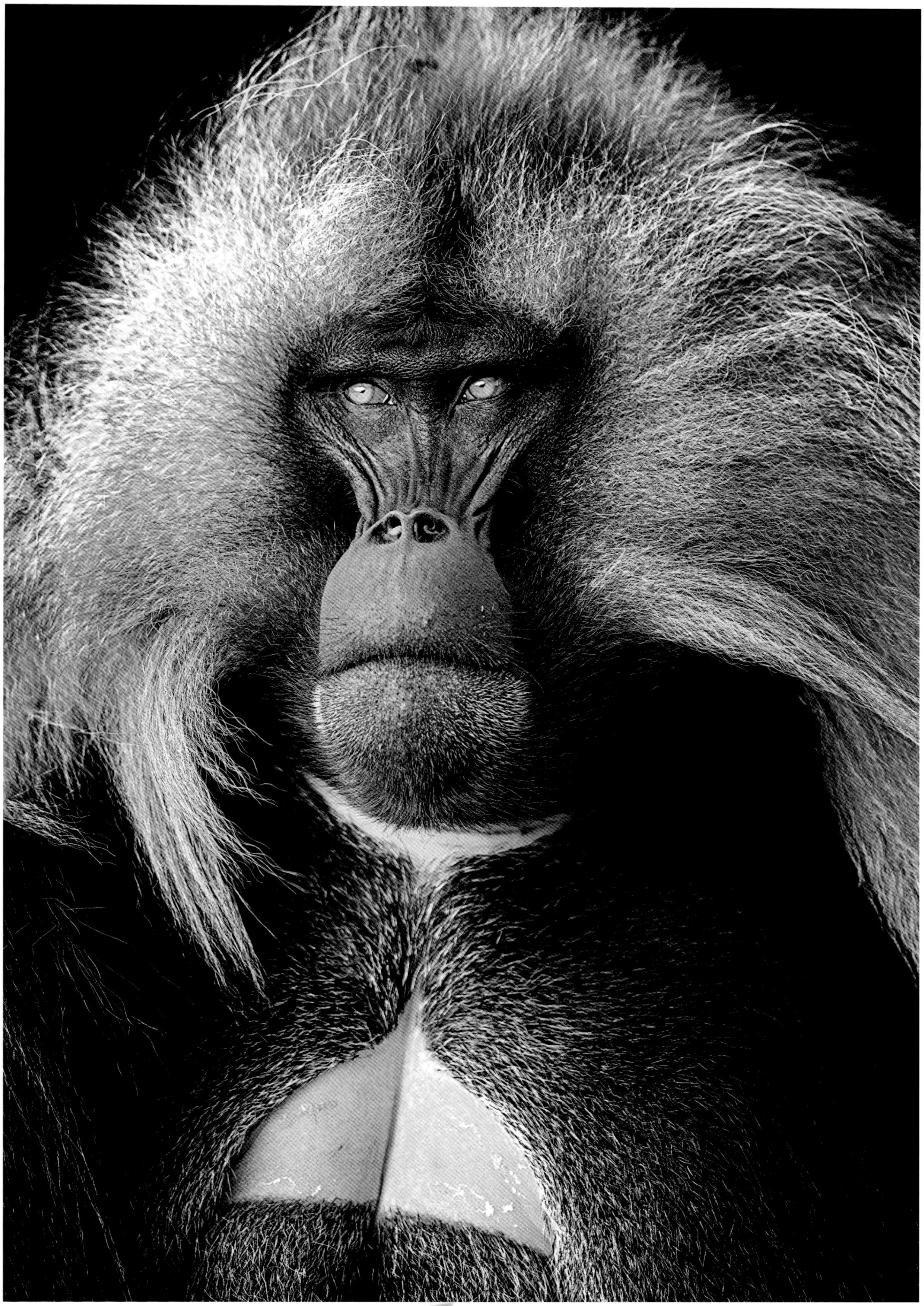

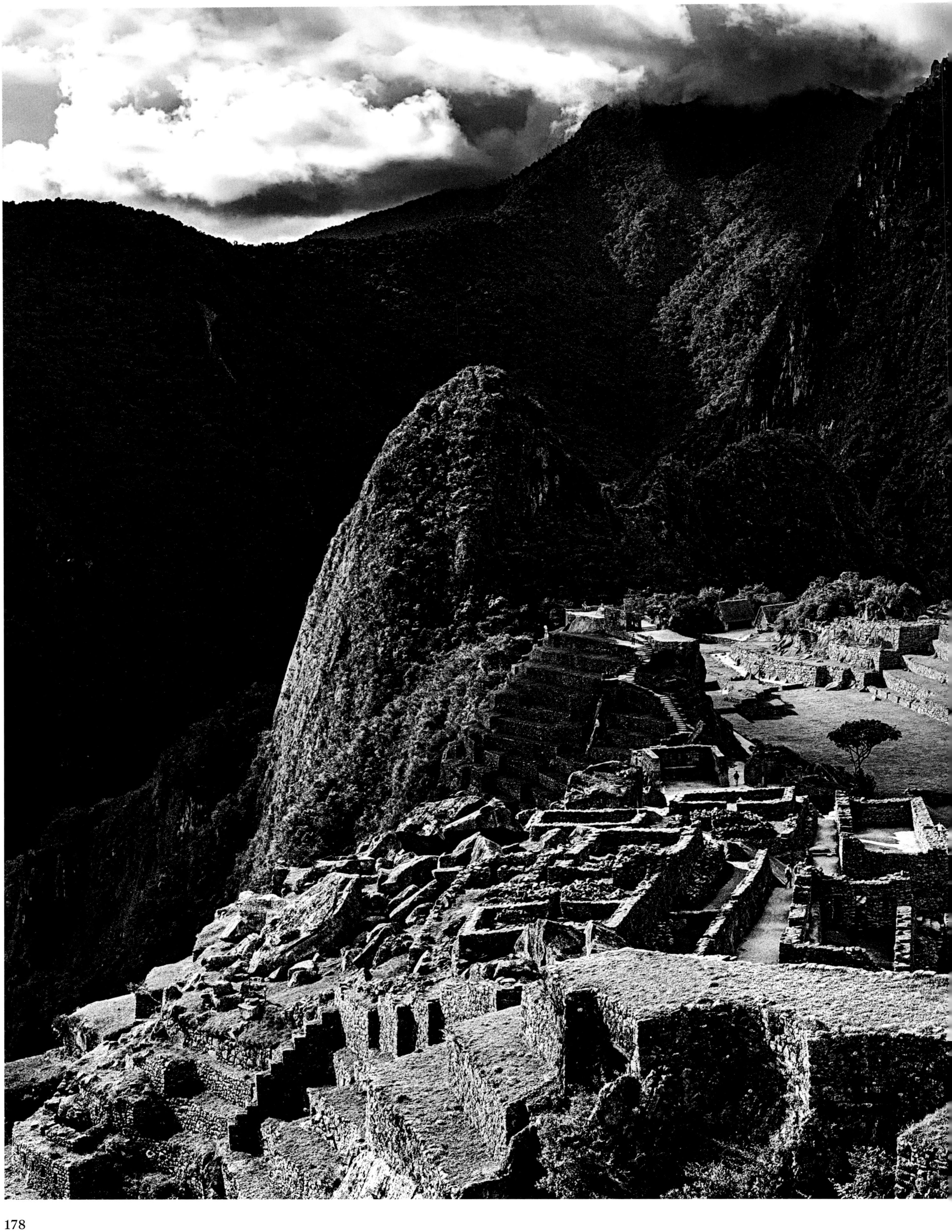

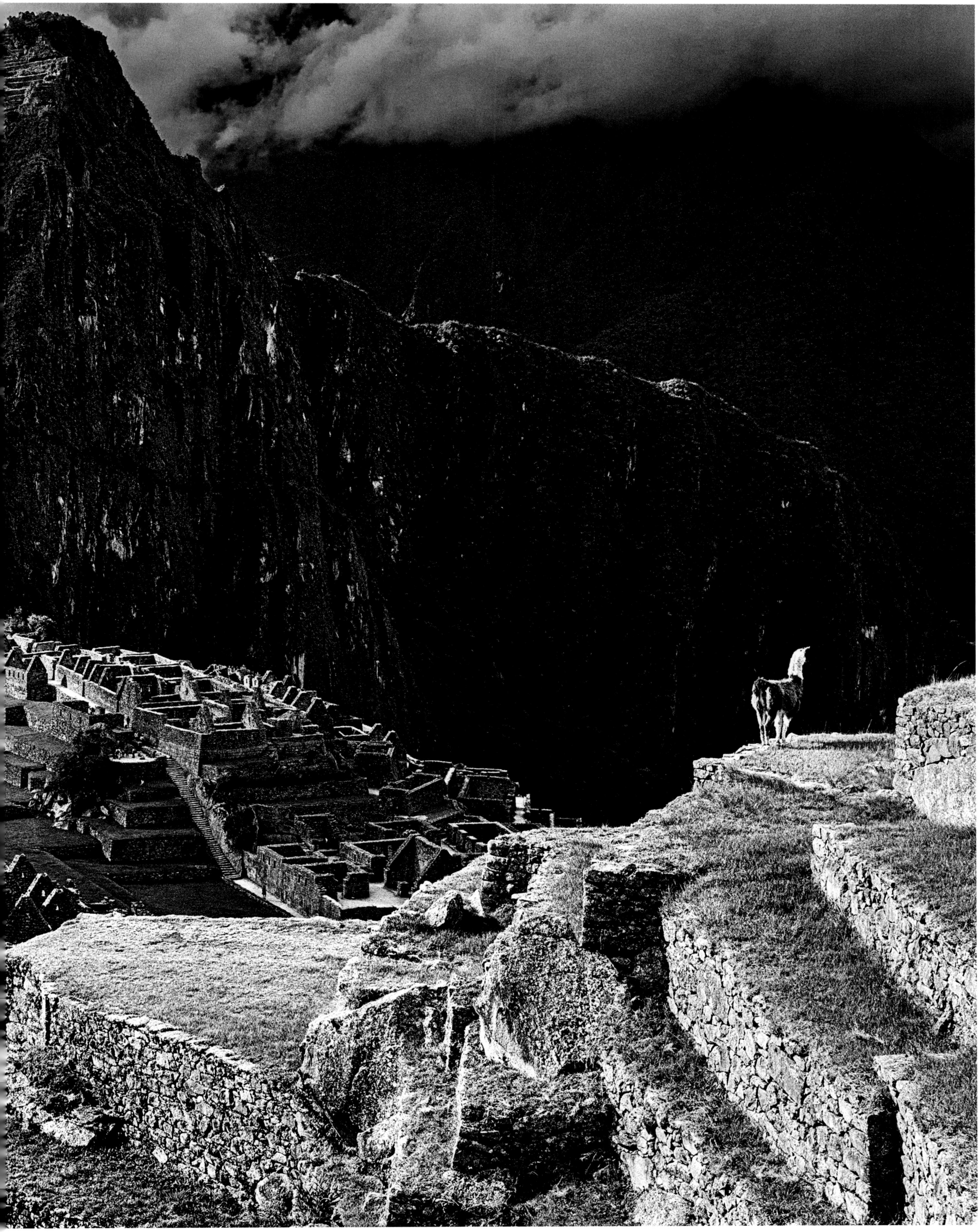

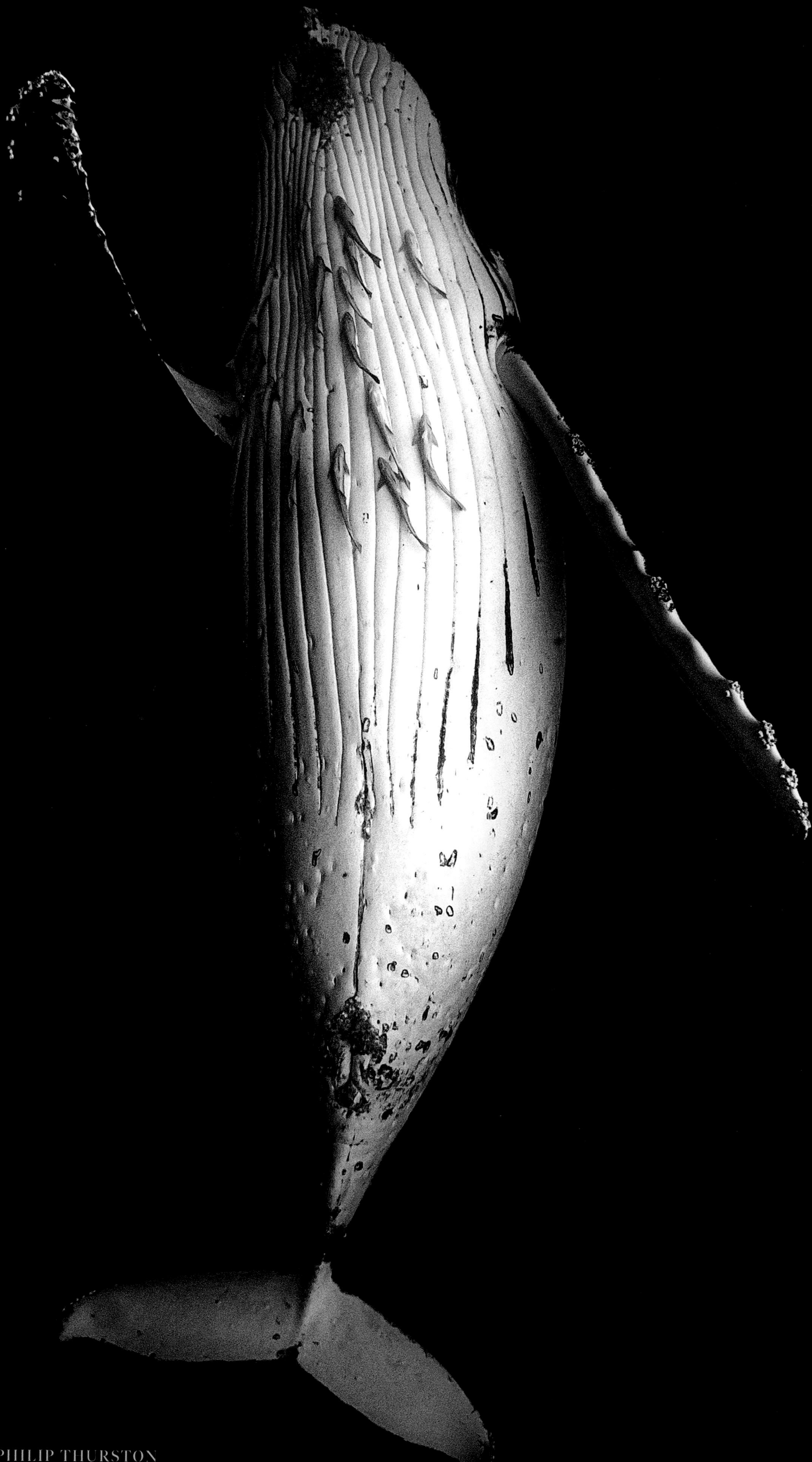

PHOTO CREDIT: PHILIP THURSTON

Chapter Five

BLUE PLANET

To stand at the edge of the sea, to sense the ebb and flow of the tides, to feel the breath of a mist moving over a great salt marsh, to watch the flight of shore birds that have swept up and down the surf lines of the continents for untold thousands of years, to see the running of the old eels and the young shad to the sea, is to have knowledge of things that are as nearly eternal as any earthly life can be.

— Rachel Carson

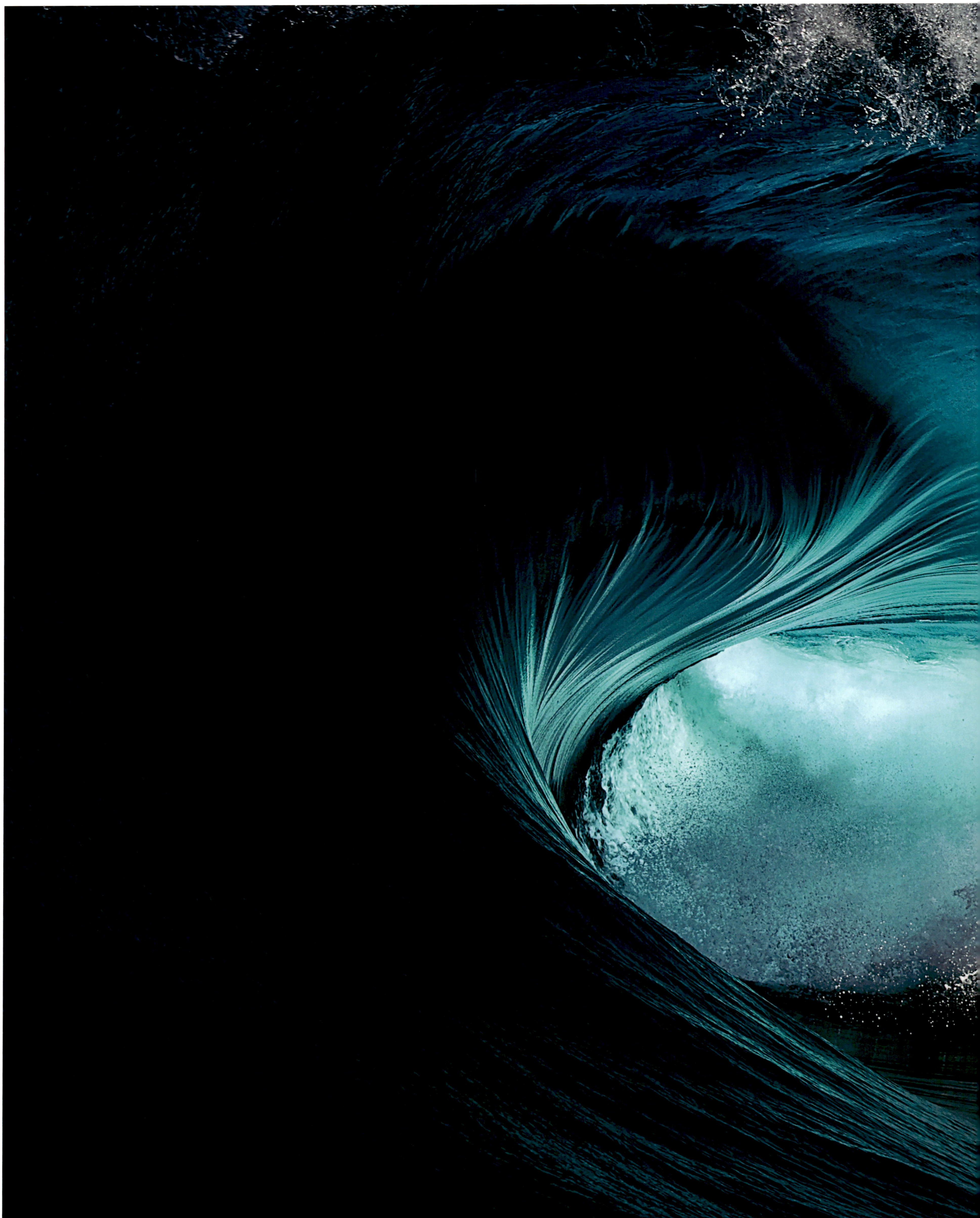

 PHOTO CREDIT: PHILIP THURSTON

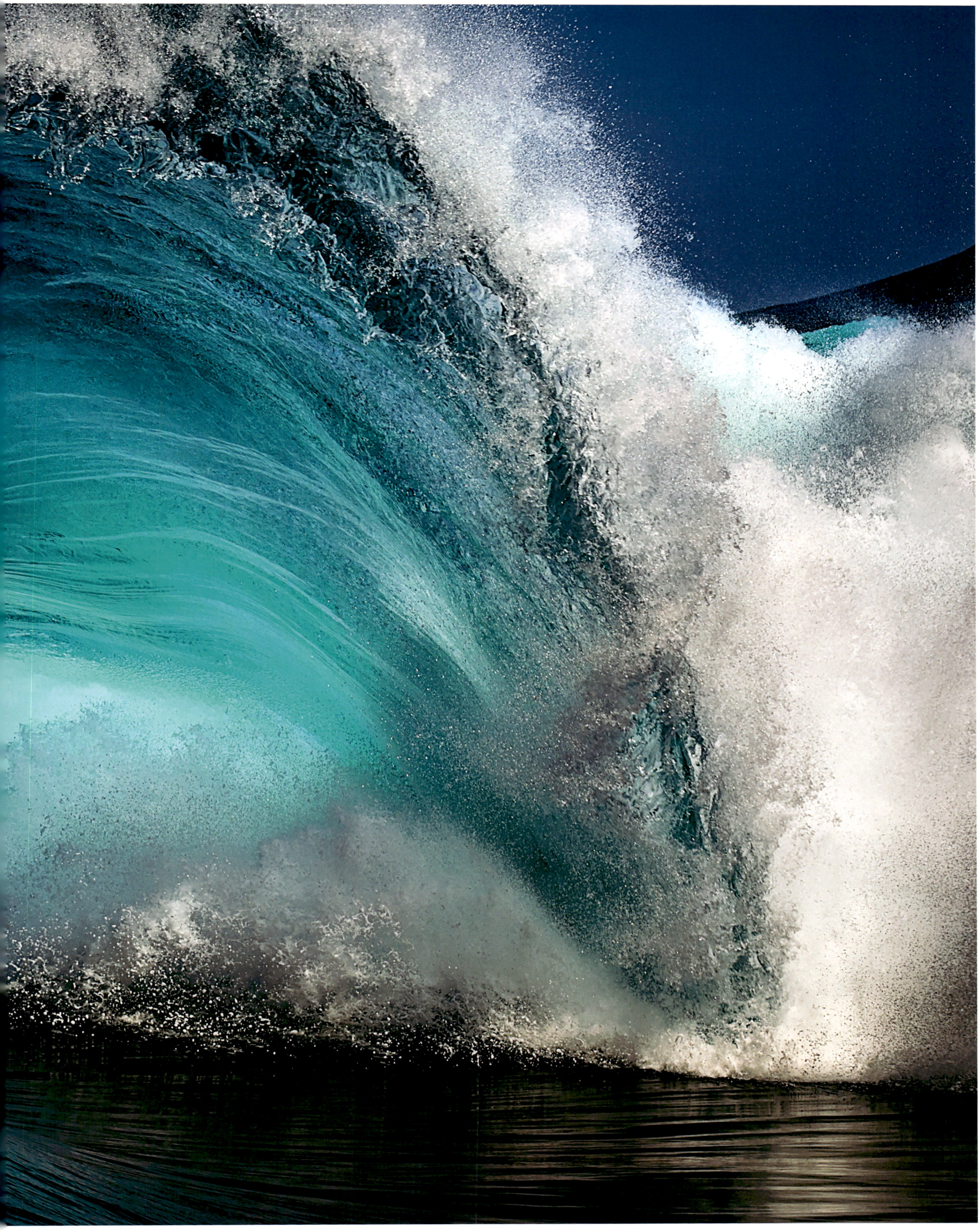

05

Water

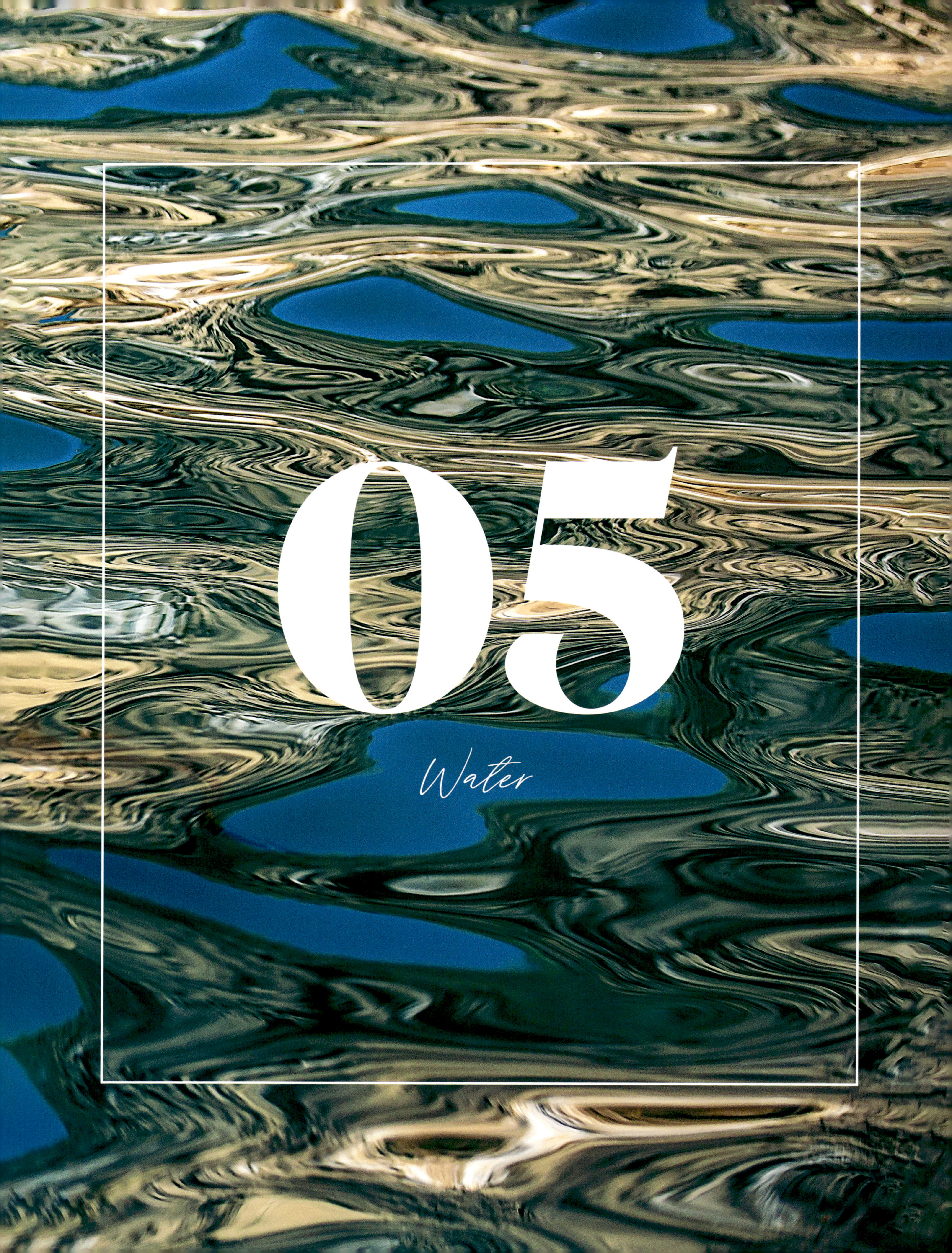

Water thrills the senses with a thousand faces. The thunderous roar of a waterfall writ large, the miracle of snowflakes falling softly on a carpet of white or cobwebs sparkling with droplets of dew as radiant as diamonds in sunlight. The raw power of water has the ability to provoke fear and terror as easily as it can induce a sense of calm and wonder. For thousands of years water has been used to communicate the sacred value of life across human cultures, symbolising purification, protection and healing. It comprises 70 per cent of our bodies, forms the matrix of our cells, lubricates our joints, regulates our body temperature and flushes waste products from our system. We are bathed in it before birth, we drink it when thirsty, wash in it to clean and refresh our bodies and minds. Without water we would die within days.

On the planetary scale, water is vital to maintaining the composition of our atmosphere, cycling moisture through evaporation from oceans and lakes that nourishes the cloud-filled skies, then replenishes those same oceans and lakes with rainfall. Planet Earth is far enough from the sun for it not to lose its water to the runaway greenhouse effect, yet close enough for low temperatures not to cause all the water to freeze as ice. By moving heat from the equator towards the poles, ocean currents play an important role in controlling the climate and are vital to sea life. They carry nutrients and food to organisms that live permanently attached to one place, and carry reproductive cells and ocean life to new locations.

Where did this miraculous solvent come from? New research suggests that Earth's water came both from rocky material, such as an asteroid bombardment in the days of the early solar system, and from the solar nebula, the vast cloud of dust and gas remaining after the sun's formation. Some 70 per cent of our blue planet is covered with water, with the oceans holding almost all of it. Only 2.5 per cent of it is fresh water and, of that, just 1.2 per cent is surface water. Though the grandeur of our rivers, lakes, icecaps and glaciers catches the eye, 97 per cent of the planet's liquid fresh water is buried beneath the ground in sponge-like aquifers, the primary source of drinking water for more than 1.5 billion people worldwide.

In an ever more thirsty world, the warning signs of our impact on weather systems are staring us in the face: hurricanes and tsunamis wreak devastation on human settlement, while melting glaciers and rising tides are further indications of our destructive impact on the planet. Of all the Earth's ecosystems, those composed of fresh water have suffered most from human activities – farming and industry, water extraction and pollution, over-harvesting of species and the introduction of invasives, along with climate change. More than 20 per cent of the 10,000 known fresh-water fish species have become extinct or imperilled in recent decades.

Angie is a child of the ocean. Little wonder. She was born in the coastal city of Alexandria in Egypt, and spent her childhood in Dar es Salaam in Tanzania, where boats, water-skiing and photography were her passions. She loves nothing more than to explore the coral reefs, to wander barefoot along the sandy places with the surf massaging her feet. Africa's warm seas and rich wildlife, diving the deep and exploring savanna landscapes, have defined her life. Yet, vast and unspoilt as the deep blue might seem, humankind's careless and extravagant ways are imprinted throughout its watery void, with a tide of plastic bottles and refuse as common as seaweed. Even more insidious is the devastation at a microscopic level, with man-made waste embedded in the heart of organic life and in its cells.

Angie's love of the sea has taken us round the world, from the enchanted Galapagos islands that inspired Charles Darwin's theory of evolution to the world's second largest island country of Madagascar with its endemic lemurs and chameleons. More recently, we visited Sri Lanka – the pearl of the Indian Ocean – with its mix of stunning wildlife viewing (leopards, elephants and blue whales) and 6,000 Buddhist monasteries. We sailed the southern archipelago of Myanmar with Robinson Crusoe moments, such as kayaking to a deserted coral beach where spectacular giant hornbills glided between the tree tops. There were wild-cat pug marks visible in the sand and not a trace of a human footprint to spoil our reverie, though the flotsam of plastic bottles and other non-biodegradable litter fringed the vegetation. The lights of fishing boats twinkled all around at night as they voraciously plied the waters for fish and squid. We have snorkelled the waters of the Red Sea at Hurghada in Egypt and explored the island of Mauritius, once the home of the dodo (*Raphus cucullatus*), an odd-looking flightless bird standing a metre high and weighing up to 20 kilograms. First discovered by Dutch sailors in 1598, within a hundred years it had gone.

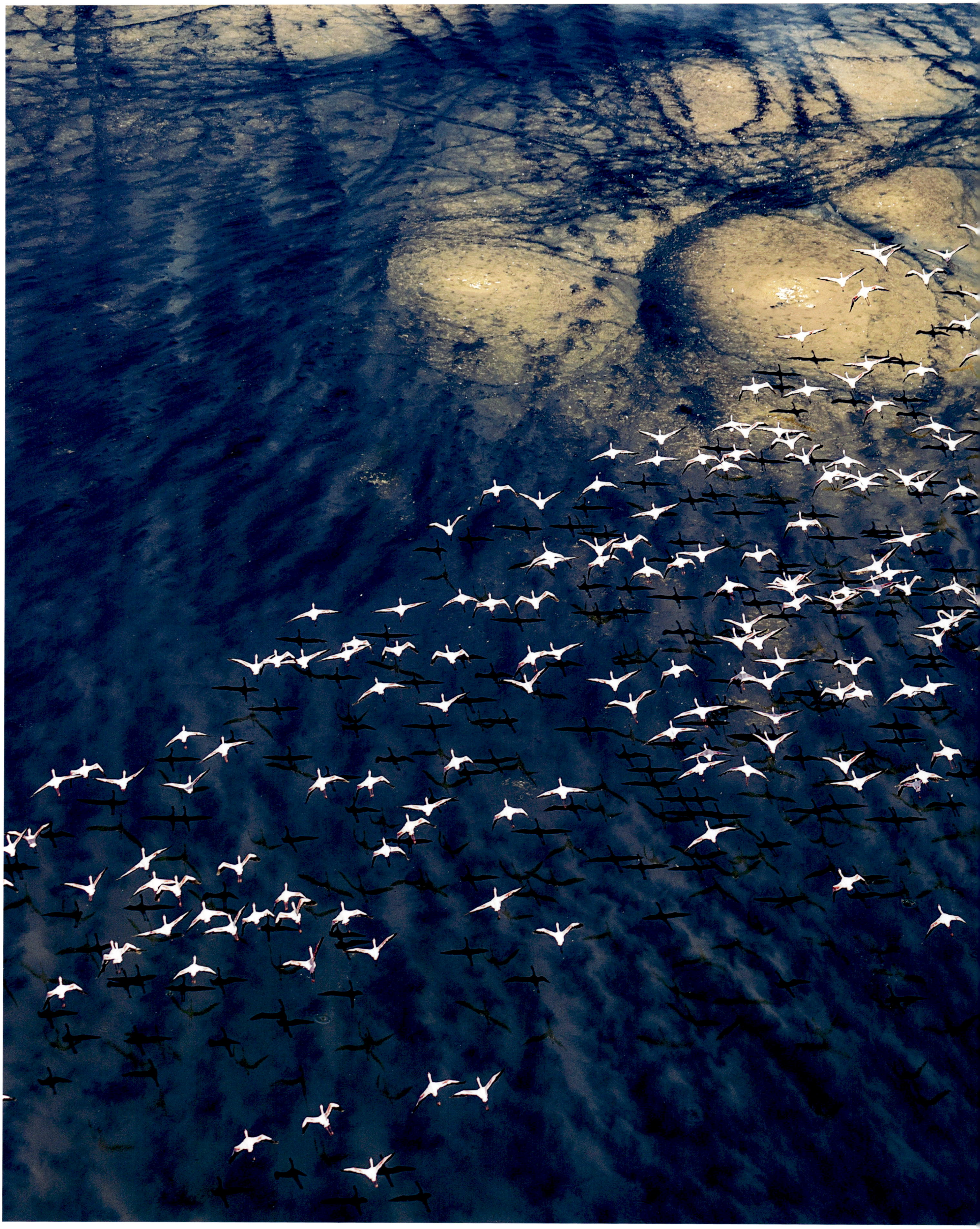

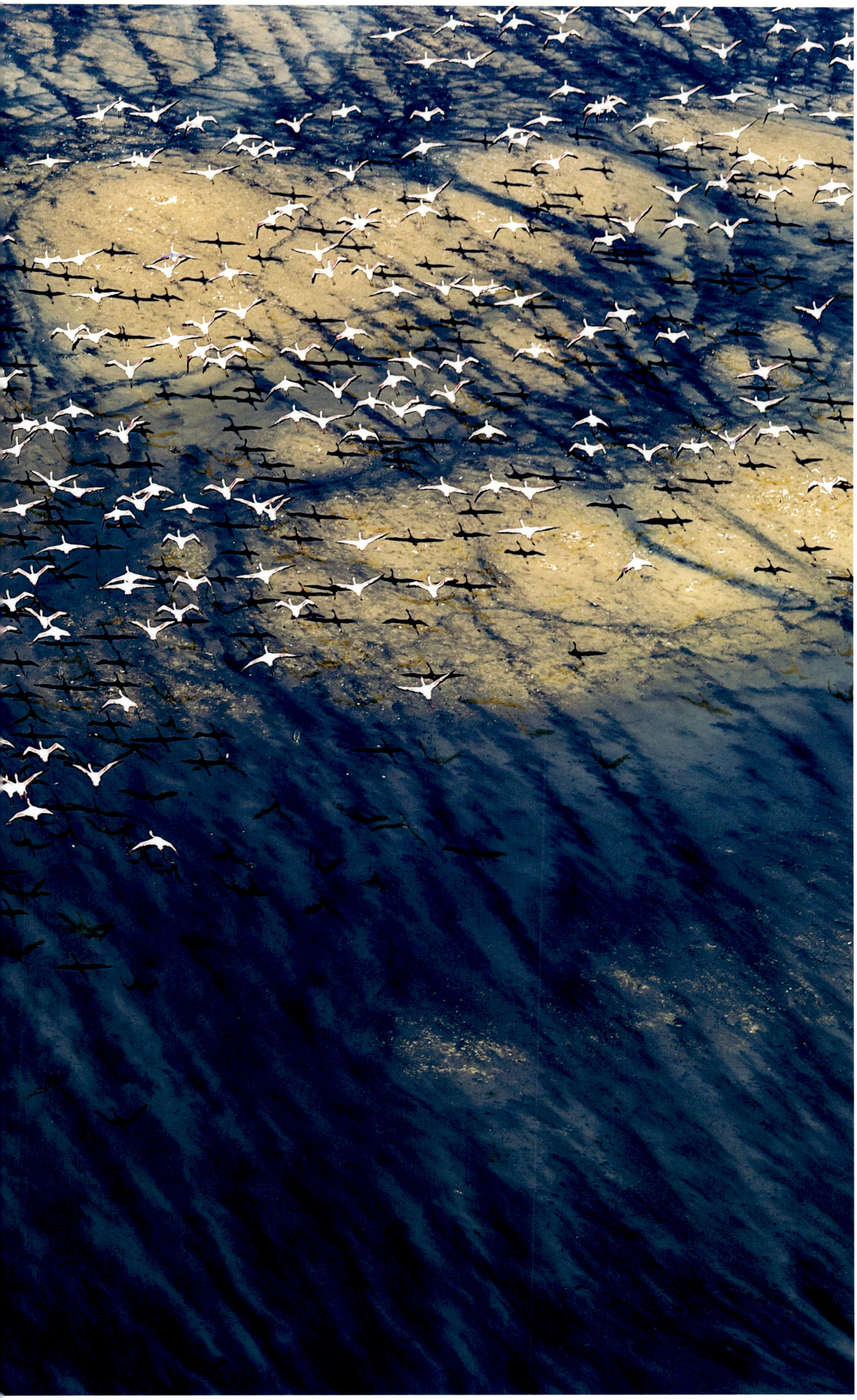

The entrancing beauty and allure of islands and oceans continue to flood our thoughts. Close to home, Diani Beach on the Kenya coast has the bluest water and whitest beaches we had ever set eyes on, until we visited the island nation of the Maldives. Immersing yourself in the Maldives' oceans soothes away the chattering voices stirred up a storm of sand that attracted an audience of fishes. Nearby, an octopus sought refuge in a sinkhole in the coral, morphing from pink to speckled browns and white, while a moray eel as thick as a man's arm swirled sinuously through the labyrinth of crevices among the coral heads.

Suddenly its just you and the fishes and a deeply relaxing silence, your breathing creating a rhythm as soothing as the sound of a child's heartbeat

of urban living, the incessant hum of cars and trains, the endless throbbing music. Suddenly it's just you and the fishes and a deeply relaxing silence, your breathing creating a rhythm as soothing as the sound of a child's heartbeat, reminding you of the miracle of your own existence. Every shade of pastel was spread before our eyes: lilacs and purples, the softest pinks and mustard yellows, the coral carved into patterns as varied and delicate as snowflakes. Shoals of fishes danced like leaves blowing in the wind, the shafts of sunlight spotlighting their silvery armour of scales. They swirled this way and that in perfect formation, approached then drifted away again, holding us in their thrall. We could hear the rasping jaws of parrot fish as they chiselled away at the coral, all dazzling greens and blues. Pairs of angel fish glided in perfect formation as a two-metre-long stingray danced on the ocean floor, its huge eyes blinking as it

The most notable wild residents of the Maldives resort of Velassaru were the grey herons with their quirky looks and flashy head plumes. Standing nearly a metre tall but weighing in at a wispy two kilograms, they were as eye-catching as a serpent: half bird, half God, denizens of the watery places so loved by humans. The herons would dive straight into the depths, harpoon-like bills lancing forwards at almost 160 kilometres an hour to skewer one of the tiny fish that clustered in dark clouds near the shoreline. They monitored the ebb and flow of these swarms as black-tipped reef sharks patrolled the shallows, occasionally lunging with electrifying speed, mouths wide open, sending a shower of sparkling silvery bodies into the air and straight into their open bills. On our penultimate evening, we set sail in a multi-decked fishing boat with Angie eagerly accepting the chance to stand in the crow's nest for a 360-degree view of the setting sun as the waves created patterns mirroring the orange and pink of the storm-clouded sky. We had come to the Maldives to flee from the madding crowd and found a watery paradise along the way.

As an island nation with a long history of isolation, Japan has always had a reputation for a distinctive culture and unique traditions. Art and innovative design permeate every fabric of the society, from the elegant beauty of the written language to the exquisite floral and stone gardens and Buddhist and Shinto temples. In a world where discipline and order have so often been cast aside in favour of the cult of the individual and free expression, the sense of respect and politeness we discovered in Japan proved a welcome respite. Highlights were almost too numerous to describe, from tree-lined avenues and canals alive with the cherry blossom of sakura trees in March and April to snow monkeys bathing in the hot springs at Yudanaka Onsen. To wander through a bamboo forest was a thing of wonder, the beauty of the grey bark and lush green leaves creating a symmetry that finds a natural expression on trellises and partitions in people's dwellings. We savoured a traditional tea ceremony in Nikko before meeting with a Zen master at the Kodaiji Gesshin-in Temple for an introduction to traditional Zazen meditation. The chief priest challenged us to contemplate the world without using language to describe it, an all-embracing wisdom radiating from his moon face, bathing the meditation room with a sense of calm and reverence. To live in the moment, to accept life as it is, to understand that nothing – our life, our thoughts – is permanent, believing that there is always room for change: these are universal truths that transcend religion.

In 2018 we were invited to join our great friend and fellow photographer Griet van Malderen on her quest to photograph humpback whales during the calving season in Tonga. On our first day on the ocean we had an encounter with a mother and her two-week-old calf that will live with us forever. Later, overcome with emotion, Angie described her feelings as the dark shape of the leviathan rose unwaveringly towards her, spot-lit by a shaft of light – so huge, so gentle, so quiet. She remained motionless, transfixed with amazement, revelling in the heart-stopping experience of being within touching distance of such a creature. She was entranced by the texture of the whale's barnacled head and radiant white throat pleats, exalting as the whale looked at her with its liquid all-knowing eye. Then with a massive exhalation of air and spume it melted back into the blue with its calf. Although humans are unable to communicate verbally with other life, there was no doubting the sense of wonder we all felt in the startling blue waters of the South Pacific. Griet's photograph of Angie and the whales illuminates perfectly a kinder, more considerate and loving relationship between humans and their wild relatives. It was a moment of deep connection, a sense of an ultimate reality that passeth all understanding.

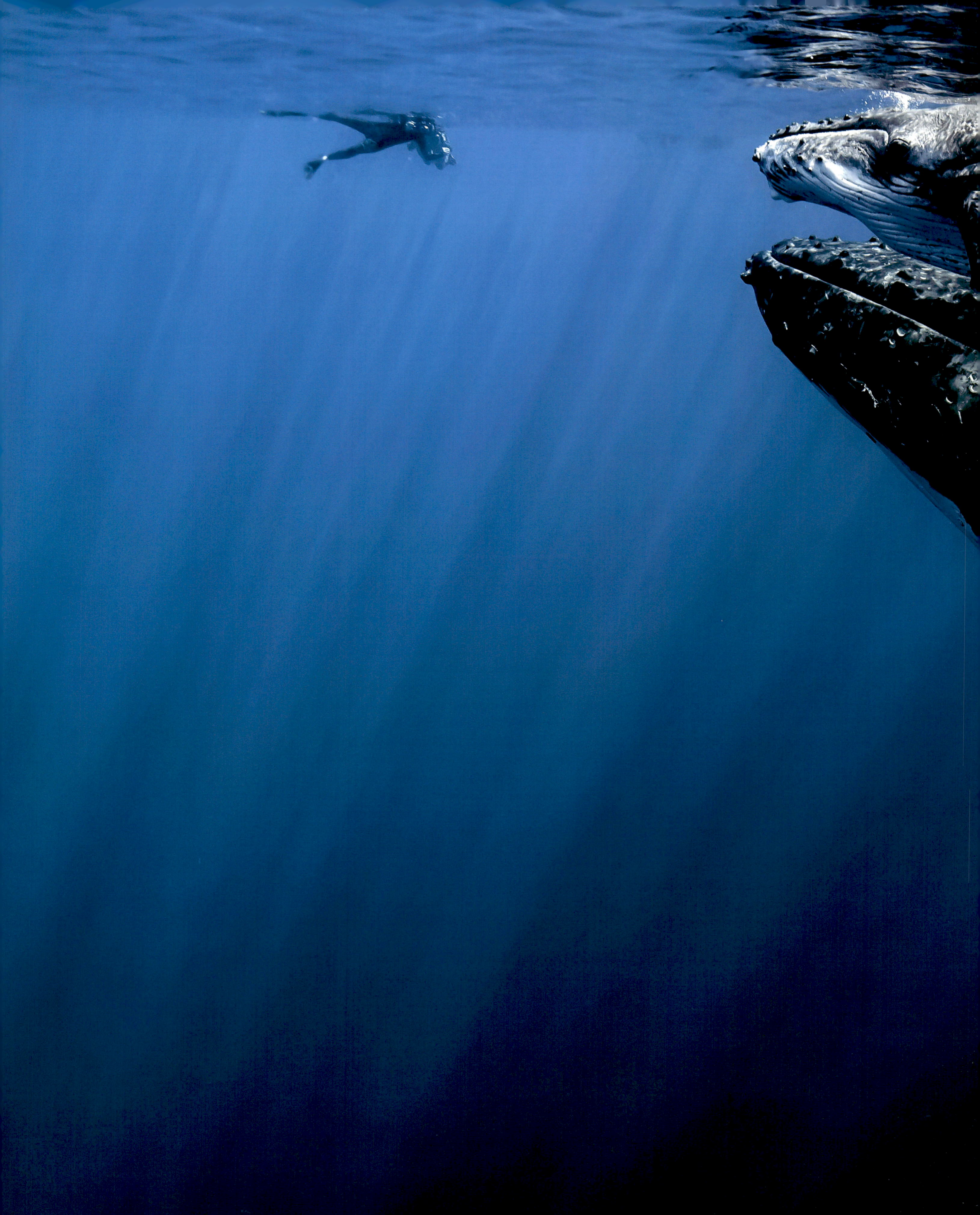

PHOTO CREDIT: GRIET VAN MALDEREN

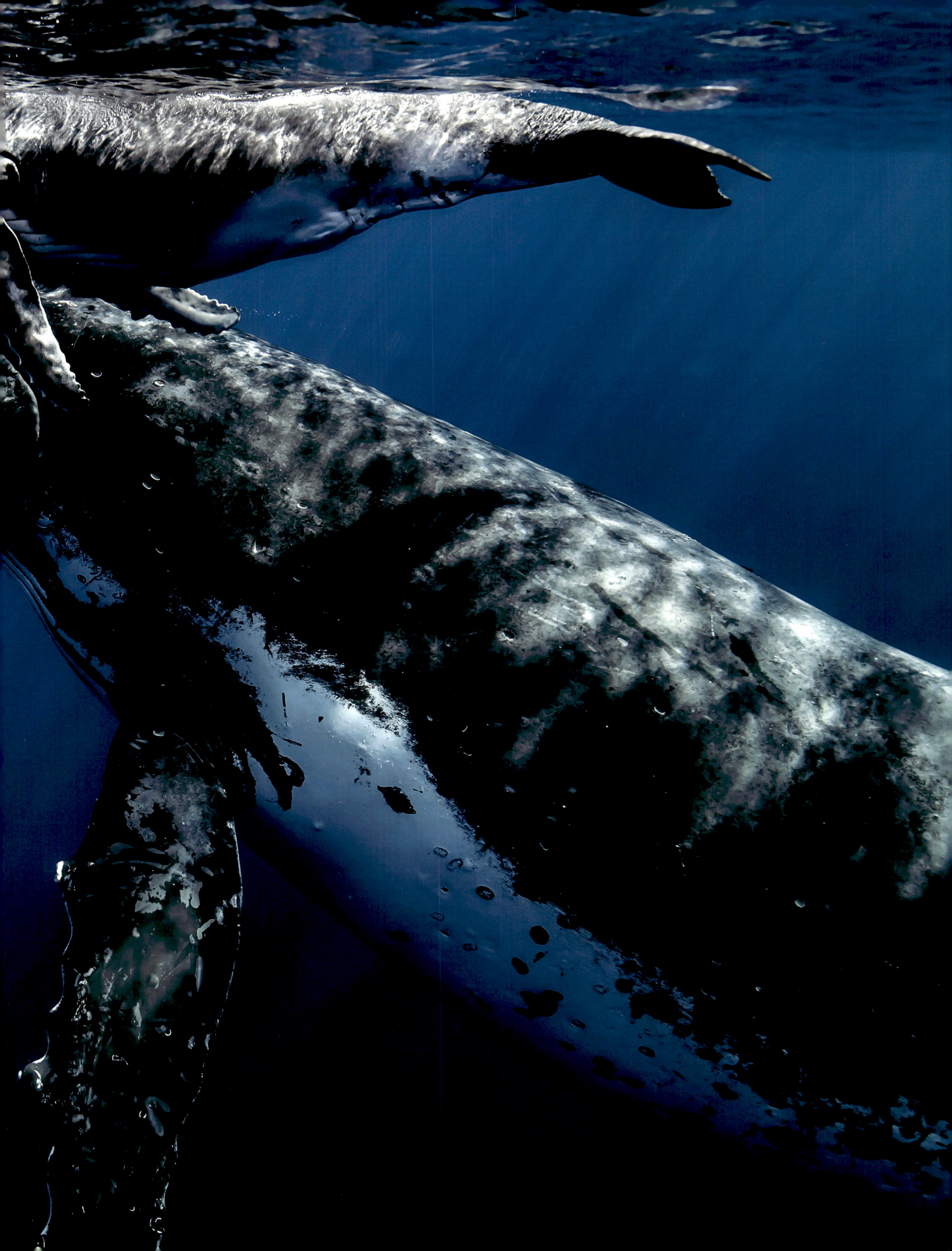

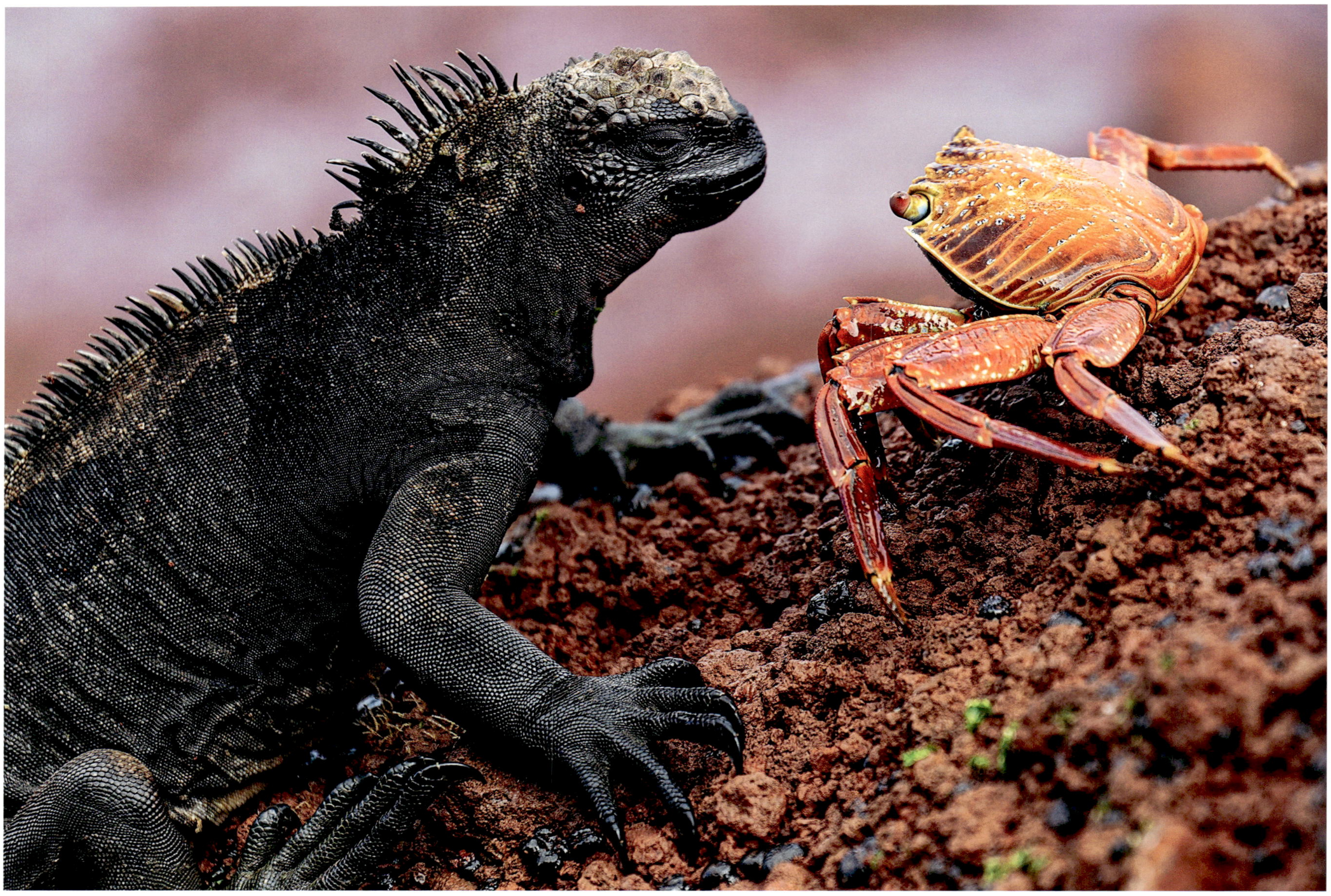

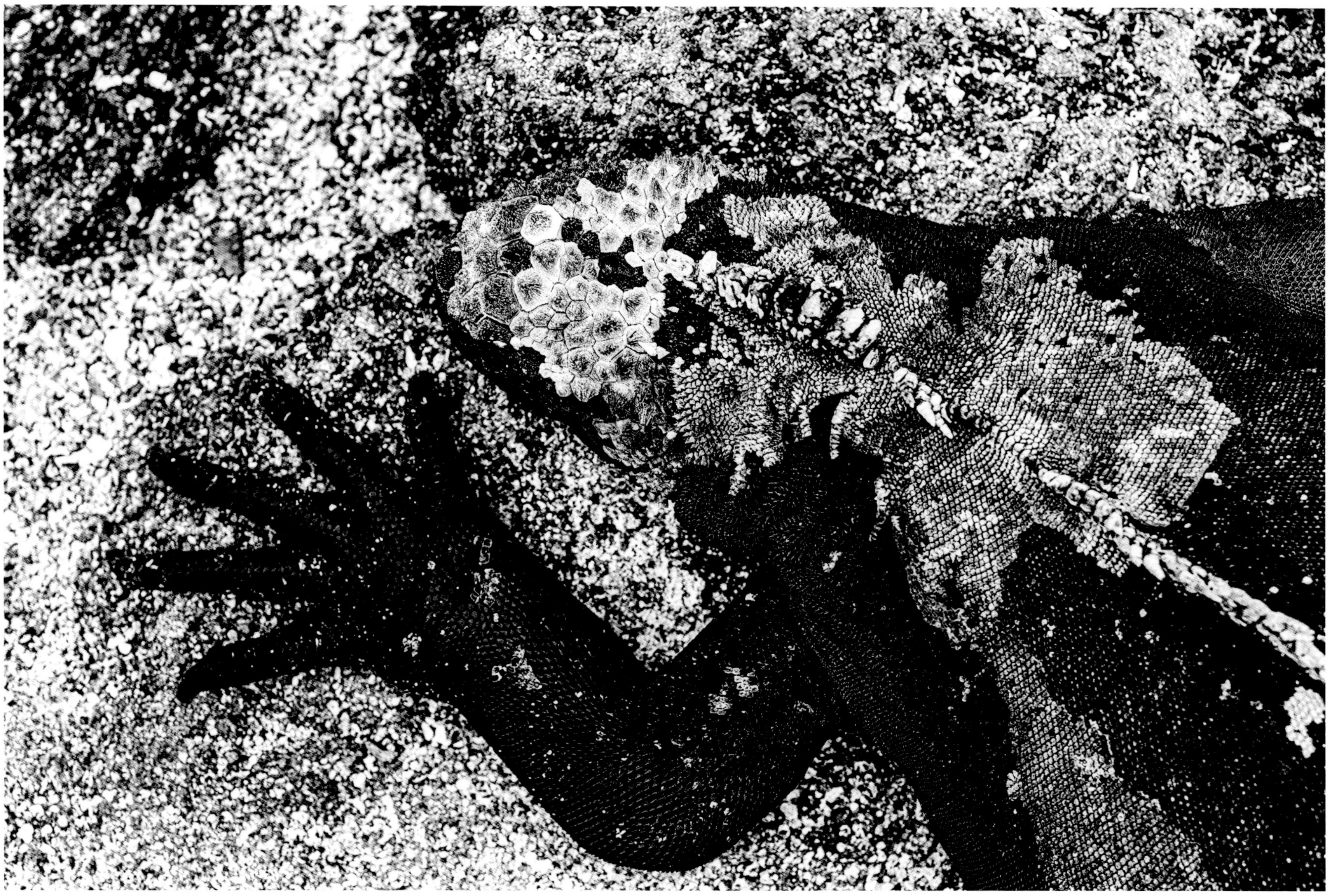

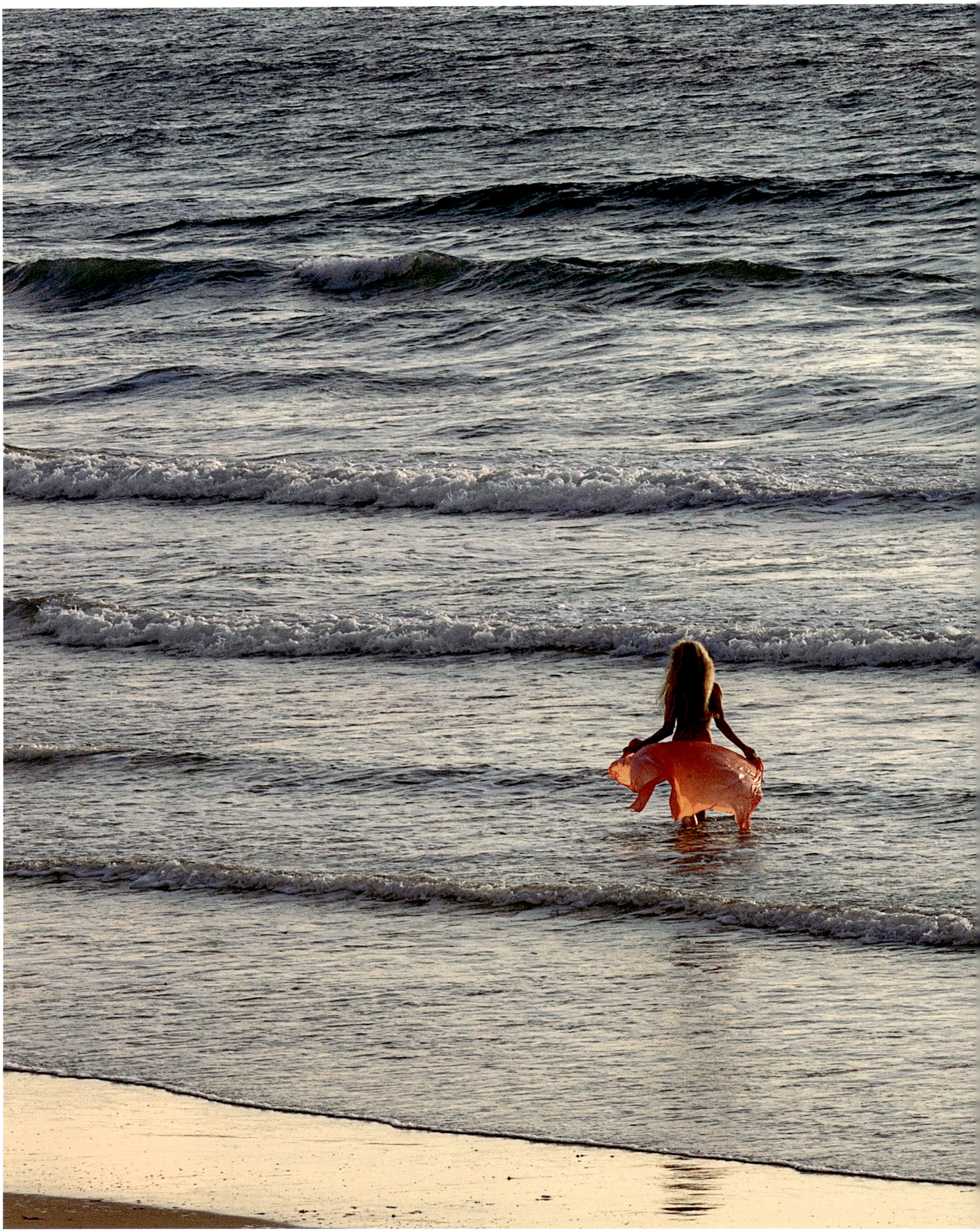

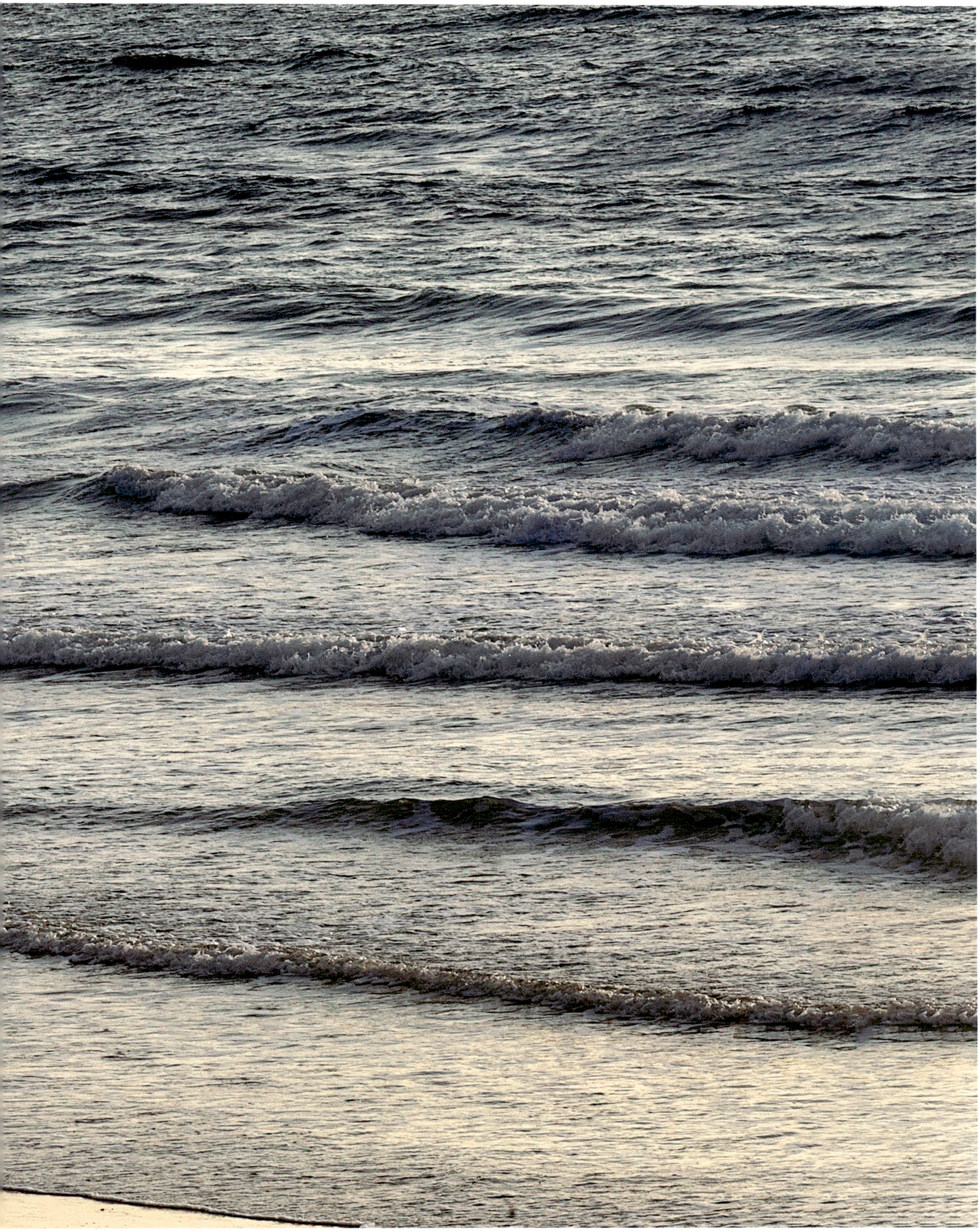

The least movement is of importance to all nature. The entire ocean is affected by a pebble.

— Blaise Pascal

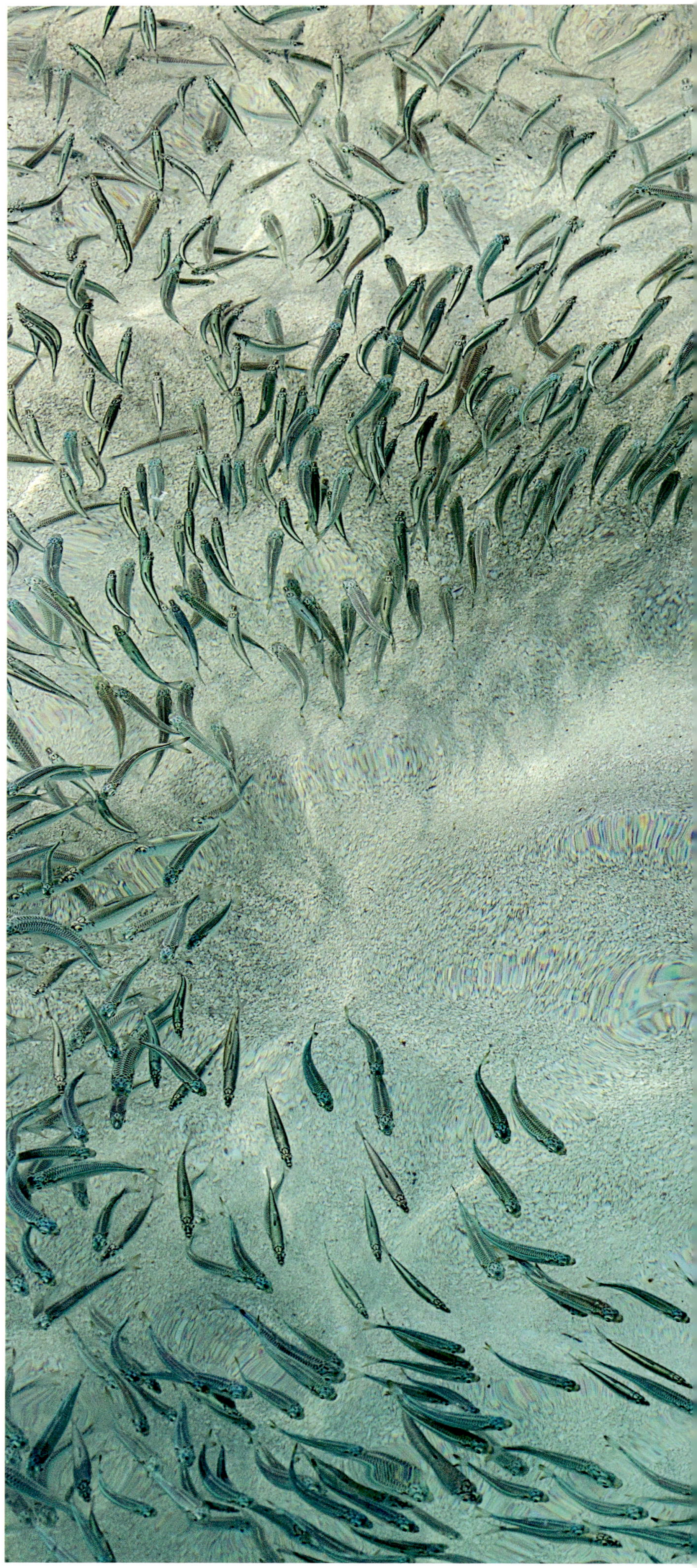

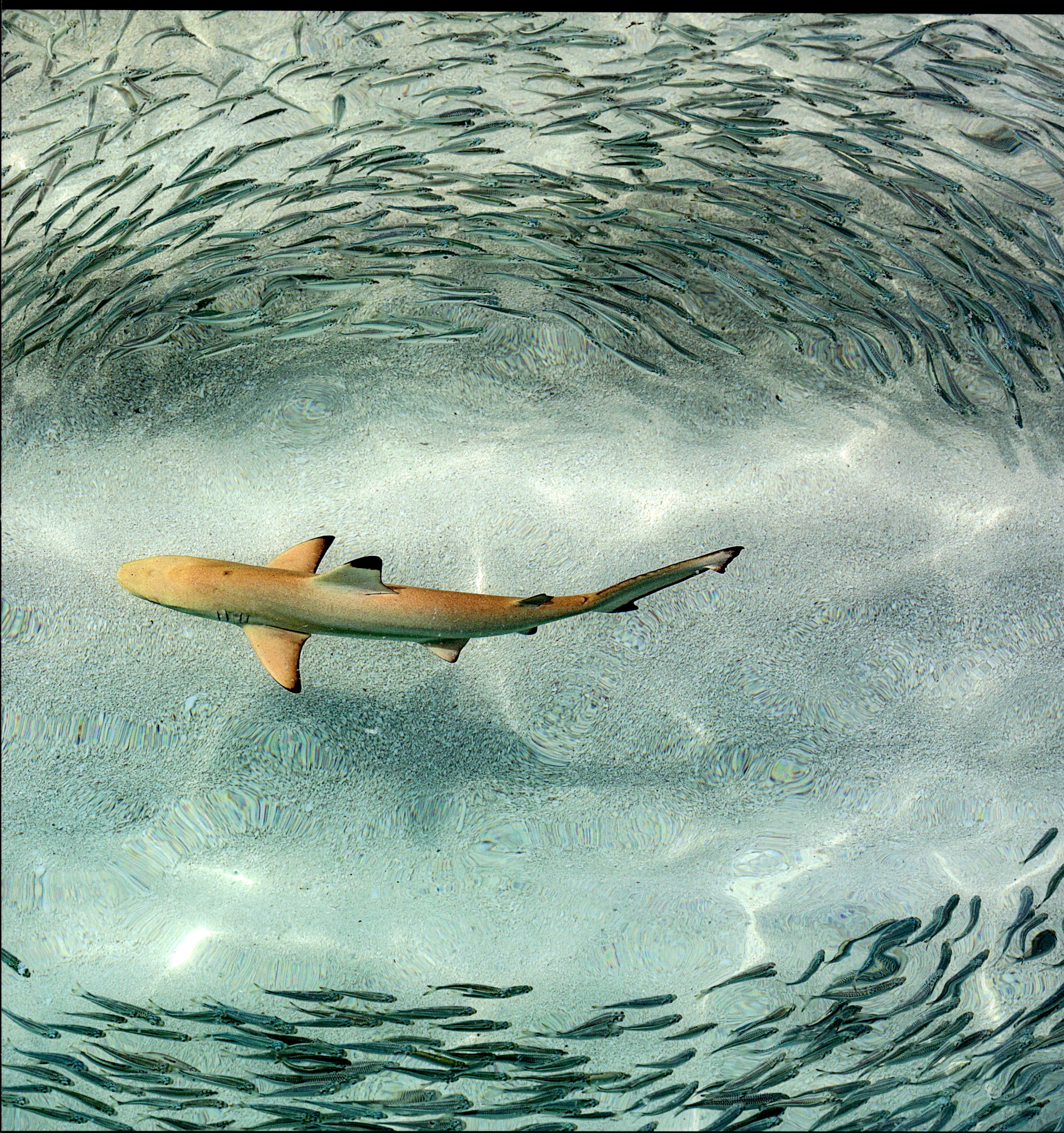

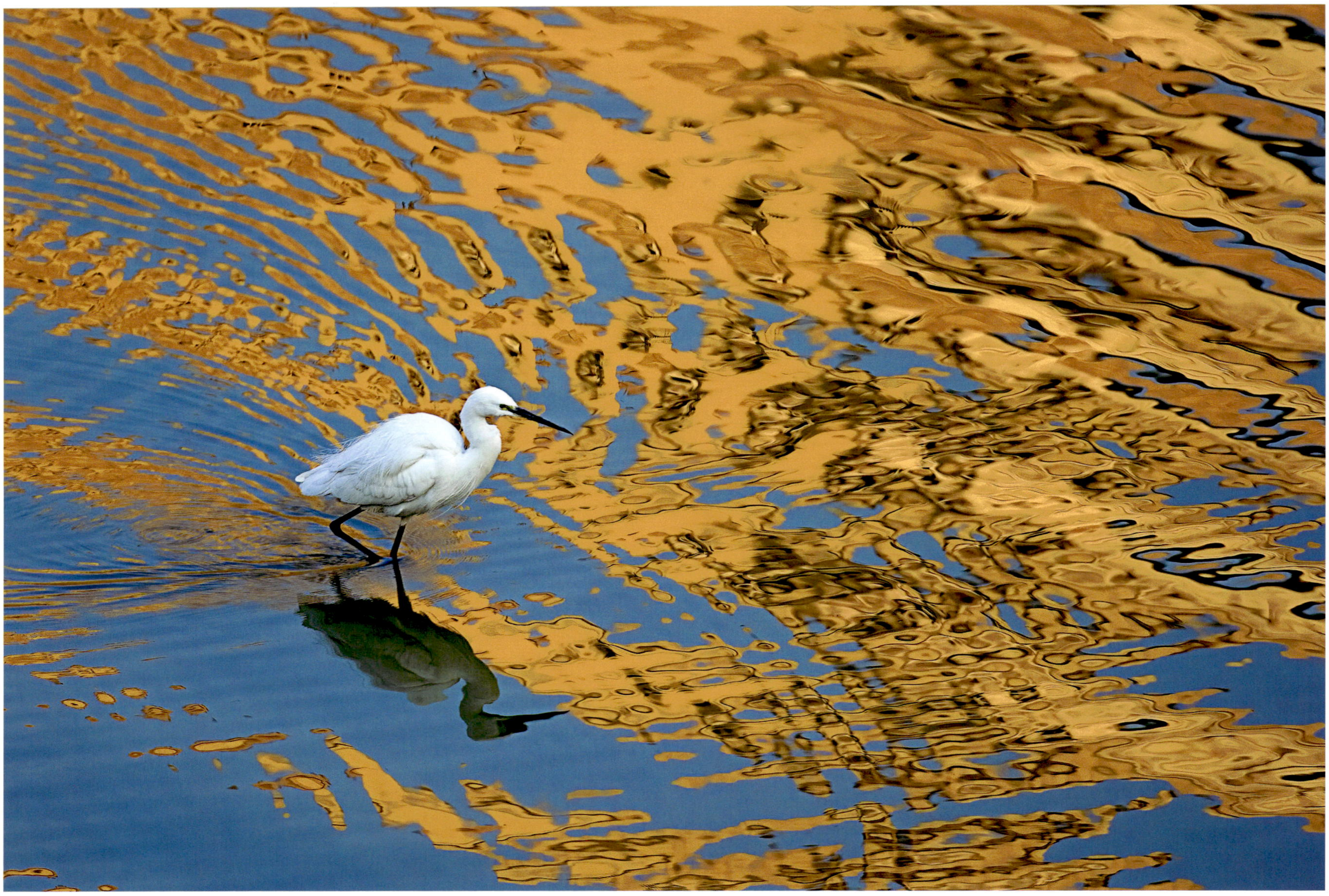

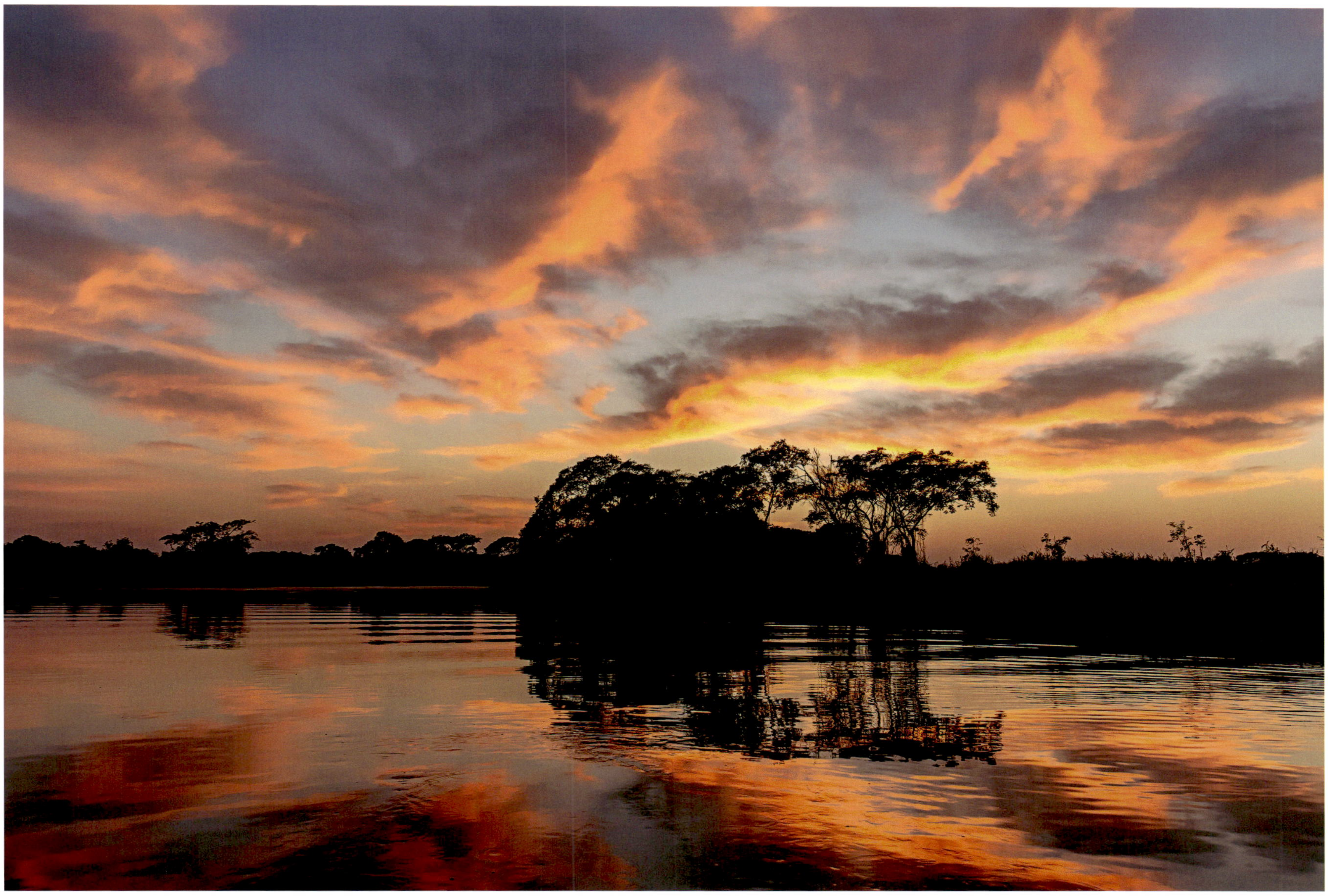

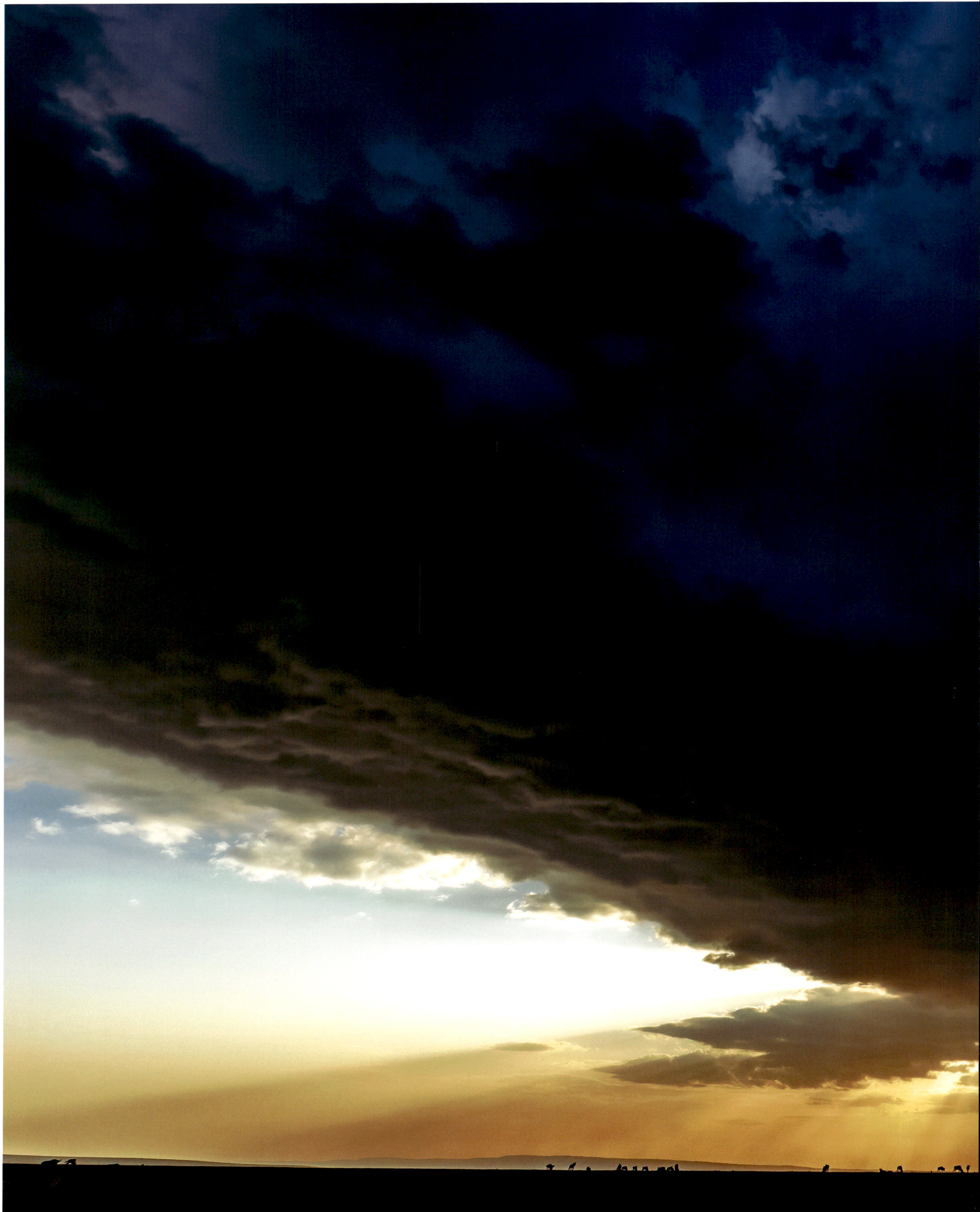

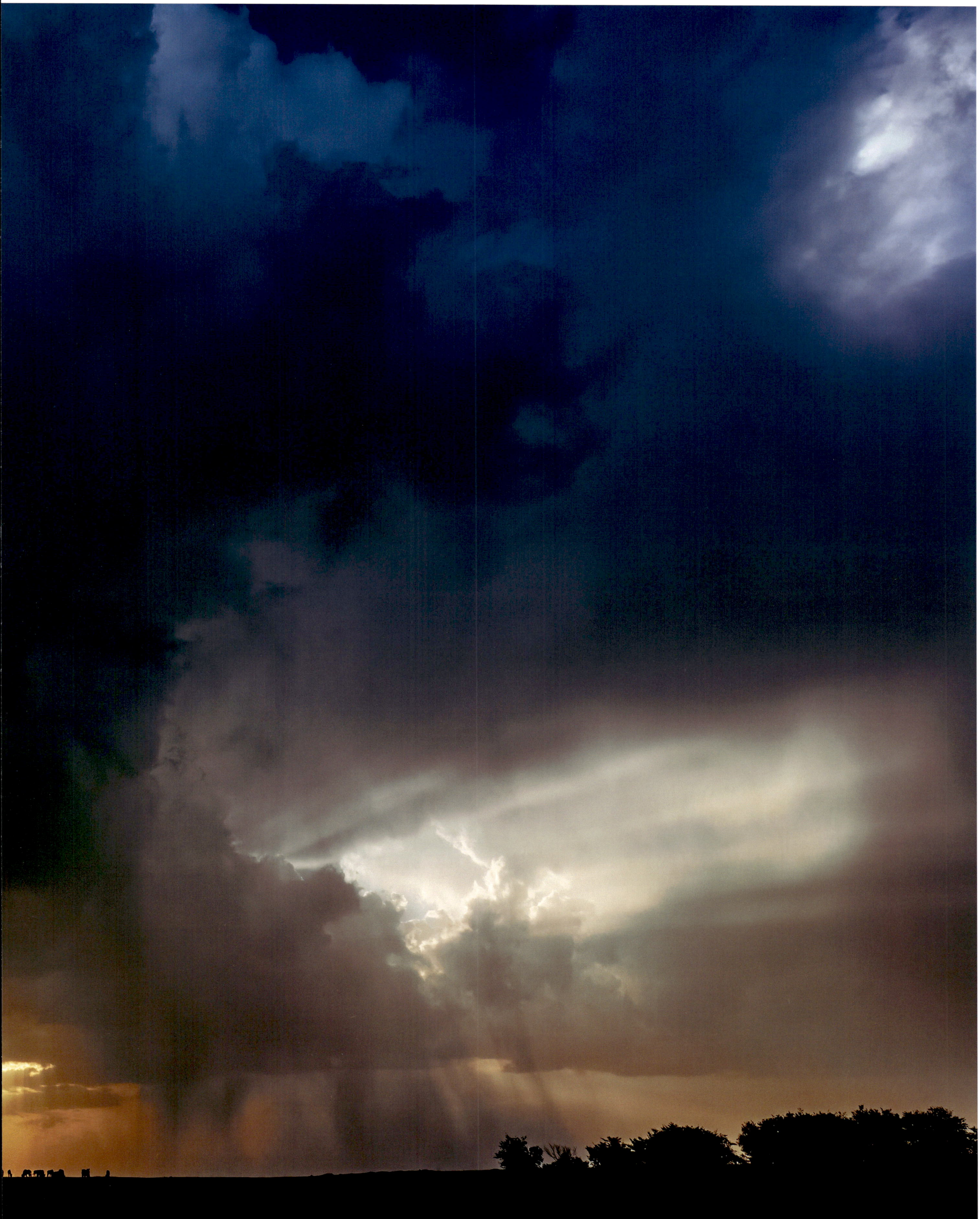

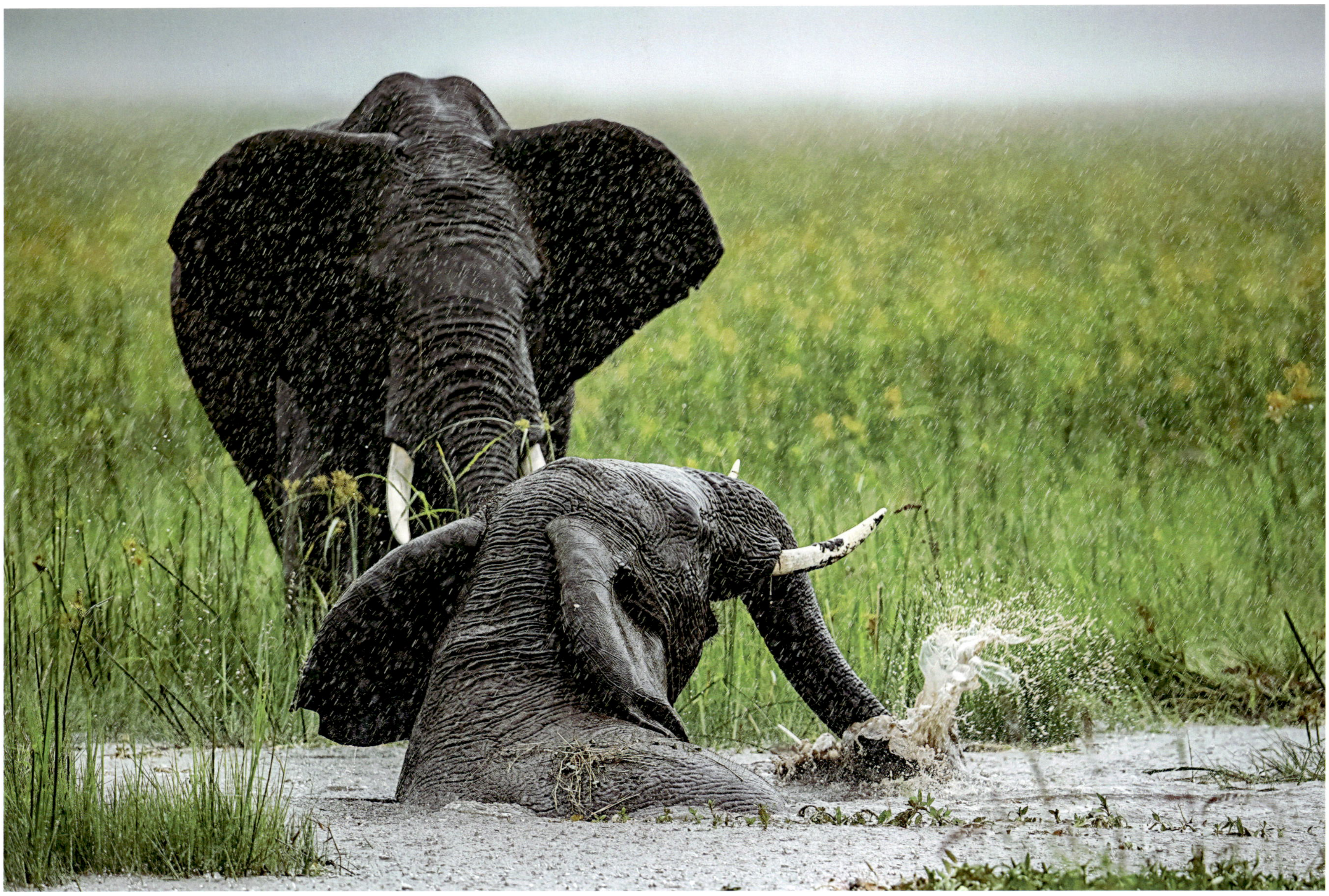

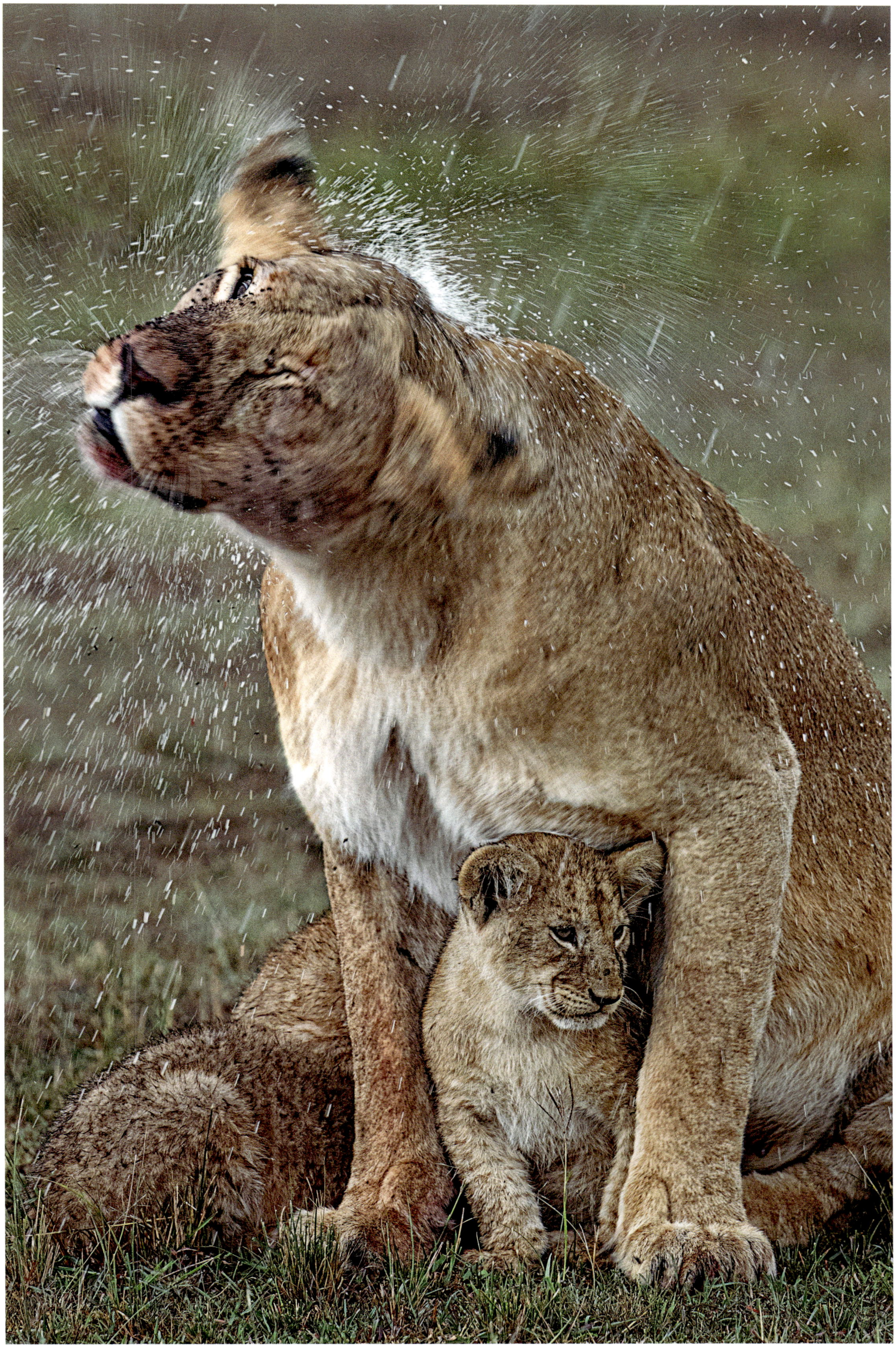

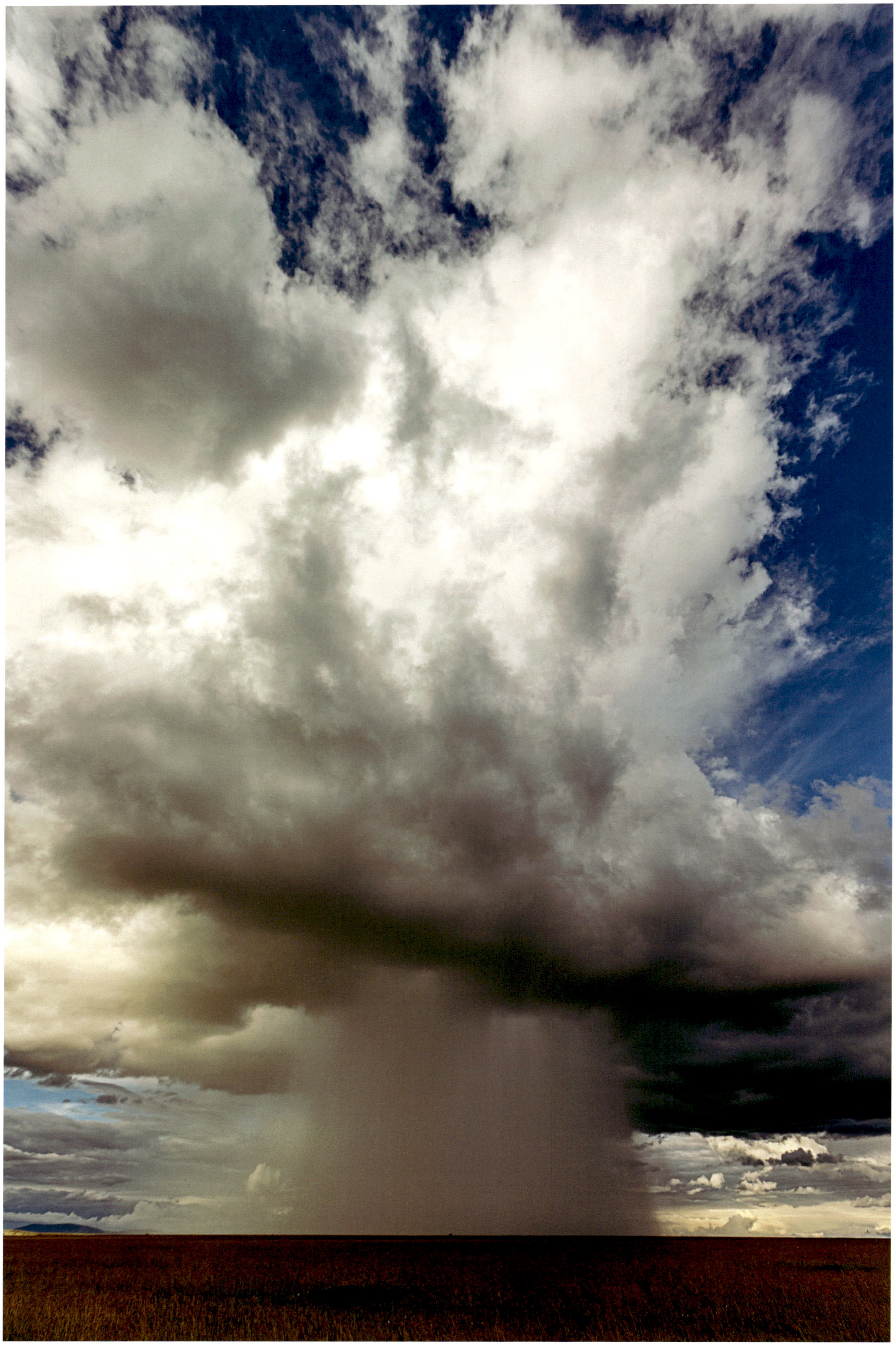

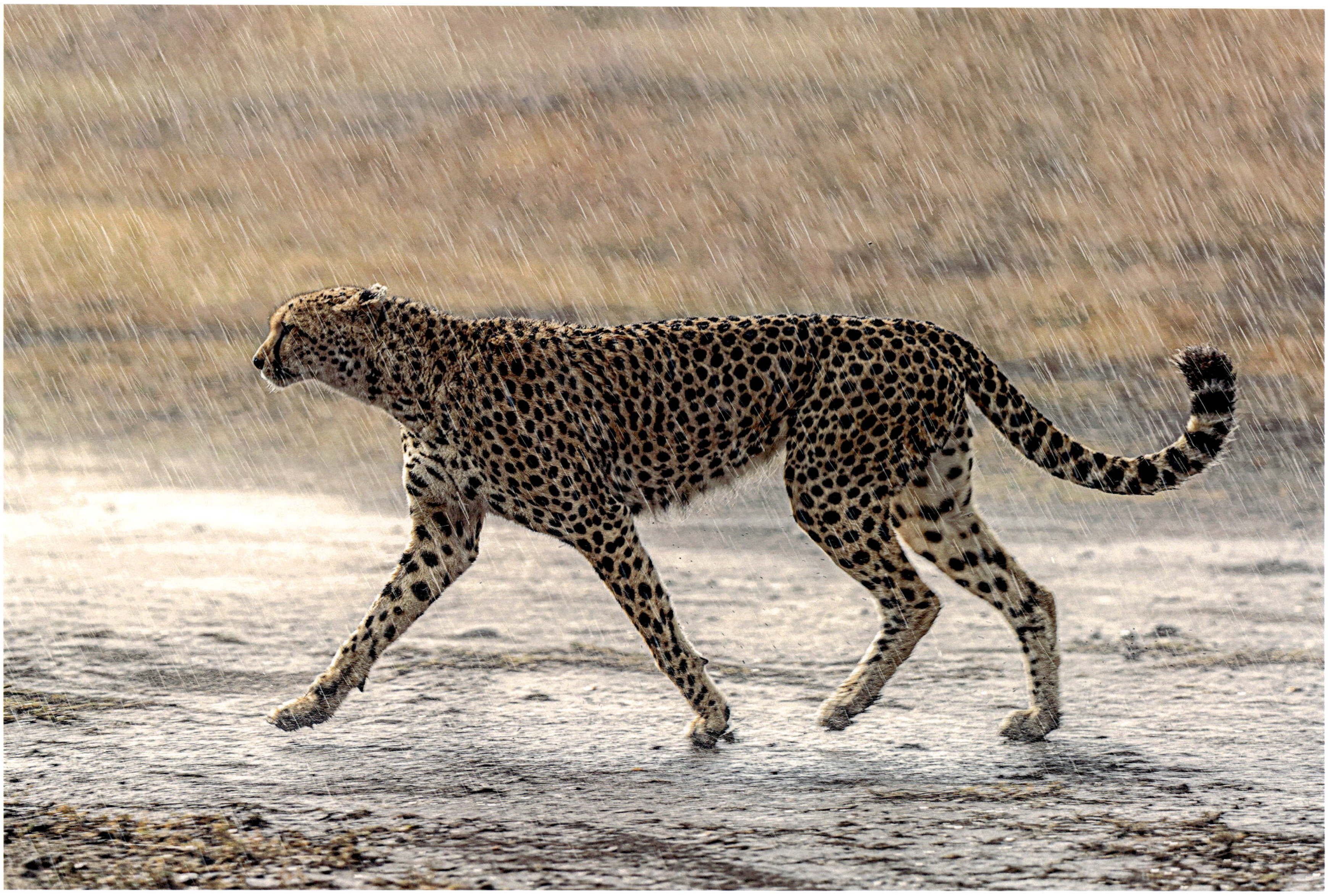

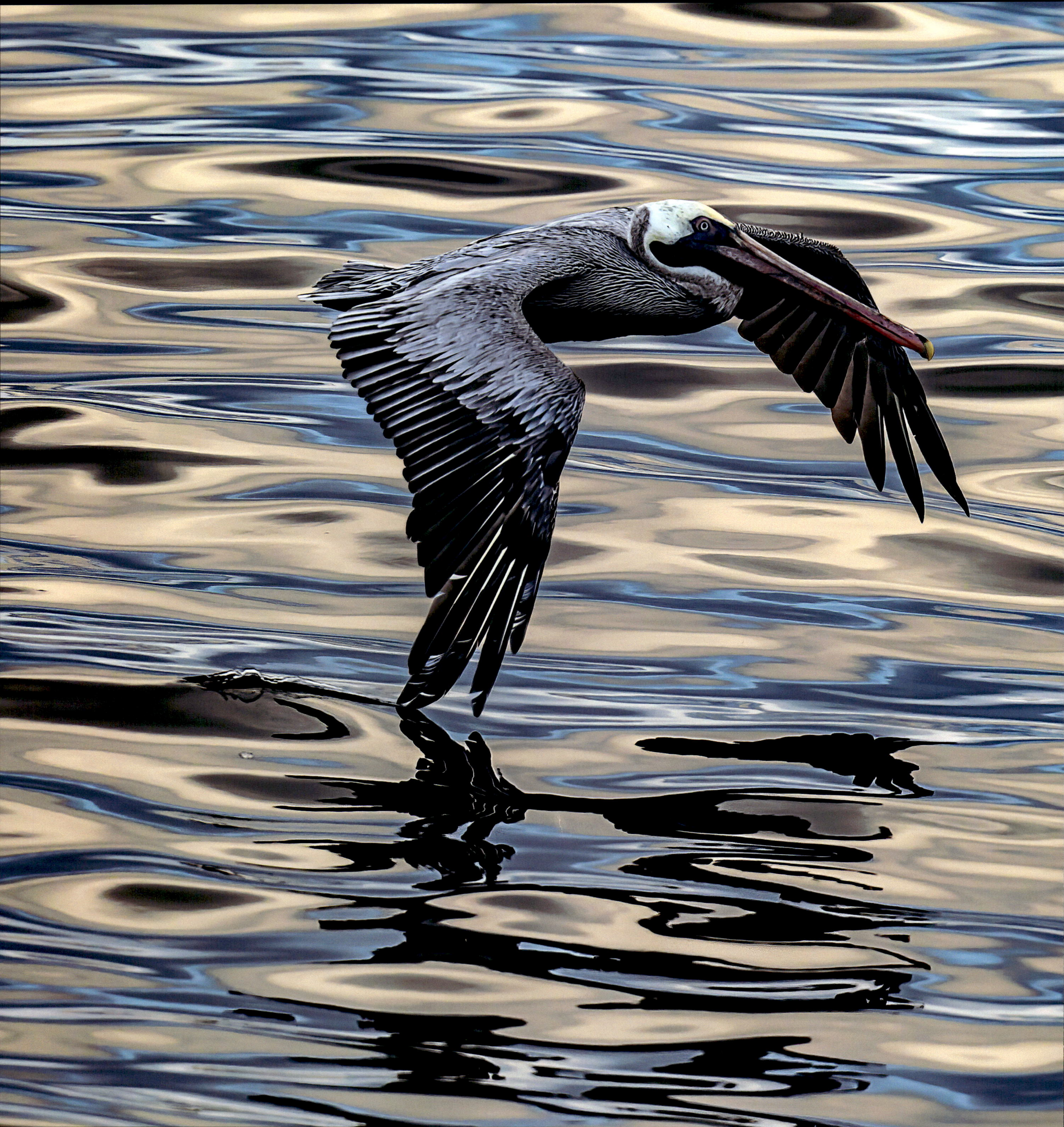

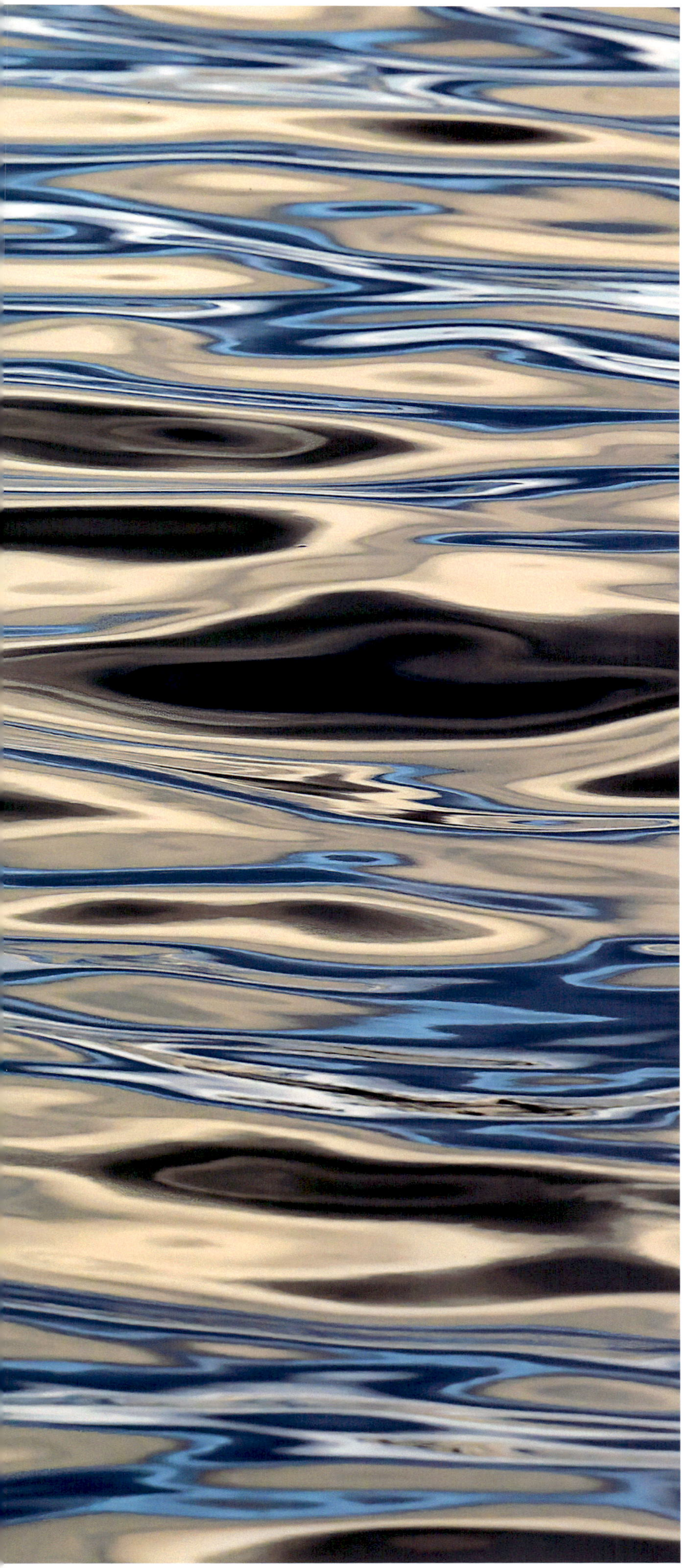

The sea, once it casts its spell, holds one in its net of wonder forever.

— Jacques-Yves Cousteau

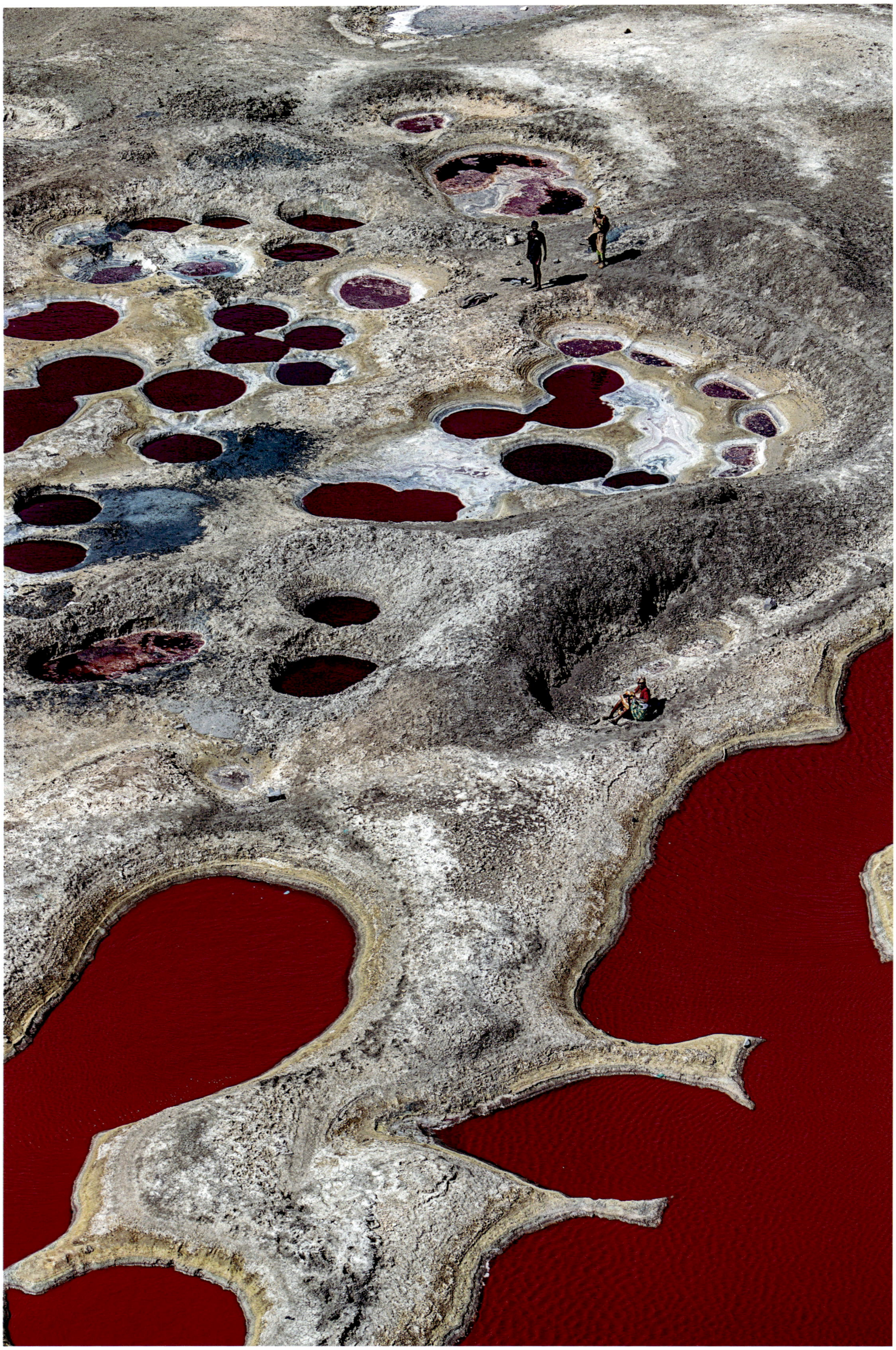

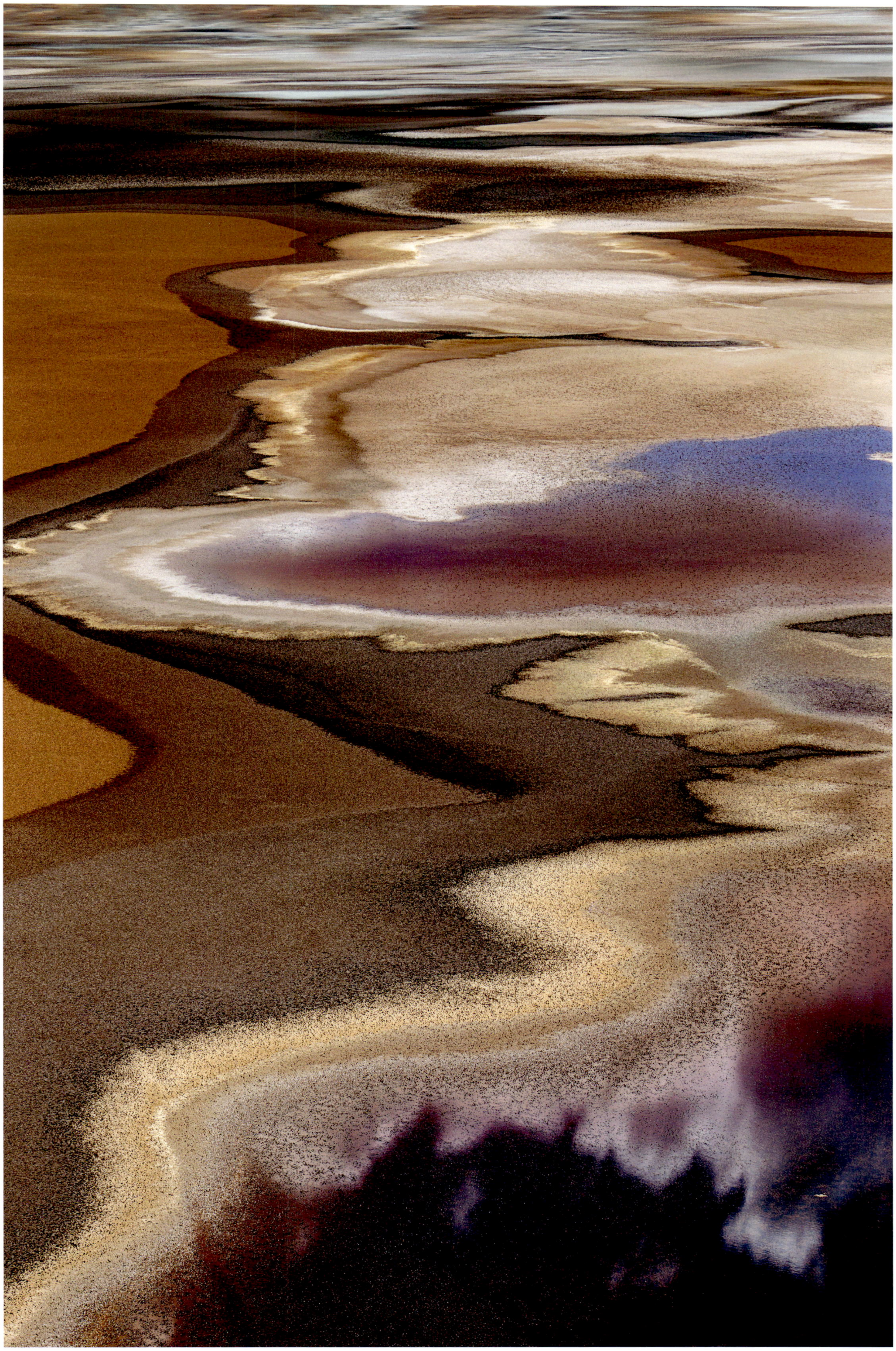

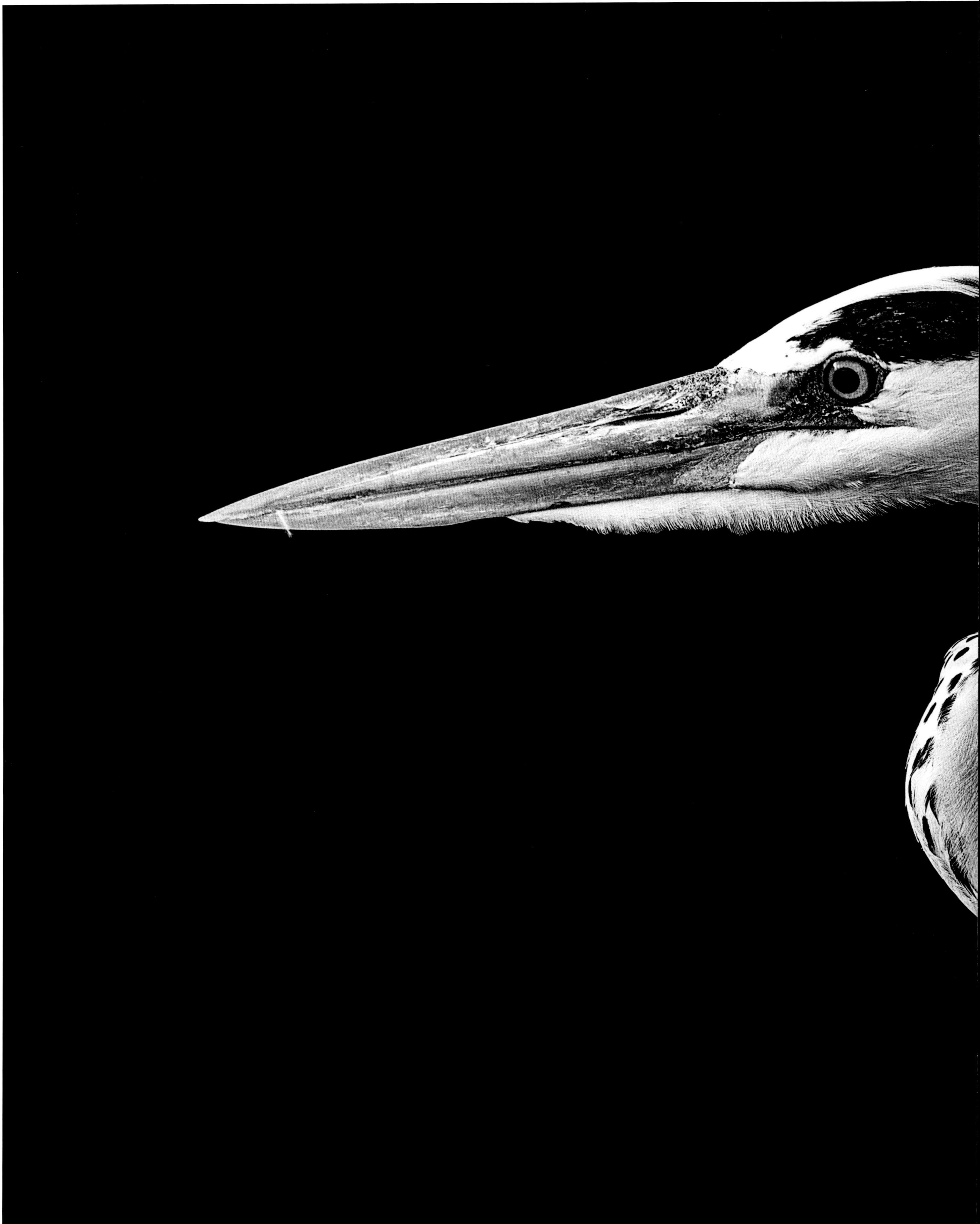

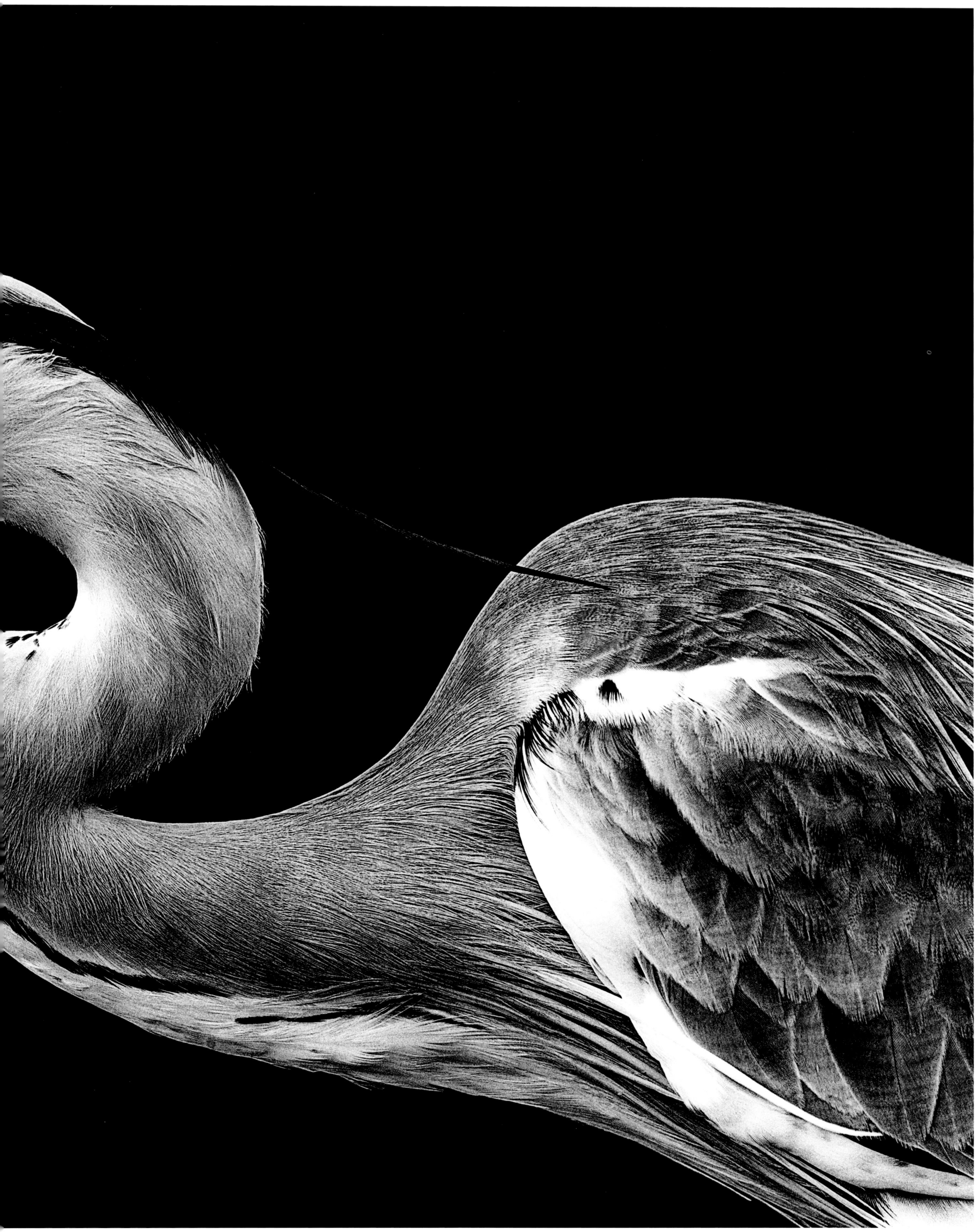

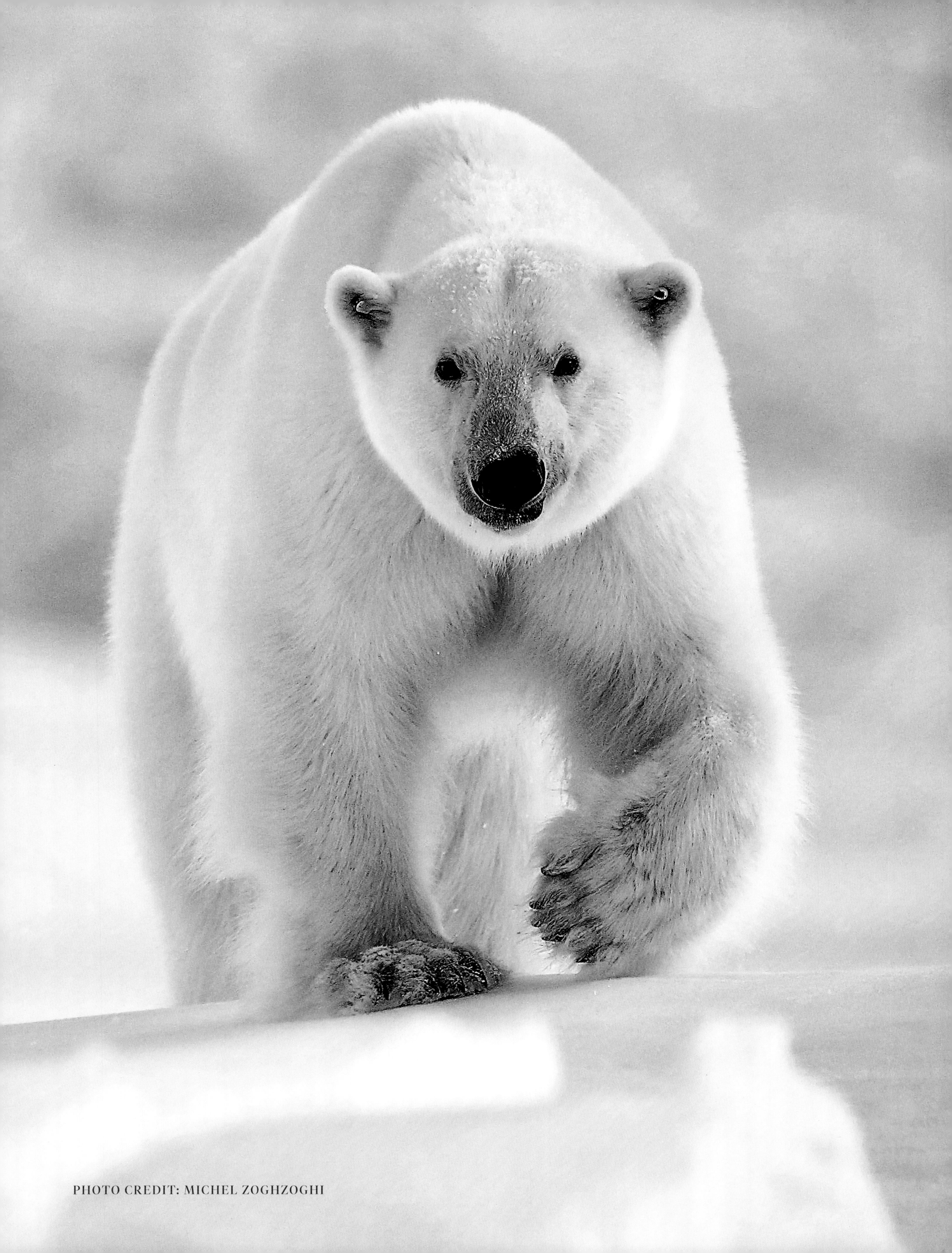

PHOTO CREDIT: MICHEL ZOGHZOGHI

Chapter Six

CRYSTAL DESERTS

In memories we were rich. We had pierced the veneer of outside things ... We had seen God in His splendours, heard the text that Nature renders. We had reached the naked soul of man.

— Sir Ernest Shackleton

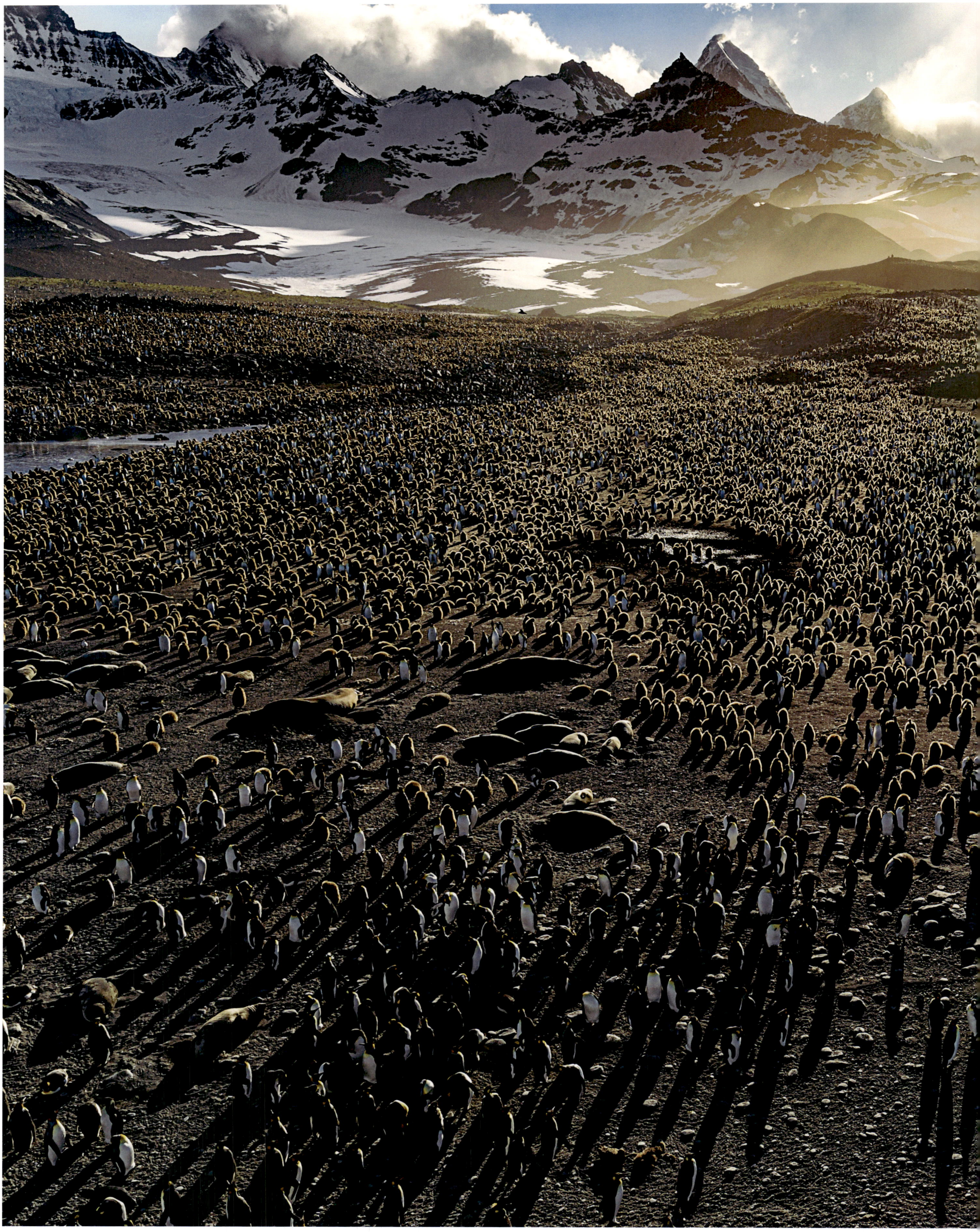

 PHOTO CREDIT: ABRAHAM JOFFE ACS

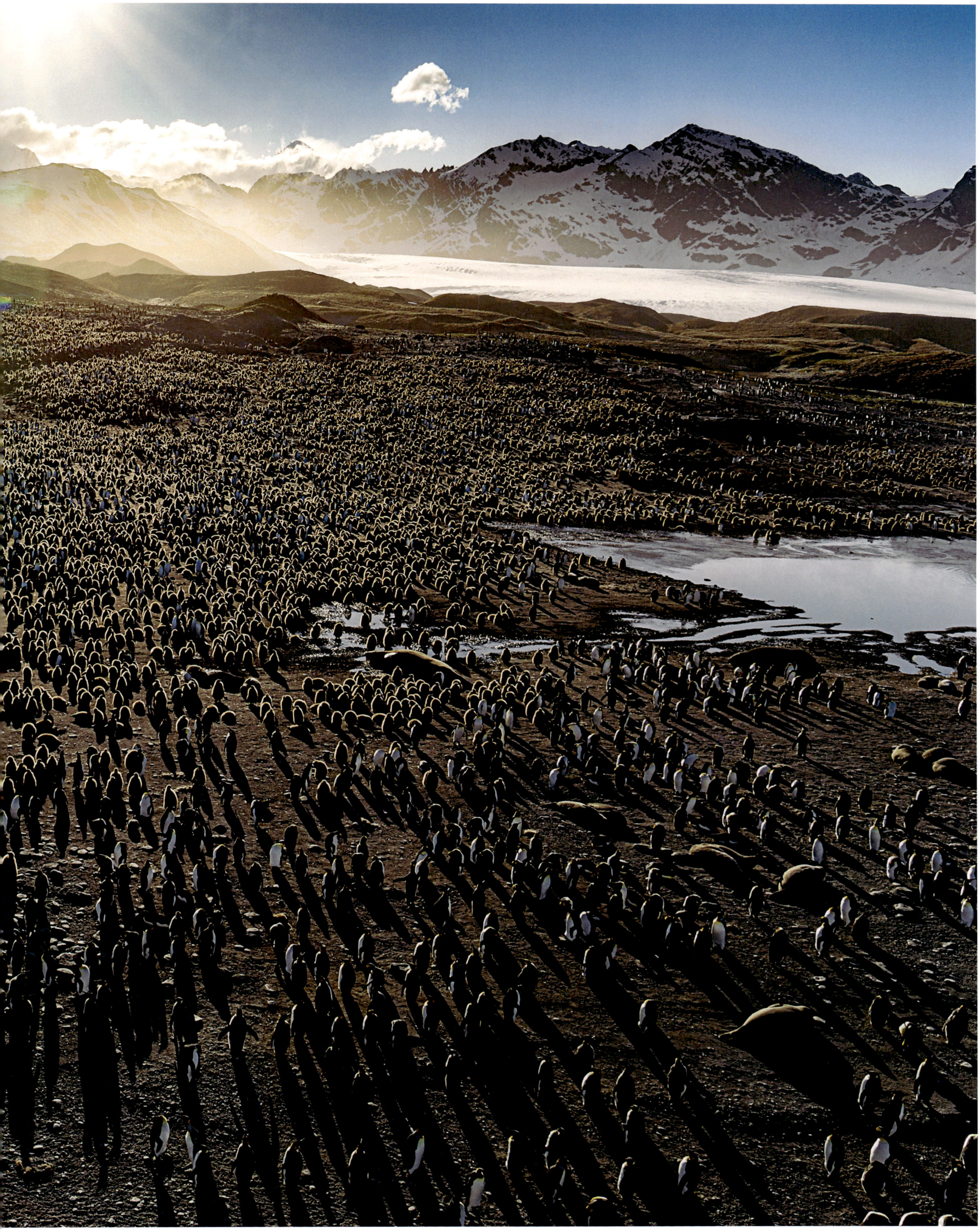

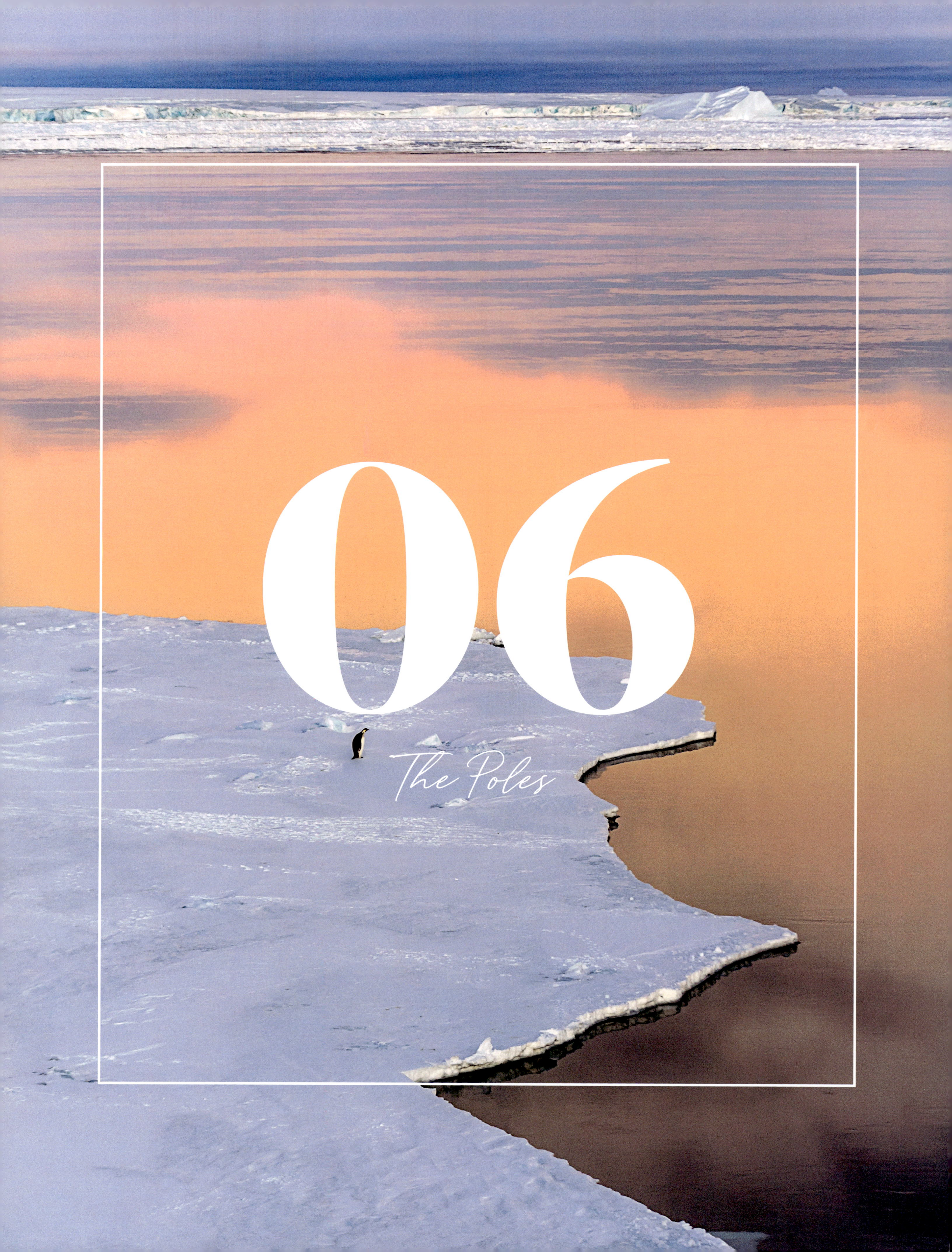

06

The Poles

Deserts, mountains, oceans, icescapes all convey the indomitable face of nature. Each represents an extreme of some kind to be conquered. While other life has taken millions of years to adapt to difficult conditions, we humans have found ways to mask our physical limitations through the power of our technology. We have navigated deserts by forging an alliance with camels, scaled mountain peaks with crampons, ice picks and oxygen, braved the ocean depths with aqualungs and submersibles, survived the bitter cold of polar regions with Gore-Tex jackets and mitts. We have even walked on the moon.

When it comes to suffering for a cause, nothing comes close to polar exploration. The legacy of three men towers over their contemporaries in the annals of the 'Heroic Age' of Antarctic exploration that began at the end of the 19th century and ended after the First World War: Robert Falcon Scott (an Englishman), Roald Amundsen (a Norwegian) and Ernest Shackleton (an Irishman). Each set his sights on being first to the South Pole. Shackleton had been a member of the 1901–04 British National Antarctic Expedition, accompanying Scott and Edward Wilson on a sledging journey that reached a record farthest south of 82° 17'. Five years later he was back and in January 1909, with three companions, reached a new farthest south of 88° 23', just 180 kilometres short of the Pole. In 1911, Amundsen and Scott struck out across the ice to claim the prize for king and country, with Amundsen and his four companions arriving at the pole on 14 December, five weeks ahead of Scott and his men, who perished in their tent from cold, starvation and scurvy on their return journey.

The attitudes and emotions exemplified by these heroic figures say much about human nature. Amundsen created a meticulous plan predicated on science and common sense rather than national pride. He knew and trusted each of his team based on a cool appraisal of their physical and mental strengths and weaknesses. Scandinavians like Amundsen are born to ski, with snow and ice their childhood companions. He intended to kill the sledge dogs that hauled their supplies as they weakened, adding the meat to his stores. Scott meanwhile put his faith in Empire and destiny, imposing a hierarchy of class and order cultivated by years in the Royal Navy. His methods were exemplified by the British tradition of 'man-hauling' sledges laden with provisions, relying on grit and stoicism to see them through. He ignored sound advice offered by explorers such as another clear-thinking Norwegian, Fridtjof Nansen: 'Don't take ponies, kill and eat the dogs along the way (an unpalatable suggestion to Scott and his compatriots) and ensure all your men can ski proficiently.' These examples offer insight into how we may or may not free ourselves from our present circumstances as 'failed' guardians of the planet. We would do well to learn from the Great Law of the Iroquois: to think seven generations ahead (about 140 years into the future) and decide whether the decisions made today would benefit our children seven generations from now.

For much of human history Antarctica was an idea rather than a place. The ancient Greeks reasoned there must be a great continent in the south as a counterweight to the known landmasses of the north. They called this unknown land *Antarktike*, meaning 'opposite of Arctic', a name that evoked dreams of a fertile paradise rich in timber and minerals for anyone daring and hardy enough to lay claim to it. The rounding of the Cape of Good Hope and Cape Horn in the 15th and 16th centuries proved that if the Antarctic existed it must be a continent in its own right and in 1773, James Cook and his crew became the first to cross the Antarctic Circle, sailing within 250 kilometres of the continent without sighting the mainland. That prize was claimed nearly 50 years later, on 27 January 1820, when a Russian expedition led by Fabian Gottlieb von Bellingshausen and Mikhail Lazarev discovered what is today known as the Fimbul Ice Shelf.

Antarctica's visible face is unlike anything else on Earth: a continent covered with ice surrounded by ocean, while the Arctic is an ice-covered ocean almost completely surrounded by land. Antarctica is a frozen desert: the coldest, driest, highest and windiest continent on the planet with snowfall less than five centimetres a year in the interior and air drier than the Sahara. Yet, the profusion of Antarctica's wildlife and the grandeur of its scenery glimpsed on a summer's day are unrivalled: an artist's canvas run wild with broad sweeps of whites and blues and greens, icebergs tinged with turquoise, snow of a dazzling brightness amid a swirling ocean of

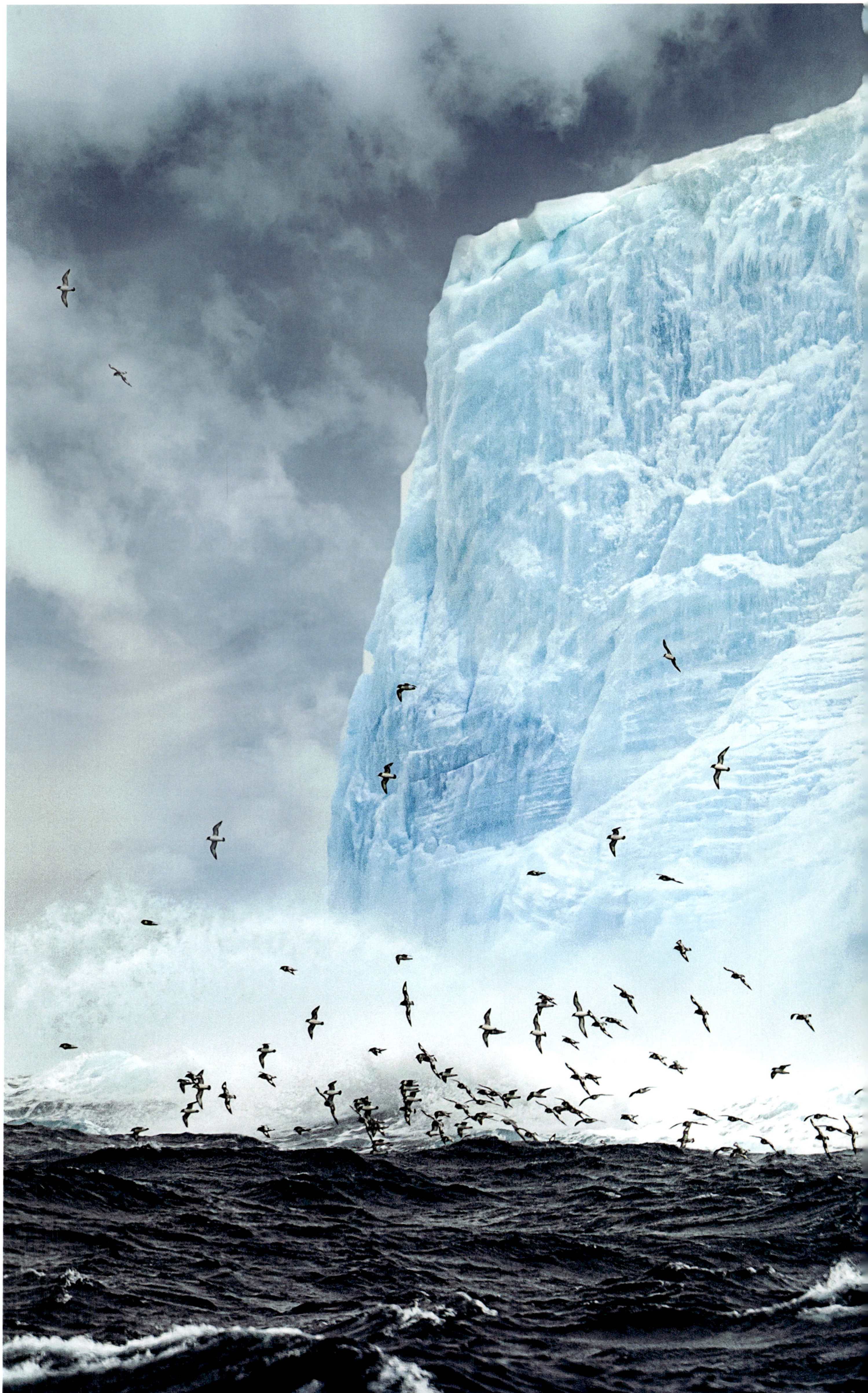

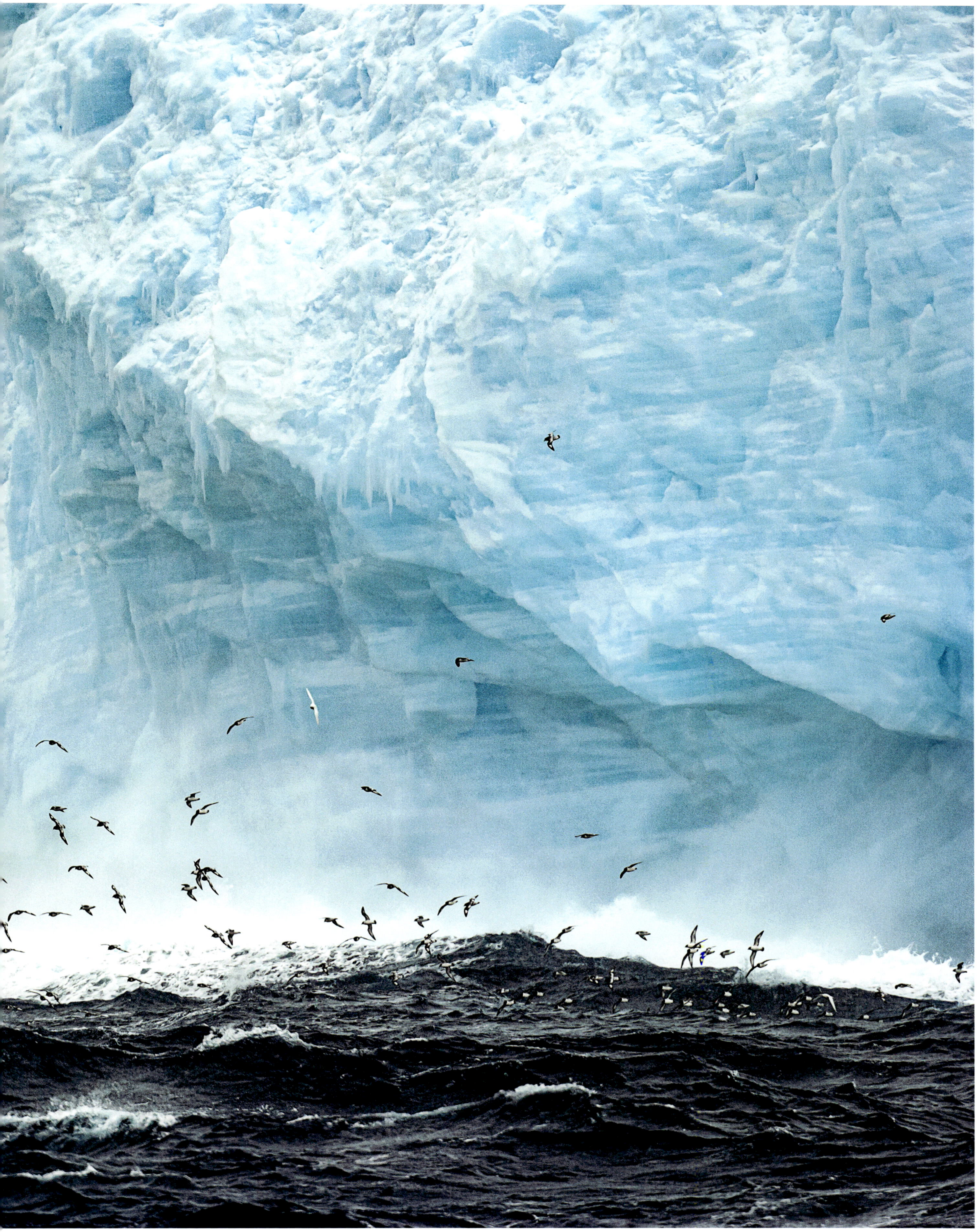

the deepest blue. It is Turner and Chagall at their most exuberant. Add to the mix the spectacle of millions of penguins and seals, creatures with aquiline contours that spend most of their time at sea in the Southern Ocean, venturing onto land only to breed during the brief Antarctic summer when the ice melts along the fringes of the Peninsula, the continent's wiggly tail of bare rock. There may be fewer species here than in the Serengeti and less variety of habitat than in East Africa, but the sheer volume is overwhelming.

Most people who travel to the Antarctic do so once. So adding a pilgrimage to the rugged island of South Georgia is a must if you can afford it. Situated halfway between the southeast coast of Argentina and the Antarctic continent, South Georgia lies within the area known as the Antarctic Convergence – where cold, northward-flowing waters meet the relatively warmer waters of the sub-Antarctic, making it part of the Antarctic realm. As the chilled Antarctic surface water sinks, it causes upwelling or overturning of the nutrient-rich depths of the Southern Ocean. At the heart of this ecosystem is a tiny shrimp-like crustacean known as krill, one of the most abundant species in the world, nourishing whales, seals, squid, icefish, penguins, albatrosses and many other birds. Baleen and blue whales can eat as much as four tonnes of krill per day, and krill is increasingly sought after to feed farmed seafood, livestock and poultry, while its omega-3 fatty acids and other nutrients are popular as krill oil. Krill needs both sea ice and cold water to survive, while rising temperatures reduce the growth and abundance of the plankton that it feeds on. Loss of sea ice removes habitat that shelters both larval krill and the organisms it eats, so when Antarctic sea ice declines, as is happening, so does krill.

You only have to spend a day ashore on South Georgia to experience its fickle character. There is a jagged-edged abruptness to its coastline of deep bays and fjords, with dark slippery slabs of volcanic rock creating a forbidding fortress-like visage for any seafarer hoping to come ashore. Given that it rains on more than 200 days a year and that even in summer 75 per cent of the island is covered in snow, ice and glaciers, you can only pray for clement weather during your visit. But seen on a good day, the island's beauty is unforgettable, part Swiss Alps part Alaska. The pioneering tour operator Lars-Eric Lindblad was the first to host tourists to Antarctica, in 1966 aboard a chartered Argentinian navy ship. For many years afterwards, he operated his own vessel, the MS *Lindblad Explorer*, fondly referred to as the Little Red Ship, that became the byword for polar expeditions.

Angie and I enjoyed many Antarctic adventures aboard the *Explorer* in the 1990s, including a number of landings on South Georgia. An afternoon out on deck cruising the Antarctic Peninsula and Lemaire Channel, soaking up crisp blue skies and snowcapped mountains reflected on the ocean's glassy surface, or stepping ashore on Salisbury Plain on South Georgia, are never-to-be-forgotten moments, not least for those mugs of piping hot chocolate laced with a generous tot of brandy to keep the chill wind at bay.

During summer, South Georgia is host to four million Antarctic fur seals, 400,000 southern elephant seals and millions of penguins. Sinuous leopard seals patrol just offshore in the kelp, ready to pick off fur seal pups and gentoo, macaroni and chinstrap penguins as they move back and forth from colony to sea. Taking centre stage are an estimated 500,000 breeding pairs of king penguins, which clog the bays and coves with their eye-catching presence. Intermingling with the black and white adults are their comically attired chicks, fat as butter in russet down coats, huddling together for warmth and protection in the world's largest crèche.

Witnessing this profusion of animal and birdlife today, one is mindful of the slaughter that occurred here within living memory; humanity's tendency to exploit other forms of life balanced against nature's ability to recover. While the mineral wealth of the continent (in the form of coal and oil deposits) remains buried beneath the ice, the discovery of South Georgia in the 18th century by Captain James Cook unleashed a gold rush of sealers and whalers eager to ply their trade in and around the Southern Ocean. The glut of fur and whale oil created fortunes overnight for sea captains and their owners. By 1825, around 1.2 million fur seals had been slaughtered to satisfy the hunger for sealskin coats and boots, principally in the UK and China. Whalers soon followed, killing the slower swimmers first: right whales, humpbacks and sperm whales; their oil and blubber provided lighting, margarine, soap, fertiliser and food supplements for farm animals. With the invention of fast, steam-powered catcher boats and explosive harpoons in the early 1900s,

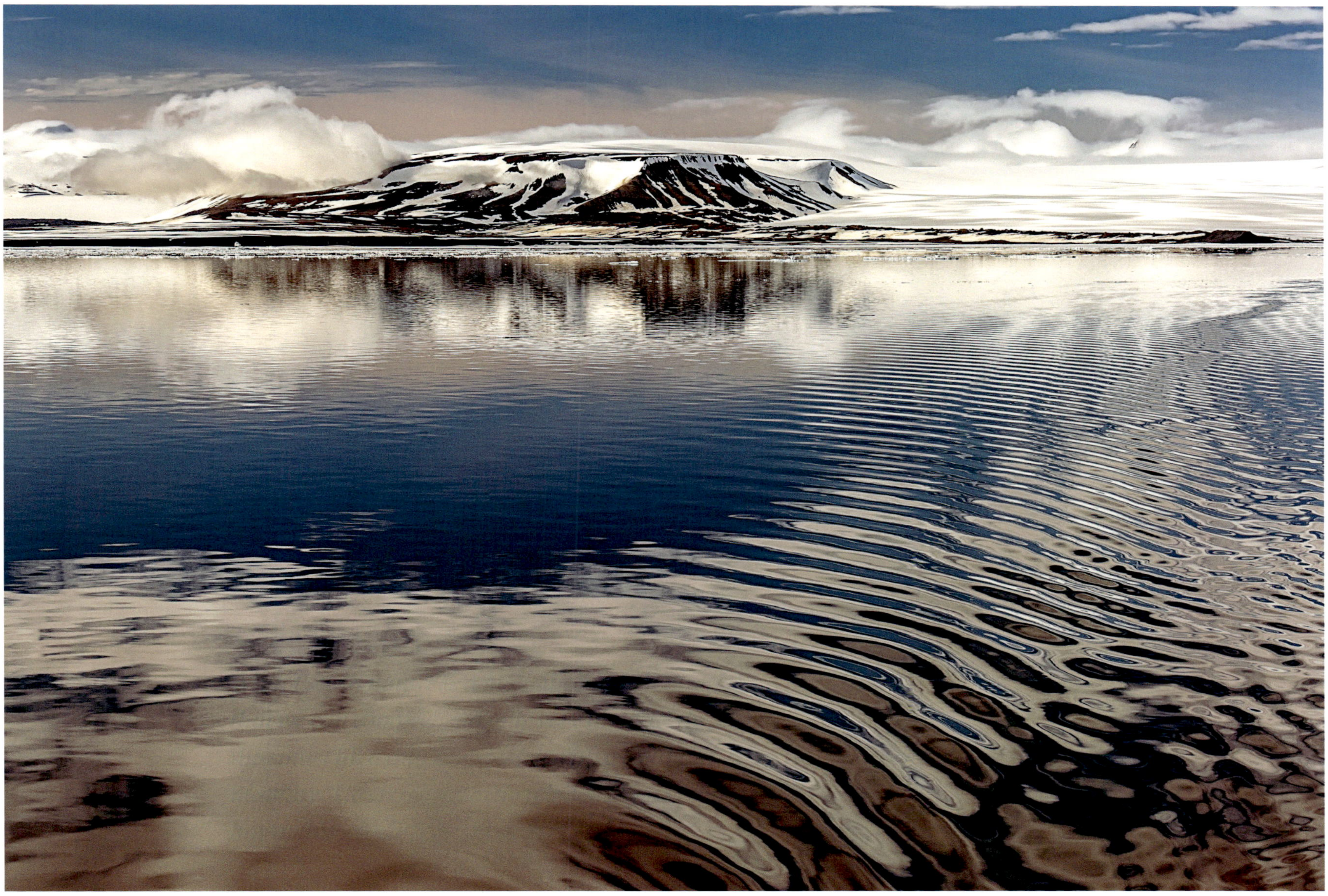

South Georgia became home to whaling stations such as Grytviken and Stromness that targeted the big, fast baleen species, the fin and blue whales. From the opening of Grytviken in 1904 until the time it closed its doors some 60 years later, 175,250 whales were processed, including a record female blue whale more than 33 metres long, killed in 1912. In just four decades, the largest creature ever to live was almost wiped out. Today it is the whaling stations that are extinct and whales are a common sight around South Georgia again, while both fur and elephant seals have made spectacular recoveries.

Most people who visit Antarctica will travel there in summer for just a week or two. The thought of experiencing the continent in winter chills the heart. It's a time of bitter darkness, an alien world to humans. Yet, this is breeding season for the most remarkable bird on the continent: the emperor penguin. Emperors stand one metre tall and are dressed in the finest downy fleece, with the highest feather density of any bird at 15 feathers per square centimetre of skin. Their white breasts sparkle with a necklace of gold, water droplets spilling off their bodies like showers of diamonds as they launch themselves out of the water. During Scott's doomed 1910–13 expedition, he allowed three of his companions – Edward Wilson, Henry 'Birdie' Bowers and Apsley Cherry-Garrard – to undertake what became known as the Winter Journey, a six-week trek to the emperor breeding colony at Cape Crozier. The primary aim was to establish whether or not the emperor might prove an evolutionary link between birds and reptiles, something that Wilson had set his heart on discovering. To do that scientists at the Natural History Museum in England needed to examine embryos at an early stage in incubation.

On 27 June 1911 – midwinter in the southern hemisphere – the three men set out, man-hauling their sledges across the Ross Ice Shelf in complete darkness and temperatures of –40° Celsius. It took 19 days to travel the 100 kilometres to the rookery and, on 5 July, the temperature fell below –61° Celsius. Arriving at the rookery on 15 July, the men built an igloo from snow blocks, stone and a sheet of wood they had brought for the roof. The igloo was almost destroyed in a three-day blizzard with force 11 winds that carried away their precious tent and many of their supplies, compelling them to endure the last day of the storm in their sleeping bags, half-covered in snow, expecting to die. Miraculously, Bowers found the tent blown against some rocks less than a kilometre away. Barely alive and badly frostbitten, the three men arrived back at Scott's base at Cape Evans on 1 August. The eggs they had risked their lives to collect would later prove not to contain embryos and Wilson's theories have been shown to be incorrect.

The emperors arrive at their rookery in March or April, by which time the sea ice has frozen solid for the winter season, providing the stable platform the birds depend on for breeding, feeding, moulting and as a refuge from predators. After an elaborate courtship, the female deposits a single hand-sized egg on the ice; her partner then quickly scoops it up on to his feet, enveloping it in a warm covering of skin and feathers. There he must stand, huddling together for warmth with hundreds of other males in temperatures that plummet to –40 degrees Celsius with winds raging up to 150 kilometres per hour. After 65–75 days, the tiny chick emerges from its egg and is fed a meal of 'crop milk', rich in fat and protein. By the time the female returns from feasting on krill, squid and fish for two months – if she survives the orcas and leopard seals – the male will have lost almost half his body weight; only then can he return to the ocean to replenish his energy stores. Both parents take turns feeding and protecting their chick through September and October, then in November chicks begin to grow their protective feathers, and the parents stop feeding them. In December, adults and chicks (now fully fledged in waterproof feathers) abandon the colony and return to the ocean.

For summer visitors like Angie and myself, penetrating the emperor penguins' icy abode on Snow Hill Island in the Weddell Sea relied on all the ingenuity and technology at humanity's disposal, including icebreakers and helicopters. In 2006, we made the journey aboard *Kapitan Khlebnikov*, at times struggling through knee-high snow to reach the rookery of 4,000 breeding pairs. When we arrived, surrounded by a cacophony of penguins trumpeting their individually recognisable greeting calls, we could only stand in silent tribute to the extraordinary tenacity of nature and the human urge to overcome the most brutal elements.

Penguins act as indicator species of climate change. With some hundred emperor breeding colonies scattered around the Antarctic continent, in recent times their ability to breed successfully has been hindered in some of these locations by the fast ice melting before the chicks are ready to enter the ocean. Scientists warn that emperors could go extinct by 2100 unless the world delivers on limiting global temperature rises to 1.5° Celsius. If that were to happen, the decline would be less than a third. But it isn't just the emperors that are feeling the effect of global warming. Populations of Adélie and chinstrap penguins are in decline on the Antarctic Peninsula, which has warmed by 5° Celsius in the past 60 years. The ice of Antarctica, like that of Greenland – but unlike Arctic ice – rests on land. Ice is slippery when wet and the more widespread the water beneath it, the greater the chance the ice will become unstable and slide into the sea, something that is thought to have happened dozens of times over the past six million years. If it happened again, sea levels could rise by as much as 60 metres. Though this is unlikely, West Antarctica, which is divided from the rest of the continent by the Transantarctic mountain range, is already witnessing a significant retreat, with the potential to raise sea levels by between one and three metres by the end of this century.

Thanks to analysis of ice cores, the last continent to be discovered, a land beyond reality, is providing us with a unique record of what our climate has been like over the past one million years. While Antarctica is among the most vulnerable to climate change, it is also one of the greatest natural assets to mitigate it, with the Southern Ocean playing a vital role in the planet's atmospheric pressure, humidity, air temperatures and wind patterns. Antarctica represents the largest surface area of snow and ice with the greatest albedo effect, a measure of the amount of solar heat bounced back into space that would otherwise become trapped in the Earth's atmosphere. The current retreat of ice and snow makes it inevitable that more heat will accumulate over time, causing ever more reflective sea ice to melt and potentially leading to a catastrophic runaway greenhouse effect.

As legendary physicist Stephen Hawking noted, pollution coupled with human greed and stupidity are still the biggest threats to humankind.

Antarctica is the only continent on Earth without indigenous human inhabitants, though the scientists and staff from 30 countries who live on about 70 bases (40 year-round and 30 summer-only) number 4,000 people in summer and 1,000 in winter. For the moment it is a potent symbol of our good intentions towards the planet, a grand experiment in restraint. A place dedicated to science where no nation is permitted a military presence, it is a land of peace, a global laboratory with an obligation to protect the environment. If ever there was a case for establishing Antarctica as the planet's first World Park, as envisioned by Greenpeace back in 1987, surely this must be it.

At the other end of the world, the Arctic is drowning. Even as the ice melts beneath the giant fur-covered feet of the north's iconic polar bears, nations are scrambling to lay claim to its watery depths, with a quarter of the planet's oil and gas at stake. World powers such as Russia, Canada and the USA have an unprecedented chance to win navigation rights and resources in the Arctic seabed, untouched since its emergence during the twilight of the dinosaurs, with little concern for its original human or animal inhabitants. Unlike in the Antarctic, which is protected by international treaties, there are a host of issues that remain dangerously unresolved in one of the world's most fragile and life-sustaining regions. On 2 August 2007, in a record-breaking dive, two Russian mini-submarines reached the seabed more than four kilometres beneath the North Pole. They planted a one-metre-high titanium Russian flag on the underwater Lomonosov ridge, which Moscow claims is directly connected to its continental shelf. Andrei Ionin, a Russian military expert, commented, 'This race shows that intellect is not the main thing but that resources still rule the day.' As legendary physicist Stephen Hawking noted, pollution coupled with human greed and stupidity are still the biggest threats to humankind.

There could be no more powerful symbol of the state of the planet than the fate of the last 20,000 polar bears, a wild creature immortalised by the ancient Greeks, who named the bright shining northern constellation Arktos, the Bear. By this century's end, polar bears could vanish as a result of the shrinking sea ice they depend on as a platform to hunt seals, a direct consequence of global warming and our part in it. The life force of the great bear is dimming and flickering towards extinction at the hand of humankind.

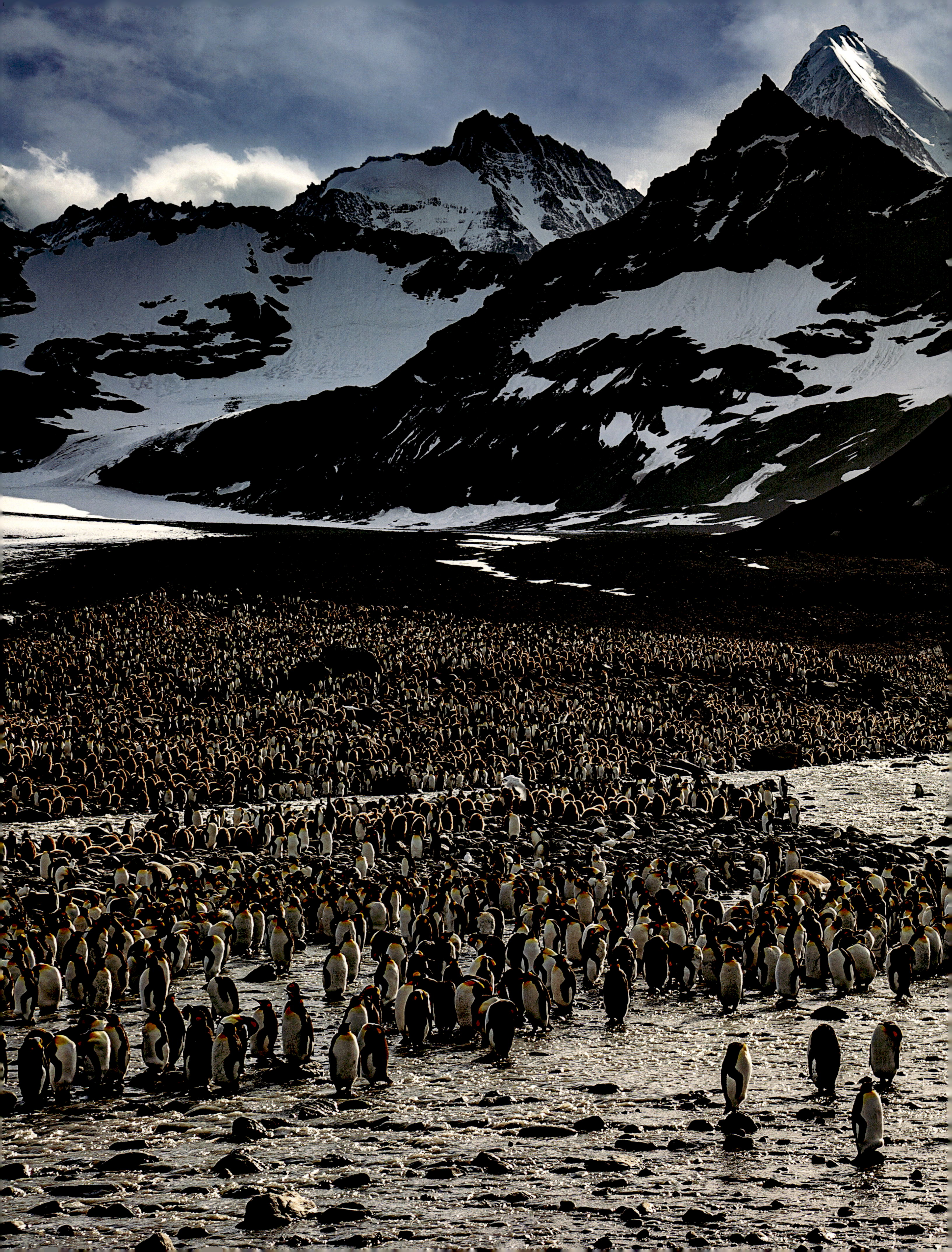

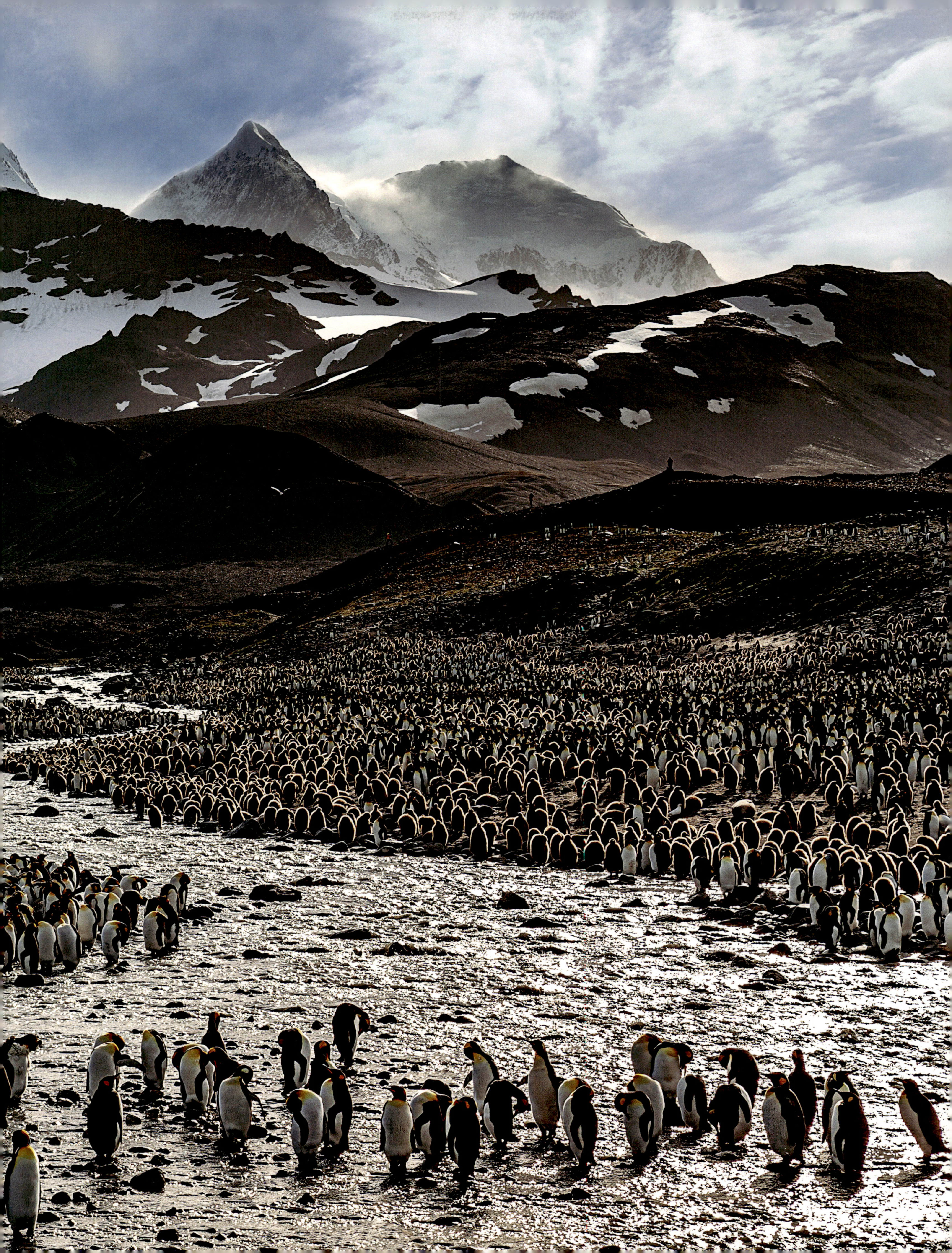

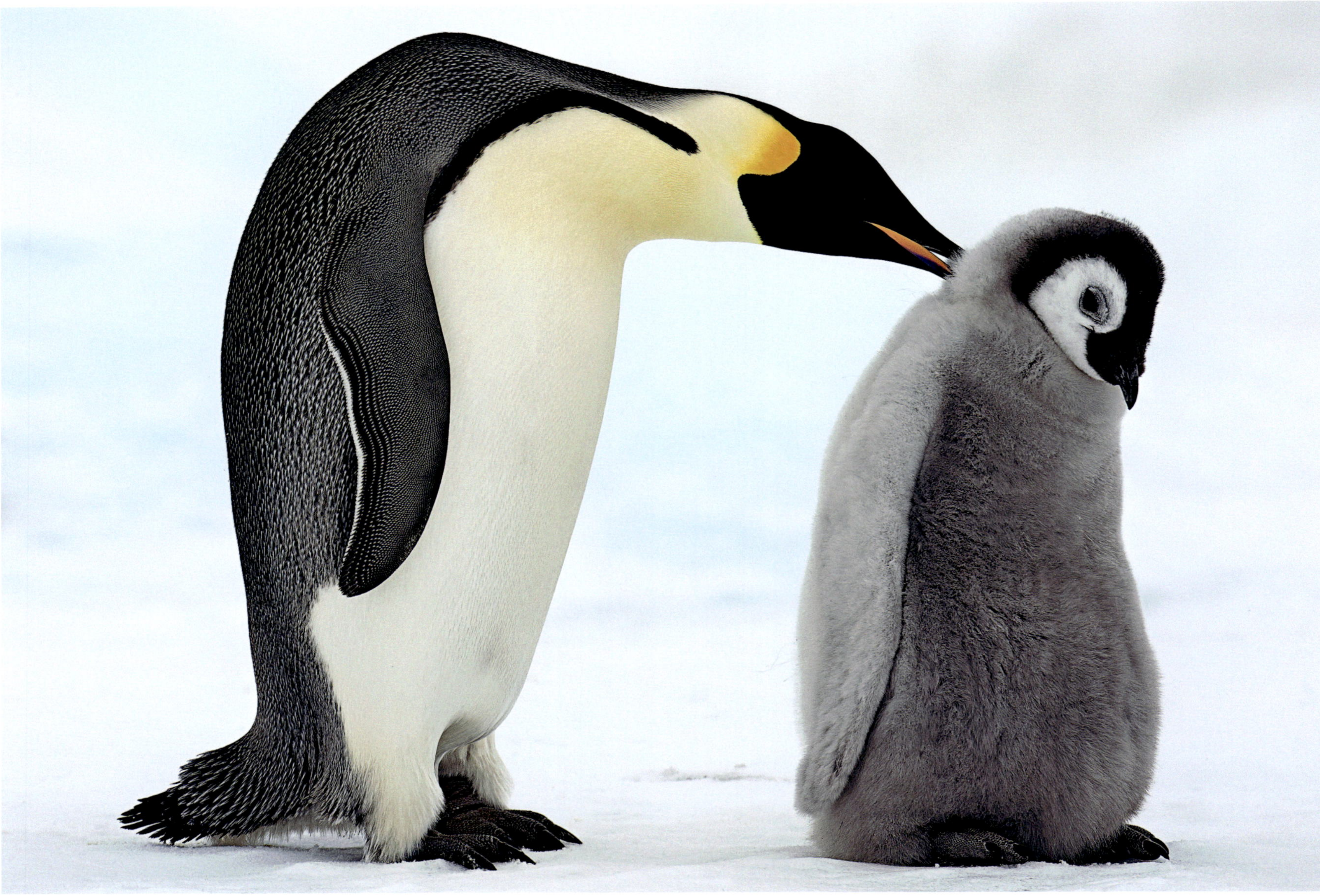

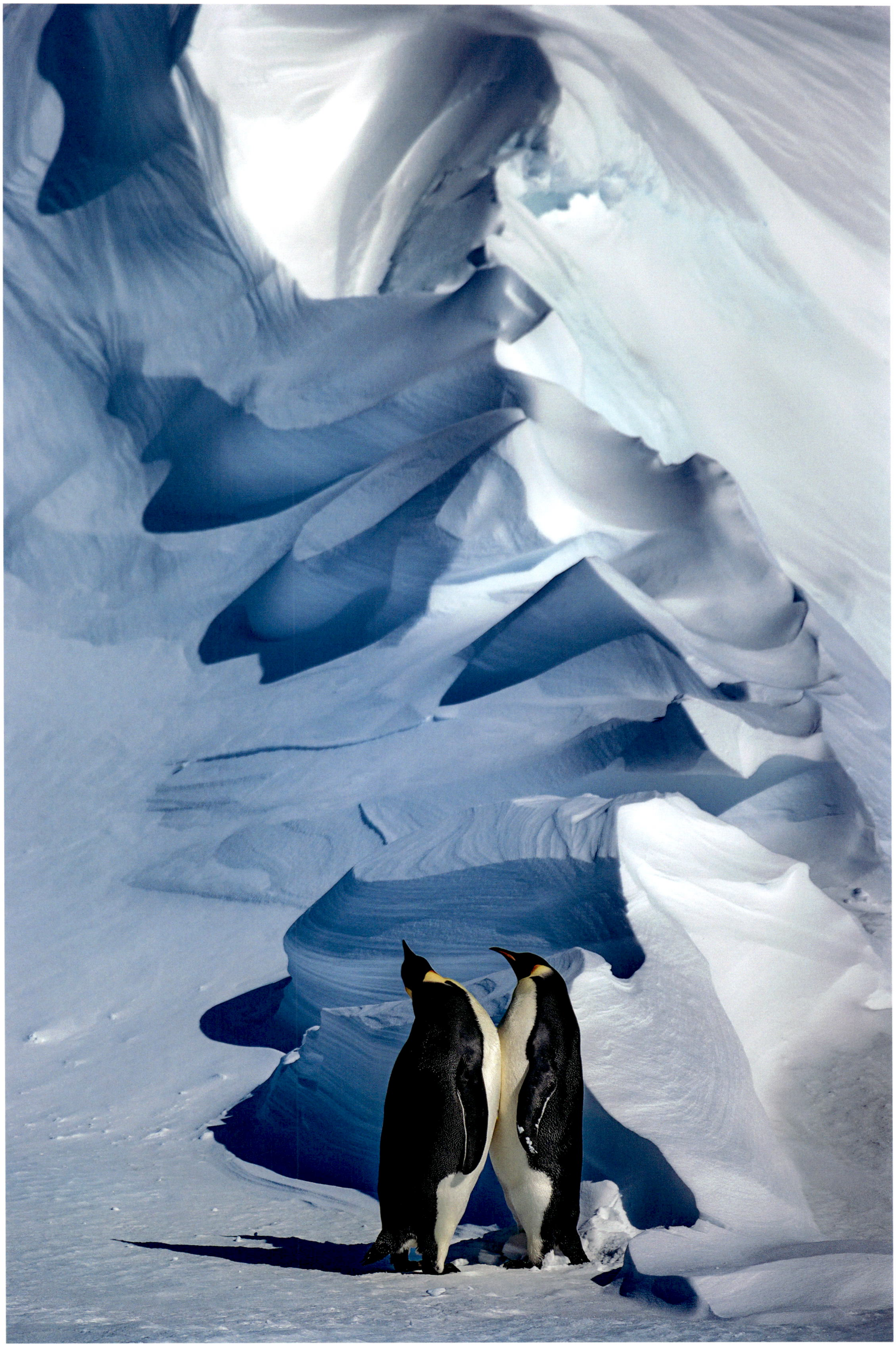

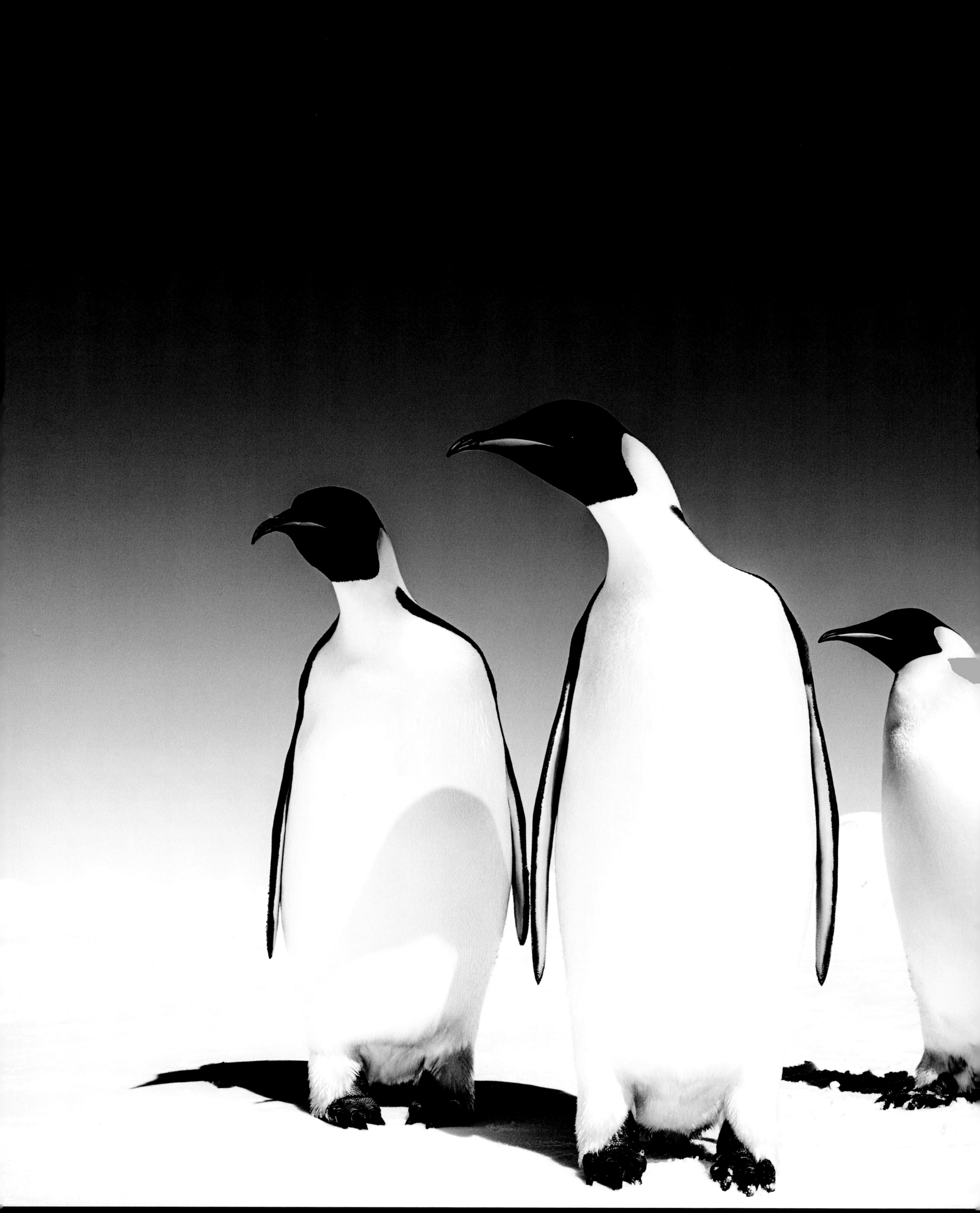

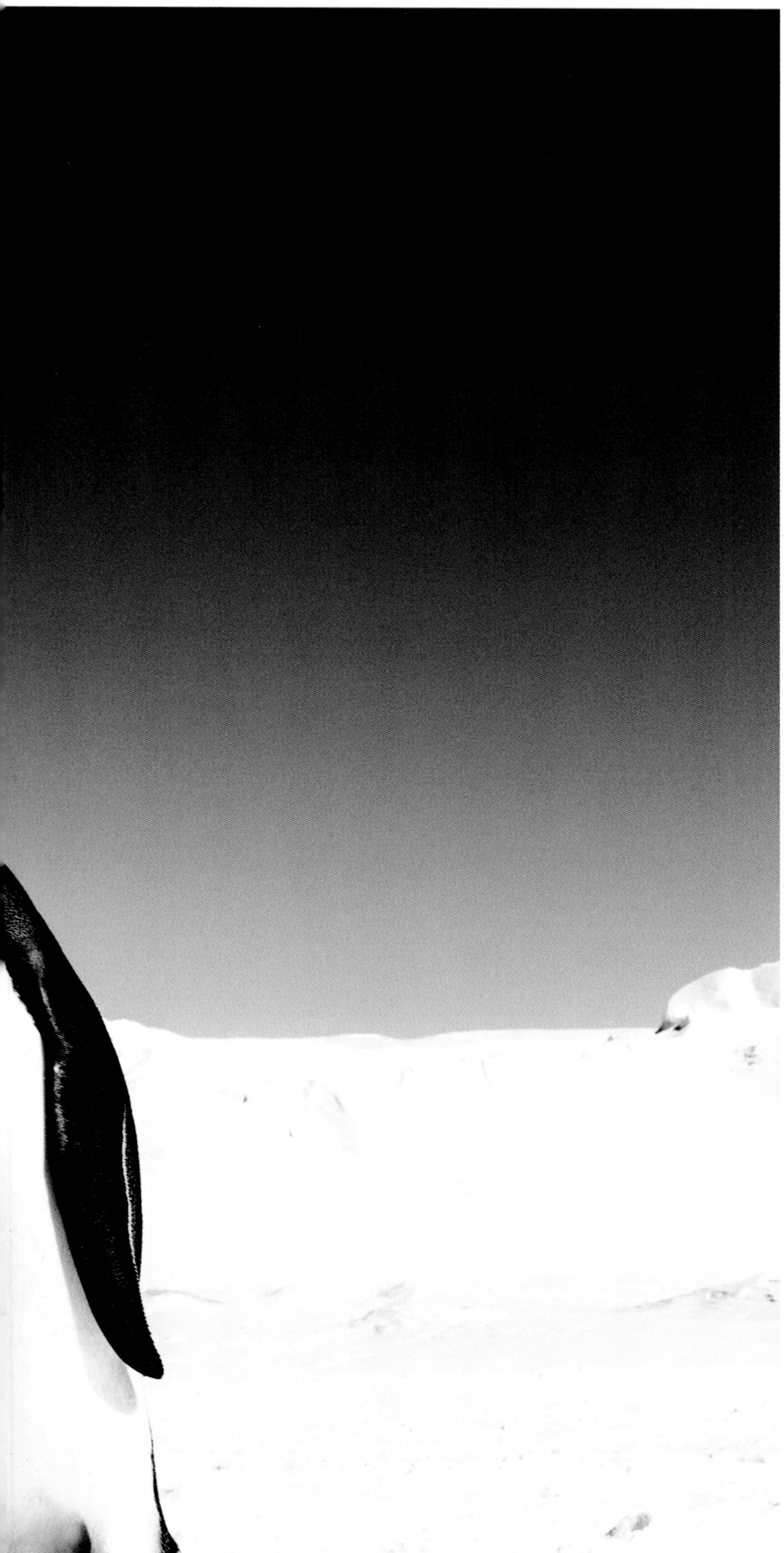

Everyone has an Antarctic – the inner white space of clarity and reflection that you feel when you visit Antarctica.

— *Thomas Pynchon*

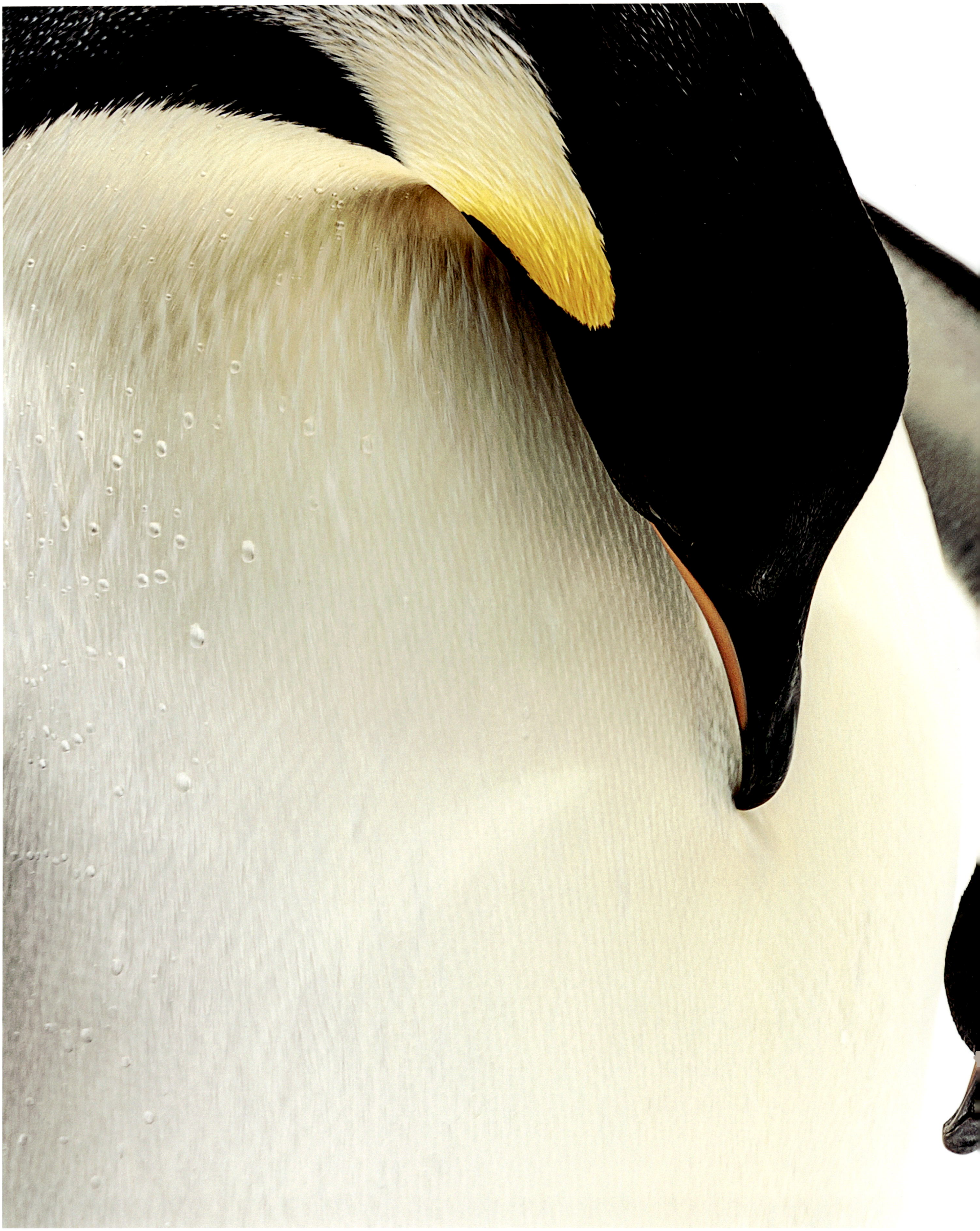

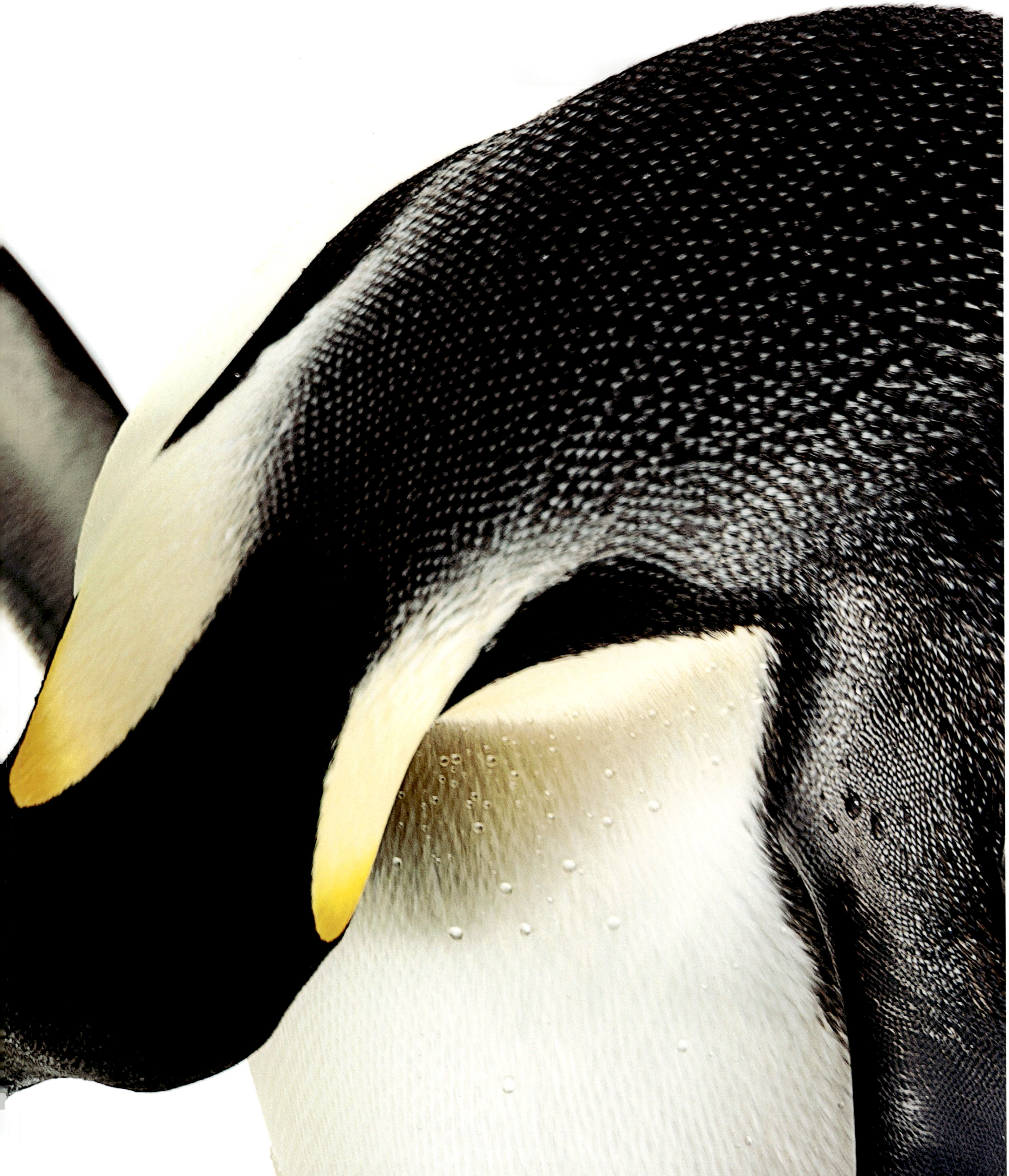

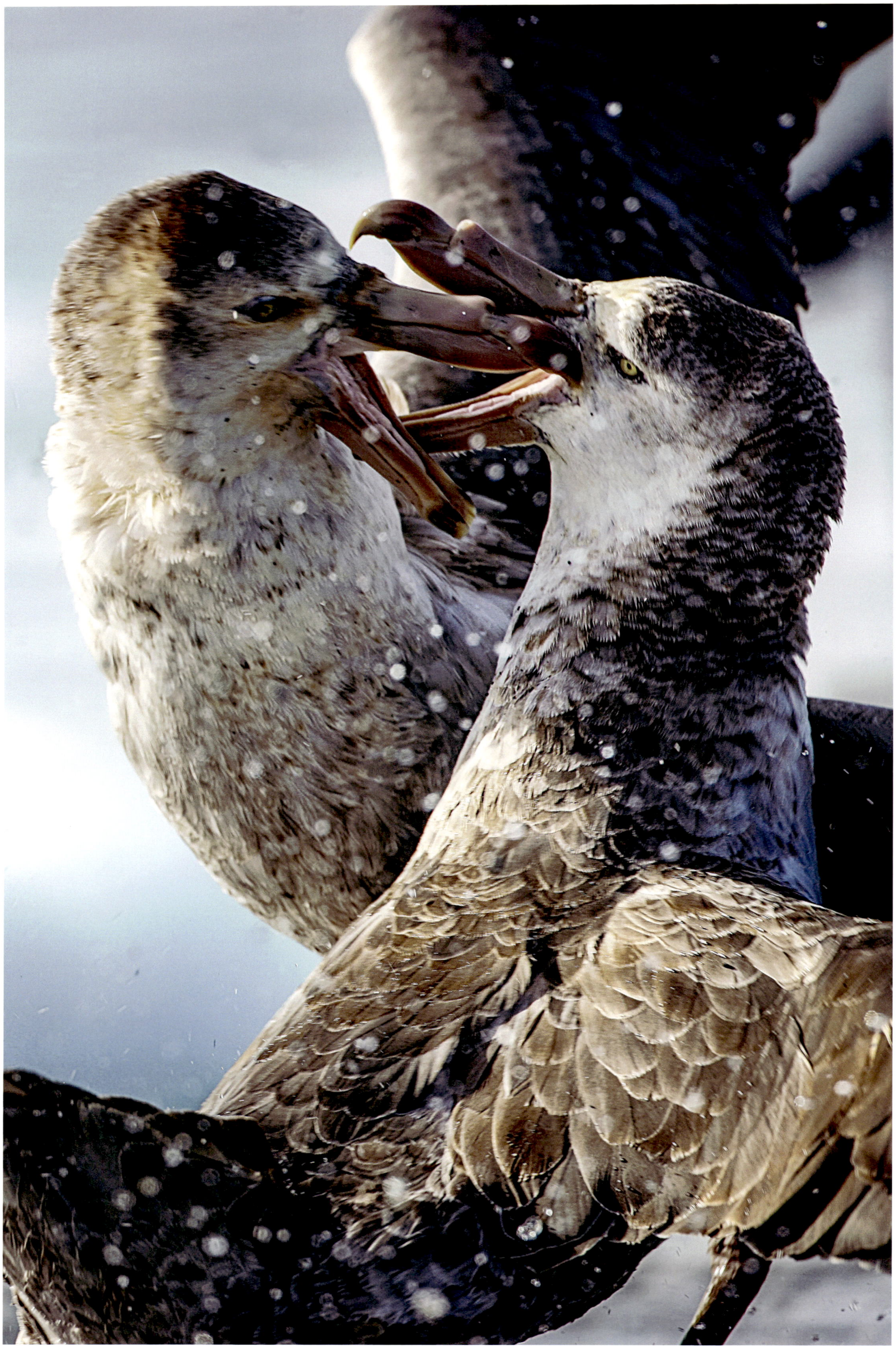

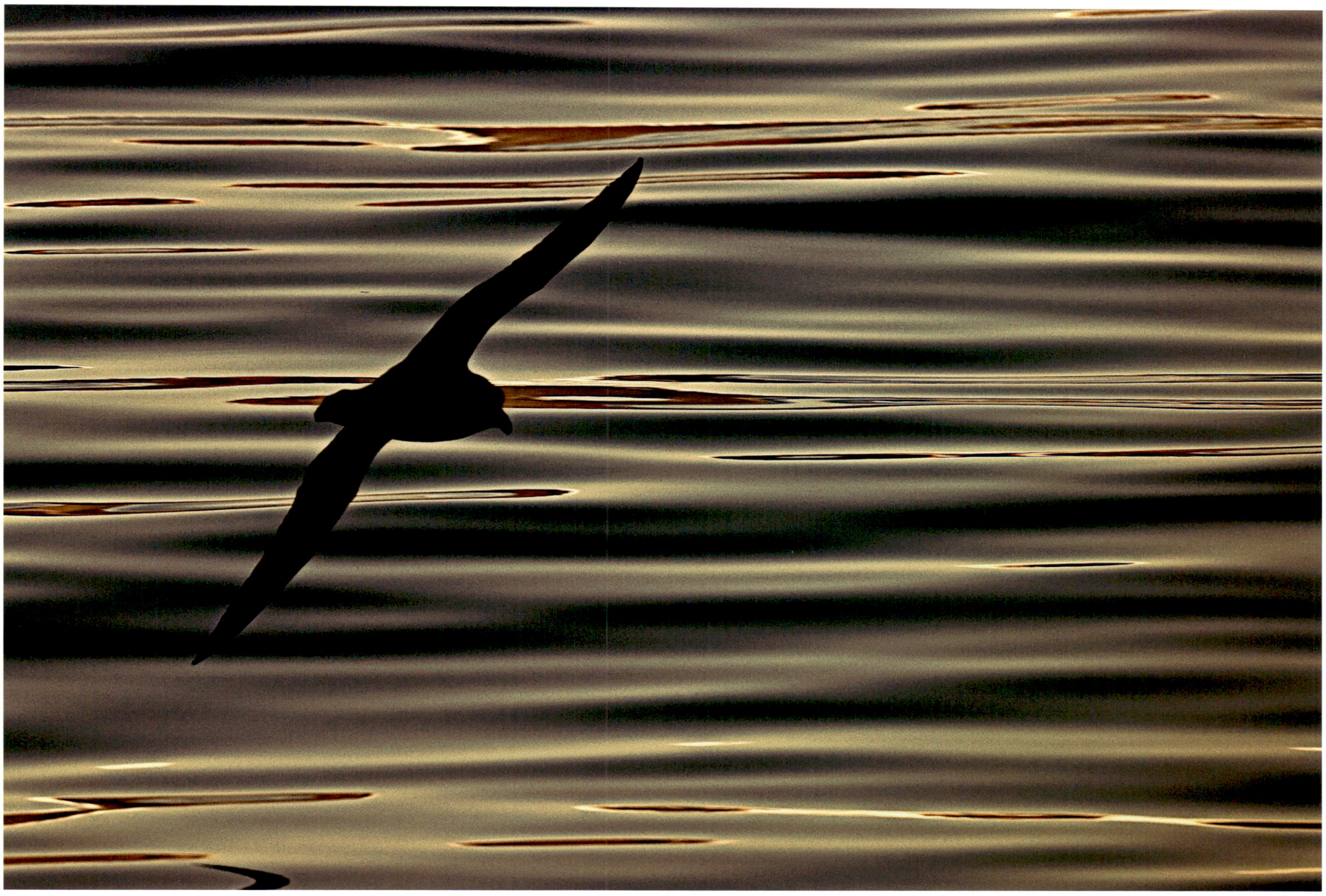

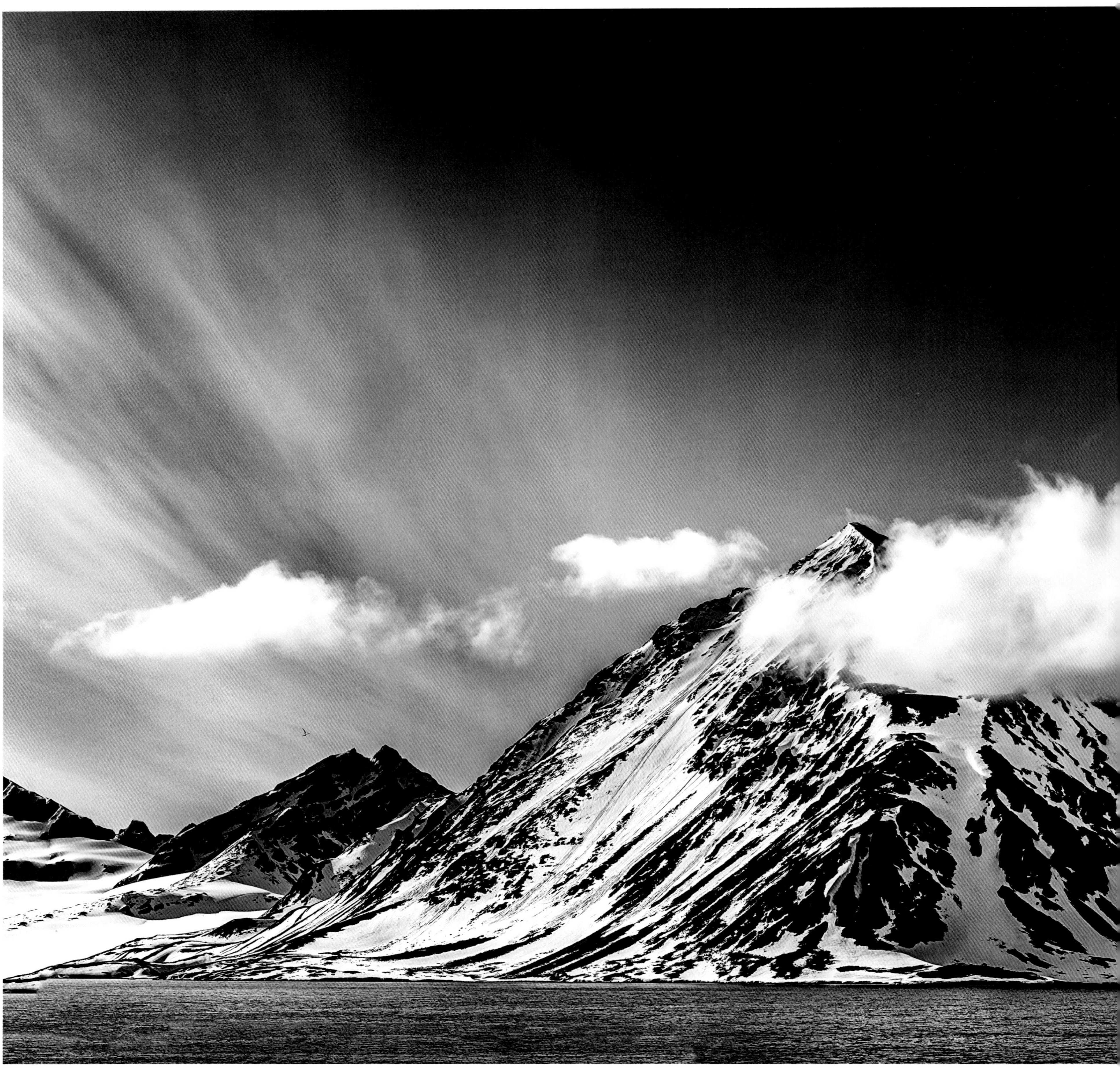

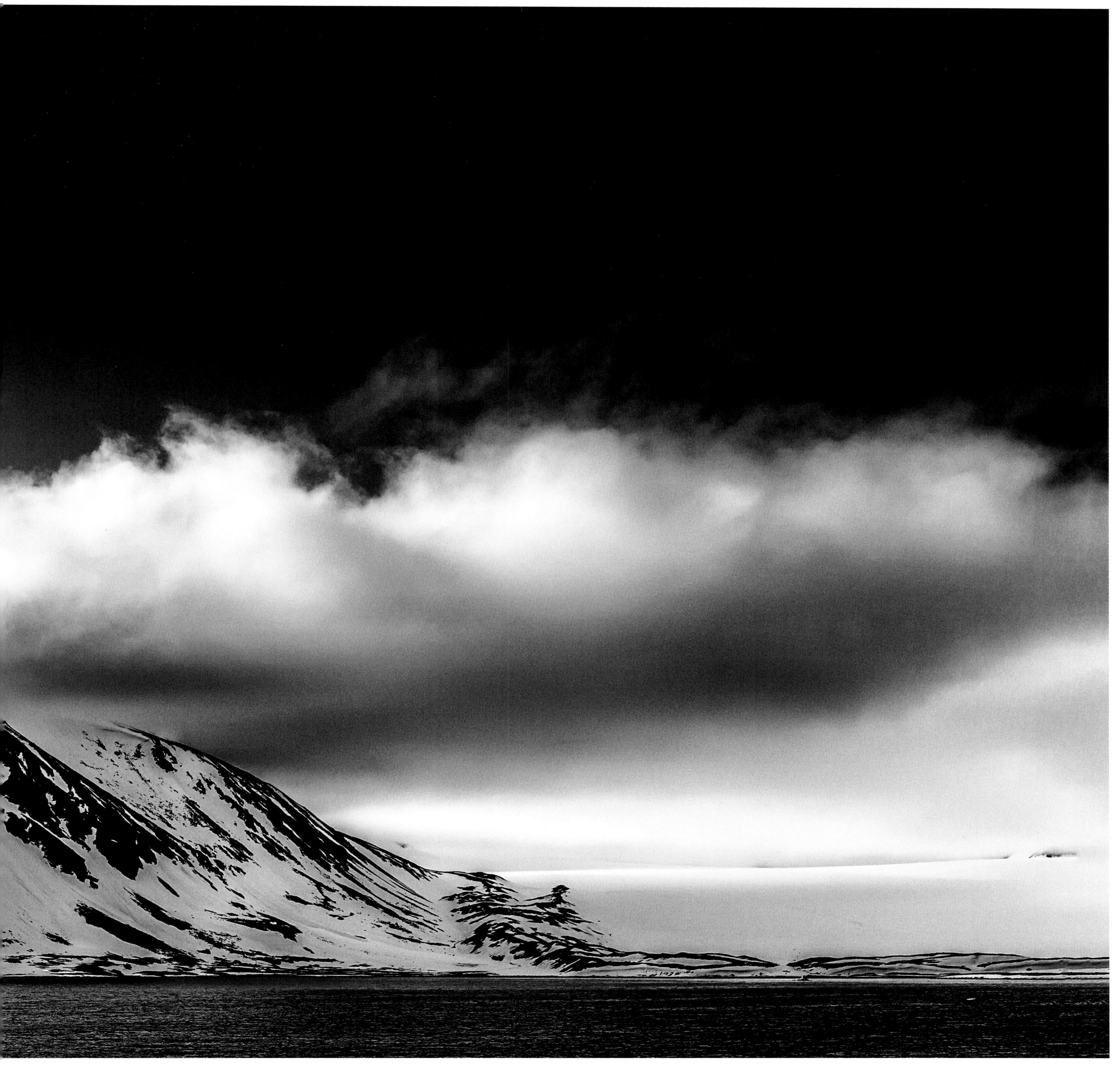

In nature, we never see anything isolated, but everything in connection with something else which is before it, beside it, under it and over it.

—Johann Wolfgang von Goethe

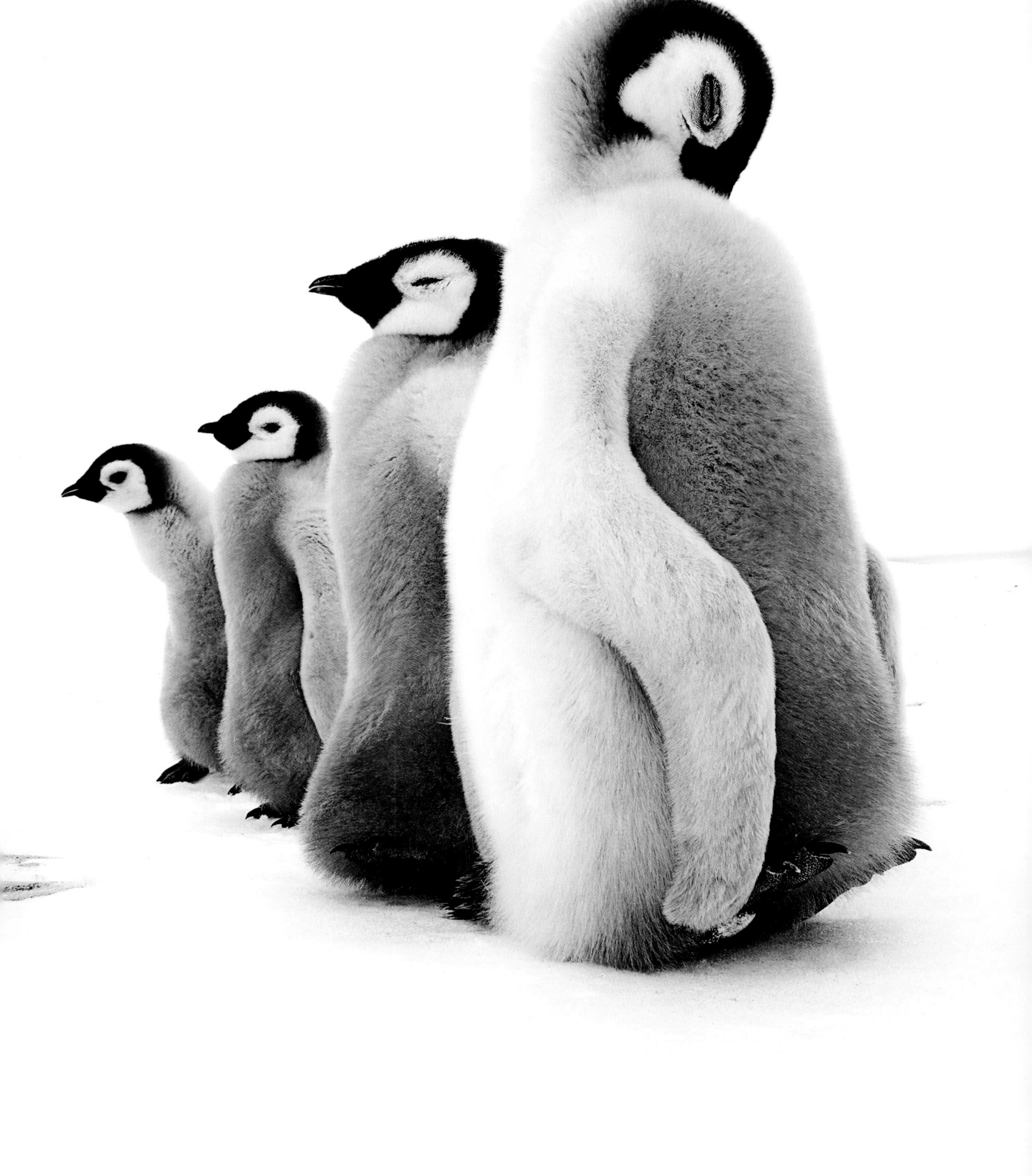

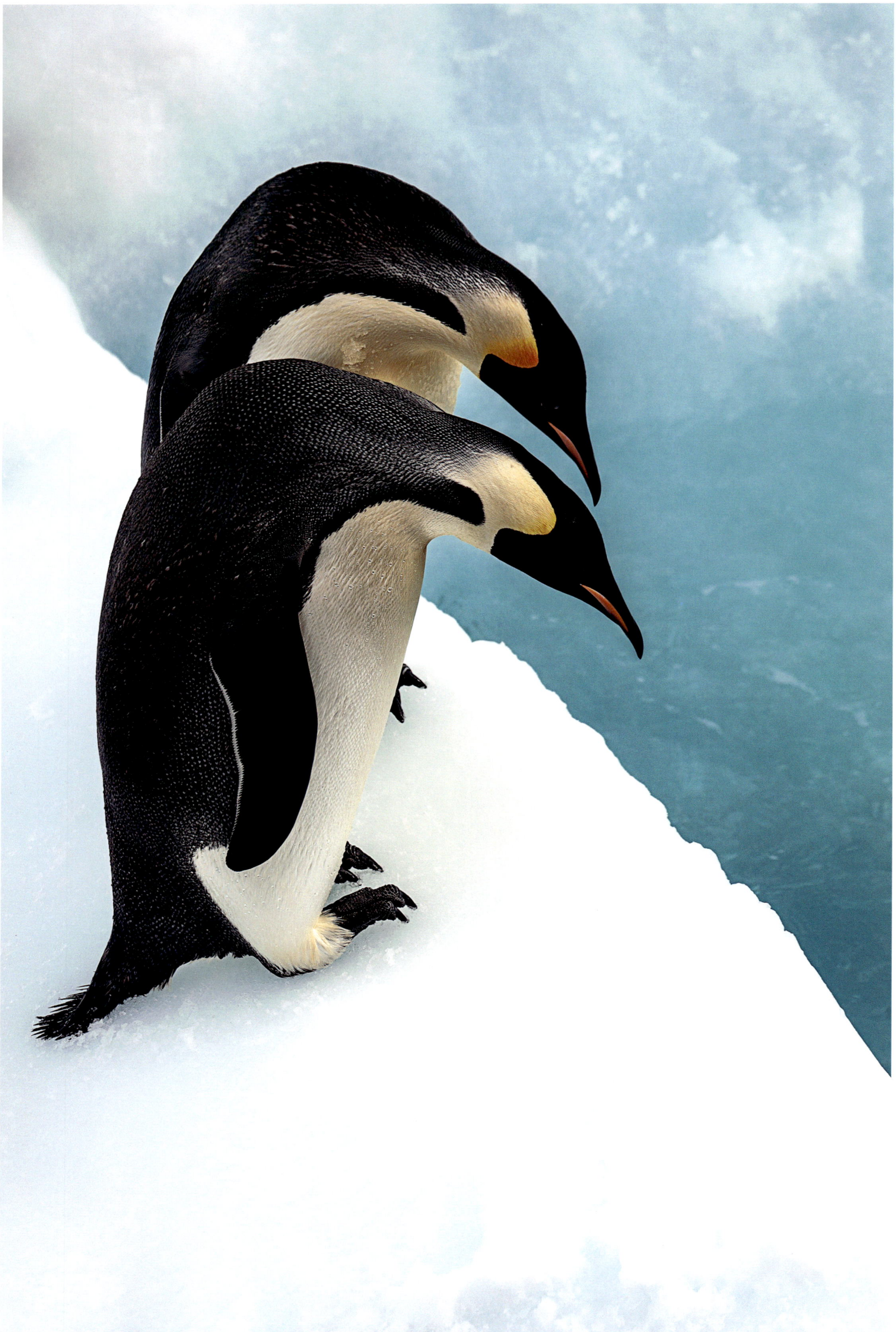

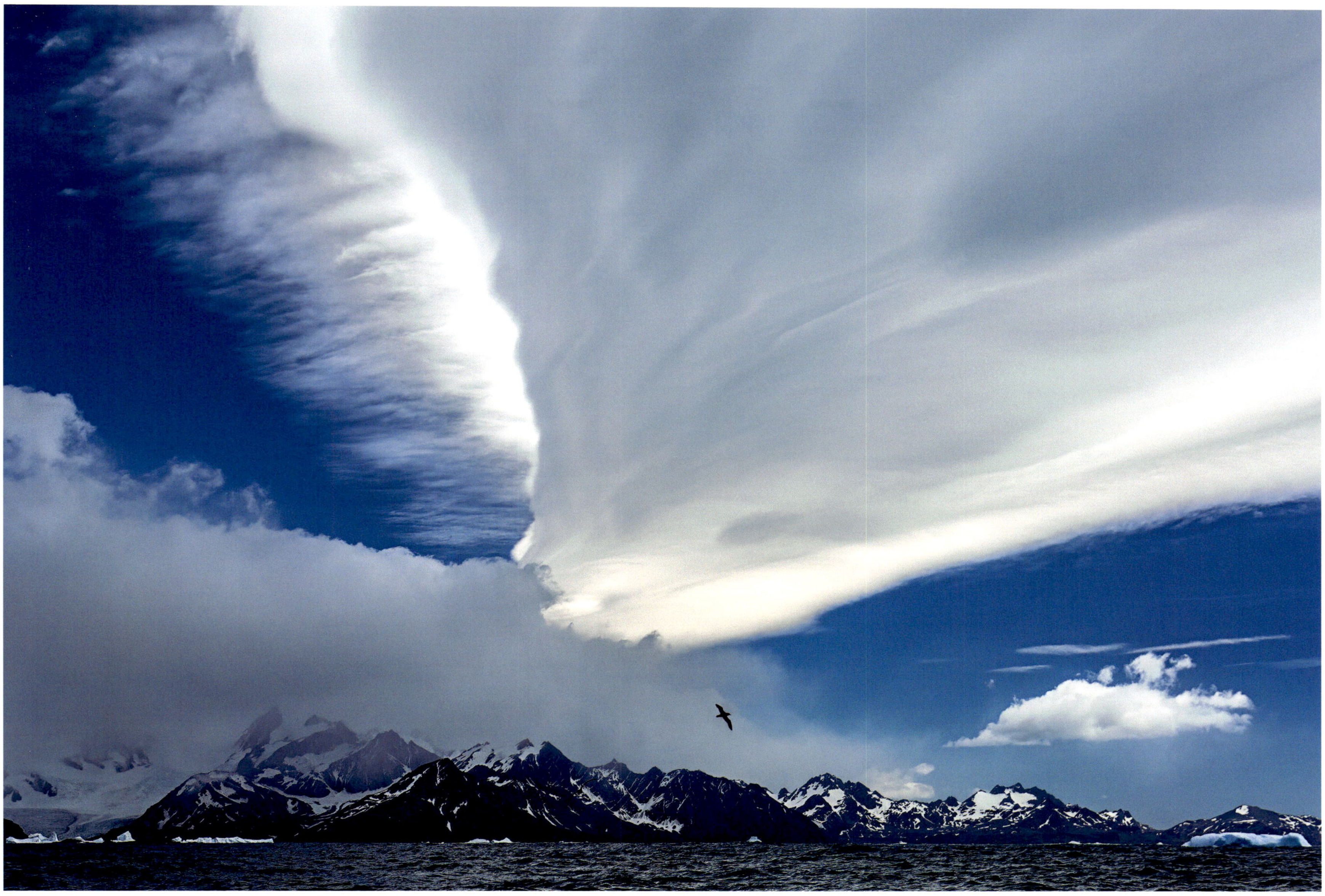

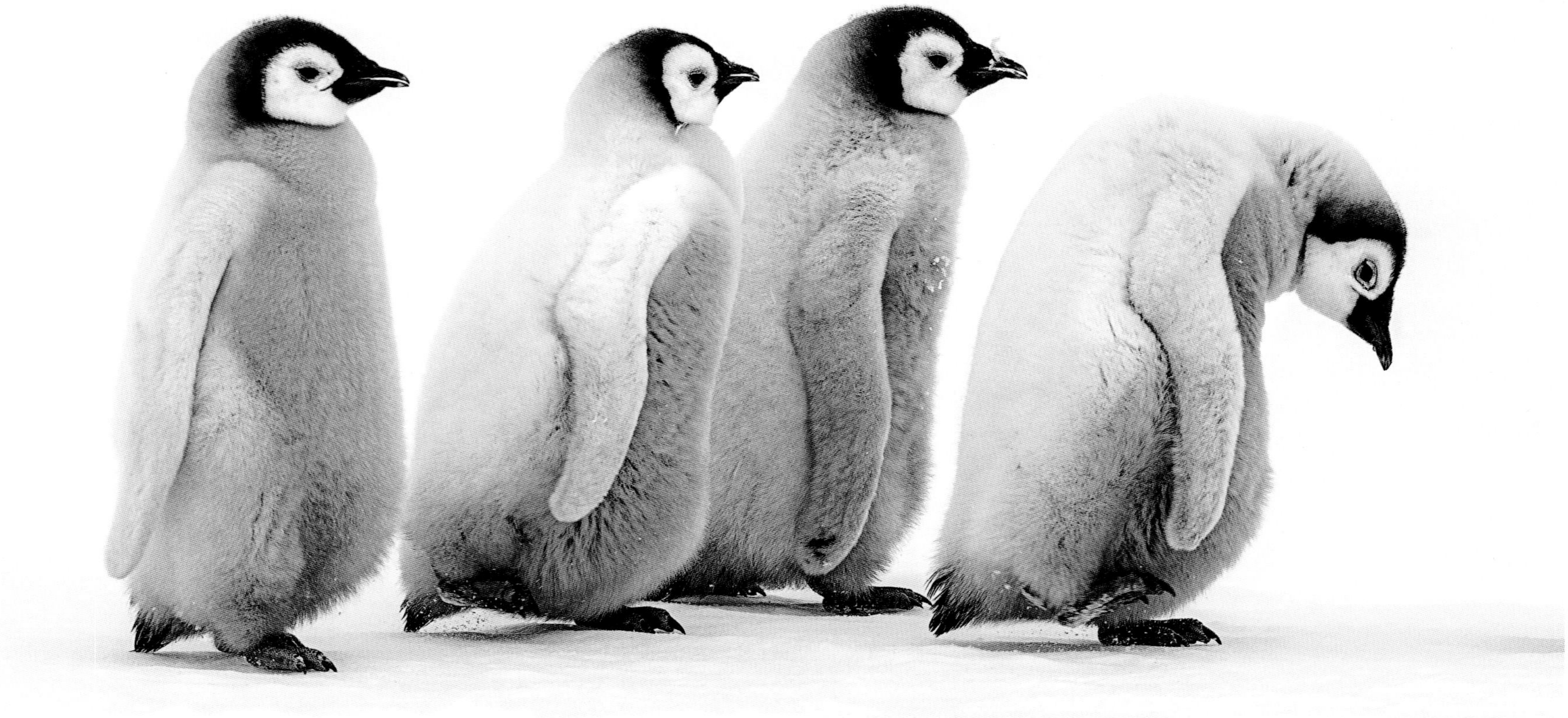

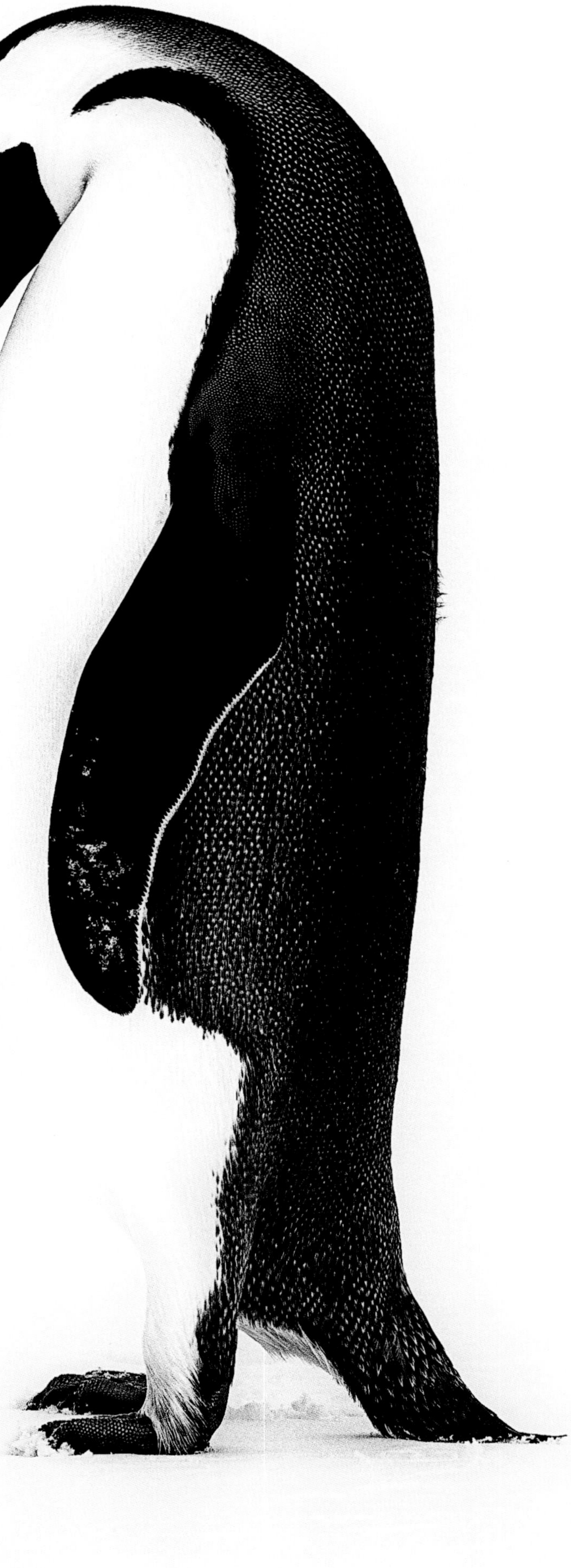

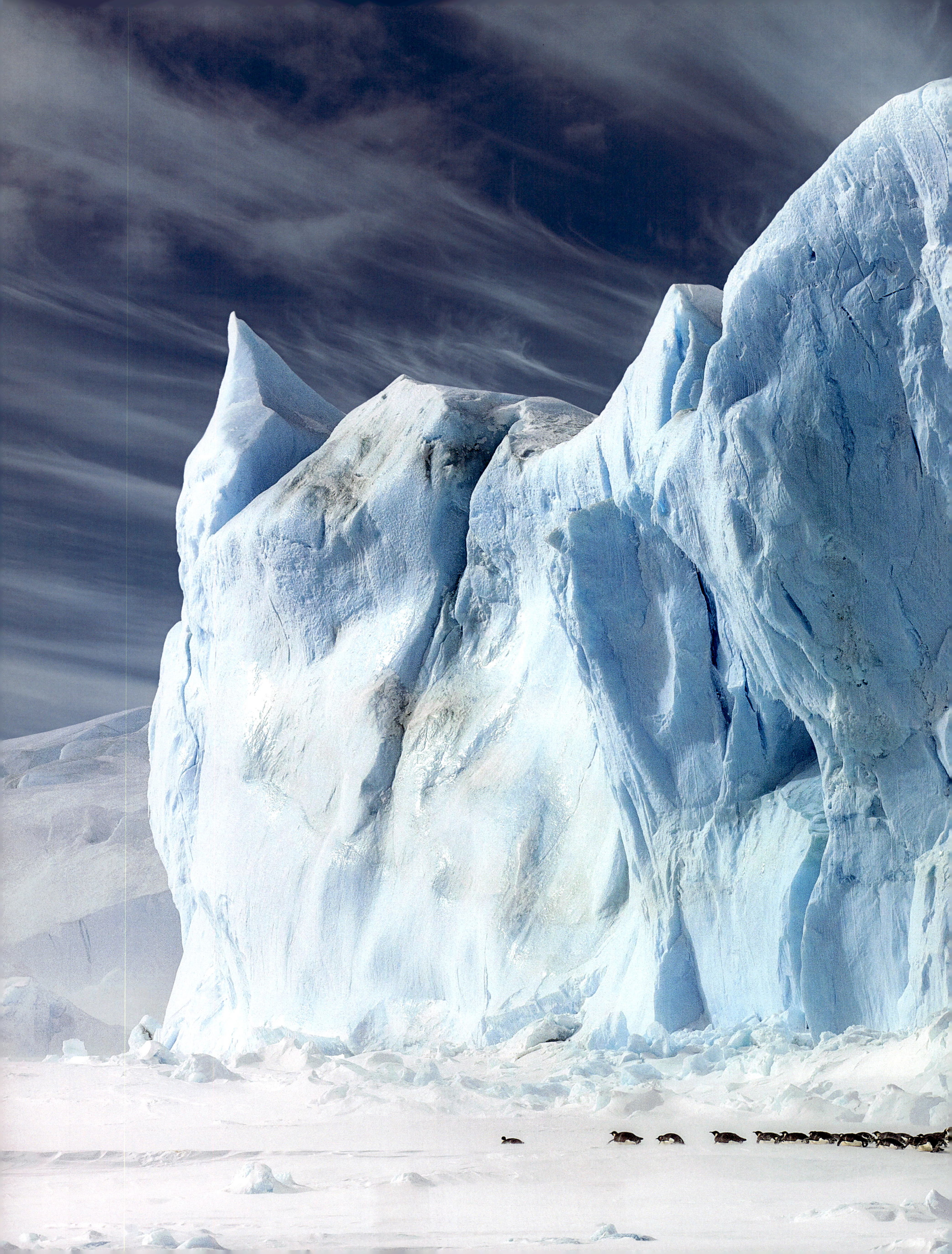

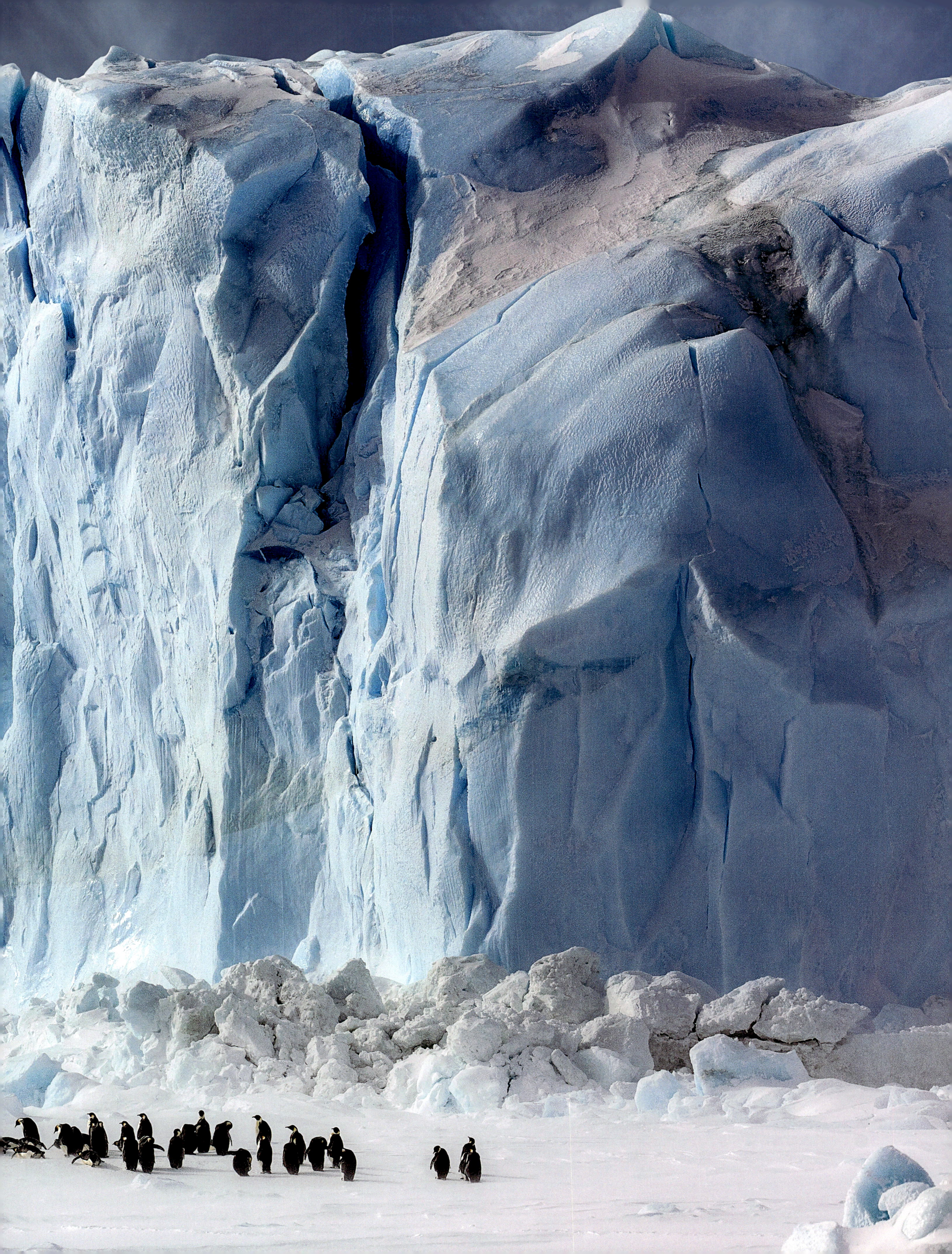

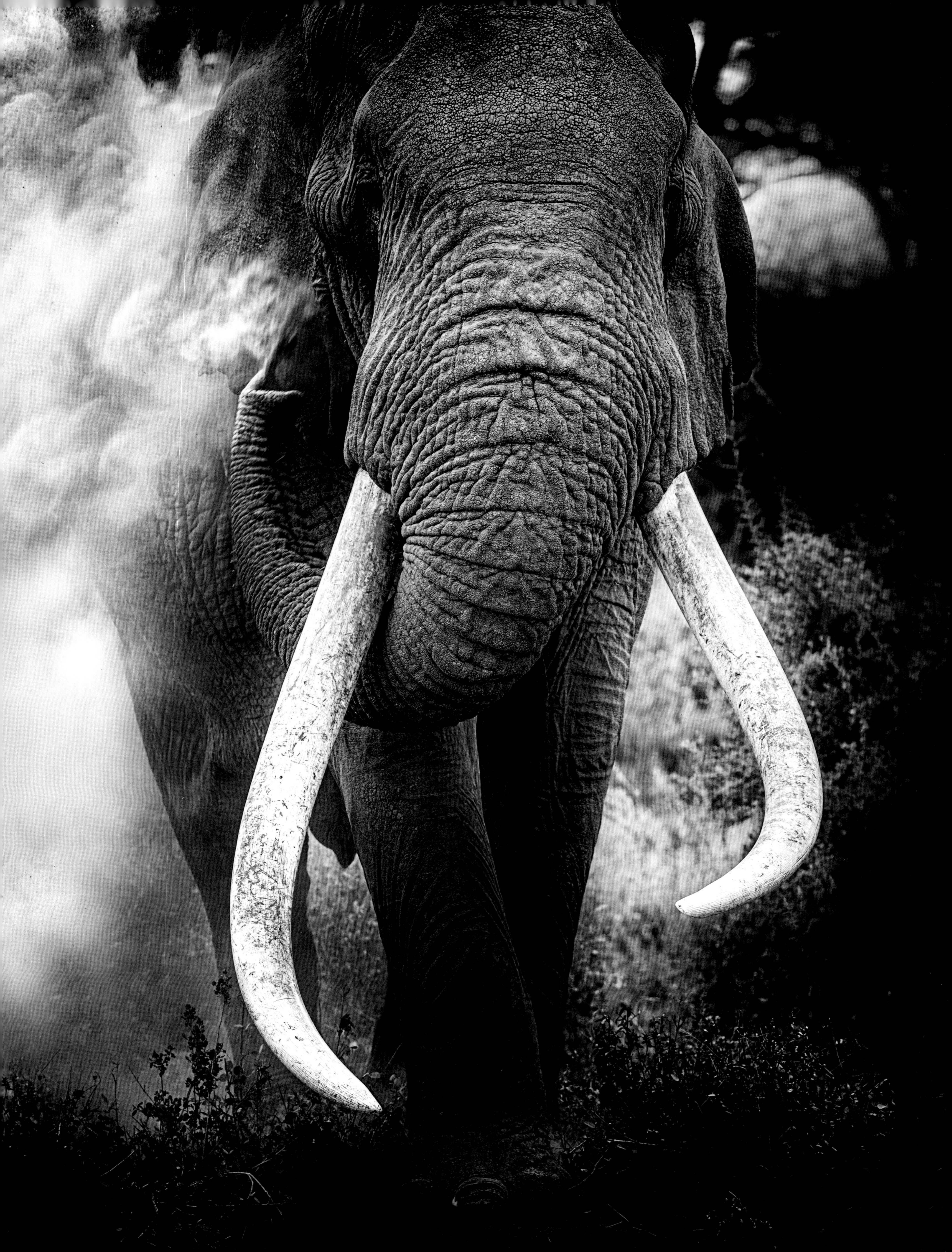

Epilogue

REASON FOR HOPE

Silence in the wild, solidarity from society's static noise, allows harmony with the universe, giving our inner voice the ability to speak and demanding the attention of our external self revealing life purposes, exposing latent gifts and talents and promoting unselfish values ringing the bells of truth about our true spiritual nature within.

— Benjamin Powell

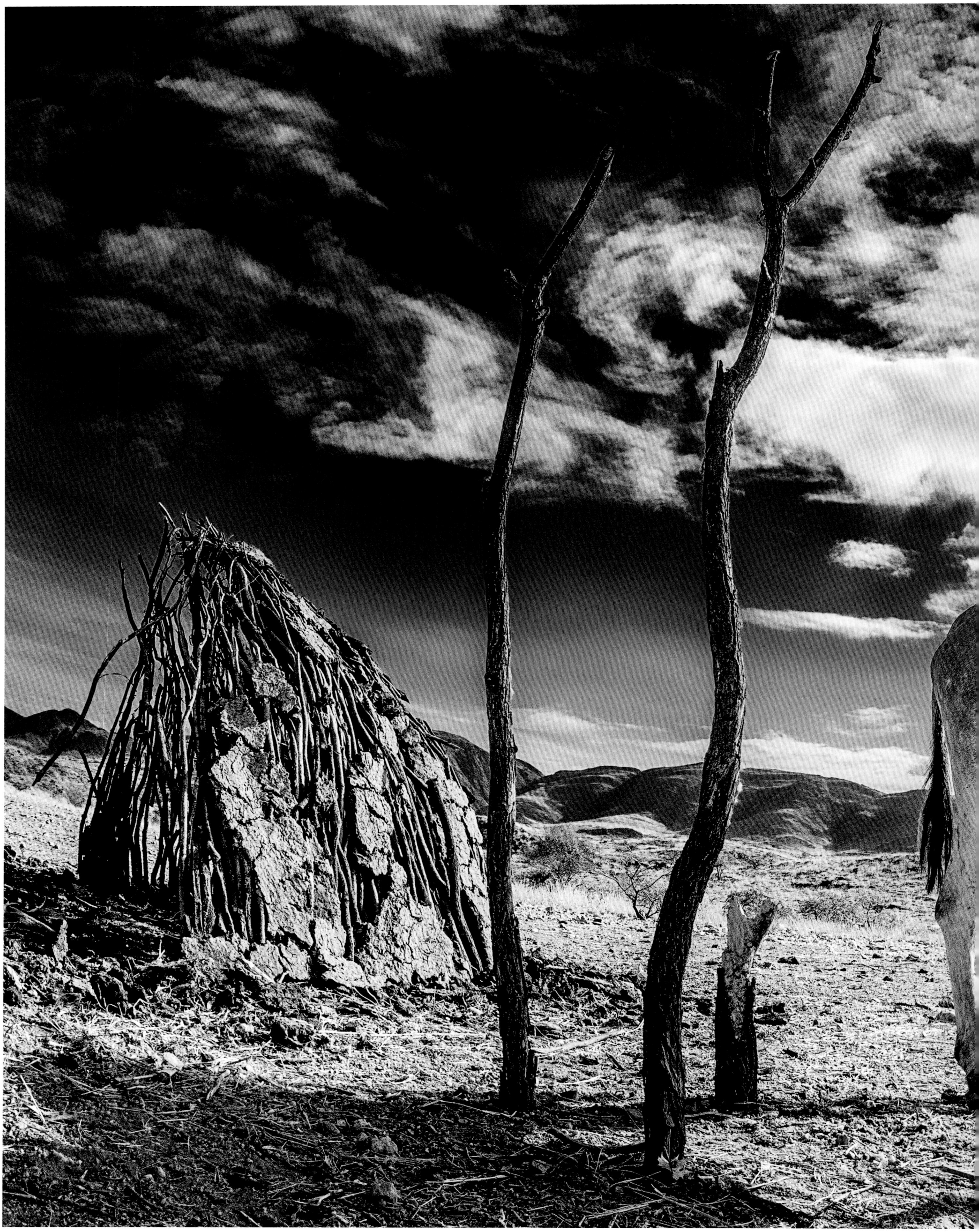

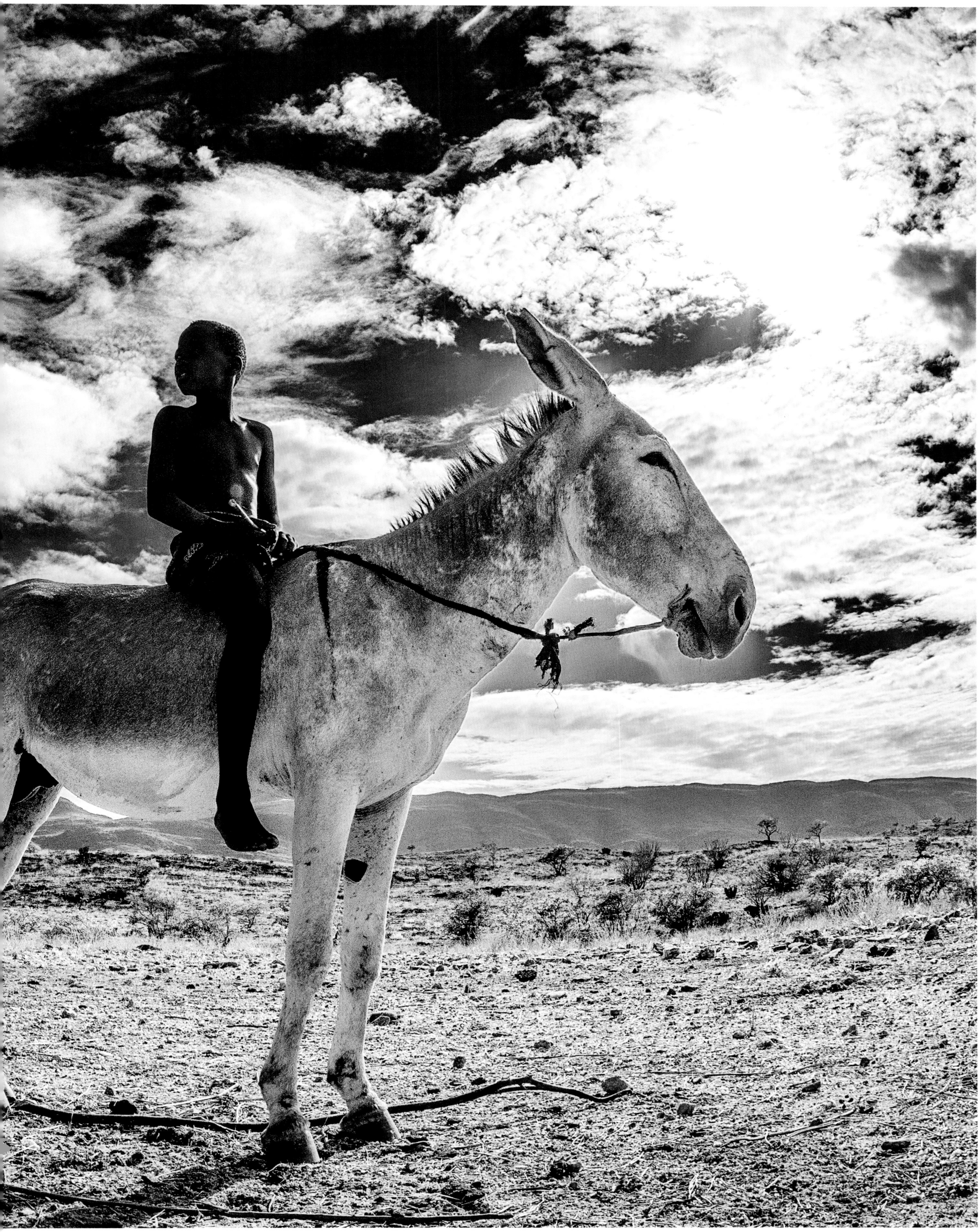

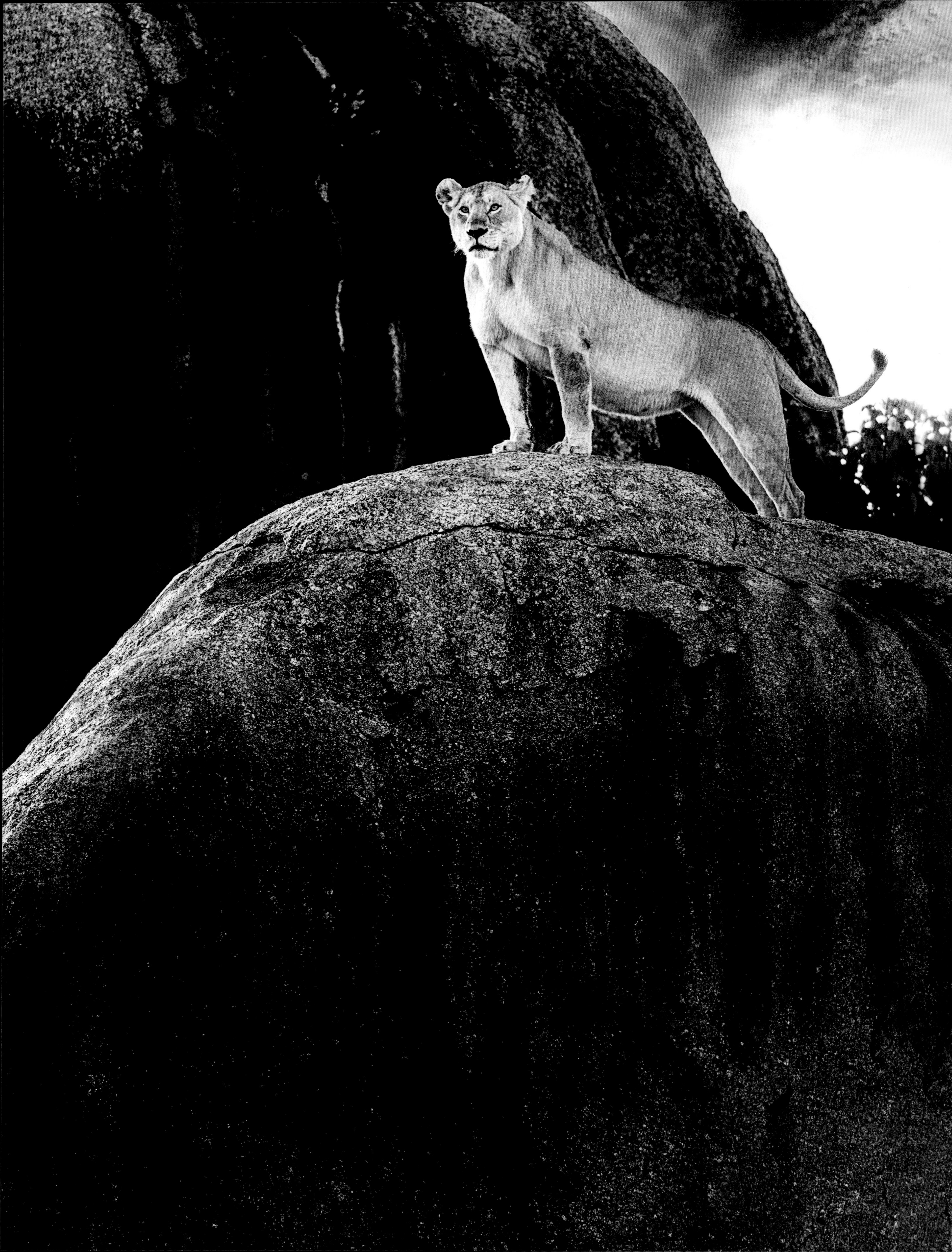

For the majority of our time on Earth, we were just one more species struggling to survive, the direction of our lives determined by the natural environment. Only when humans began to create their own environment shut off from nature's temperance did we lose contact with reality, with the fact that nature is the provider of all things, creating stability between our species and all other life. The advent of agriculture and the domestication of animals and plants sounded the death knell to that way of being. It allowed us to replace wilderness with towns and cities. If we look around us we see that all other life forms are both sustained by nature and linked by an unspoken covenant with the environment, ensuring they remain in balance. By contrast, we humans have broken free from many of the restraints imposed by our environment; in their place we have created an artificial set of scenarios that has prompted a population explosion. With 7.7 billion people already swamping the planet and the likelihood this figure will rise to 11 billion by 2100, we are rapidly exhausting the Earth's natural resources. We can no longer plead ignorance of this fact. Without an instruction manual of how to manage Planet Earth, we need to proceed with the utmost caution.

The guiding light that burns within all of us, that sense of spirituality that transcends all beliefs and understanding, enables us to express our wonder and gratitude for the gift of life and creativity of nature. The sublime vision of a snowcapped mountain glimpsed against a sky of the most radiant blue or the cascading sound of a rapturous chorus as birds of many colours shuffle their feathers and salute the dawning of a new day does not require explanation. It evokes emotions and feelings on which we all thrive. In that moment we experience a sense of belonging. There is a word for this deeply felt love of all that is alive: biophilia, the urge to connect with nature and the natural environment.

So why isn't everyone conscious of our connection to nature? Why isn't everyone a conservationist? Anthropologist Kay Milton argues that in Western society science and capitalism dominate our world view. By exploiting nature to fuel our economy we have become conditioned to viewing it primarily as a commodity, a resource to be owned and used as we please. In taking this approach, we have lost any sense of moral responsibility for nature.

Indigenous communities have long highlighted the spiritual importance of stewardship and caring for the Earth. Science alone cannot evaluate the emotional connection people feel towards nature, weighing its merits against the market interests embedded in an economic model that prioritises growth at all costs. Equally it is impossible for economists to account for all the hidden costs of exploiting the natural environment or accurately assessing the value of ecosystem services, those hidden benefits that nature provides free of charge. However, if the positive benefits of nature need quantifying by science, then help is at hand in Florence Williams' excellent book *The Nature Fix: Why Nature Makes Us Happier, Healthier, and More Creative*. Her message is simple: we suffer from an 'epidemic dislocation from the outdoors', a nature-deficit disorder that is damaging to our mental and physical health. More time spent in nature makes us healthier and happier, promoting reflection and innovation and strengthening our relationships, helping to improve mood, alertness and creativity by enhancing our capacity to think clearly.

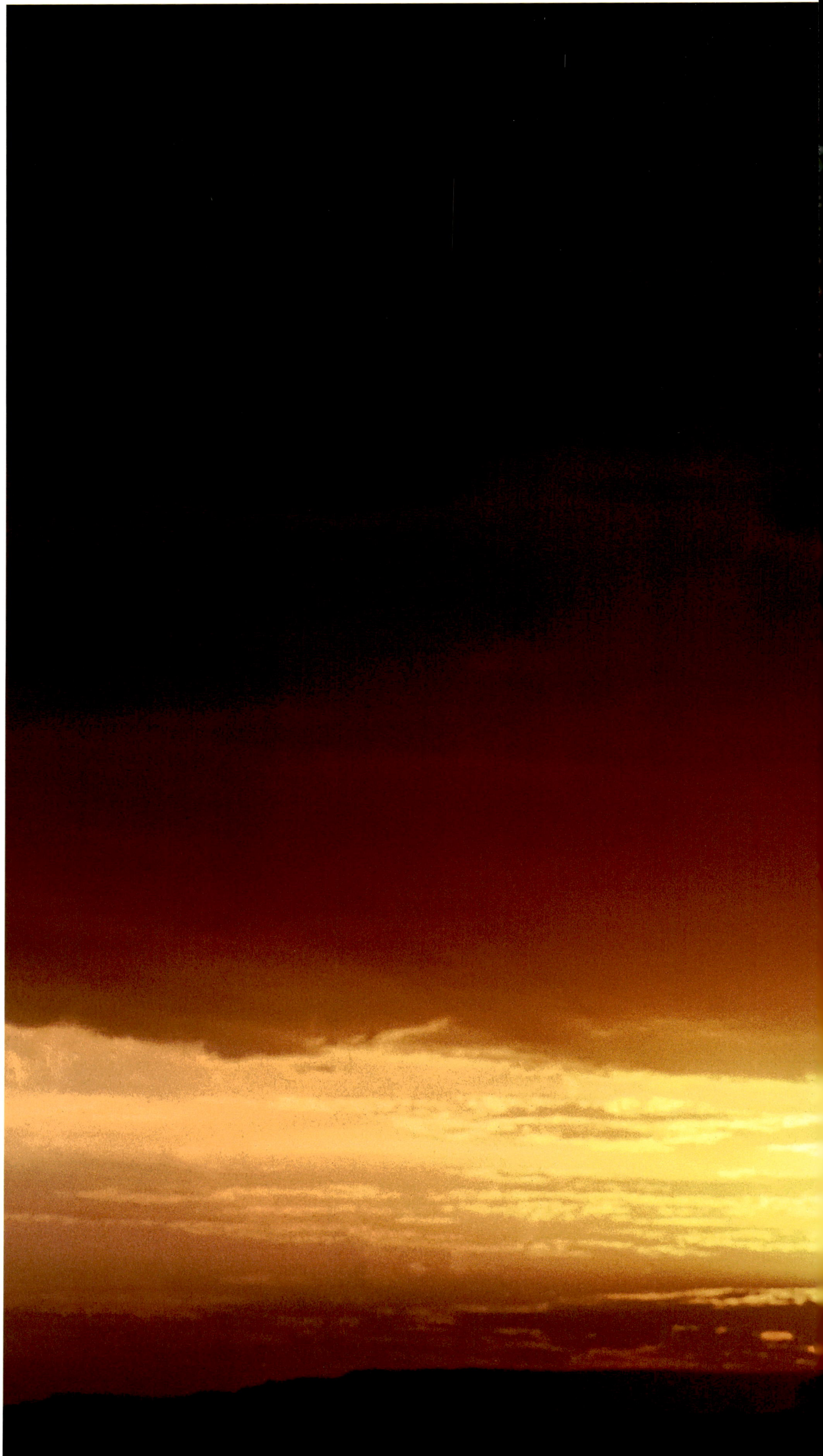

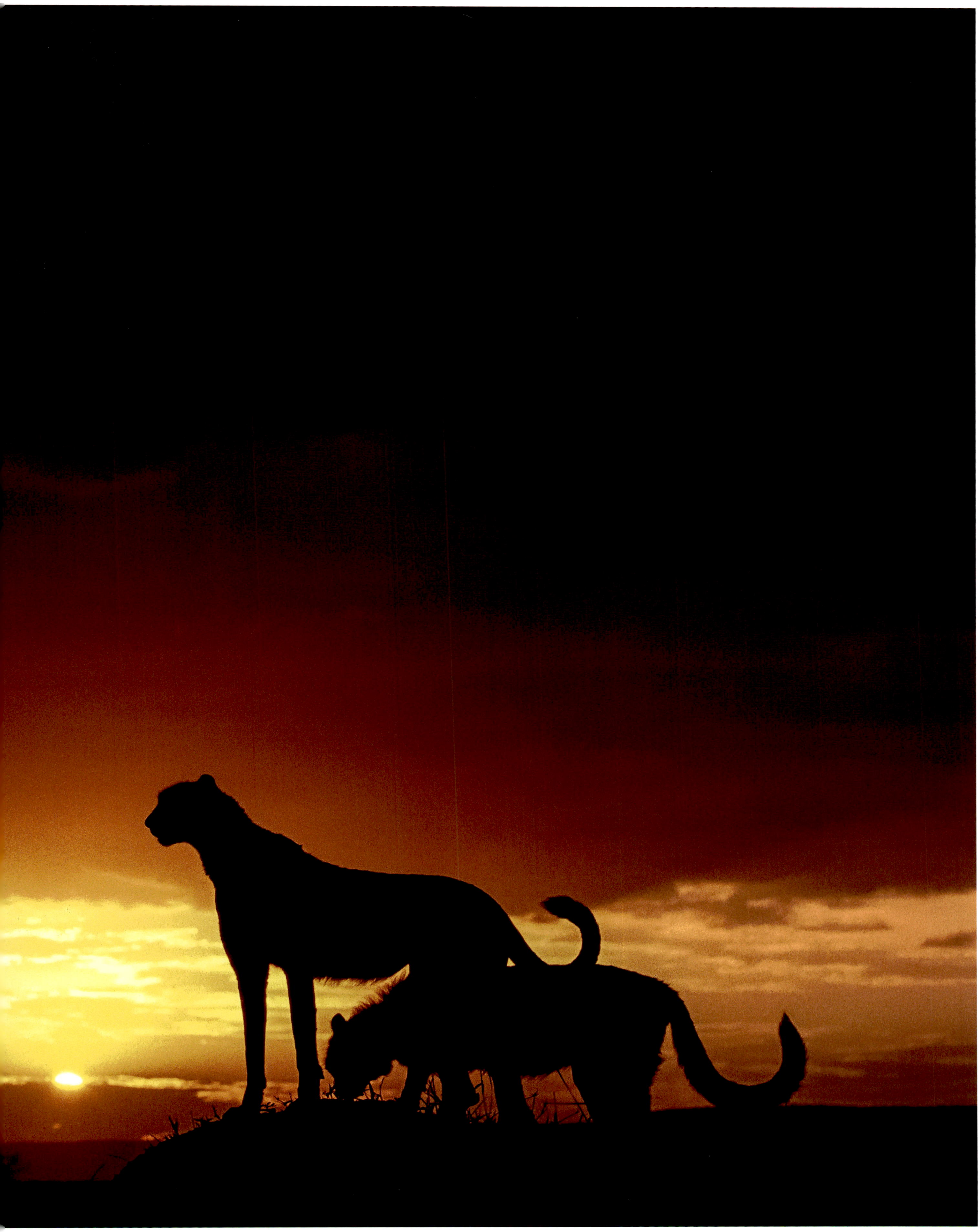

There is a word for this deeply felt love of all that is alive: biophilia, the urge to connect with nature and the natural environment.

The therapeutic value of nature knows no boundaries, from tree bathing trails in Japan and healing fragrant cypress forests walks in Korea that boost respiration while acting as mild sedatives, to therapy gardens in Sweden with their glass-domed greenhouses, water features, flower beds and vegetable gardens. Nature provides an antidote to the overstimulation caused by the urban environments in which most of us live. Two elements seem particularly potent at refreshing body and soul – the sight and sound of water and birdsong – just as contact with sentient beings like dolphins brings joy at a deep subliminal level to children with special needs. Spending time outdoors offers tangible relief to those suffering paralysing episodes of post-traumatic stress disorder (PTSD), while children with attention-deficit hyperactivity disorder (ADHD) derive significant benefits from adventure-based school-time in nature, far healthier than administering drugs and forcing pupils to sit still in a conventional classroom. Believing that the only way to keep children safe is to keep them off the roads, away from woods and fields and open spaces for fear of abuse or violence is a great mistake. Communing with nature is not optional. It is a necessity, evoking a powerful sense of connection to the larger community of life, and allowing us to rediscover the sacred in nature.

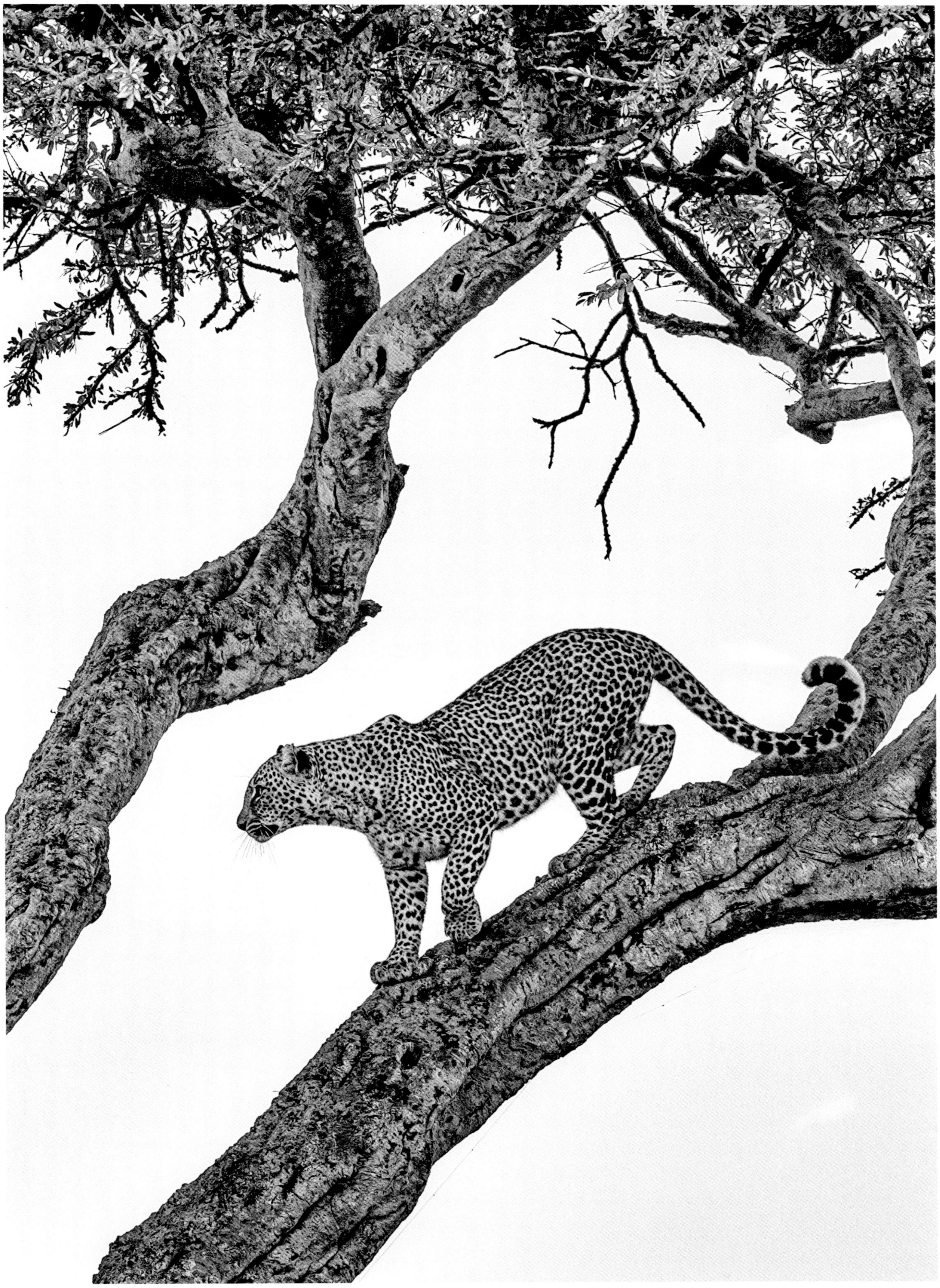

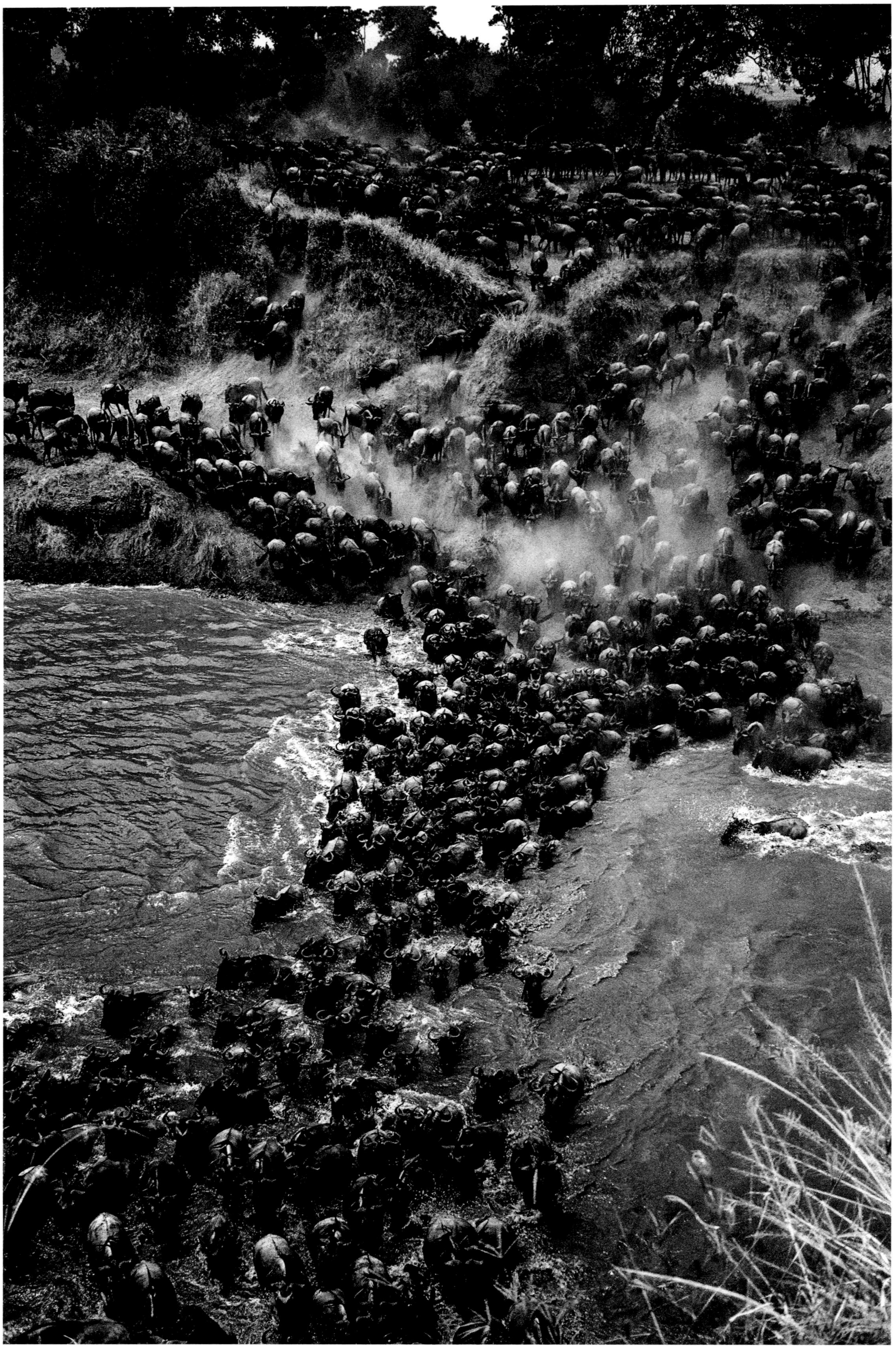

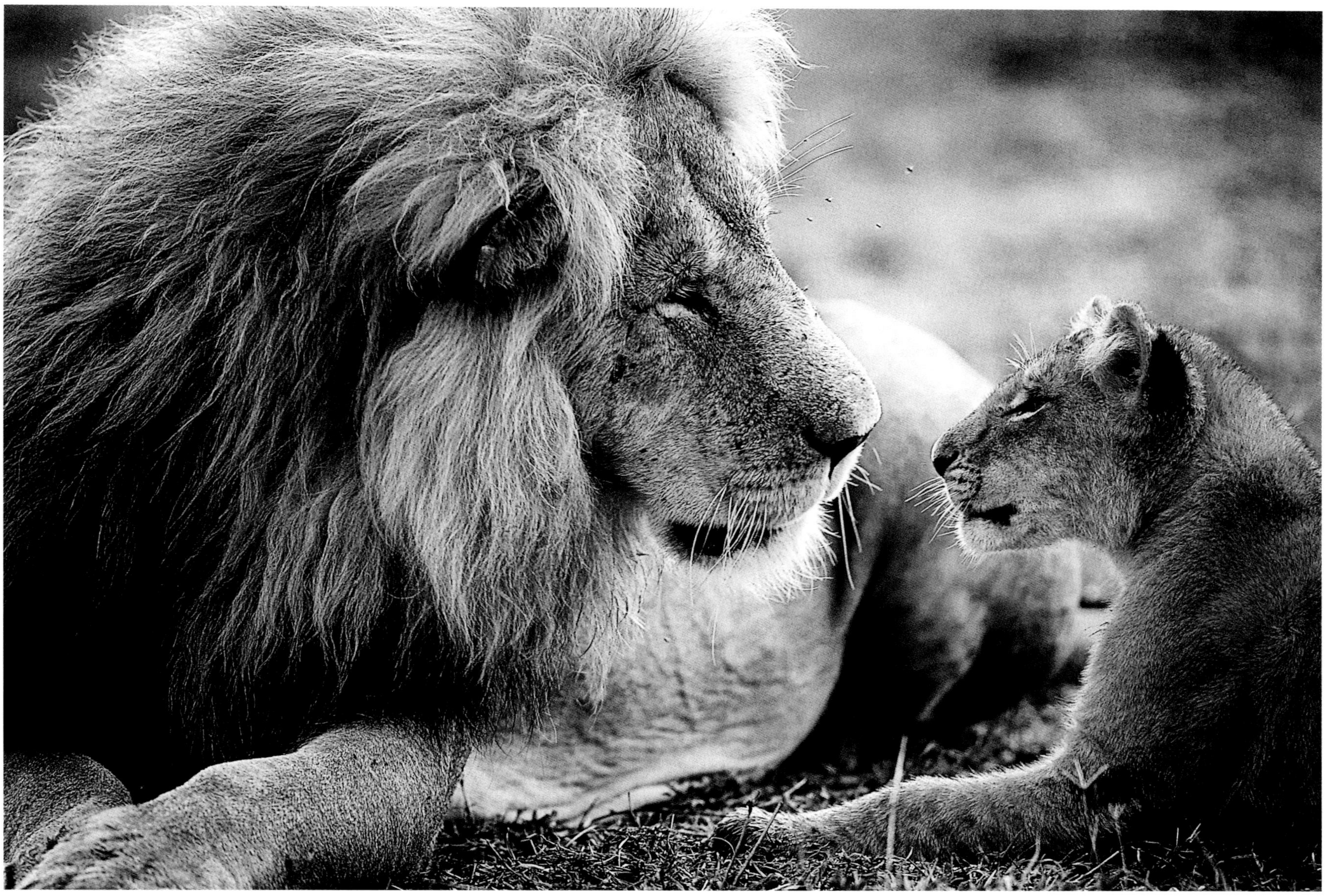

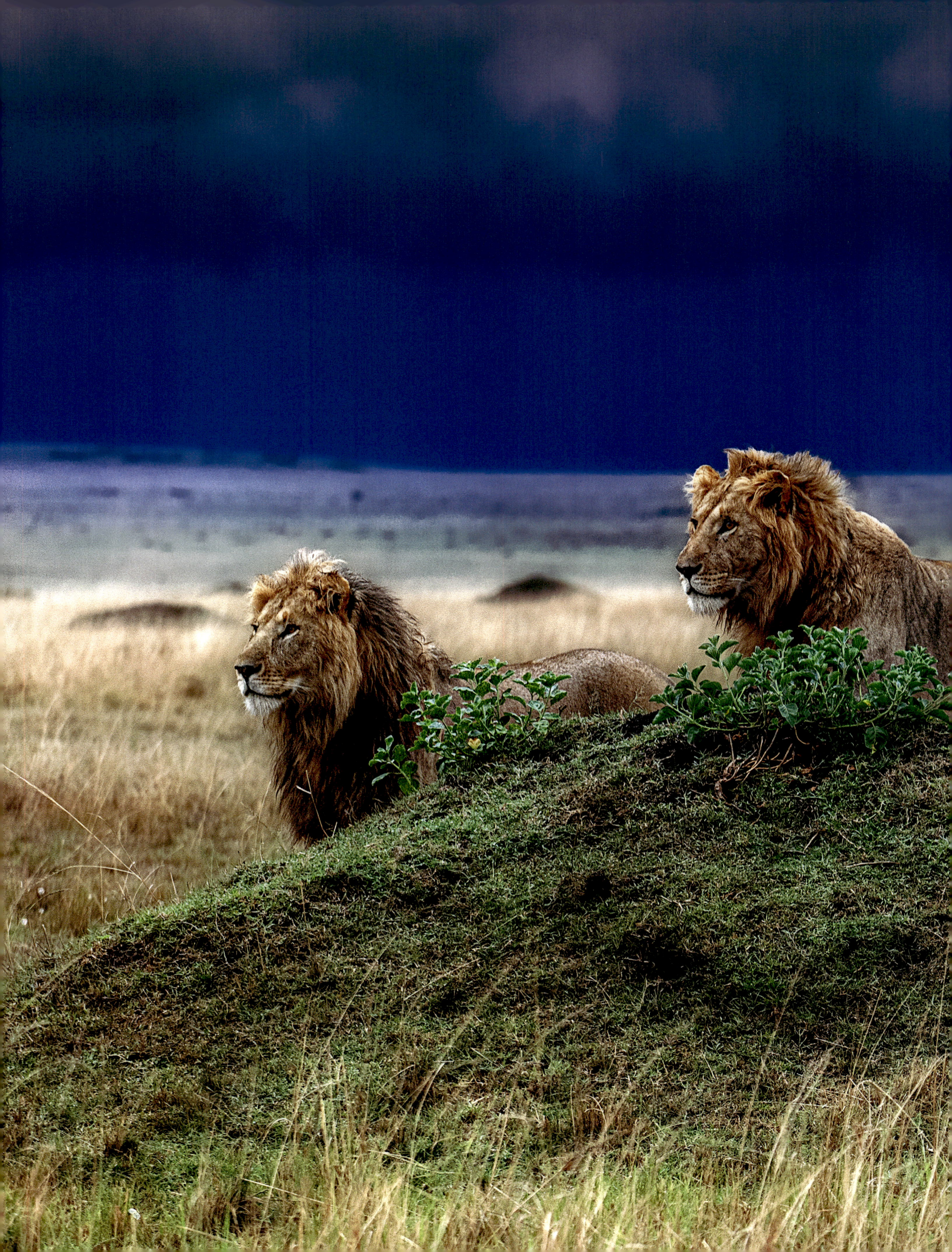

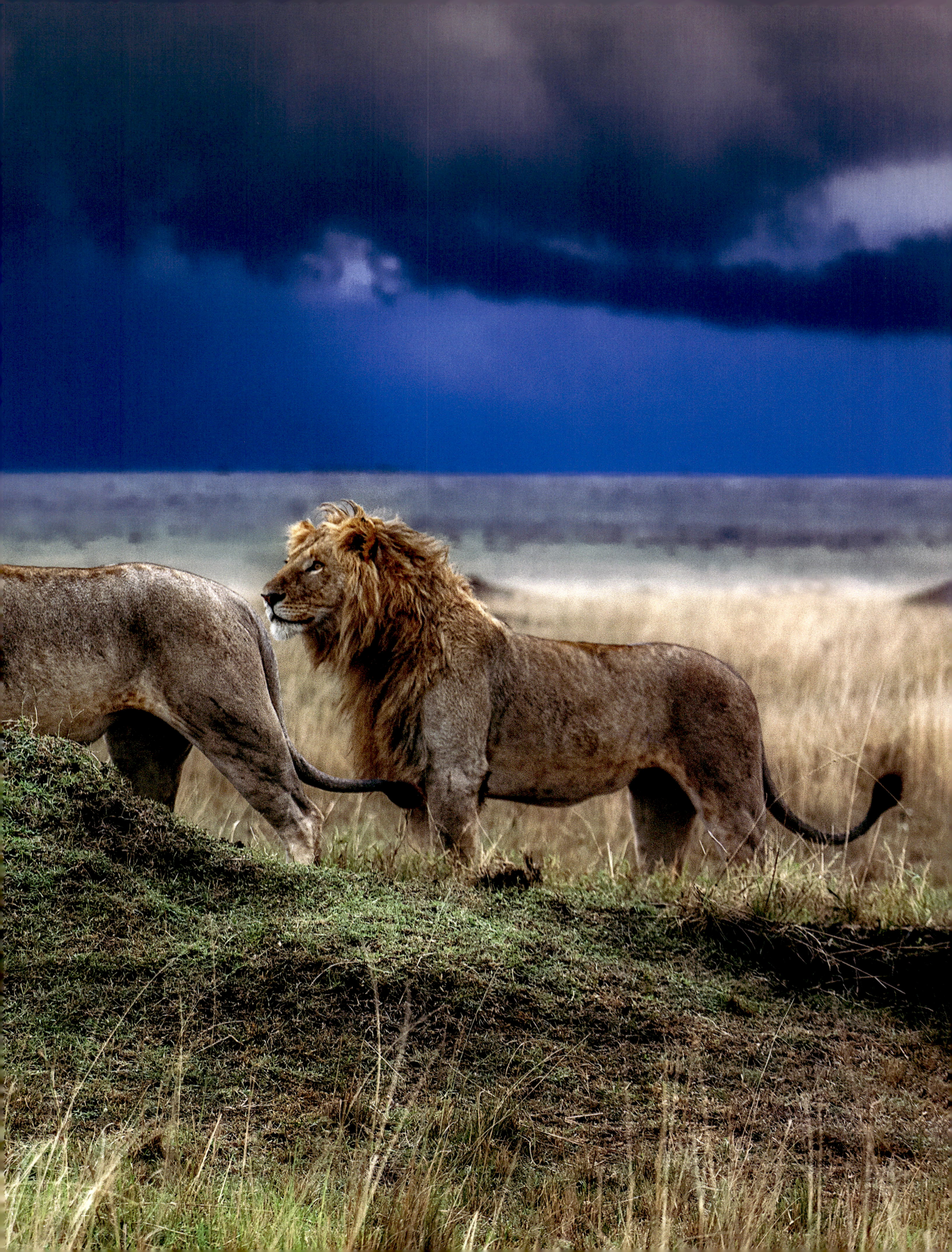

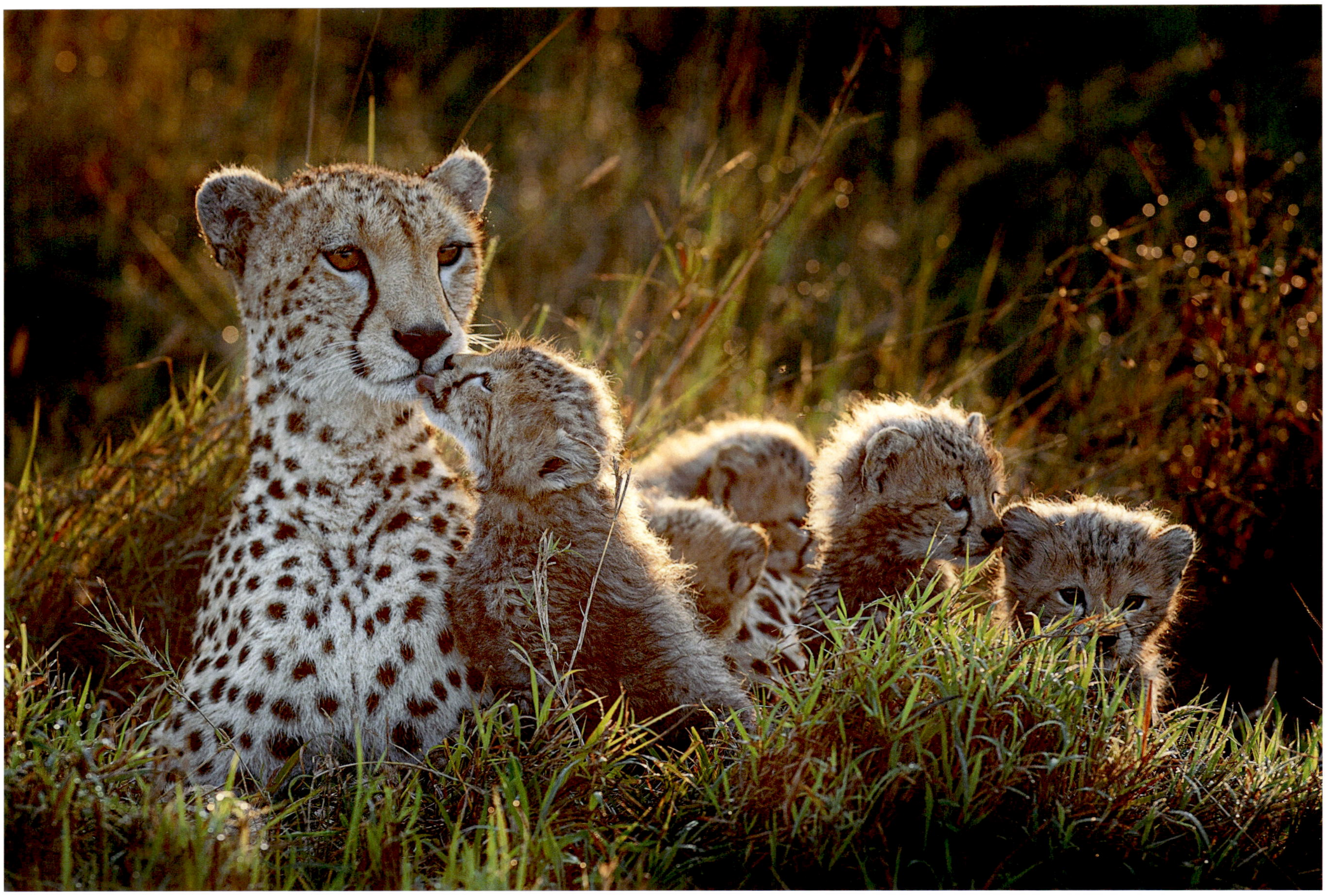

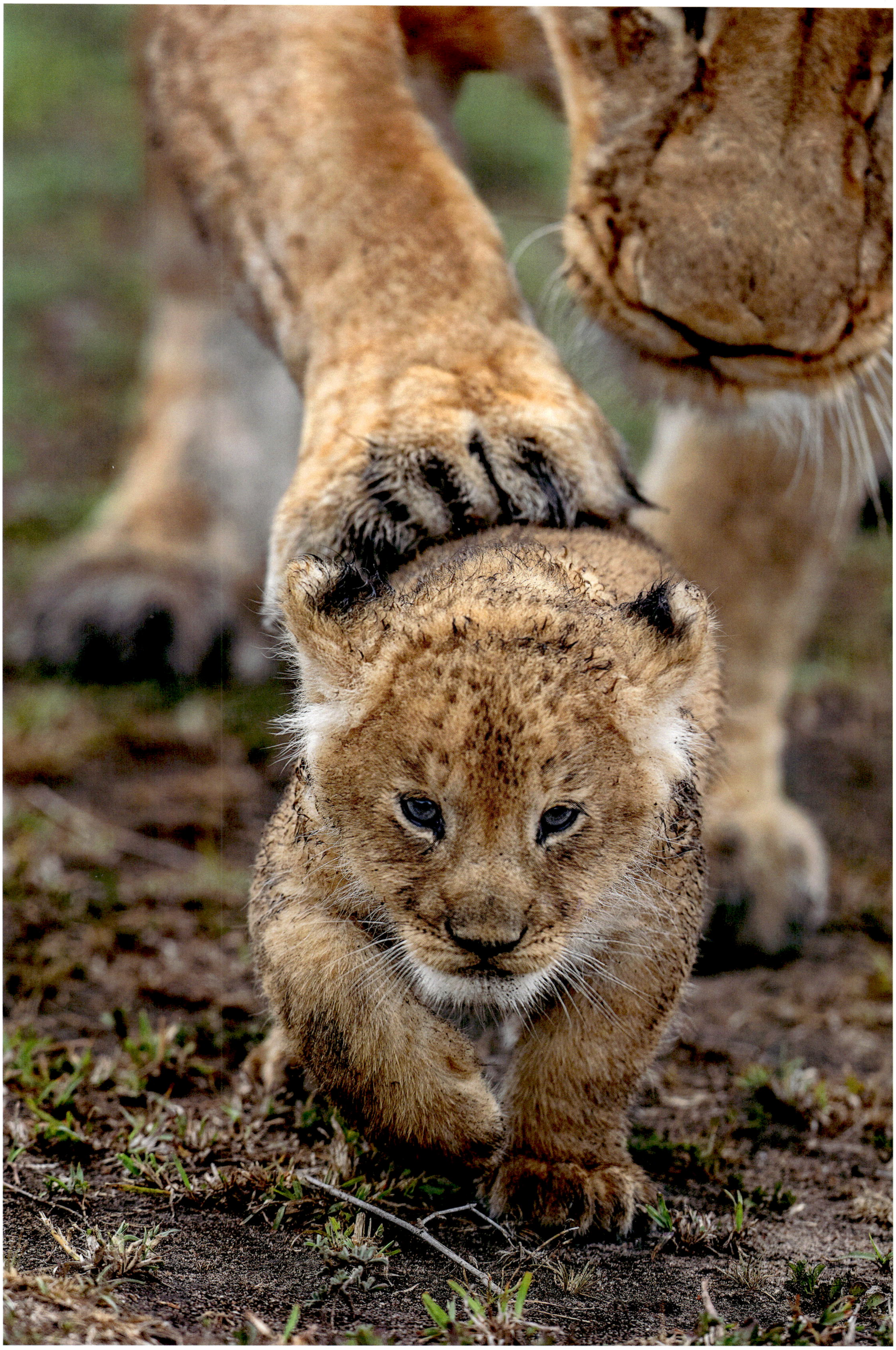

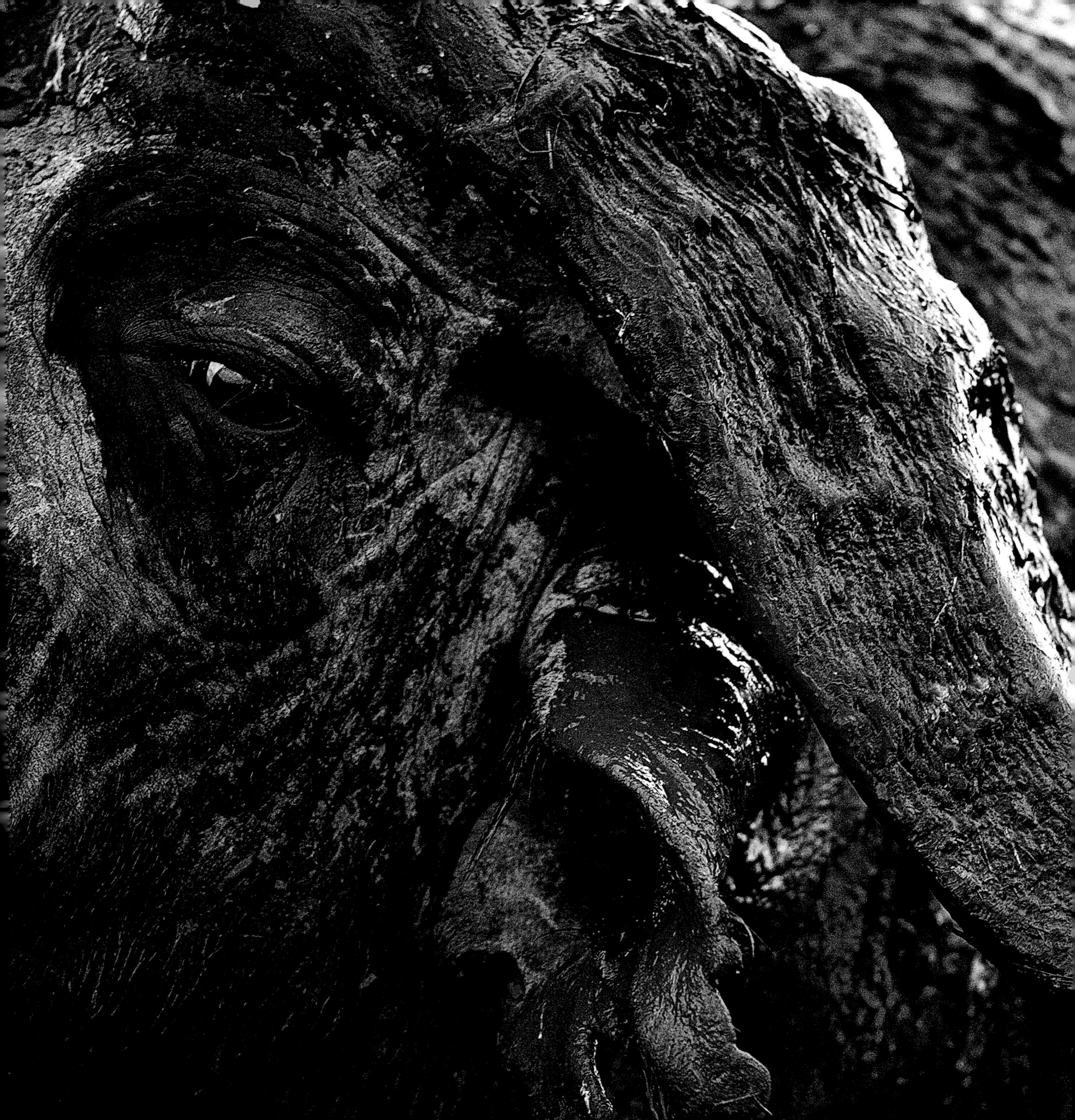

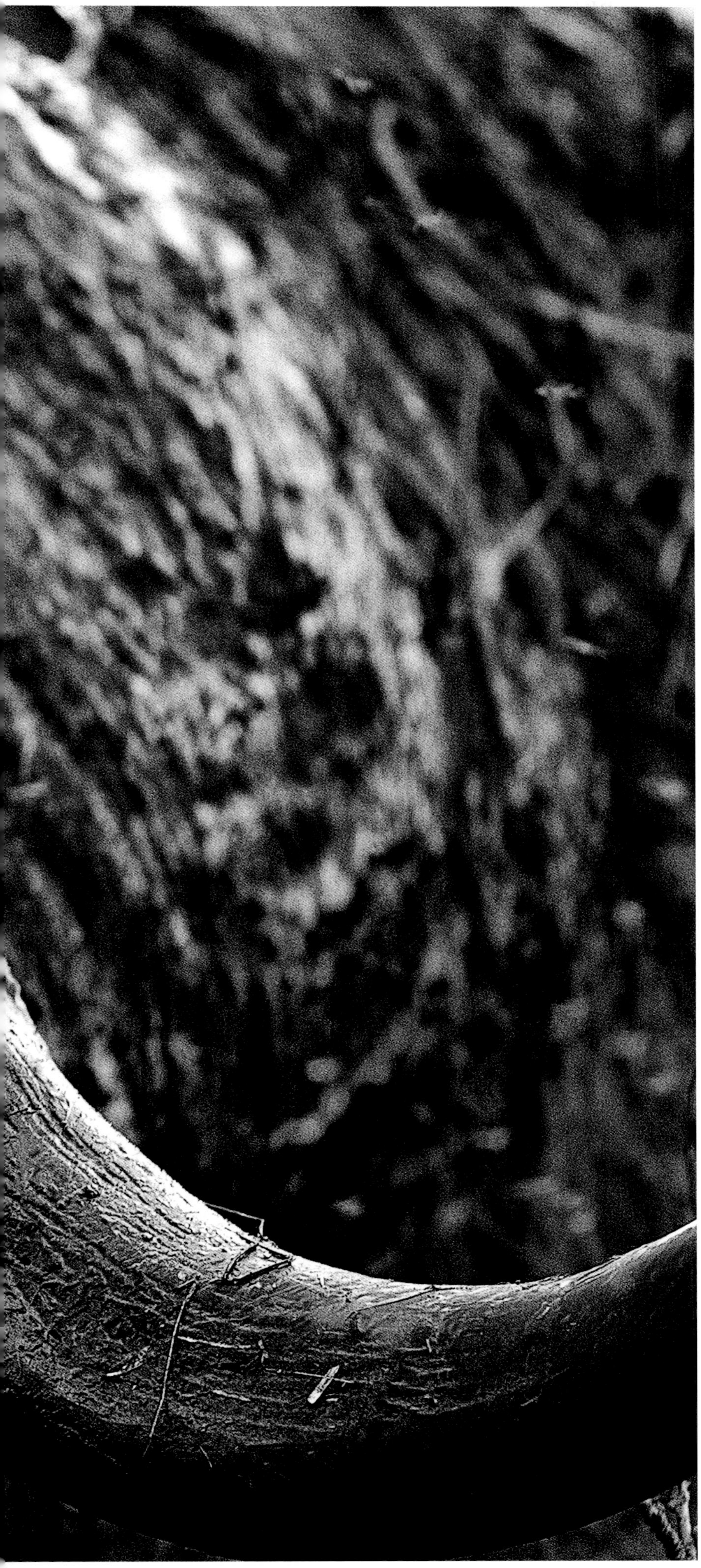

What is life? It is the flash of a firefly in the night. It is the breath of a buffalo in the winter time. It is the little shadow which runs across the grass and loses itself in the Sunset.

— Crowfoot of the Siksika First Nation

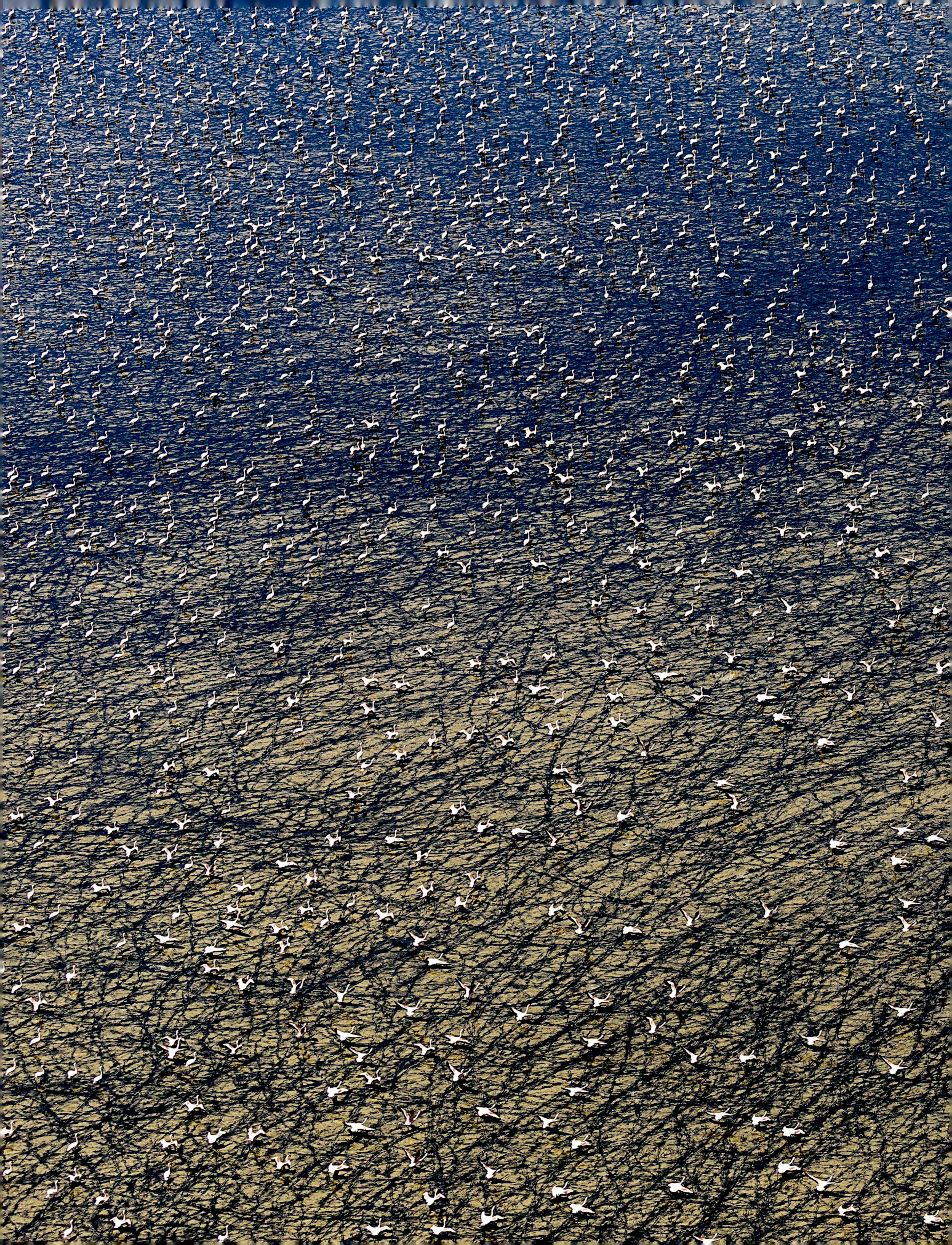

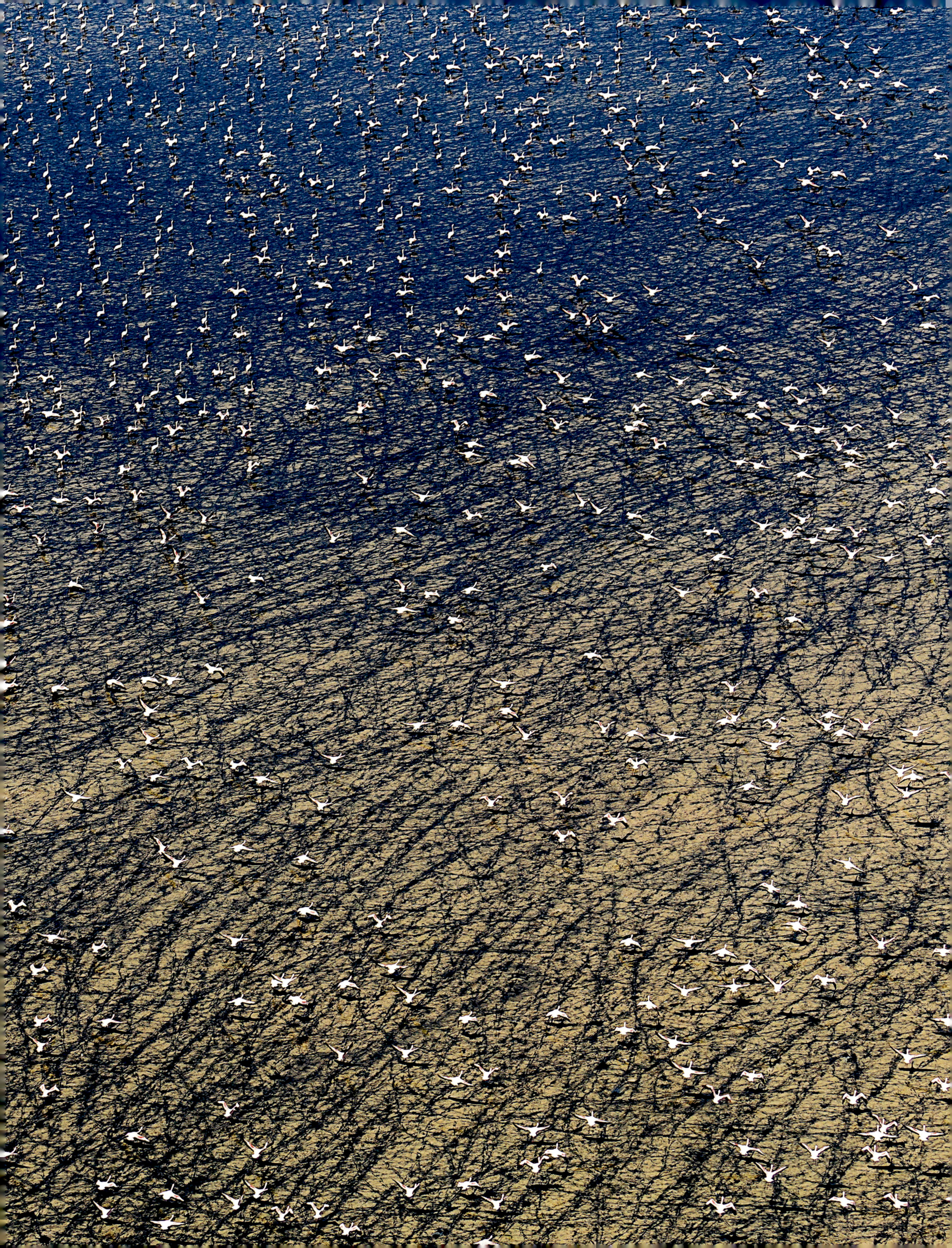

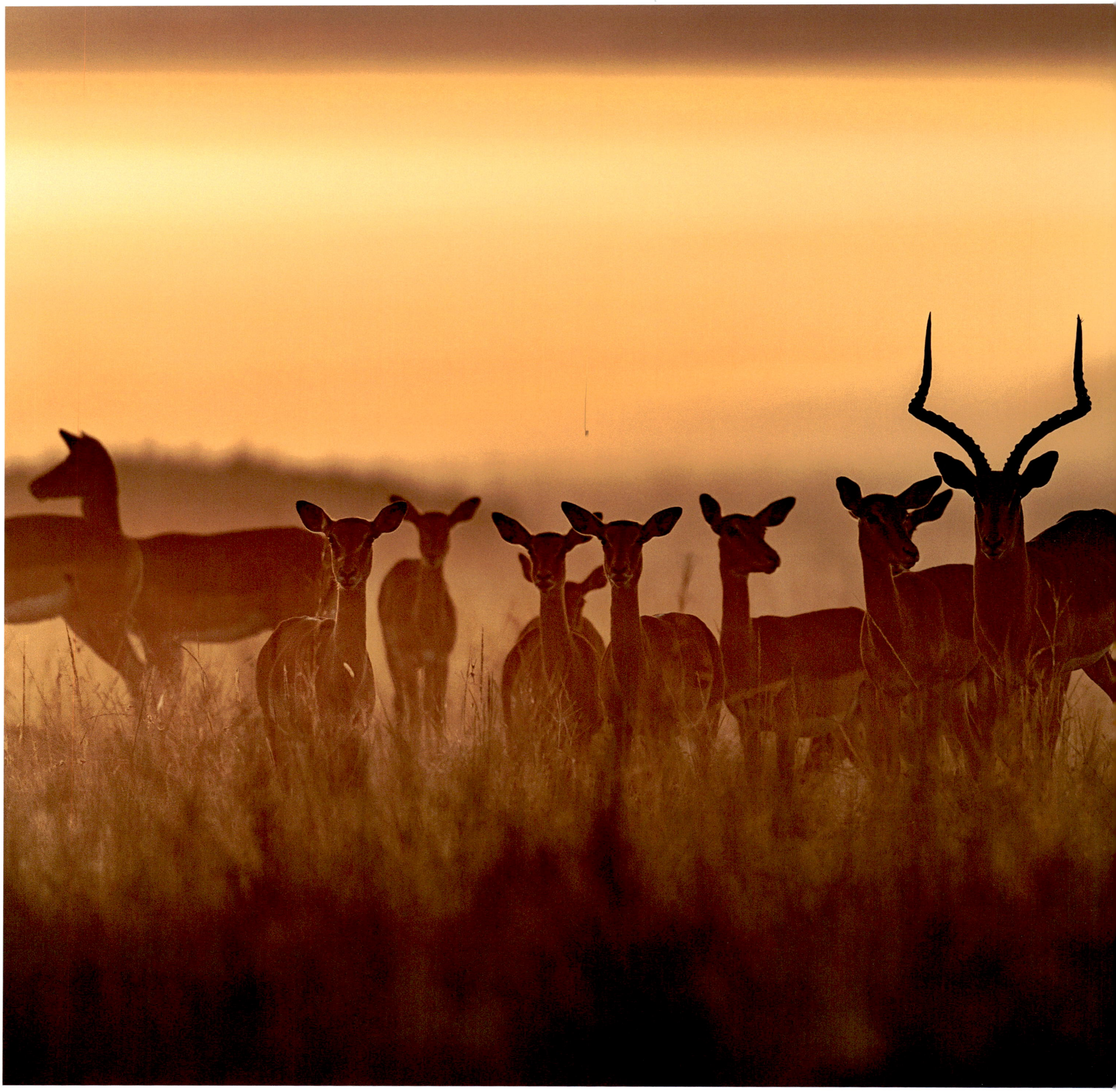

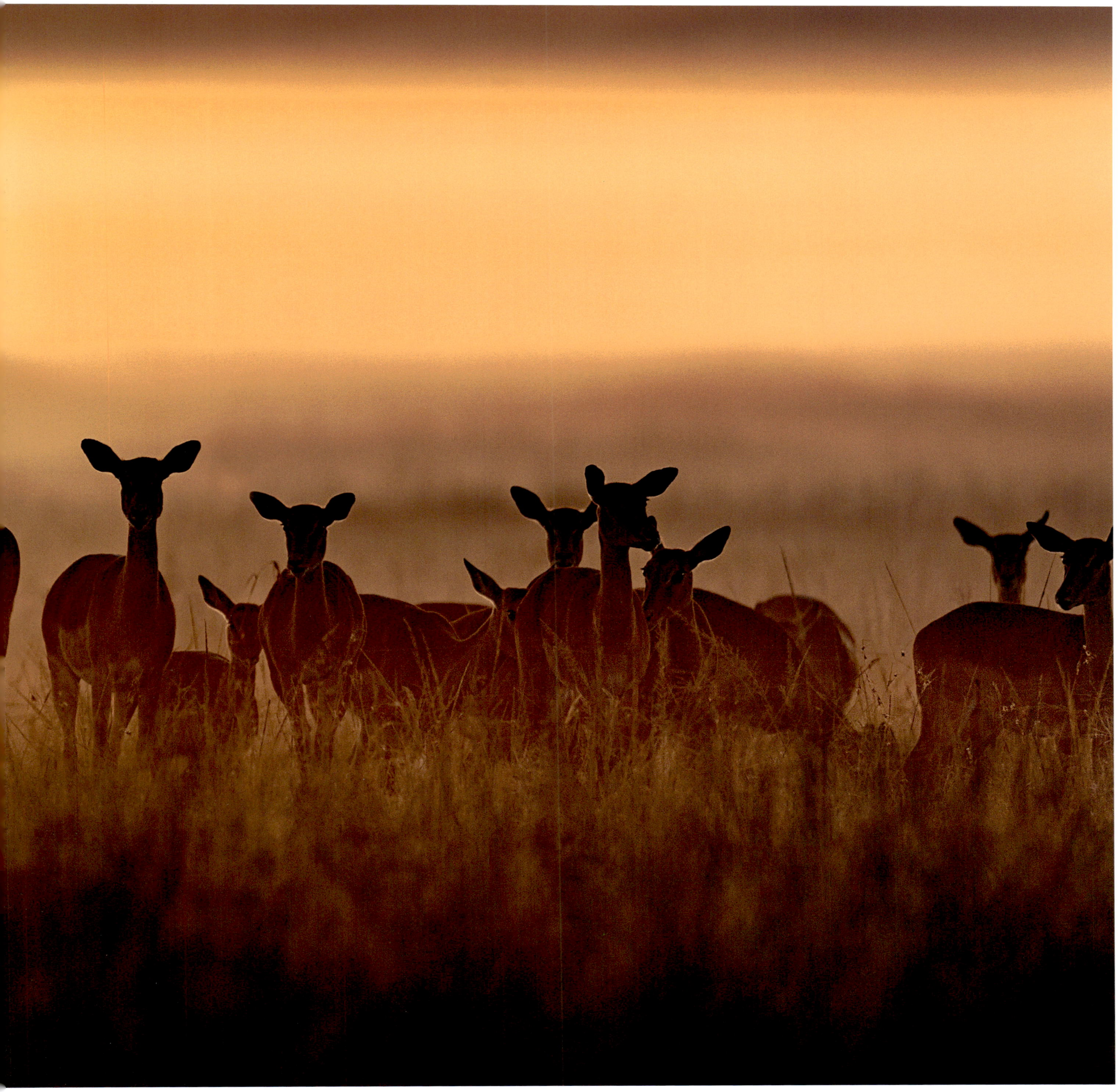

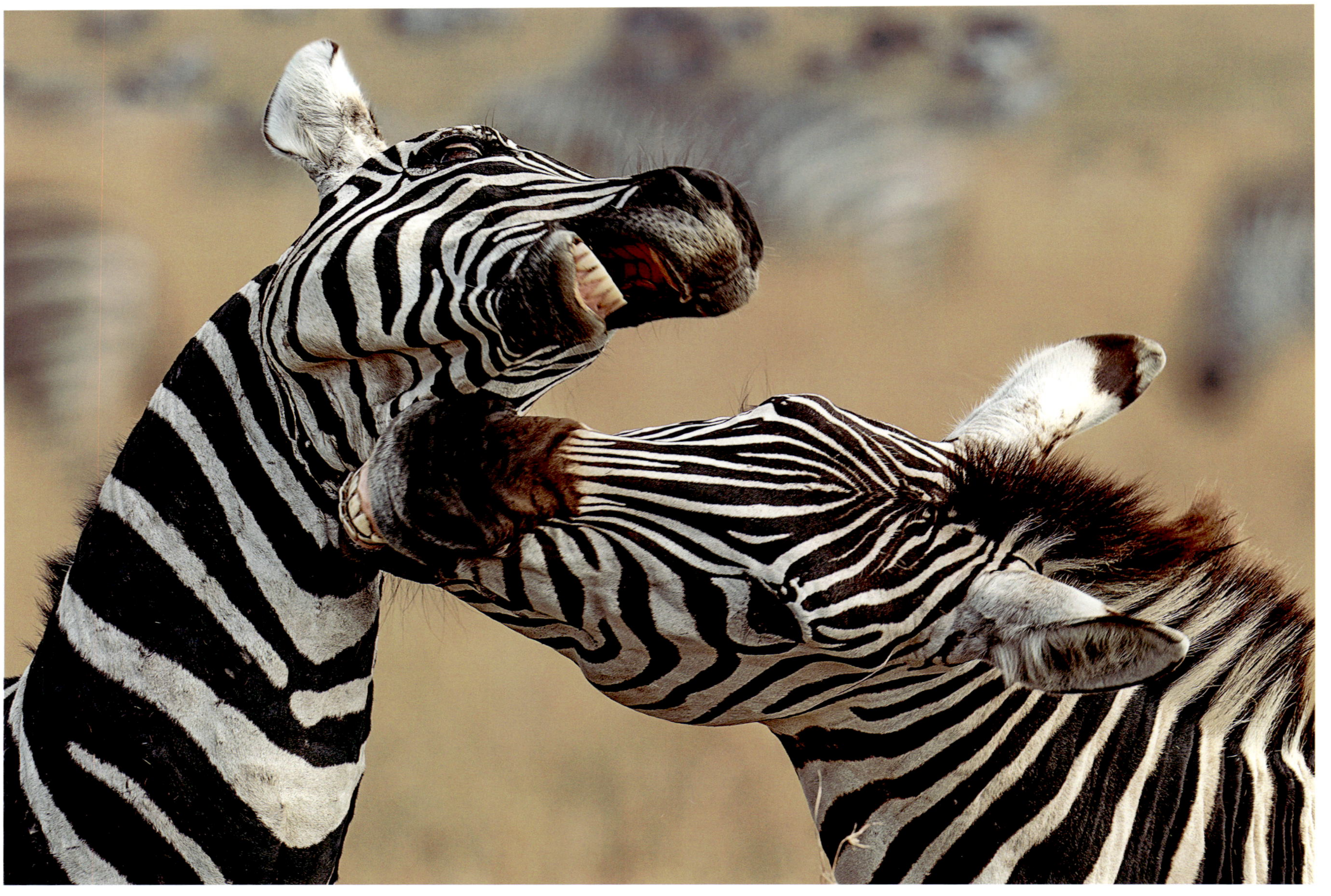

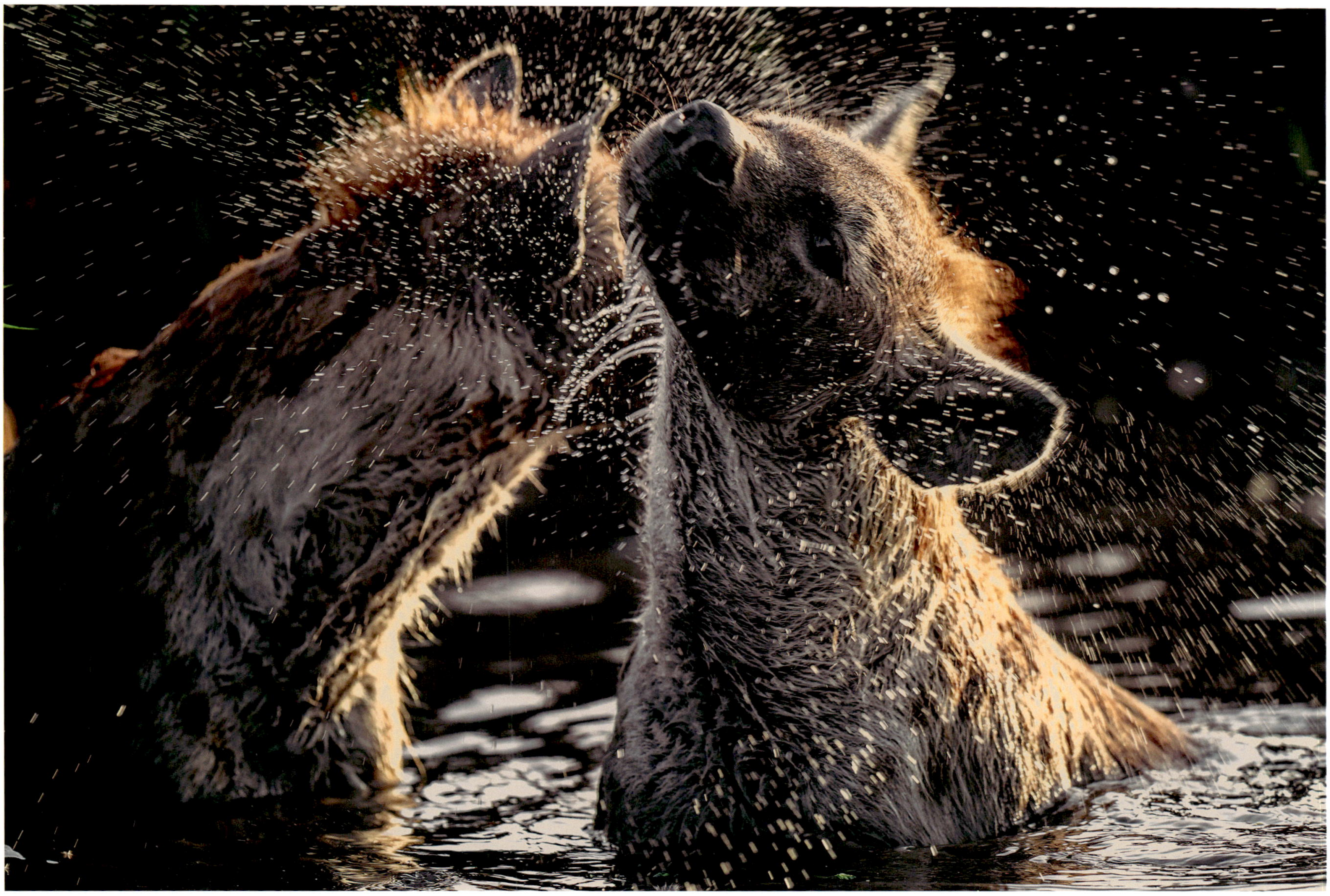

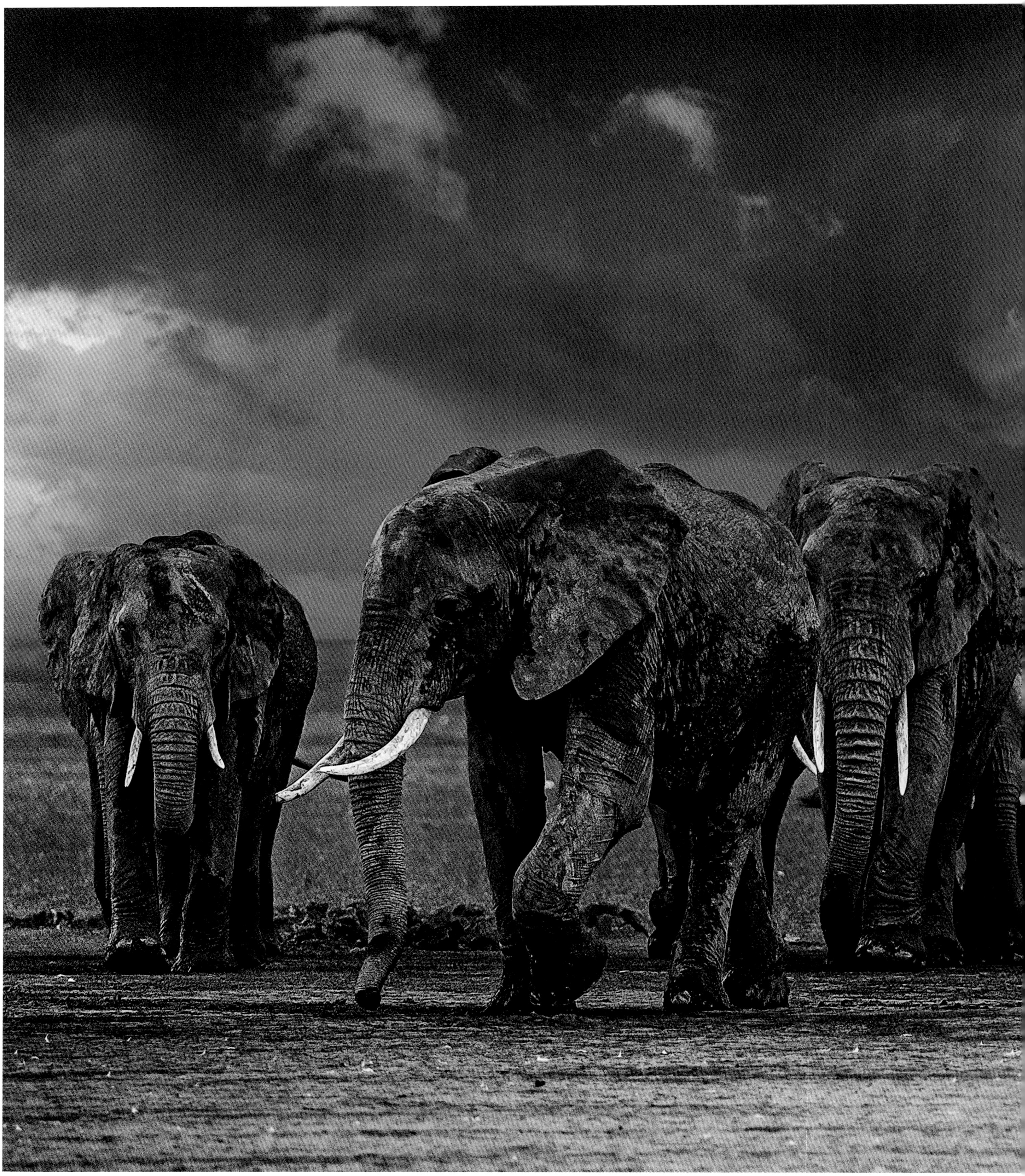

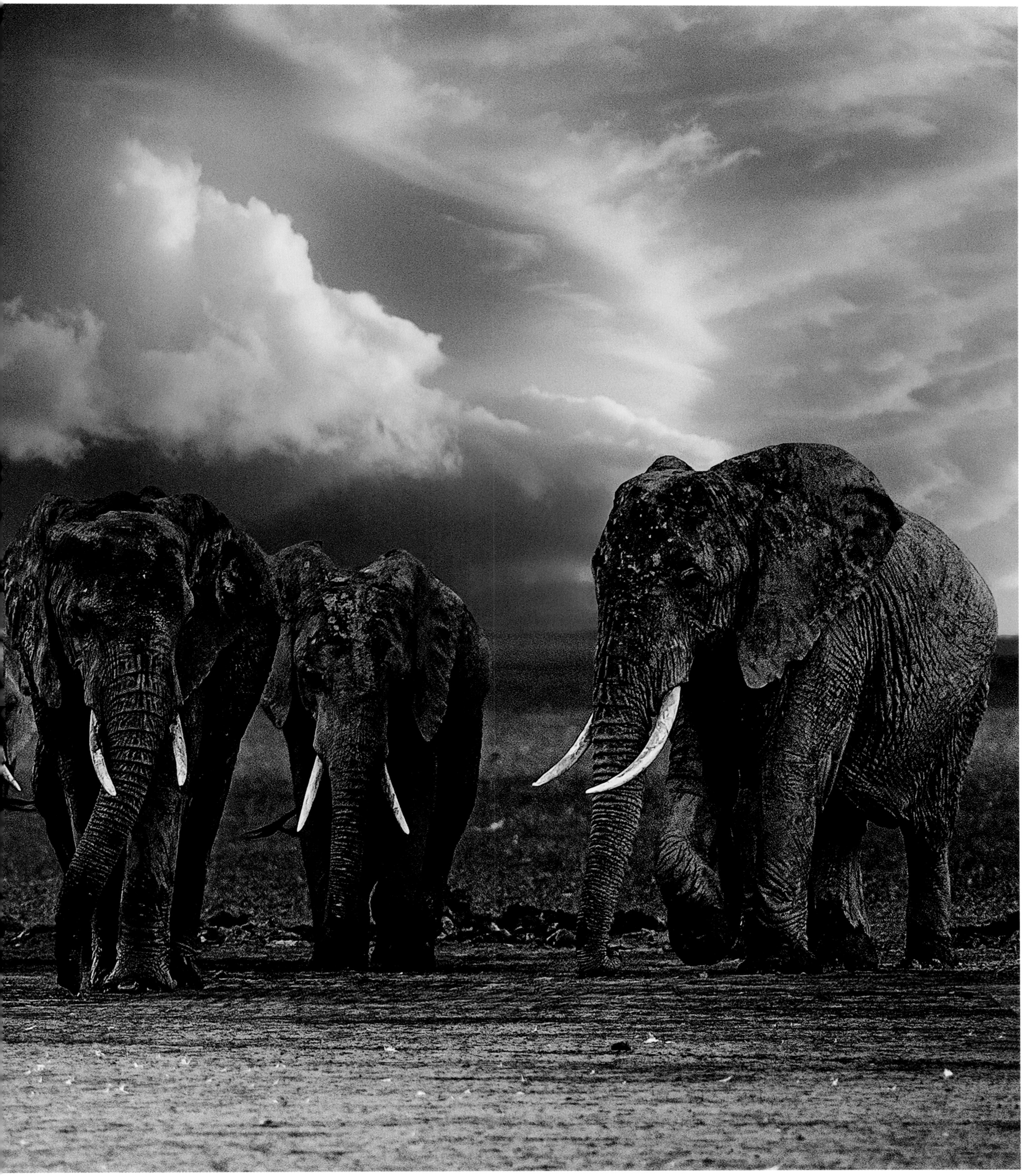

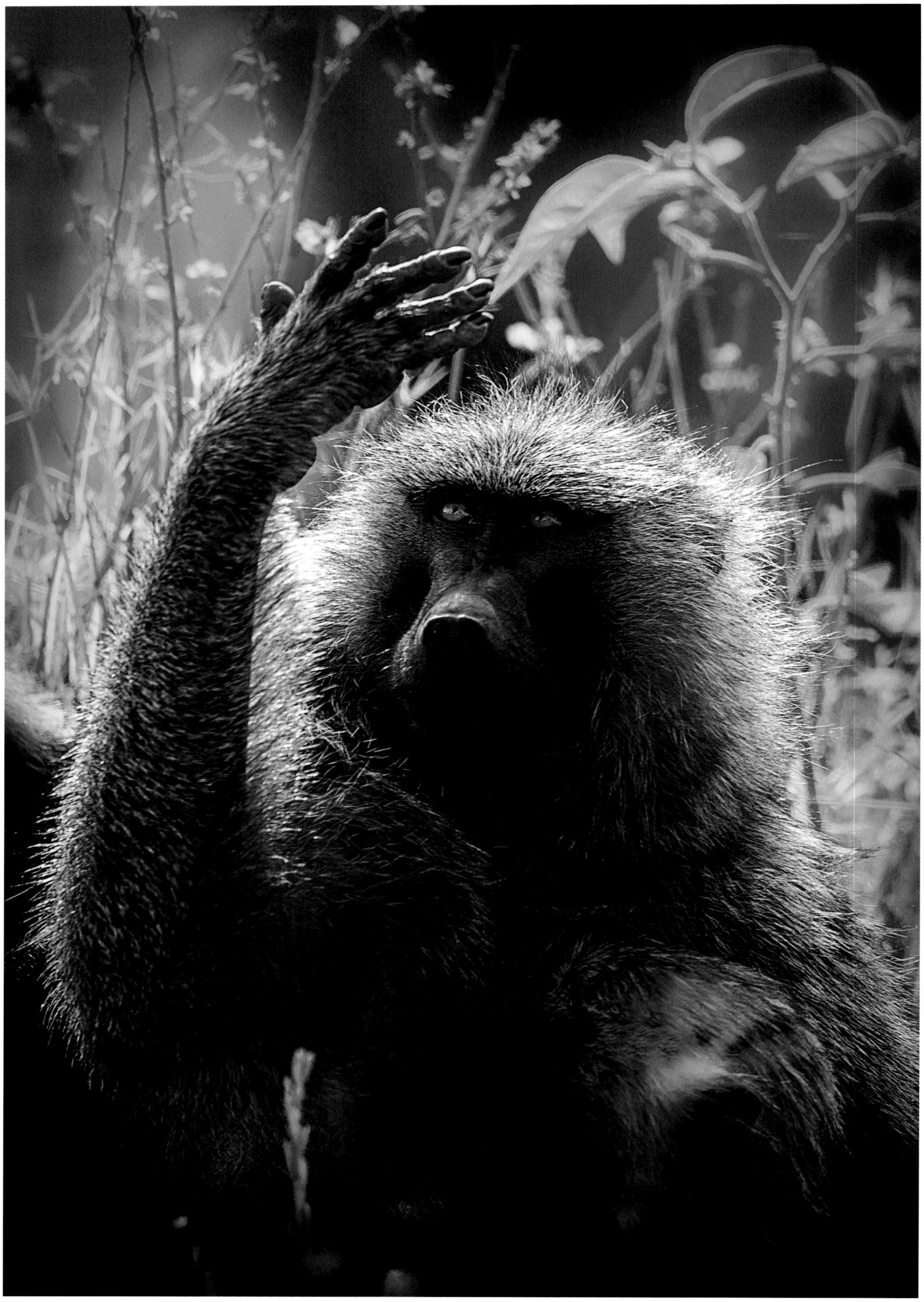

This world is indeed a living being endowed with a soul and intelligence ... a single visible living entity containing all other living entities, which by their nature are all related.

— *Plato*

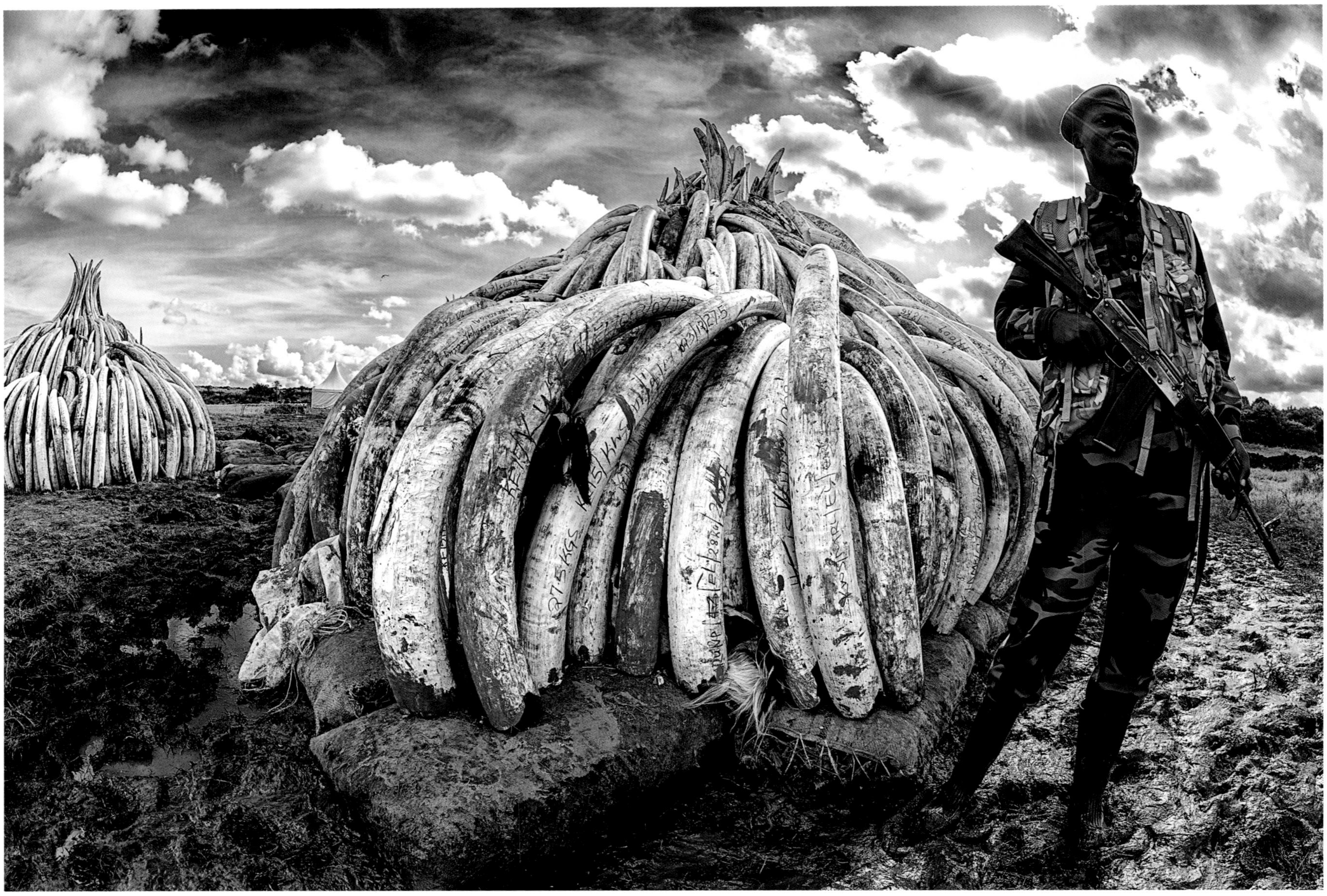

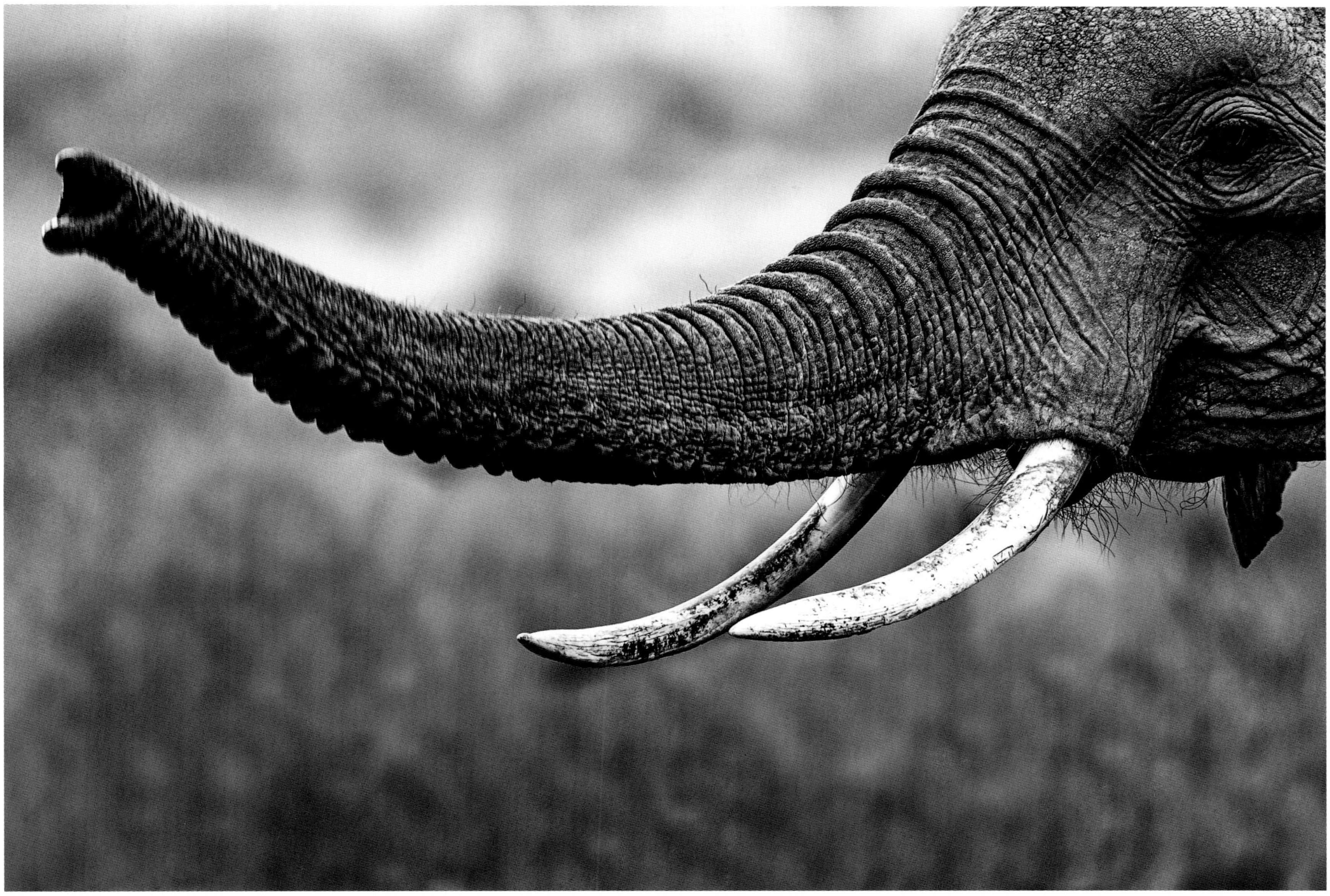

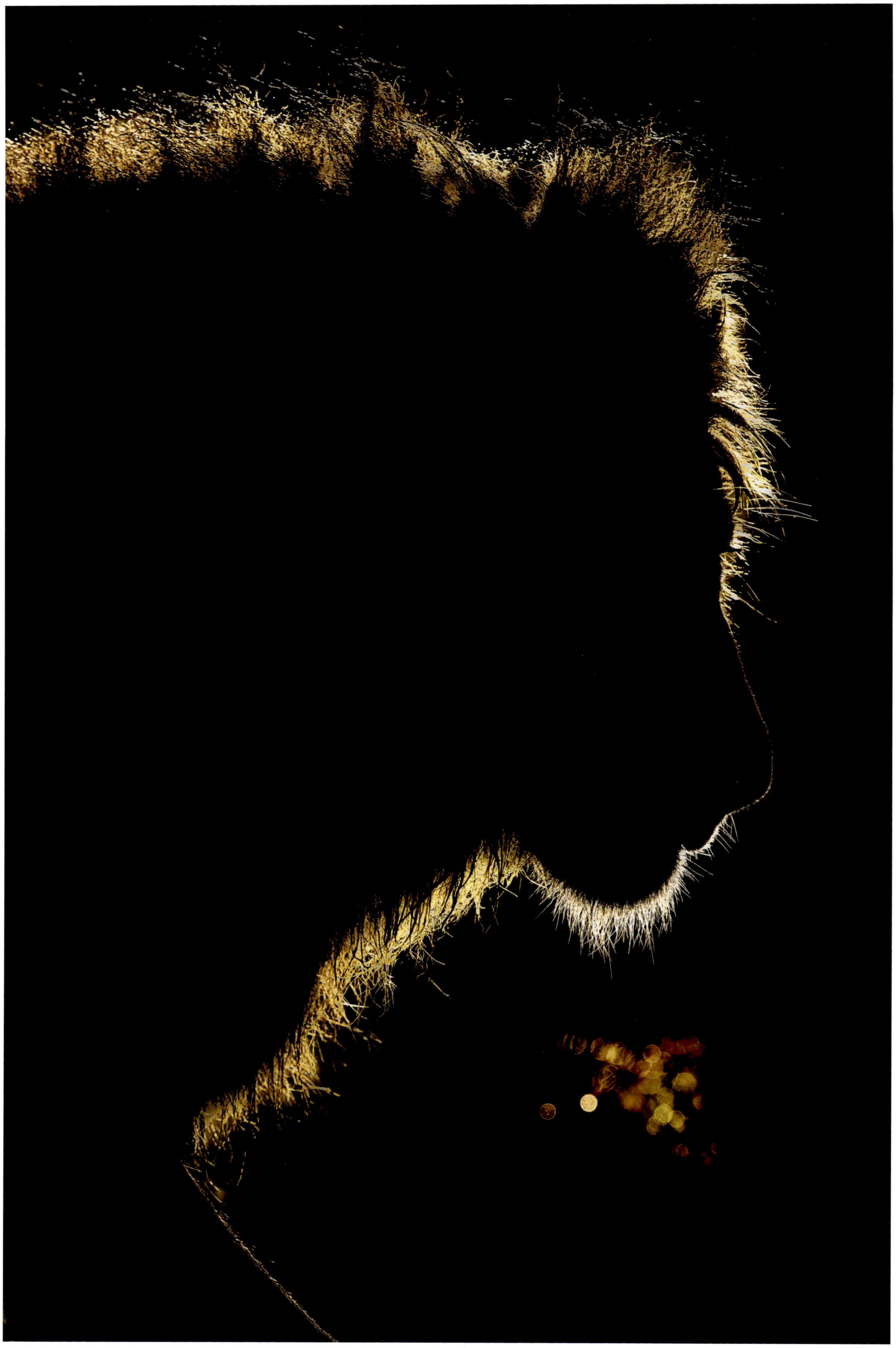

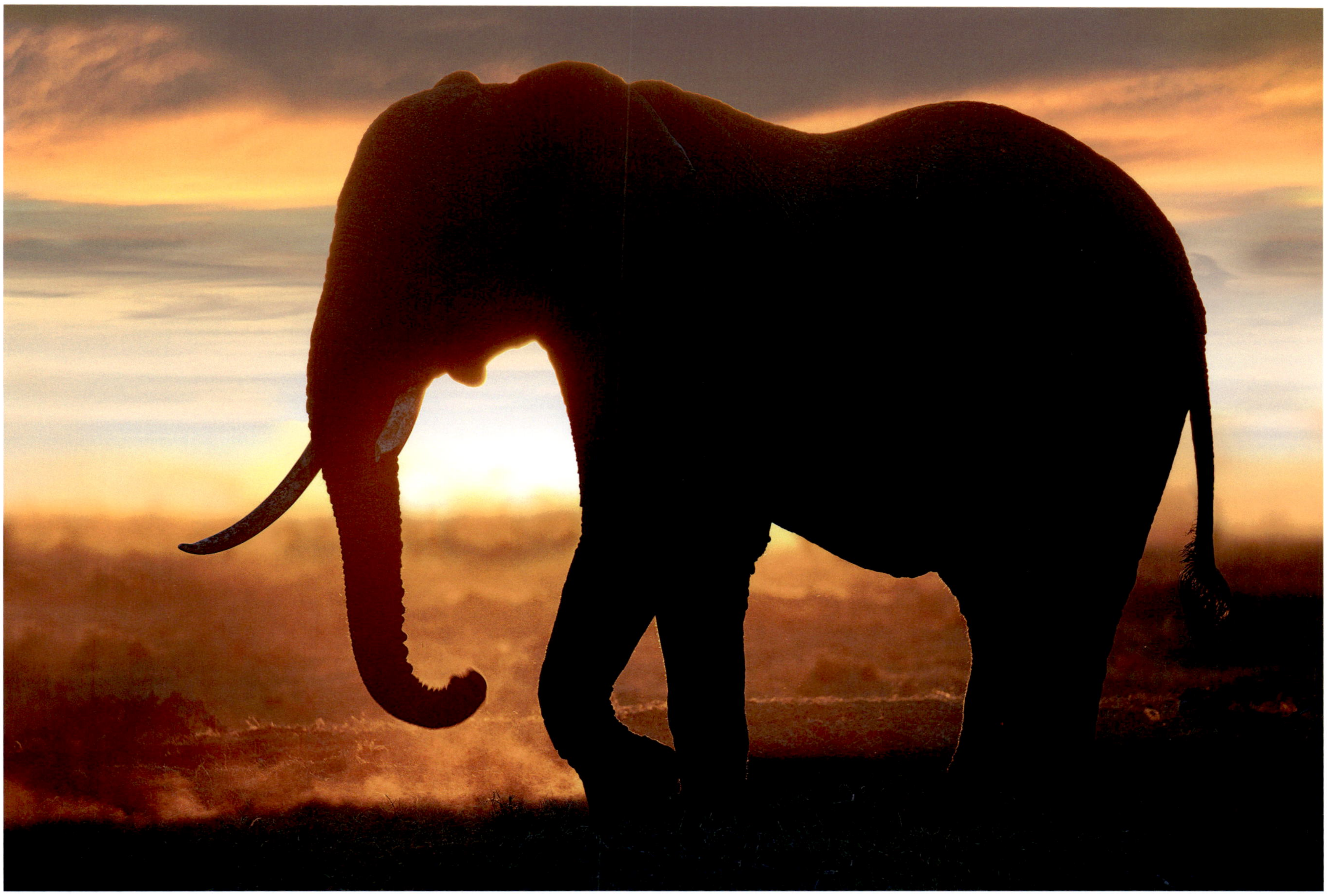

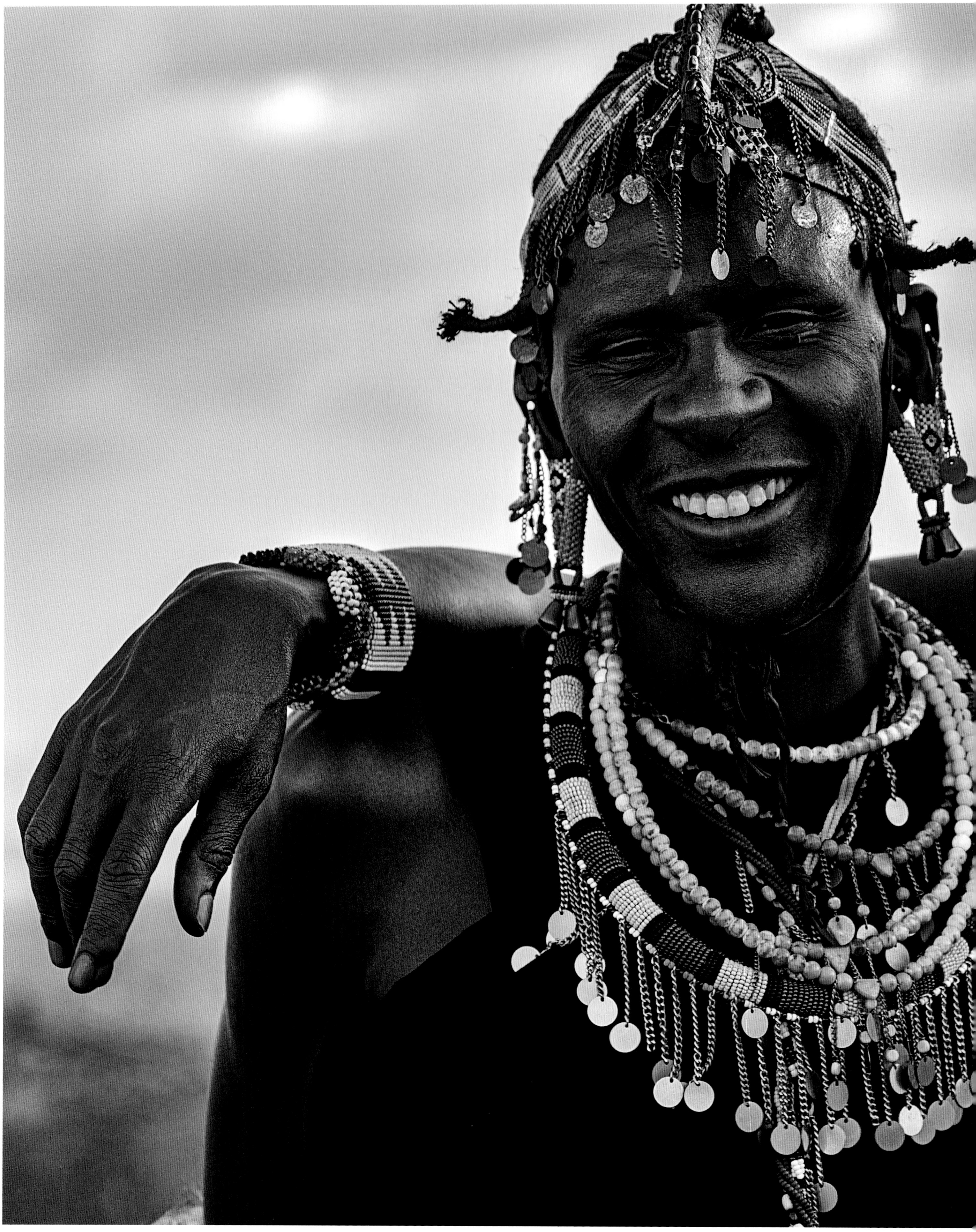

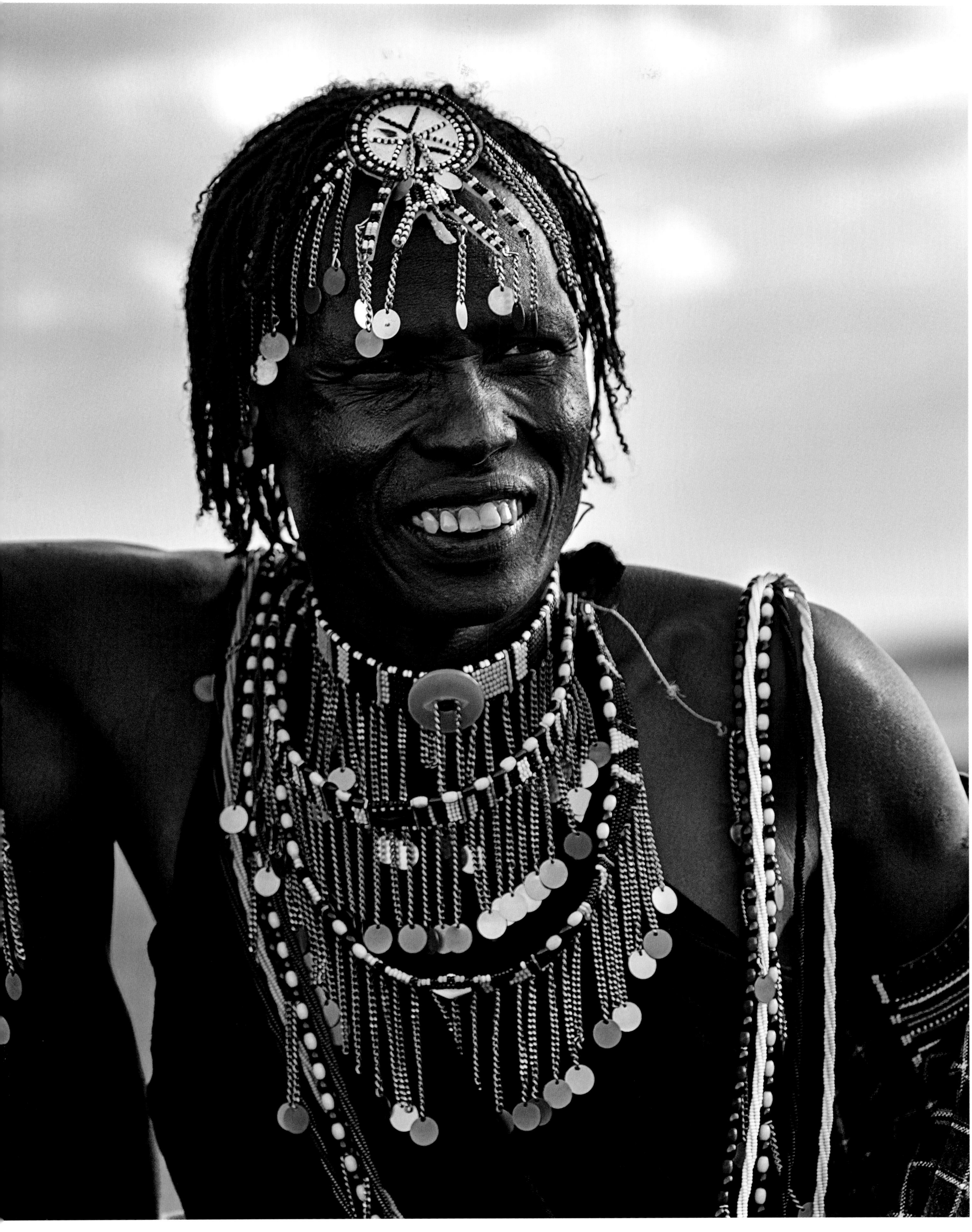

Captions

KEY:

NR = National Reserve, **NP** = National Park,
CA = Conservation Area, **GR** = Game Reserve

EQUIPMENT: **CANON CAMERAS AND LENSES**

EOS-IDX Mk1 & MkII, EOS5D MkIV & 5DSR with Canon Lenses: EF200–400mm F/4L IS USM Extender x1.4, EF600mm F/4L IS II USM, EF800mm F/5.6L IS USM, 1.4x extender Series III, EF100–400mm F/4.5/5.6L IS II USM, EF24–105mm f/4L IS USM, EF16–35mm F2.8L II USM

—	PROLOGUE: **PARADISE LOST**
Pg 03	Young male leopard, Maasai Mara NR, Kenya
Pg 08	Bull elephant, Africa Born mobile camp, Kitirua Conservancy bordering Amboseli NP, Kenya
Pg 10–11	William ole Pere and friends, Mara North Conservancy, Maasai Mara, Kenya
Pg 12	Balanites tree, Maasai Mara NR, Kenya
Pg 17	Male lion, Maasai Mara NR, Kenya
Pg 18–19	Romi, female leopard, Maasai Mara NR, Kenya
Pg 20	Marsh Pride: Cloudy Eye and daughter, Musiara Marsh, Maasai Mara NR, Kenya
Pg 21	Marsh Pride: Red and Spot with cubs, Maasai Mara NR, Kenya
Pg 23	African fish eagle, Musiara Marsh, Maasai Mara NR Kenya
Pg 24–25	Male lion, Maasai Mara NR, Kenya
Pg 26	Lesser flamingos, Lake Logipi, Suguta Valley, northern Kenya Rift Valley
Pg 27	Ol Doinyo Lengai ('Mountain of God' in Maa), an active volcano, south of Lake Natron, Tanzania
Pg 28–29	Lionesses resting up on Simba Kopjes, Serengeti NP, Tanzania
Pg 30	Marsh Pride: the Four Musketeers feeding on buffalo carcass, Maasai Mara NR, Kenya
Pg 31	Nomadic males, Maasai Mara NR, Kenya
Pg 32–33	Young male leopard, son of Olare (also known as the Kaboso female), Maasai Mara NR, Kenya
Pg 34–35	Sunrise, Musiara Marsh, Maasai Mara NR, Kenya
Pg 36–37	Male lion, Maasai Mara NR, Kenya
Pg 38	Plains or Burchell's zebras, Maasai Mara NR, Kenya
Pg 39	Maasai giraffes, Maasai Mara NR, Kenya
Pg 40	Grey-crowned cranes, Maasai Mara NR, Kenya
Pg 41	African buffaloes with attendant red-billed oxpeckers, Maasai Mara NR, Kenya
Pg 42–43	Wildebeest crossing Mara River, Mara Triangle, Maasai Mara NR, Kenya

—	CHAPTER 01: **SAVANNAS OF OUR BIRTH**
Pg 44	Notch 2 mating with Ridge Pride lioness, Maasai Mara NR, Kenya
Pg 46–47	Maasai giraffes and boscia tree, Maasai Mara NR, Kenya
Pg 48	Sunrise, Maasai Mara NR, Kenya
Pg 50–51	Marsh Pride: Dada and Kabibi, Maasai Mara NR, Kenya
Pg 54–55	Elephants at sunset, Musiara Marsh, Maasai Mara NR, Kenya
Pg 56	Marsh Pride: Cloudy Eye and Kabibi, Maasai Mara NR, Kenya
Pg 57	Marsh Pride: Scarface, Maasai Mara NR, Kenya
Pg 58–59	Lions feeding on wildebeest in intermittent watercourse, Maasai Mara NR, Kenya
Pg 60–61	Lions feeding on wildebeest in intermittent watercourse, Maasai Mara NR, Kenya
Pg 62–63	Nomadic male lion, Rhino Ridge, Maasai Mara NR, Kenya
Pg 64	Coalition of five male cheetahs known as Tano Bora ('Magnificent Five') hunting wildebeest, Maasai Mara NR, Kenya
Pg 65	Lion mother and cub, Maasai Mara NR, Kenya
Pg 66–67	Leopard female, Maasai Mara NR, Kenya
Pg 68	Marsh Pride: Kali and young cub, Maasai Mara NR, Kenya
Pg 69	Spotted hyenas, Musiara Marsh, Maasai Mara NR, Kenya
Pg 70–71	Wildebeest, Lake Ndutu, Serengeti NP bordering Ngorongoro CA, Tanzania
Pg 72	Ridge Pride: Maasai Mara NR, Kenya
Pg 73	Leopard female Zawadi and daughter Safi, Fig Tree Ridge, Leopard Gorge Conservancy
Pg 74–75	Leopard female, Maasai Mara NR, Kenya
Pg 76–77	Marsh Pride: Cloudy Eye and Kabibi at Dave's Tree den site; male buffalo watchful, Musiara Marsh, Maasai Mara NR, Kenya
Pg 78–79	Marsh Pride: lioness chasing male African buffalo, Musiara Marsh, Maasai Mara NR, Kenya
Pg 80–81	Elephants at salt lick, Musiara Marsh, Maasai Mara NR, Kenya

—	CHAPTER 02: **FOR THE LOVE OF TREES**
Pg 82	Leopard, Maasai Mara NR, Kenya
Pg 84–85	Japanese garden
Pg 86	Detonix regia, the Flamboyant Tree or Flame of the Forest, native to Madagascar, introduced to tropical and sub-tropical countries worldwide.
Pg 88–89	Young female tiger hunting, Bandhavgarh NP, Madhya Pradesh, India
Pg 93	Tiger, Kanha NP, Madhya Pradesh, India
Pg 94	Cherry blossom, Miyajima Island, Japan
Pg 95	Chital (spotted deer) greeting, Kanha NP, Madhya Pradesh, India
Pg 96–97	Sunrise, Ranthambore NP, Rajasthan, India
Pg 98	Mother chital approaching fawn, Kanha NP, Madhya Pradesh, India
Pg 99	Young Northern Plains gray langur, Kanha NP, Madhya Pradesh, India
Pg 100	Male African buffaloes, Maasai Mara NR, Kenya
Pg 101	Sal forest, Bandhavgarh NP, Madhya Pradesh, India
Pg 102–103	Peacock displaying, Ananda in the Himalayas, Rishikesh, India
Pg 104–105	Territorial male jaguar, Corixo Negro river, Pantanal, Brazil
Pg 106	Tigress, Bandhavgarh NP, India
Pg 107	Ranthambore NP, Rajasthan, India
Pg 108	Former alpha male chimpanzee, Kibale NP, Uganda
Pg 110–111	Jaguar, Porto Jofre area, Pantanal, Brazil
Pg 112	Flower garden, Ndali Lodge, near Kibale NP, Uganda
Pg 113	Parson's chameleon, Madagascar
Pg 114–115	Leopard, India

—	CHAPTER 03: **GRAINS OF SAND**
Pg 116	Afar girl, northeastern Ethiopia
Pg 118–119	Dune Valley, Serra Cafema, northwestern Kunene, Namibia
Pg 120	Sossusvlei, Namib-Naukluft NP, Namibia
Pg 122–123	Gemsbok (a species of oryx), Hartmann Valley, Serra Cafema, northwestern Kunene, Namibia
Pg 125	Dune 45, Sossusvlei, Namib-Naukluft NP, Namibia
Pg 126–127	Hot springs, Danakil Depression, Afar Triangle, northern Ethiopia
Pg 128	Cheetah chasing lure, Cheetah Conservation Fund, Namibia
Pg 129	Sossusvlei, Namib-Naukluft NP, Namibia
Pg 130–131	Desert elephants, Hoanib Skeleton Coast Camp, Damaraland, Namibia
Pg 132–133	Sossusvlei, Namib-Naukluft NP, Namibia
Pg 134	Gemsbok, Sossusvlei, Namib-Naukluft NP, Namibia
Pg 135	Dry river bed, Namibia
Pg 136–137	Female cheetah, Maasai Mara NR, Kenya
Pg 138–139	Fog sweeping in from the Skeleton Coast, Little Kulala Camp, Namibia
Pg 140–141	Mother leopard and cub, Londolozi Private GR, South Africa
Pg 142	Cheetah Conservation Fund, Namibia
Pg 144–145	Bedouin (meaning 'desert dweller') gather for camel-riding displays during Eid al-Fitr celebrations marking the end of Ramadan, the Islamic holy month of fasting, Eastern Oman
Pg 146–147	Jabal Samhan mountain range, rising to 2,100 metres in southern Oman

—

CHAPTER 04: STONES OF SILENCE

—

CHAPTER 05: BLUE PLANET

—

CHAPTER 06: CRYSTAL DESERTS

—

EPILOGUE: REASON FOR HOPE

—

THE SACRED NATURE INITIATIVE

Dedication

Our pride and joy: David and Tori, Alia and Michael, Romy, Miki and Paloma, Artemisia and Ian: the younger generation at the heart of our amazing family. Cherish the Earth.

First Edition August 2021
ISBN 978-0-6398318-4-8

Publishing

HPH Publishing
www.hphpublishing.com

Photography & Writing

Jonathan & Angela Scott
www.jonathanangelascott.com

Copy editing

Caroline Taggart

Design

David John Scott
www.davidjohnscott.com

Photographic Equipment

Canon

Fine Art Photography

Photographic prints available at:
www.thuranima.com

THURANIMA COLLECTIVE
FINE ART

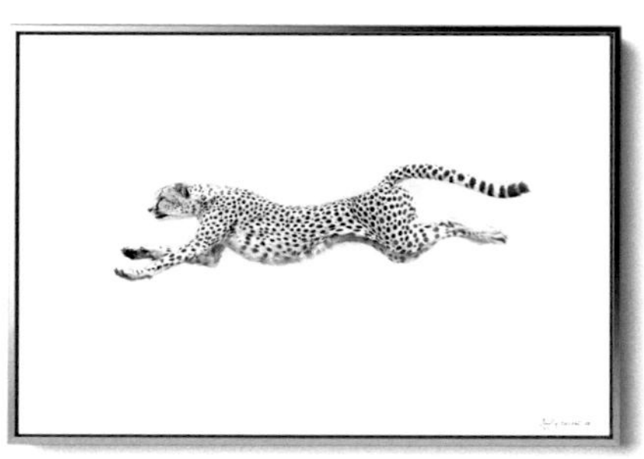

Acknowledgments

We are immensely grateful to our son David for his vision in turning a dream into a stylish and original work of art. Thank you as well to David's fiancée Tori for her invaluable role as the newest member of our Big Cat Family and to our daughter Alia, grandson Michael and all the other members of our family for their love and support. To Carole Wyman for being the wonderfully generous soul and friend she is; Gabriel and Deborah Brenner, Brad Chatellier, Vicky Coombe and Sarah Kennedy (what gems!), Charles and Lindsay Dewhurst, Brian Hall, Hamish Hurley, Ray Johnston, Griet van Malderen, Biki' and Vikram Oberoi, Nigel Pavitt, Michel Zoghzoghi, Vanessa Raven, Sylvia and Peter Szapary, Jock Anderson and Boris Tismimieszky (Jonathan's long-suffering Kenya chums), Christos Tolias, Dr Mauro Saio, Dr David Silverstein, and Cissy and David Walker for their unconditional support and friendship. To Heinrich van den Berg and HPH for allowing us to create volume 2 of a book first conceived by Angela, and for sharing their wealth of experience in repro and printing.

For insights and inspiration: *The Power of Myth* (and other works) by Joseph Campbell in conversation with Bill Moyers; *The Social Conquest of Earth* and *Consilience* among the many classic works of Professor EO Wilson; *The Nature Fix* by Florence Williams, *Loving Nature: Towards an Ecology of Emotion* by Kay Milton, *Sapiens* and *Homo Deus* by Yuval Noah Harari, *Reinventing the Sacred* by Stuart A Kauffman, *Origins* by Lewis Dartnell, and *A History of the World* by Andrew Marr. *The Last Place on Earth* and *Three Levels of Time* by the late Harold TP Hayes had a profound impact on our thinking. He wrote effortless prose, was greatly loved and sorely missed.

Our thanks go also to editor Caroline Taggart for her magic literary wand; Jonathan Pegg for his friendship and loyal and deft touch on contractual matters.

The governments of Kenya and Tanzania generously gave us access and support to enable us to live and work in their spectacular wildlife parks and reserves; for many years, the Grammaticas family has provided us with a base at Governor's Camp in the Maasai Mara in the heart of Marsh Pride territory, for which we are eternally grateful; our thanks also go to the late Patrick Beresford and his family and the team at Governor's Workshop for their good humour and dedication in keeping us on the road.

The two volumes of *Sacred Nature* are flagships for the Sacred Nature Initiative. Caro and Scott Greenhalgh, whom we hosted on safari in the Mara in 2018, were pivotal in transforming that idea into a reality, alongside friends and colleagues Richard Damania, Mike Eldon, Philip Jespersen, Abraham Joffe, Sarah Kennedy, Ranjit Majumdar, Chris and Miriam Parel, Steve Shelley, Marley Sianto, Nicholas Soikan, Philip Thurston, Michael Turner and Ed Wilson.

It is with tremendous gratitude and respect that we acknowledge the role played by four special friends who have generously allowed us to use their iconic images in *SN2* – images that demonstrate the power of a photograph to speak for a thousand words: Philip Thurston (humpback whale, pg 180, and waves, Australia, pg 182–3), Griet van Malderen (humpback whales, Tonga, pg 190–1), Michel Zoghzoghi (polar bear, Spitzbergen, pg 212) and Abraham Joffe (king penguins, South Georgia, pg 214–5). We have been blessed to share safaris in our beloved Maasai Mara with all of them as well as breathtaking journeys to Ethiopia and Uganda with Griet, and to the Pantanal, Namibia and Botswana with Michel (without whose extraordinary generosity publication of the first volume of *Sacred Nature* would not have been possible). Abraham Joffe ACS (CEO of Untitled Film Works, Ltd: www.untitledfilmworks.com.au) featured us in Season Two of *Tales by Light* (Netflix); as lead cameraman he also co-produced Season 1 and 2 of *Big Cat Tales* for Animal Planet. During filming in the Mara, we met ocean art photographer and inspirational author Philip Thurston (www.thurstonphoto.com), a wonderful free spirit who shares Angie's deep love of the ocean.

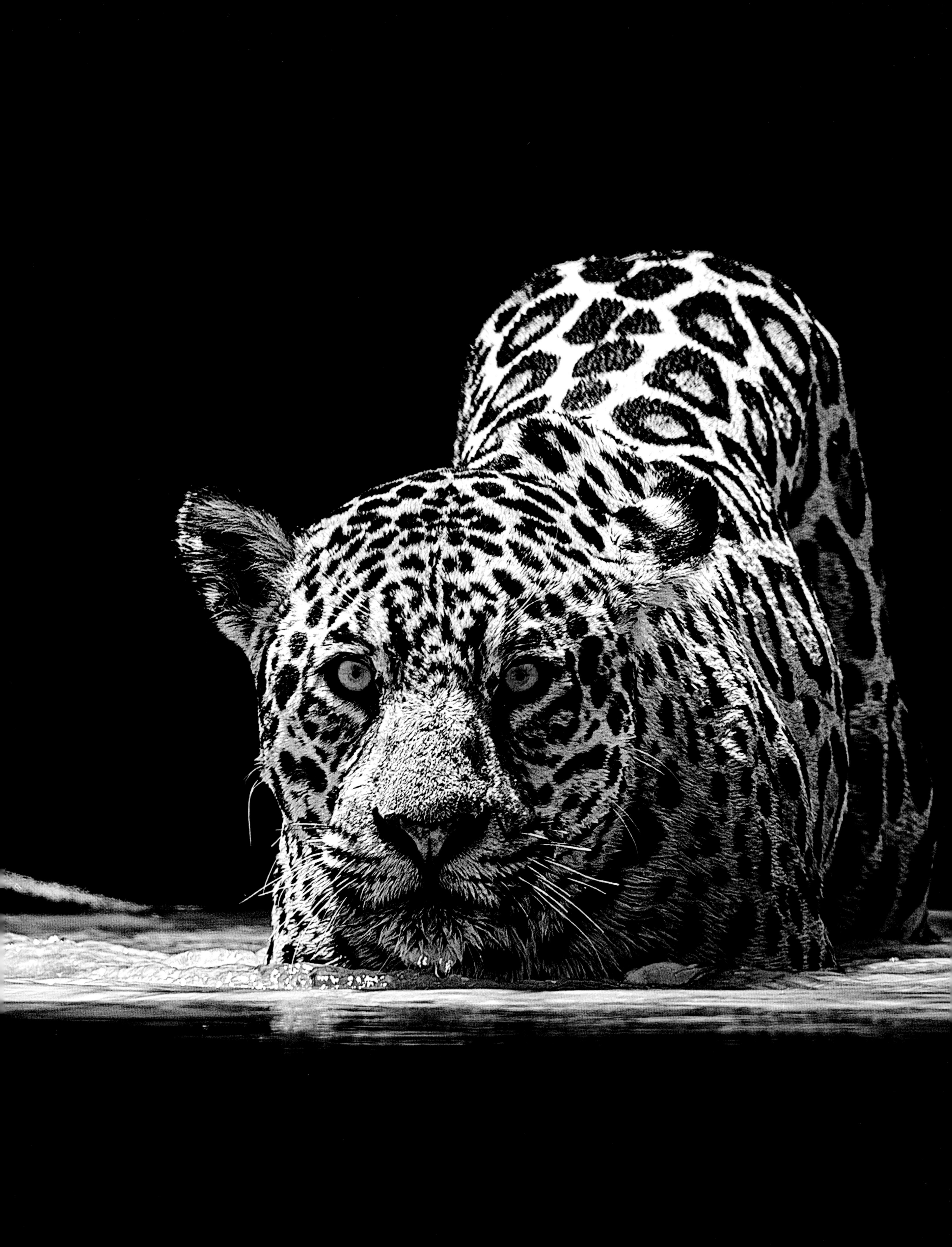

THE

SACRED NATURE

INITIATIVE

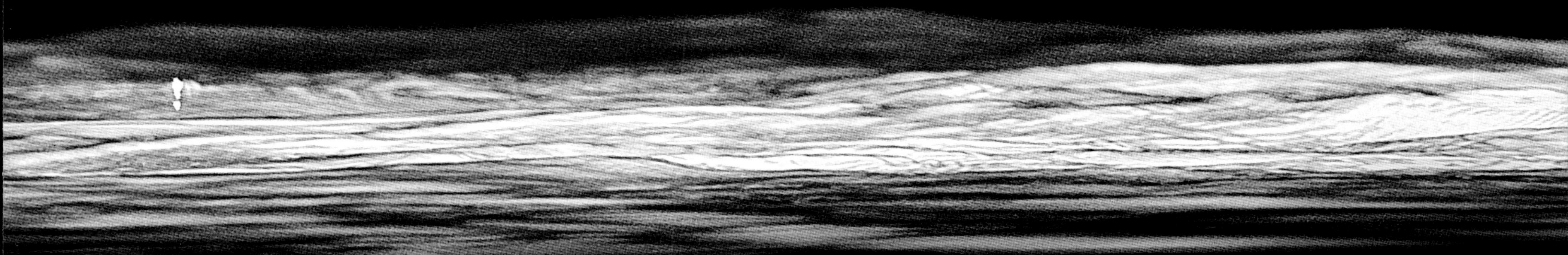

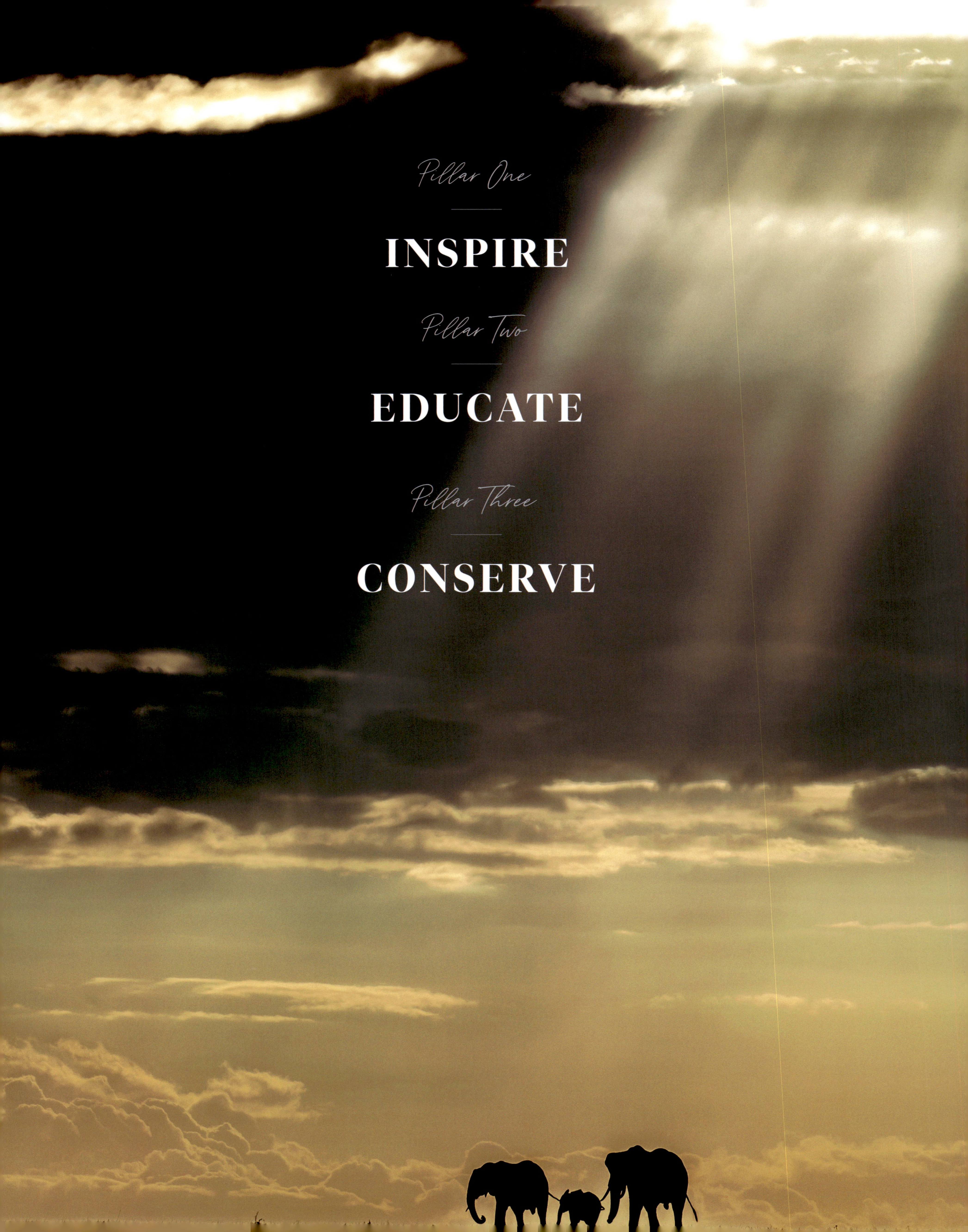
Pillar One
INSPIRE
Pillar Two
EDUCATE
Pillar Three
CONSERVE

About SNI

These past 40 years we have travelled the world in search of adventure and stunning vistas, set foot on every continent, roamed the far horizon. Yet, it is Africa that is closest to our hearts. Angie was born here; I have lived here for more than 40 years. It is our home.

The genesis of *Sacred Nature: Life's Eternal Dance* (HPH) – the companion volume to this one – was Angie's vision. It is Angie who brings artistry to our work, Angie who has forced us to try to find a different, more spiritual way of looking at nature. For her each tree and flower is a work of art, each leaf something to marvel at, each vein of each leaf distinguishing it as surely as each row of whisker spots tells us that two lionesses are different long before we come to know them as individuals. It is this sacredness of nature that Angie feels so deeply. And with the world of dance etched deep in her veins, she has awakened me to the natural rhythms that permeate the African bush, illuminating life's eternal dance. It is what we have tried to capture in our images and prompted us to found the Sacred Nature Initiative (SNI): the intention of which is to help ensure a sustainable future for all life on Earth. For that to happen, we must plan for the long term, embrace environmental stewardship, adopt sustainable practices that promote the provision of clean energy and the equitable use of natural resources. These ideas mirror the Great Law of the Iroquois – a historical indigenous confederacy in northeast North America – which holds appropriate to think seven generations ahead (about 140 years into the future). Adopting similar principles, in 2018, the Welsh Assembly passed the Future Generations Act requiring all public organisations to take into account the long-term effects of any decision they make on the prosperity of the nation, its environment, culture and communities by developing non-party political solutions to issues like poverty, ill health, poor air quality, low-quality jobs.

How does it work?

SNI is a new entity incorporated in the UK and dedicated to conserving the planet's natural wonders. Its approach is holistic and targeted, committed to rigorously analysing needs and feasible interventions in areas of concern. To achieve this, it will assess likely outcomes and create or support donor-funded projects with designated results, time frames and accountabilities. Solutions in ecosystem restoration and maintenance must be sustainable and significant.

It is essential that everyone – children, parents, teachers, business leaders, politicians – understands the importance of nature, that the natural environment sustains all life. Equally, we must adopt a new convention that says we do not own nature, that land isn't a commodity to be used as we please. Nature is something to be respected and nurtured, held in trust by each generation for the benefit of future generations. Something sacred.

Though the SNI is global in its scope and ideals, Phase 1 will focus on the place we know best: the Mara-Serengeti ecosystem spanning the border between Kenya and Tanzania (see Chapter 1: Savannas of Our Birth).

By purchasing this book, you have already supported SNI because a percentage of the profits from the sale will be donated to projects supported by the Initiative.

If you'd like to learn more about SNI and how you can Reconnect to Nature please visit:
www.sacrednatureinitiative.com

"

The goal of life is to make your heartbeat match the beat of the universe, to match your nature with Nature.

Joseph Campbell

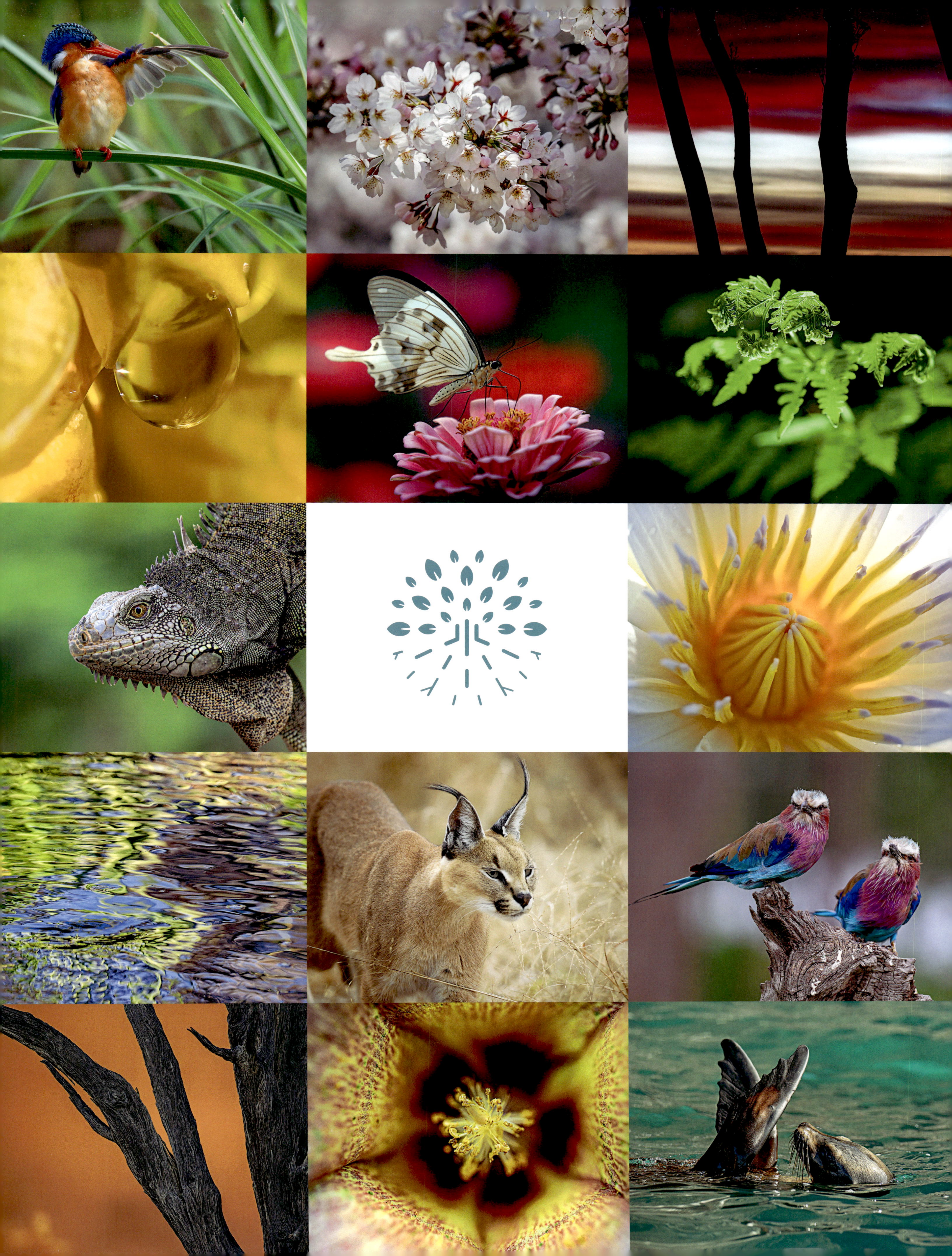

Sponsors

Heartfelt thanks to the people and companies listed below for believing in the ethos of Sacred Nature 2 and the Sacred Nature Initiative and for contributing so generously to making it happen:

Platinum

Carole Wyman

Michel Zoghzoghi
@michel_zoghzoghi

Fredrick & Anne Fisher

Griet van Malderen
www.grietvanmalderen.com/en

Canon Europe
www.canon-europe.com

Gold

Karen & Don Lang

Sarah & Gordon Sanders
www.runwoodhomes.co.uk

SanDisk
www.sandisk.com

Gabriel Brenner

Silver

Victoria Coombe
www.victoriacoombe.com

Oberoi Hotels & Resorts
www.oberoihotels.com

Peter & Liz Jarman

Michael & Denisa Sofaer

Swarovski Optik (UK)
www.swarovskioptik.com

Frank, Alex & Max Moore
www.moorepolaroids.com

John & Gail Coombe

Carole & Paul Nicholson

Darrin & Michelle Johnson

Kim, Nicky, Carla, Holly & Jessica Gottlieb

Camila Leigh & Peter Williams
www.adlingtonhall.com

Sue Tweddell

Paul Jackson & Julia Rainbow

Margi & Gerard Moss

Digital Ink Ltd
www.digitalinkgb.com

Phillip Coulson

Brad Chatellier

Ninian Stewart Richardson

Pippa Millard

RUNWOOD HOMES
SENIOR LIVING

Canon

DIGITAL INK
EXPERTS IN INDUSTRIAL AND COMMERCIAL INK

SanDisk®

VICTORIA COOMBE

GRIET VAN MALDEREN PHOTOGRAPHY

mp

SWAROVSKI OPTIK